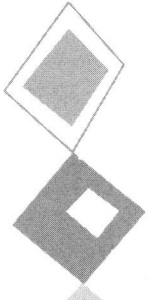

Nyae Nyae !Kung
Beliefs and Rites

Peabody Museum Monographs
Harvard University • Cambridge, Massachusetts
Number 8

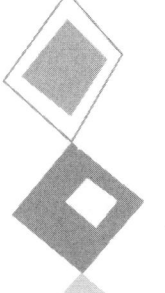

Nyae Nyae !Kung
Beliefs and Rites

Lorna J. Marshall

Peabody Museum of Archaeology and Ethnology
Harvard University • Cambridge, Massachusetts
1999

Illustration Credits:

Cover illustrations: Inset background: detail of map of southern Africa from *Atlas of the World*, enlarged 2d edition, National Geographic Society, 1966, reproduced courtesy of the National Geographic Society; left: Gao Feet (Gao Medicine); right: Ritual Healing Dance viewed from the top of the expedition truck. Both left and right photos were taken by John Marshall.

Page 82: The drawing of the Rain-Eland Scale is reproduced courtesy of Nicholas England.

Page 215: The drawing of the n≠abbi, bull-roarer, and the text describing it are reproduced courtesy of Nicholas England.

Text Credits:

Chapters 1, 3, 7, and 13 contain text that was previously published elsewhere. See the source notes for each chapter for more information about first publication of the material.

Production Credits:

Editing: Megan Biesele and Tim Cullen
Design: LeGwin Associates, Cambridge, Massachusetts
Copyediting: Donna M. Dickerson
Composition: Donna M. Dickerson and LeGwin Associates
Proofreading: Donna Dickerson, Janice Herndon, and Amy Hirschfeld
Indexing: Lynn Hutchinski
Line art scanning: Henry N. Sawyer Printing, Charlestown, Massachusetts
Photo scanning: LeGwin Associates, Cambridge, Massachusetts
Printing and binding: Sheridan Books, Ann Arbor, Michigan

CONTENTS

FIGURES

FOREWORD

From the beginning, Lorna Marshall's ethnographic work has been part of a family endeavor comprising complementary projects. In 1950 Laurence Marshall, Lorna's late husband, retired and resolved to spend more time with his family. Together, he, Lorna, and their two children, Elizabeth and John, planned a trip to southern Africa. By and large, Laurence was to attend to the logistics of the travel through roadless deserts; John was to make his now-famous ethnographic films; Elizabeth was to write the narrative account of their experiences that became the widely acclaimed book *The Harmless People* (1959). Lorna herself was to devote her time to a detailed ethnographic record.

Born in 1898, Lorna Marshall grew up in a world in which automobiles were few and airplanes even fewer. She recalls receiving news of the Great San Francisco Earthquake. She has seen two world wars, a moon-landing, and many other technological wonders. When Lorna went to university, Franz Boas had recently established ethnography as a scientific and systematic endeavor, and Bronislaw Malinowski's work was beginning to be published. Anthropological method was shifting from armchair generalizations based on the observations of colonial administrators and missionaries to first-hand experience. The participant ethnographic method with all its plethoric detail was taking the place of essentially cerebral grand schemes, usually of an evolutionary nature. But, at that time Lorna's interests lay elsewhere, and she read English for her Bachelor of Arts degree (1921) at the University of California, Berkeley, and for her Master of Arts degree (1928) at Radcliffe College.

When, just over two decades later, Lorna Marshall began her southern African work, the writing of ethnography had become well established as a central and distinguishing feature of cultural and social anthropology. Accepting that she was not a trained ethnographer, she read appropriate books and consulted some of the leading figures of the day: Clyde Kluckhohn was one of them, and J. O. Brew, then director of the Peabody Museum, Harvard, appointed a committee to discuss the aims and procedures of the Marshall family's work. In southern Africa, the Marshalls sought the advice of Phillip Tobias, Monica Wilson, L. F. Maingard, and Raymond Dart, among others. Later, when Lorna was preparing her first publications, she consulted such people as Mary Douglas, Daryll Forde, and George Peter Murdock. More recently, she has discussed her work with Richard Lee, Irven DeVore, Megan Biesele, and many others who were associated with the Harvard Bushman Research Project, which eventually grew out of the Marshall family's work. Whatever Lorna's nonprofessional status as an ethnographer may have been, she has not hesitated to consult, at all times, the leading people in the field. Above all, Lorna wanted to conduct her ethnographic researches in the best possible way, and she left no stone unturned to achieve the highest standard.

When the Marshall family organized their first expeditions at the beginning of the 1950s, they could not find a professional ethnographer to accompany them to the Kalahari Desert. Africa was a long way from Boston, and the thought of spending a year with the Bushmen (San) did not appeal—incredibly, from the perspective of the 1990s—to professional anthropologists, not even to those on the thresholds of their careers. The Bushmen were, of course, well known for their *click languages,* their small stature, and their supposedly mysterious origins, but the "Bushman industry" had not started. Laurens van der Post's "discovery" of what he called the "lost world of the Kalahari" did not take place until later, and his musings on the Bushmen had not yet seized the public's imagination.

Not surprisingly therefore, Lorna Marshall herself points out in her first book, *The !Kung of Nyae Nyae* (1976), that it was initially not so much the Bushmen as the possibility of finding "any remnant groups of Bergdama . . . in remote parts of the Kaoko Veld living in their ancient ways" that interested her family. It was anthropologist friends who pointed out to the Marshalls that little was known about another group, the !Kung Bushman hunter-gatherers, who lived in the Kaukau Veld. On their first, preliminary expedition, Laurence and John sought in vain for any remnant Bergdama. Disappointed, they headed for northwestern Botswana to look for "unacculturated Bushmen." There, they were told of the !Kung people of Nyae Nyae, who were believed to be "living in complete independence from Bantu or white people." It was not until the following year, 1951, that they, together with Lorna and Elizabeth, were able to reach Nyae Nyae.

Today, four decades and much anthropological research later, the "independence" of the Nyae Nyae !Kung, the Ju/'hoansi as they are also known, and indeed the very notion of looking for unacculturated communities are much debated. The so-called Kalahari Revisionist Debate has raised the question of the "authenticity" of the Nyae Nyae !Kung. Were they as isolated as people believed? Were they in any sense pristine hunter-gatherers? As they came to be perceived, were they little more than a construct made by the Marshall family?

In answering these questions, it is important to remember that the Marshalls themselves never believed that the Nyae Nyae !Kung had always lived totally isolated lives. As Lorna Marshall herself makes plain, the !Kung knew both white and black people, and they used many artifacts obtained from those communities. Moreover, some !Kung had worked, not always willingly, for periods of varying duration for members of other communities. But it was the !Kung's apparently unacculturated way of life, rather than their contacts with other people, that principally interested the Marshalls at first, and Lorna Marshall has made no secret of this interest. In his essay "Filming and Learning" (in *The Cinema of John Marshall,* edited by Jay Ruby), John reports a shift away from his own early, exclusive interest in "traditional" or "real" !Kung life, a shift that was associated with his family's growing concern for the well-being of the Nyae Nyae people: "In 1955 I was still cleaning tin cans out of shots to make Ju/'hoansi in Nyae Nyae look real. By 1958, I was filming the people being themselves."

Whatever cleaning up may have taken place, Lorna Marshall has made it clear that her own ethnographic work pertains to the years 1951 through 1955. Although the Nyae Nyae !Kung of that time knew of and had met other people, they themselves lived wholly by hunting and gathering; they had no agriculture, cattle, or even dogs. Lorna Marshall's ethnography does not deal with what may have happened in the remote past in Nyae Nyae, nor with what happened after the mid-1950s. It is other writers who have extrapolated her work to other times; Lorna Marshall herself warns against taking her work as timeless. She simply says that if the !Kung had, in some remote or not-so-remote period, lived pastoral or agricultural lives, she found no evidence of it. Though the point has been contested, the Marshalls and other anthropologists believe that the Nyae Nyae !Kung of the early 1950s were long-standing hunter-gatherers, not lapsed herders.

On the other hand, the people at Nyae Nyae had no knowledge of flaked stone artifacts; they said that their grandfathers had used metal arrowpoints and knives, just as they themselves did. They had not previously noticed the stone artifacts that Robert Dyson, an archaeologist and member of the 1951 Marshall expedition, found at various localities. Trade in iron and other goods had been part of their lives for many years, perhaps for as long as several hundred years.

Yet, despite the contacts that Lorna Marshall chronicles, the people of Nyae Nyae saw themselves as different from their neighbors in a number of significant ways: unlike their neighbors, they lived entirely by hunting and gathering, and they spoke a distinct click language. Moreover, their physical appearance, beliefs, and rituals were all clearly different.

The Marshalls realized that their own presence impacted on the !Kung: groups, or bands, gathered where the Marshalls camped, interested to see and to talk to them. Interaction between the !Kung and the Marshalls was considerable. When they left at the end of their 1952–1953 expedition, the Marshalls gave the !Kung presents, things that, after much consideration, they thought would be useful and appropriate. But this was done with many misgivings: as Lorna says in *The !Kung of Nyae Nyae* (1976), "The people were enchanted with their gifts, and we departed still searching our souls and wondering if we had done the right thing." When the Marshalls were with the !Kung, the now-institutionalized self-flagellations of post-modernism had not become fashionable, but honest self-reflection was nevertheless real enough. Indeed, soul-searching was the hallmark of the Marshalls' contact with the Nyae Nyae !Kung and the other Bushman communities whom they visited.

Today a secondary industry has grown up around ethnography. It purports to deconstruct ethnographies and to show how ethnographers work selectively, how they make their work persuasive, and how Westerners construct their own identities by seeing themselves in comfortable contrast to economically less-complex societies. A distinction between the status of primary ethnographic research and that of secondary work of this kind is being increasingly blurred as anthropologists return to their armchairs to work with ethnography compiled by others. Sir James Frazer, I read somewhere, was once asked if he had ever lived with, or even seen, any of the people whose strange and wild customs he chronicled in *The Golden Bough*. Aghast, he exclaimed, "God forbid!" Today it is the strange and wild customs of earlier ethnographers that seem to be of greatest interest to some anthropologists. No doubt their intellectual inquisitions have value; all researchers need to be self-critical, and no one should take the statements of others at face value. But I suspect that long after the inquisitors have gone the way of the grass of the African veld, the great ethnographies on which they battened will continue to be read, whatever their faults and limitations. Certainly, Lorna Marshall's 1950s Nyae Nyae ethnography, written as it was at particular times and in particular places, will be revisited and critiqued at future times and in other places. The processes of reinterpretation will change with each revisit, but the ethnography itself, as a self-conscious, invaluable record of a particular time, will endure. As Marcus and Fischer remark in their book *Anthropology as Cultural Critique*, the "classic works of anthropology remain vitally relevant, and their materials are a perennial source for the raising of new conceptual and theoretical problems."

Lorna Marshall's earlier work, *The !Kung of Nyae Nyae* (1976), is one of those enduring, classic works. It is principally concerned with the Nyae Nyae !Kung's successful hunting and gathering way of life in what many people see as a dangerously marginal environment. Bringing together some of the papers she had published earlier in the journal *Africa*, she considered !Kung social structure, kin terminology, and the ways in which talking, sharing, and giving relieved social tensions. She ended with a chapter entitled "Music for Pleasure."

Now, in this latest work, she deals with another kind of music and the whole belief system in which it was set. She describes the Ritual Healing Dance and its powerful, transforming *n/um* (or "medicine") songs; beliefs about the gods; ritual food avoidances; concepts of childbirth; hunting rites; and beliefs about *n!ow* (the power that can cause rain to fall).

Concepts about n/um and n!ow are at the heart of !Kung belief. For the !Kung there are two worlds: this world of hunting, gathering, living, and dying; and another world that is inhabited by the gods and nameless spirits of the dead, the *//gauwasi*. Passage between these two worlds is achieved by those who learn to control n/um so that it can boil within them and carry them across the frontier of the spirit. These people are the *n/um k"xausi*, the possessors of n/um, the "medicine people" or shamans. N!ow is something different; it is possessed by ordinary people, not only by n/um k"xausi. In a way that is difficult to understand in strictly scientific or regulated terms, a hunter's personal n!ow can interact with the n!ow of an animal so that it changes the weather in specific ways, which the hunter himself comes to know.

Belief in these two powers, n/um and n!ow, must have been very widespread among Bushman groups, for detailed records that Wilhelm Bleek and Lucy Lloyd made in the 1870s show that the /Xam, who lived in what is now the Northern Cape Province, also believed in them, or at any rate, in powers very like them (Bleek and Lloyd 1911). These powers, especially n/um, lie behind much of the splendid rock art for which southern Africa is known. Although the !Kung themselves do not make rock paintings or engravings, Lorna Marshall's ethnography has made and continues to make a significant contribution to our understanding of southern African rock art. Her work, together with Bleek and Lloyd's nineteenth-century records, has contributed to an appreciation of some of the ways in which the artists worked with the beliefs and key metaphors of their cosmos to produce powerful, visual statements, which continue to impact upon our consciousness so many years, and even centuries, later.

N/um, n!ow, and the cosmos that these powers permeated are, of course, difficult matters for an ethnographer to understand; indeed, many of the early travelers and missionaries who interviewed Bushmen despaired of ever comprehending what they believed. Perhaps fortunately, Lorna Marshall found no *Ogotemmêli* or *Ihembi*, those ritual and religious specialists who sometimes provide ethnographers with a ready-made, structured cosmological framework. More realistically, Lorna Marshall's !Kung friends often said that they simply did not know or that they had never thought about what she wanted to know—frustrating, perhaps, for an ethnographer looking for a neat (but very possibly misleading) "system," but, for Lorna Marshall, an important part of the fabric of daily life. There are many things that people do not know, and Lorna Marshall does not gloss over them. The very fact that people have never considered an issue put to them by an ethnographer is part of the pattern of those people's lives.

With elegant transparency of style, Lorna Marshall leads the reader through the intricacies, ambiguities, and silences of !Kung belief. Above all, she conveys the experience of actually talking to people, real people with their own views and emotions. Unlike some ethnographers, she does not adopt an Olympian detachment; always her narrative is situated in the Kalahari of the early 1950s, and we hear the voices of particular, named people. Her photographs, too, are mostly not of nameless exemplars— "a such-and-such youth" or "an old man"—as is the case in some celebrated ethnographies, but of real, named, and, without any sentimentality, much loved people whose words can be found in the text.

The impact of the work that the Marshall family conducted with those people continues to reverberate in fields and times that Lorna Marshall herself did not foresee. Perhaps the true measure of a person's work is not simply the quality of the work itself, important as that of course is, but rather what comes after it, what it leads to. Today, the work that the Marshalls started forty-six years ago, is still going forward. The comprehensive and long-term Harvard Bushman Research Project broadened the scope of the Marshalls' work, and some of the studies begun by the project are still underway.

The Marshall family's involvement with the Nyae Nyae people has, however, not been exclusively academic. The Marshalls' sensitive humanism and concern is evident in all their work. When they first arrived in Nyae Nyae, they explained to ≠Toma, leader of a Nyae Nyae group, that "they believed it good for people with different ways of life to learn to understand each other as best they could," and that they wished to learn about and understand the !Kung. ≠Toma agreed and became one of their principal teachers. In recording what ≠Toma and other !Kung people told her, Lorna Marshall does not debate social theory, nor is she judgmental; she is a self-proclaimed ethnographer, not a social or cultural anthropologist. Yet, reading between the lines, we sense that her learning about and understanding of the !Kung led to a deeply felt critique of her own society. Her generally functionalist, though tacitly so, position and even some of her paper titles, such as "Sharing, Talking and Giving," embody an indictment of Western society that flowered in and is implied by the title of Elizabeth's influential book *The Harmless People*.

As the years went by, the Marshall family was moved by the worsening plight of the !Kung. They therefore established a trust to help them to adjust to the modern way of life that was transforming their world. The comparative independence that the Marshalls observed in the early 1950s would vanish and the people would be reduced to poverty, landlessness, and political impotence during the South African occupation of what was then known as South West Africa. The Marshalls never walked away from the people whom they came to know so well. Their concern led eventually to the establishment in 1982 of the Ju/'hoan Bushman Development Foundation. Lorna's son, John, was a co-founder of the foundation. Since then, the foundation has fostered a Ju/'hoan people's cooperative that is effectively articulating the views and needs of the !Kung in a democratic Namibia.

Lorna Marshall's long-recognized role in both ethnography and social concern was celebrated in 1986 by the publication of a Festschrift, *The Past and Future of !Kung Ethnography: Critical Reflections and Symbolic Perspectives. Essays in Honour of Lorna Marshall,* edited by Megan Biesele with Robert Gordon and Richard Lee. Contributor after contributor pays tribute to her influence, encouragement, commitment, and compassion. In the same year, the University of Toronto conferred on her an honorary Doctorate of Laws. In 1994, the University of the Witwatersrand, Johannesburg, conferred on her the degree of Doctor of Literature, *honoris causa.* No one, it is widely recognized, has done more for Bushman studies and for the Bushmen themselves than Lorna Marshall.

As of this writing, she still takes an active interest in the Bushmen, and younger researchers turn to her for guidance and wisdom. They have found, as I found long ago, that Lorna's personality is aptly summed up in the title of her paper "Sharing, Talking and Giving." That paper was wisely reprinted in *The !Kung of Nyae Nyae* (1976). The present book takes its place alongside *The !Kung of Nyae Nyae;* together, these two books constitute one of the great, classic ethnographies, certainly one that will endure.

J. D. LEWIS-WILLIAMS
UNIVERSITY OF THE WITWATERSRAND
JOHANNESBURG, AUGUST 1997

[Note from the publisher: In 1999, Lorna Marshall celebrated her 101st birthday.]

REFERENCES CITED

Biesele, M., ed., with R. Gordon and R. Lee.
 1986 *The Past and Future of !Kung Ethnography: Critical Reflections and Symbolic Perspectives. Essays in Honour of Lorna Marshall.* Helmut Buske Verlag, Hamburg.

Bleek, W. H. I̊., and L. C. Lloyd
 1911 *Specimens of Bushman Folklore.* George Allen, London. Reprinted 1968 by C. Struik, Cape Town.

Marcus, G. E., and M. M. J. Fischer
  1986   *Anthropology as Cultural Critique: An Experimental Moment in the Human Sciences.*
          University of Chicago Press, Chicago.

Marshall, J.
  1993   "Filming and Learning," in *The Cinema of John Marshall,* J. Ruby, ed. Harwood
          Academic Publishers, Philadelphia.

Marshall, L.
  1976   *The !Kung of Nyae Nyae.* Harvard University Press, Cambridge.

Thomas, E. M.
  1959   *The Harmless People.* Knopf, New York.

◆ Acknowledgments

The foremost expression of my gratitude and that of my family is to the !Kung whom we knew in the Nyae Nyae region. They accepted our presence among them in friendliness and willingly helped us in our endeavor to understand their ways. We are equally grateful to the many people from the United States, Europe, and South Africa who helped us. Much of the material for this book was collected almost fifty years ago, and many people mentioned here are no longer living. We remember them all with much affection and gratitude.

Those with whom we spent the most time learning about !Kung beliefs and rites included ≠Toma of Band One, who was essentially our mentor and was with us almost constantly. It was largely from him that we learned about the beliefs and rites of *n!ow*. Lazy /Qui, Old Demi, Old Xama, Gao Beard, Old /Gaishay, !Kham, Lame ≠Gao, /Qui Hunter, /Gao Music, Old /Gasa, Ghia, and //Kushay were also extremely helpful. I am very grateful to them all. I thank Short Gao of Band 12 for telling us an important creation story, and Gao Feet, the healer, for telling us much about rain and lightning, about the magical, miniature bows and arrows, and about //Gauwa, whom he had seen. I would like to thank /Ti!kay for his insistence on counterexamples of items of belief, and Tuka N!a for the prayer songs he taught us, and also Demi, who gave us much understanding of the gods. I thank /Qui from /Gam, who told us about the Wildebeest People, as without him, we would not have heard of them. Most others around him believed there were Gemsbok People only. I also thank Old Ukwane of the /Gwi for providing us with many examples of /Gwi folklore.

I am equally grateful to Old N≠isa for helping us understand how she had been given *n/um* songs. I also respectfully acknowledge Be of Samangaigai, who shared the story of how she received the first Giraffe Song, which later became popular over much of the Kalahari. I would also like to thank //Khuga of Band 12, who helped us to understand dreams, also /Gunda and N!ai, who shared with us the dramatic events of their young lives—marriage and the apprenticeship of n/um. From them we learned much about the power of n/um. I would like to thank N!aishi for telling us how he received n/um, and also for helping us to understand burial customs. For helping us to understand food avoidances, I would like to thank /Qui. I am also grateful to Baú, daughter of N/aoka and /Ti!kay, for sharing with us the *Tshoa* Rite for the *tsi* beans she saw when we were together. I am grateful to //Kushay and her son ≠Gao for showing us the ritual of burying his umbilical cord, and to ≠Toma, likewise, for sharing with us his washing of his daughter Norna in New Rain.

I thank Old Gao of Band 1 for showing me the rite of the Meat Fire, and for explaining many things about hunting, animals, and the use of the rain horn. Likewise, I thank /Ti!kay of Kai Kai for demonstrating the rite of "Cutting with Meat."

I am equally grateful to the men who had been in *Tshoma,* the young men's initiation, for helping us to understand this event. Among these men were Old Demi, Old Gaú, Old N!aishi, Old ≠Toma, and Gao Wildebeest, who was my son John's sponsor in the practice Tshoma.

The people who helped us most with information concerning beliefs about the sun, moon, and stars included N/aoka, ≠Toma, Old Xama, Di//khao, Gao of Band 2, and Ukwane of the /Gwi. Ukwane pointed out the path of the sun and told us a number of /Gwi tales involving sun lore. He also told us more about stars including the relationship to the stars of ant lions and ant eggs. We heard first about ant lions from /Qui. Old /Gani shared Nharo moon lore with us and told us the Nharo version of "the Moon and the Hare." Our respected interpreter /Gishay made us aware of the star called Finish Fire. Yet in the context of stars, perhaps it is to Old Gaú that I am most grateful. He made me aware of the Green Leaf Horn of the Tshxum (the Pleiades) and took care to wake me in the dead of night on September 17, 1955, so that I could see both horns of the Tshxum in all their glory.

My husband, Laurence Kennedy Marshall, and I had the great pleasure of having our daughter and son working and sharing experiences with us in the field for large portions of the time. Our daughter, Elizabeth Marshall Thomas, gathered ethnographic material, as I did, and put her notes at my disposal. In some cases I am able to give her due credit for them, but in other cases our work is so merged that hers is inextricable from mine, and I can only express my gratitude for it.

The special fieldwork of our son, John Marshall, was to make a film record. The experiences of his first field trip led him to feel that the way to let ethnographic film best speak for the people it photographs, minimizing the intrusion of the observer who holds the camera, is to film events as completely as possible as they happen to occur. In producing the films, he has preferred to work with sequences rather than to construct thematic films that use material from different bodies of footage to illustrate a theme. From this film record he has since produced a number of documentaries including *The Hunters; Bitter Melons; !Kung Bushmen Hunting Equipment; N/um Tchai; !Nai, the Story of a !Kung Woman;* and many others. These films, as well as the film record in an unedited state, have been a valuable resource to me in my work.

I wish to express particular thanks to Megan Biesele, who made a collection of !Kung folktales for her Harvard Ph.D. dissertation. Her knowledge of the !Kung with whom she worked in the Dobe area, her mastery of their language, and her deep interest in all aspects of their lives made her assistance very useful indeed. She shared many of the tales with me and helped me to understand them. In addition, she supplied me with further information on the practice of Tshoma, and also on "luck" and on n!ow to supplement my original *Africa* paper on the latter topic. I also thank Megan for information about the locution "the late" in speaking of the dead. I am very grateful to her for her help in these matters. I am also grateful to her for reading the manuscripts with critical acumen and, with my daughter Elizabeth, for assisting me in the final stages of preparation of this book.

Nicholas England, who was with us in the field in 1958, 1959, and 1961, made a collection of Bushman music and is the author of a superb study of the music of Nyae Nyae, *Music Among the Zū'/'wā-si and Related Peoples of Namibia, Botswana, and Angola* (1995), which I have cited several times. His particular contribution to this work has been to further our understanding of the dance periods, as well as the practice of Tshoma. He was an unusually companionable member of our group in the field, with his flair for bringing people of all kinds into friendly relationships. Over the years, discussion with him on any aspect of our work in Bushman studies has been a benefit and a pleasure.

I have also had the pleasure and benefit of discussing this work with Nancie Gonzalez, who has been most generous with time and counsel.

I would like to thank Sigrid Schmidt for her work on Bushman folklore, especially for her paper "Tales and Beliefs about Eyes-on-his-Feet: The Interrelatedness of Khoisan Folklore" in the Festschrift she and others collaborated on for me (*The Past and Future of !Kung Ethnography: Critical Reflections and Symbolic Perspectives. Essays in Honour of Lorna Marshall*, Megan Biesele, ed., with Robert Gordon and Richard Lee 1986). Sigrid Schmidt provided me with a manuscript copy of her valuable 1973 paper "Die Mantis Religiosa in den Glaubensvorstellungen der Khoesan-Völker," whose more than 100 pages held many treasures of information about mantis beliefs. Megan Biesele made a rough translation of this paper for me while she was working as my research and editorial assistant.

Franklin Ross of the Harvard Museum of Comparative Zoology provided further information on mantises as well as on medicinal plants of the Kalahari. Theodore August Wagner awakened my interest in studying the star lore of the Bushmen and thoughtfully provided me with a copy of Norton's *A Star Atlas*. In this context, I also thank Nicolaas J. van Warmelo for his help in informing me about Canopus.

I have benefited from discussions about the supernatural travels of the n/um owners with Richard Katz, who with Megan Biesele, shared with me old K"xau's riveting story of his journey to the sky. The new book by Katz, Biesele, and Verna St. Denis, *Healing Makes our Hearts Happy: Spirituality and Cultural Transformation among the Kalahari Ju/'hoansi,* 1997) enhances my understanding of the !Kung healing tradition.

David Lewis-Williams I thank for his help in understanding the food avoidances and for his rich information on Bushman symbolism in general. Polly Wiessner helped me with a detailed description of a burial, and I am grateful to her for that. In addition, I would like to thank Bert Ramsden for giving me two magic quivers full of tiny arrows. He was our gracious host while we were in the Ghanzi area, and shared with us his collection of Nharo artifacts.

Charles O. Handley, Jr., of the Smithsonian Institution, collected small mammals while with us in 1952. He made his report to the Smithsonian available to us. I refer to it several times, and want to express my thanks.

Robert Story collected Bushman food plants in the Kalahari while with us in 1955 and 1958. His published material has been of great use to me, and he has been kind, meticulous, and entertaining in responding to my questions about the botanical identification of the food plants. In particular, his information about dagga has been important to this work. His replies have come to me from South Africa, Patagonia, and Australia.

Richard Borshay Lee and Irven DeVore organized the Harvard Bushman Research Project in 1963, which has brought scientists of several disciplines to study the !Kung. The members of this project are sometimes called the Harvard Group. Lee's work and that of others of this group have added new dimensions to Bushman studies. I have immensely enjoyed talking with several members of the group about our mutual interests in their special fields, especially Irven and Nancy DeVore, Melvin Konner, Marjorie Shostak, Pat Draper, Nancy Howell, Richard Katz, Alison Brooks, and John Yellen.

I am thankful to Drs. A. S. Truswell and J. D. L. Hansen of South Africa for their medical and epidemiological knowledge and help. Our dear friend Dr. Jacob Fine of Boston assembled the medicine chest that proved extremely helpful to us many times in the field.

It is impossible for me to name individually all the people whose abilities and efforts helped us to travel and live in the desert; I can only assure them all of our sincere thanks for their cheerful and effective cooperation. I would like to express special thanks to Philip Hameva, who was with us for many years, and also to Heiner Kretzchmar, Casper Kruger, Foppe Hoogheimstra, and Kurt Ahrens, who were with us at different times. We enjoyed their company and relied on their skills.

The major photographic contributions to the fieldwork were made by Laurence Marshall and John Marshall. Laurence Marshall worked in still photography, taking mainly color photographs but also many black-and-whites. Special credit for many fine pictures is also due to Anneliese Scherz, Daniel Blitz, and Robert Gesteland.

Many expedition members worked on sound recording—of music especially, and also of speech. Chief among them were Nicholas England, John Marshall, myself, Daniel Blitz, Elizabeth Marshall Thomas, Frank Hesse, and Hans Ernst.

For many years, my dear friend Constance Coulopoulos served as my valued assistant, organizing and typing field notes, cataloguing and filing photographs, and typing manuscripts. Julie Fair was most helpful in editing the manuscript. I am very grateful to her for her skill and patience, and for the clarification she achieved. Working with her was always a pleasure. My granddaughter, Stephanie Thomas, whose undergraduate degree was in folklore and mythology, was also helpful to me at several stages of editing this manuscript. My esteemed friend Frances Panton also helped me in immeasurable ways. Each gave me the advantage of special skills, the enjoyment of sharing an interest, and the pleasure of a warm relationship. I am grateful to them all.

I would also express my deepest thanks to Rubie Watson of the Peabody Museum at Harvard for her support of this work and for seeing it through to publication.

Finally, I wish to name with pleasure the interpreters whose work was essential to our record of the Bushmen. I am especially grateful to Kernel Ledimo, who was my interpreter on every expedition except that of 1969 and who spoke at least four languages, among them !Kung, which he had learned in his childhood. I am also very grateful to Ngani, who spoke nine languages. Both of these men understood our purposes and our methods and strove faithfully to translate as accurately as they could, not to embellish or distort information the !Kung gave us, nor to offer their own interpretation of what the !Kung meant. Rather, they tried painstakingly to unravel the misunderstandings and nonunderstandings in which we were so often entangled. In this context I would also like to thank the other interpreters who so skillfully helped us: Katukwa, Katembehe, Frederick Gaeb, /Gao, Ebsom Kopunko, Joseph Tsanigob, Wilhelm Camm, Dabe, and /Gishay. With the aid of these interpreters we were able to communicate in fifteen languages: Afrikaans, Ambo, English, //Gana, German, /Gwi, Heikum, Herero, !Ko, !Kung, Nama, Nharo, Ovambo, several dialects from the Okavango area, Portuguese, and Tswana.

NOTES ON THE TEXT

Chapters 1, 3, and 7 (section on "n!ow") in this book originally appeared as papers in *Africa,* the journal of the International African Institute. It is with the kind permission of the Institute and of Edinburgh University Press that this text is republished here. Chapter 13 originally appeared as a paper in *Contemporary Studies on Khoisan 2,* and it is with the kind permission of Helmut Buske Verlag that this text is republished here. The dates and titles of original publication are given in endnotes to the chapters.

I have made some revisions in these papers—principally changes in the order in which material is presented. Any corrections or revisions of significance are signaled in endnotes. I have also added some introductory material, a chapter on leisure and games, and a set of charts showing the composition of thirteen !Kung bands as they were in 1952 (first published in my book *The !Kung of Nyae Nyae,* 1976). In various endnotes to the chapters, I have also amplified certain points and introduced some new material of relevance.

ORTHOGRAPHY

My orthography is codified in the following key showing the values I attribute to various letters and combinations. Some letters represent more than one sound. This orthography does not transcribe the !Kung sounds with high phonetic accuracy; in many instances it allows only an approximation of the !Kung sounds:

a	*father*
e	*end*
i	*feet*
o	n*o*te
u	m*oo*n
ai, ae	*lie*
ao, au	th*ou*
aú	Ra*ú*l (Spanish)
ei, ay	s*ay*

dj	*ju*d*ge*
g	*g*ap
j	*je* (French)
kh	*k* with strong aspiration
k"	ejective *k* or "glottal croak" as Dorothea Bleek calls it in *A Bushman Dictionary* (1956:117)
n	sometimes *n*ot, sometimes si*ng*; *n* before a click is always nasalized
ng	si*ng*
tsh	*ch*ance. To avoid the ambiguity of the hard *ch* as in character and the soft *ch* as in chance, I changed to tsh.
x	no*ch* (German)

I attribute the common English values to the letters *b, d, h, k, m, s, t, w,* and *z,* and the combinations *qu* and *sh.*

In addition to the above letters, I use the standard symbols for clicks (see below), a tilde to indicate nasalization of a vowel, and an apostrophe ['] to indicate the glottal stop. !Kung has five tones: high, middle, low, rising, and falling. High tone is indicated by a line above the word as in ⁻*di,* "female"; low tone by a line on the lower level of the word as in ⌐*!ga,* "rain." Middle tone is conventionally not marked. I do not mark rising and falling tones because I could not be sure I distinguished them correctly, and I fear I·have failed to note high and low tones in every instance in which they should be noted.

Some place names that appear in this volume have established spellings that are found in maps and official publications. I have not altered these, although in some cases they conflict with the key given above. The most important of these are:

Barachu	*ch* = my *tsh*
Chadum	*ch* = my *k*
Cháassis	This name is pronounced like—in fact, it is—the French and English word for the underpart of an automobile.
Gautscha	*tsch* = my *tsh.* The !Kung pronounce this name with an initial dental click that is ignored in the established spelling; a more correct rendering would be /Gautsha.
Ghanzi	*gh* = my *x; z* = my *ts*
Nyae Nyae	*ae* = my *ai*

I am not a competent linguist and feel very humble about my rendering of the !Kung words. I do not want my spellings to be taken as authoritative. In view of the recent works of Dr. Nicholas England and members of the Harvard Bushman Research Project, I revised some spellings to conform with theirs, but for the sake of consistency with my own earlier work, I limited those changes to a few. My principal changes are as follows:

N!ai	the name formerly written !Nai (placing the *n* that indicated nasalization before the click instead of after)
Tsho/ana	a place name formerly spelled Cho/ana.
tai	"mother," formerly spelled *dai*. See chapter 6 about kin terminology in L. Marshall 1976.
k"xau	"owner," formerly spelled *kxau*.

CLICKS

Clicks are called velaric suction stops (Heffner), or velar injectives (Greenberg). There are five click sounds in the Khoisan languages. !Kung employs four, all of them lingual. (The fifth click of the southern Bushman languages is labial.) To make the four lingual clicks, one forms a cavity at the top of the mouth by pressing the back of the tongue against the velum, the sides of the tongue against the inside of the upper teeth, and the tip against the back of the front teeth or the alveolar ridge. The center of the blade of the tongue is then drawn downward (Doke, Heffner). This enlarges the cavity a little, and the air in it becomes slightly rarefied. To produce the click sounds, the closure at the velum is maintained while the tongue is released at some other point. The rush of air into the cavity makes the different click sounds according to the place of the release. To produce the fifth, the labial click, closures are made at the velum and the lips; the closure at the lips is then released with a gentle smack. In all clicks, the velar closure is released almost immediately after the frontal release; the manner of velar release is indicated in writing by the letter that follows (or in the case of *n*, precedes) the click. The release may be unvoiced (with a *k* sound) or voiced (with a *g* sound); these sounds may be aspirated or not. The click may be followed directly by a vowel or by a glottal stop. The whole click may be nasalized *(n)*.

The standard symbols for the clicks are:

/	Dental click. The tip of the tongue is placed against the back of the upper front teeth; in the release, it is pulled away with a fricative sound. English-speakers use a similar sound in gentle reproof; it is sometimes written "tsk tsk."

≠   Alveolar click. The front part of the tongue, more than the tip, is pressed against the alveolar ridge and drawn sharply downward when released. The sound produced, a snap, is often (not always) accompanied by a slight sucking sound.

!   Alveolar-palatal click. The tip of the tongue is pressed firmly against the back of the alveolar ridge where it meets the hard palate and is very sharply snapped down on release. A loud pop results.

//   Lateral click. The tongue is placed as for the alveolar click. It is released at the sides by being drawn in from the teeth while the front part of the tongue remains pressed against the alveolar ridge. The click has a fricative sound. Drivers of horses, at least American and Canadian drivers, traditionally use lateral clicks as sounds to signal their horses to start or go faster. My interpreter, Kernel Ledimo, said that in making this click the !Kung release both sides of the tongue. Doke, however, says that in all instances that he observed carefully among the !Kung, only one side, the right side, was released (1925).

⊙   Labial click. This click is found only in the southern Bushman languages. The velar closure is the same as for the lingual clicks, but the frontal closure is made with pursed lips rather than the tongue. When the lips are released, the sound is like a kiss (hence the name "kiss click").

For more detailed discussions of clicks, see Greenburg 1955:80, Greenburg 1966:66, Doke 1925:144 ff., and Heffner 1960:138.)

For other studies of !Kung, see Köhler 1971 and Snyman 1970.

VOCABULARY

I am dropping three Afrikaans words that I had formerly adopted because they seemed convenient or colorful at the time and am replacing them with English words. They proved not to be convenient; it became a nuisance to continually define them. *Veldkos* is replaced with "wild plant foods" or "plant foods"; *werf* is replaced with "encampment"; *scherm* is replaced with "shelter."

I use the term "band" for the group of people who live together in !Kung society. The !Kung word is *n//abesi*. Members of the !Kung band are bound together by ties of kinship and affinity. See chapter 6 of *The !Kung of Nyae Nyae* (Marshall 1976).

First Person Plural Pronouns

I find that I have slipped into a rather vague use of first person plural pronouns. Most often it is my family I have in mind when I say "we" in describing experiences we shared. Sometimes—and I think it can be easily deduced from the context—my "we" refers to members of the expedition as a whole. I avoid the editorial "we."

Charts of !Kung Bands

I include in an appendix charts of thirteen bands in the Nyae Nyae area (reprinted from Marshall 1976). Their principal purpose is to show the kin and affinal relationships on which bands are formed. The population in those charts is the count we made at a specific period of time, August through December 1952. In the charts each person has been assigned a number comprised of the number of the band of which he is a member and a number within the band according to the place in which his name falls in the chart. Thus ≠Toma is 1.16, !U, his wife, is 1.15.

Identification of Certain Individuals

Several individuals are referred to much more frequently than others. Instead of endlessly explaining who they are, I shall identify them herewith. The list does not give every member of each family. For the complete family, see the charts in the appendix.

≠Toma [1.16], called ≠Toma Word

!U [1.15], wife of ≠Toma

Tsamgao [1.17], son of ≠Toma and !U

/Gaishay [1.18], son of ≠Toma and !U

!Ungka Norna [1.19], daughter of ≠Toma and !U, named for ≠Toma's sister and for me. Norna is the !Kung rendering of Lorna. The !Kung cannot or do not pronounce *l.*

Lame ≠Gao [1.14], brother of !U

/Qui [1.24], called /Qui Navel by the !Kung. (We called him Neanderthal; Claude McIntyre called him Lazy /Qui.)

//Kushay [1.23], wife of /Qui

Little ≠Gao [1.26], son of /Qui and //Kushay

Old Gaú [1.20], father of //Kushay

!Ungka [1.21], daughter of Old Gaú, sister of //Kushay

/Gishay [1.22], son of Old Gaú, brother of //Kushay

Gao [1.8], called Gao Feet. (We called him Gao Medicine.)

N/aoka [1.7], first wife of Gao

//Khuga [1.4], daughter of Gao and N/aoka

Crooked /Qui [1.5], husband of //Khuga

Di!ai [1.9], second wife of Gao, sister of !U

N!ai [1.12], daughter of Di!ai by a former husband, Gumtsa

/Gunda [2.23], husband of N!ai

/Gao Music [1.1], husband of Gao's daughter N≠isa [1.2]

Old /Gaishay [4.1], father of Gao

Old Di//khao-!Gun≠a [4.2], wife of Old /Gaishay

Old ≠Toma [2.16]

Old /Gam [2.17], wife of Old ≠Toma

//Ao [2.20], son of Old ≠Toma and Old /Gam, called //Ao Wildebeest

Old /Gasa [2.35]

Gaú [2.25], son of Old /Gasa

Be [2.26], first wife of Gaú

Khuan//a [2.24], second wife of Gaú, mother of /Gunda [2.23]

Short /Qui [2.37], husband of Old /Gasa's daughter N/aoka [2.36]. (We called him
    /Qui Hunter.) This is the man who lost his foot as a result of a puff adder
    bite. He is described by Elizabeth Marshall Thomas in *The Harmless
    People*, Chapter 13. We took him to the hospital in Windhoek, where the
    gangrenous part of his leg was amputated and a wooden leg was made for
    him by a furniture maker. When /Qui returned to Nyae Nyae, he was able
    to walk and even run, though not as swiftly as before. He hunts success-
    fully. When he needs a new wooden leg, he carves one out for himself. I
    add this note because everywhere we go people who have read *The
    Harmless People* ask me about /Qui Hunter.

Gao Beard [2.9]. (At first we called him Gao Helmet.)

//Kushay I [2.10], first wife of Gao Beard

Xama [2.14], daughter of //Kushay I and Gao Beard

//Kushay II [2.8], second wife of Gao Beard

Old Xama [2.7], mother of Gao Beard

/Ti!kay [9.8]

N/aoka [9.7], first wife of /Ti!kay. She will be so identified each time to distinguish her from Gao's first wife

Baú [9.6], daughter of /Ti!kay and N/aoka

N!ai [9.9], second wife of /Ti!kay. N/aoka and N!ai are sisters. This N!ai will be distinguished from N!ai [1.12] by being called /Ti!kay's wife.

Old Demi [6.4]

Short Gao of Band 12 [12.6]

Old /Gaishay, the bachelor [3.8].

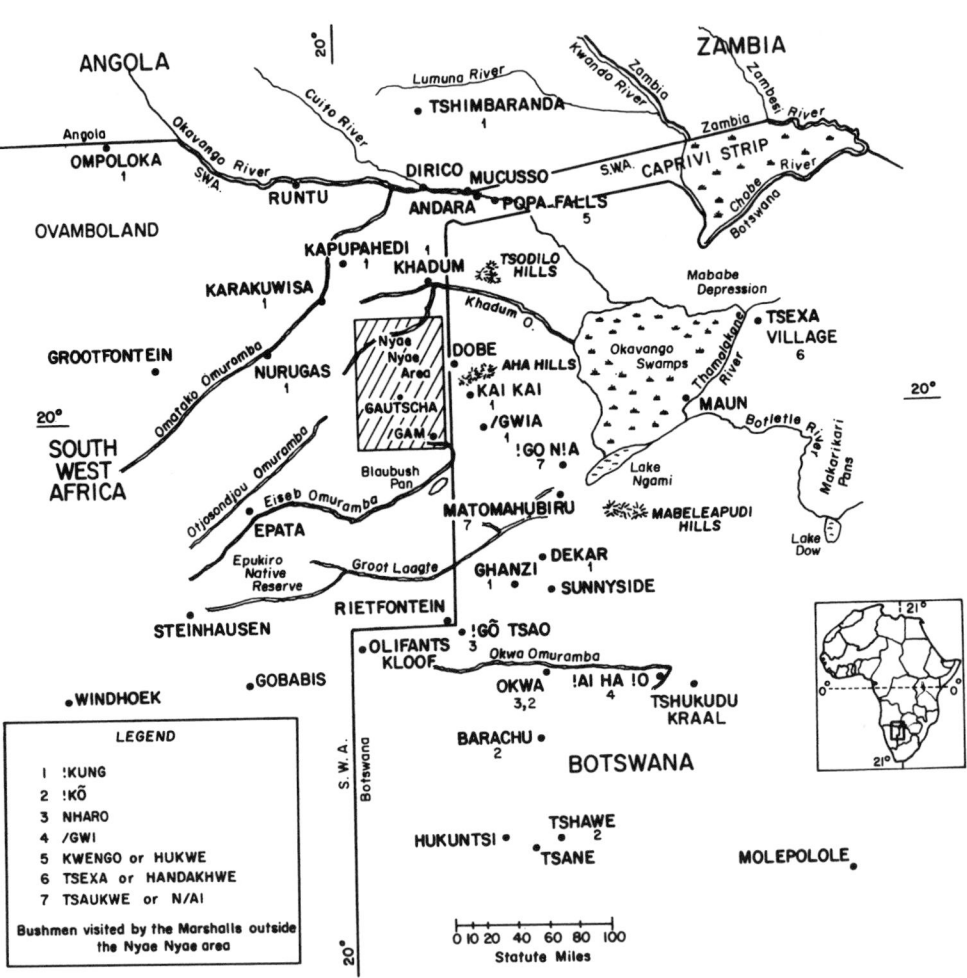

Map of the Nyae Nyae and surrounding areas visited by the Marshalls.

INTRODUCTION

Elements of the Supernatural

This book is a companion volume to *The !Kung of Nyae Nyae* (Marshall 1976). In that book I described the social system of the Nyae Nyae !Kung and their methods of procuring food. Those were mundane matters, matters of the world of nature and human relationships. In this volume I describe the beliefs of the Nyae Nyae !Kung about the supernatural world. The book is largely devoted to describing the rites and informal ritual practices that the !Kung perform to utilize the beneficent elements of that world and to protect themselves from its dangers in order to safeguard life and health. The two worlds, the natural and the supernatural, are one reality to the !Kung.

The dominant elements in the !Kung supernatural world are personified deities and certain unpersonified supernatural forces. The !Kung believe that the deities and the supernatural forces interact with man and the natural world and that they account for much of the mystery of life and the vicissitudes of the good and evil that befall mankind. Neither the deities nor the supernatural forces are totally good or totally evil in their influence on man. The great god is both the life-giver and the death-giver. There are forces that heal as well as forces that destroy. The deities and the forces are the source of the ills man suffers, but, as the source of beneficence also, they offer hope of help and protection.

Foremost in the !Kung system of beliefs are the those about the deities. The !Kung gods are two powerful anthropomorphic male sky gods. The more powerful of the two, the omnipotent creator, lives in the eastern sky where the sun rises. One of his names is "≠Gao N!a." The lesser god, best known by the name "//Gauwa," lives in the western sky where the sun sets. The gods have wives and children. With the great god in the east live all the spirits of the dead, the //gauwasi. All the sky beings are immortal.

These beings, the gods, their families, and the //gauwasi, although they live in the sky, are not aloof from mortals. On the contrary, mortals are their great concern, and they are constantly acting for the good or the ill of mortals. The gods may descend to earth to do so. More often they send the spirits of the dead as messengers.

The !Kung for their part communicate freely with the gods in personal, verbalized prayer or in reverie. Sometimes they dream that the gods come to them and they communicate face to face. Usually people plead humbly for favors in their prayers. In certain circumstances, however, the !Kung take their gods to task, shouting blasphemies and curses at them. Chapter 1, "The Gods," describes the gods and the other sky beings and man's relationship with them.

Intermingled with the beliefs about the gods and the other sky beings is the !Kung belief in unpersonified supernatural elements, which I have called supernatural forces.[1]

The forces are conceived of as being unpersonified, incorporeal, immaterial, invisible, and powerful. They have innumerable effects. I imagine that the beliefs about them are an agglomeration of ancient concepts about occult forces and magic practices. In my effort to understand these beliefs in their current forms, I came to the conclusion that the !Kung do not believe that there is a single undifferentiated force, like a single essence or substance, some of which exists in different places and operates in different contexts. The forces, instead, are multiple, and they are differentiated. They have their existence in certain people, animals, plants, and inanimate objects. They are not diffused in the universe or in the air around the earth, nor are they conceived of as spirits that enter people or animate inanimate objects. Among the !Kung we found no concepts of people, healers, or others being possessed by spirits, or of things such as trees or water being animated by spirits. The forces are as unpersonified as electricity.

The !Kung behave toward the forces as though they believed them to be autonomous, and they try to control them directly by various rituals and practices. When they must answer an ethnographer's questions and explain the relationship of the seemingly autonomous forces with the great omnipotent god, the creator and controller of all things, they make a logical explanation and say that the great god created the forces as he created everything else and put them into the people, animals, plants, or objects that they are in. He created the forces to be as they are, to act as they do. He does not wield them or direct their every action—he allows them to act autonomously. However, according to the !Kung, the great god could negate their power, stop their working, or control their action any time he wished to do so. Apparently he does not wish to do so, for the age-old forces are constantly at work, their ancient powers unabated, and acting upon man and nature.

I think of !Kung beliefs about the supernatural forces as lying in different strata. Two of the forces have current importance in !Kung culture. These forces are clearly conceived, and they are named—*n!ow* and *n/um*. In another stratum of beliefs is a presumably old assortment of supernatural forces existing in substances or in people—forces that can cause harm and death. They are described in the chapter entitled "Sorcery" (chapter 11). These beliefs have minor importance in !Kung culture.

N!ow is a force that interacts with weather. N!ow exists in all people and in certain animals. The n!ow is believed to enter a child in the womb at the moment the mother's uterine fluid flows onto the ground. Each individual possesses his own n!ow but has no voluntary control over it. A person can only observe what interaction his n!ow has with weather. N!ow is described in chapter 7.

The beliefs about n/um (plural *n/umsi*) pervade this book so much that I must try at the beginning to give an overall view of them. N/um defies a brief definition. The !Kung say, for example, that the great god has n/um that no humans possess—the strongest n/um of all. The Old Old People, the ancestors of the !Kung, also had special n/um that gave them extraordinary powers; people no longer have those n/umsi or those powers. The !Kung who live at Gautscha said that they possess the n/um of a certain Giraffe Song, one of the songs sung at the great Ritual Healing Dances, but they do not possess the n/um of the Honey Song; the people of N//o !Gau possess the Honey Song n/um.

N/um exists in many diverse beings and things. Much n/um is present at the Ritual Healing Dances, which are called n/um dances, *n/um tshxaisi*. The songs have n/um, and the men who are the healers of sickness have such powerful n/um in them that they are called *n/um k"xausi* (owners of n/um). There is n/um in the sun, in falling stars, and in rain. A fire that has been specially kindled with fire sticks for ritual purposes has n/um. Ostrich eggs, bees, and honey have very strong n/um. Blood and milk have n/um. The n/umsi of menstrual blood and women's milk are especially strong. Elands and giraffes have exceedingly strong n/um. Aardvarks and redwing partridges have n/um, but it is not strong. Many plants and trees (to be described and identified later) have n/um, including *sha sha, ≠khali, //gwey, mai,* and the *zao* and */ana* trees. I call the plants "medicine plants" and distinguish them from food plants. This list is not exhaustive. It was compiled as n/um was mentioned when we observed and discussed with the !Kung the many rites we saw performed, and when we discussed the gods and any matters of the supernatural. In all probability, there are more things with n/um in them that we did not know to ask about and the !Kung did not think to mention to us.

The n/um forces have a multitude of different effects. Some are beneficent, curative, or protective; others can cause numerous ills: sickness, death, thinness, madness, or loss of hunting powers. The n/um in the n/um k"xausi, for example, enables them to cure the sick. The n/um in ostrich eggs can cause madness in men and women in their procreative years; only the young and the old can safely eat ostrich eggs.

In some instances, a beneficent n/um can counteract a dangerous n/um. For example, if young men should sit by a fire at which a menstruating woman is sitting, the n/um of her menstrual blood would weaken their power to hunt. In !Kung concept, hunting powers can be weakened or destroyed by female procreative powers. However, if a sliver of the root of a plant called sha sha is burned in the fire, sha sha protects the young men. Sha sha (*Pelargonium* near *senecioides*)[2] is a plant used in many rituals, not as a curing agent but for its supernatural element as a protective agent.

When the !Kung are asked to explain the nature and workings of n/um, they say that n/um is strong, and having said that, they seem to think that they have explained all that need be explained. All n/um is strong, but some is especially strong. The stronger the n/um is, the more potentially dangerous it is, or in the case of the n/um of the healers, the more powerful in healing.

Referring to the strength of n/um, the !Kung call it a "death-thing" (*!khi tshi*). This is not an expression that would be applied to something like a weapon or poison that can cause death. It is a metaphor applied to anything very strong and potentially dangerous. The sun, for example, is a death-thing.

The !Kung pair the word "n/um" with a "respect" word, "*shibi.*" Many words in the !Kung language are so paired. The !Kung say that respect words are not as strong as other words, although they have identical denotations. The !Kung apparently believe that words act as conductors. The word for something harmful can conduct harm to the person who speaks it. Respect words are presumably less likely to conduct the harm. For example, the word for rain is "*!ga*"; the respect word is "*n/oi.*" If one of the fearsome Kalahari thunderheads bursts over you, you would say "n/oi" instead of "!ga," lest the word "!ga" bring so fierce a storm that the people would perish in it. Or if you looked up and saw a lion staring at you from the edge of the firelight, it would be prudent to say "*n!hei*" instead of "*//ka*," unless even more prudently you quickly said only "*kuri, kuri*" (look out, look out). So it is with n/um; in the presence of strong n/um, the word should be avoided and the respect word "shibi" used instead.

In ordinary circumstances, the words may be spoken aloud, but there are times when the n/um is so very strong that, in a deeper degree of precaution, the words should be whispered or not spoken at all. The !Kung sometimes paraphrase them. If the n/um at a Ritual Healing Dance was believed to become exceedingly strong and a person wanted to remark upon it, he could say, "The dance is *n!a.*" (N!a means "old" or "big.") At these times people should also avoid speaking the names of the songs of the Ritual Healing Dance—Giraffe, Honey, Sun, Rain, and others.

How is it that elands, aardvarks, and redwing partridges, for instance, have n/um? Why and how does the n/um in ostrich eggs cause madness and the n/um of the healers enable them to cure? We probed these and many similar questions in vain, searching for a philosophic concept or a mythic lore, or possible examples of association of ideas, concepts of sympathetic magic, or perhaps historical events that might lie behind the beliefs about n/um and explain them. The !Kung say they do not know any lore that explains the whys and the wherefores of n/um. They said their ancestors had taught them what they must do with respect to n/um but had not explained more. I sincerely believe that the !Kung were not hiding secrets from us in making these claims. N/um is mysterious and eludes understanding but the beliefs about it are not held in secrecy. I believe that the !Kung culture simply does not preserve the background of beliefs.

The belief in the first two supernatural elements that I have mentioned, the personified sky beings and the unpersonified forces of n/um and n!ow, actively influences !Kung thinking and behavior. The prayers to the gods and the rites and practices that are performed to manipulate the force are a part of daily life. Of major importance in !Kung life are the healers who, with their strong n/um, heal and protect, especially at the great Ritual Healing Dances that bring the whole community together.

The !Kung believe supernatural forces exist that can cause harm and death as well. They are apparently differentiated from the n/um forces in !Kung thinking. Their nature seems to be less defined, and they have much less importance in the life of the !Kung than the healers' n/um. The magic bow (the so-called Bushman revolver) is believed to kill by such a force. A few substances are believed to have the power to kill—the hair of a corpse, for example. And some persons, men or women, are believed to have a force within themselves that they can project into others to harm or kill them. I am calling the use of these occult forces sorcery. We found no socially structured institution of sorcerers among the !Kung. The individuals we were told about who were believed to have the supernatural inner power to kill were few. They were not in the service of others. They acted simply as individuals for personal vengeance. Instances of the believed use of sorcery are described in chapter 11.

The !Kung have a large number of folktales.[3] An important cycle of their tales tells of an ancient time when ≠Gao N!a, now the great sky god, lived on earth. He was a trickster then. Animals were people in those ancient times. They could talk, and they lived together with the humans and intermarried with them. ≠Gao N!a, the animal-people, and the humans all had marvelous powers. For example, they could change form, fly through the air, and be killed and come to life again, as in myths and folktales everywhere. Eventually a new order came. The animals became the animals they are today, the humans lost their marvelous powers, and the earthy old ≠Gao N!a became a lofty sky god.

In many of their deeds, the beings of the old tales display the dark side of human nature. They were greedy and selfish, foolish and stupid, cunning and deceitful, touchy, short-tempered, jealous, vengeful, and lustful. They cheerfully and nonchalantly committed, by !Kung standards, the most heinous antisocial acts—cannibalism, incest, rape, and murder. To the !Kung this was wicked, unthinkable behavior. But the tales are not told with an emphasis on the evil of the deeds, or as solemn moral lessons. Instead they are told as though the way of life of those ancient folk was to them the normal, expected, proper way of life. This egregious attitude is hilariously funny to the !Kung, who shriek and howl with laughter in telling the tales.

The !Kung have no structured storytelling occasions, no specialized storytellers, no formalized memorized version of the tales. Individuals tell the tales as they remember them, with many variations. They tell them for enjoyment when they happen to be in the mood. Our asking for the tales seemed to put everyone in the mood, and groups gathered to hear the tales and to participate in the telling. Grown-ups would call the children when a session was beginning, "Come, we are going to tell a story. Come and learn something." The flow of talk, the imitation of the voices of the various characters, the miming of gestures, and the uproarious laughter made storytelling sessions a highly entertaining experience.

None of the beings of the folktales is believed to exist today except the protagonist, ≠Gao N!a, now the great god. However, the !Kung tell of three quite other supernatural peoples who are said to exist in the present. They are the Gemsbok People, the Wildebeest People, and the people who have no knees, called the Knee Knee None, who are also called the People Who Eat the Sun. None of these peoples are thought to be threatening to the !Kung, and the beliefs about them are not given much importance. Some !Kung seemed vaguely uncertain of the continued existence of these peoples. I describe them in chapter 12, where I also mention some beliefs about lions and the supernatural qualities ascribed to millipedes and the praying mantis (Mantis religiosa).

Bordering on the supernatural are the first ancestors of the !Kung, called the Old Old People. They lived very long ago. They were human, not supernatural beings, but they touched upon the supernatural in having unique n/um and extraordinary powers, and they were so wise and so able they might be considered to be superhuman. They were the recipients of all knowledge. The great god himself taught them everything that Bushmen know. He taught them to make bows, arrows, and arrow poison, and to hunt. He taught them to know which plants they should gather to eat. He taught them to dig with digging sticks, and to make all the things that Bushmen need and make. He taught them that they should marry and have children, and that people should avoid fighting and live properly together. The Old Old People taught their young people, and the knowledge has been passed from generation to generation.

When the !Kung we spoke with did not have an answer to our inquiries and thought we might therefore consider them ignorant, they became embarrassed and defensive and put the blame on the Old Old People, explaining that the Old Old People had not taught them whatever it was we wanted to know. Turning the point of discussion into a question, as they so often did, they would say they were young and ask how they could be expected to know if they had not been taught. The Old Old People pervaded many of our discussions.

When the Old Old People died, they became spirits of the dead (//gauwasi). They are not differentiated from all the other people who have died since. The !Kung respect the memory of the Old Old People as founders of the !Kung way of life and refer to them often, but they do not honor or fear them as spirits of the dead. They do not worship them or perform rites for them.

The !Kung belief in the several supernatural elements varies in strength and clarity. The Gemsbok People and the Knee Knee None have no influence on !Kung lives, and the beliefs about them have a remote, unimportant quality. The Old Old People are believed to be actual ancestors of the !Kung, but they are remote in time and without present influence. The strongest, clearest beliefs in the supernatural are the beliefs about n/um and about the gods. These beliefs constantly influence the daily lives of the Nyae Nyae !Kung.

PART I

RELIGIOUS BELIEFS

1  THE GODS

The !Kung of Nyae Nyae conceive of the cosmos as having three layers: the earth that people see and walk upon; the sky that contains the sun, moon, stars, rain, lightning, and wind; and above that sky another sky, which cannot be seen from earth.

The earth and the sky of the sun, moon, and stars belong to what we call the natural world. The sky above the natural sky belongs to the supernatural world, and it is in that sky the !Kung have placed their gods and other sky beings. We make a distinction, but the natural and the supernatural are one reality to the !Kung. They do not believe in an underworld, a Hades or a Hell; nor do they believe that supernatural beings of any kind—demons or others—live inside the earth.

Bushmen of several language groups have held various beliefs about the sky beings and the celestial bodies. One concept was that the spirits of the dead live in the sky and that the stars are their hearth fires. Another concept was that the stars are the eyes of the dead. Some Bushmen have worshiped the moon or stars and have prayed to them (Schapera 1930:172ff.). The !Kung do not hold these beliefs. They believe that the celestial bodies belong to the world of material things. For instance, ≠Toma said that the moon looks like stone to him. Material though the celestial bodies are, to the !Kung they are mysterious. Their substance is not known, their motion not understood. The !Kung say that there are things of the sky so distant that they are beyond man's knowledge.

The upper sky, the abode of the sky beings, cannot be seen from earth, but it is very much like the earth, according to the !Kung. It has sandy ground, grass, trees, plant foods, and water. The sky beings walk about on it as people do on earth.

The sky beings are two powerful anthropomorphic male gods, their wives and children, and the spirits of the dead. All are immortal. The great god, ≠Gao N!a, lives where the sun rises; the lesser god, //Gauwa, lives where the sun sets. All the spirits of the dead live with ≠Gao N!a at the place of sunrise. Although their dwelling places are at opposite sides of the sky, the two gods maintain a close relationship and act together in their dealings with mankind.

They interact a great deal with mankind, most often using the spirits of the dead as agents, or messengers, as they involve themselves in human affairs. The !Kung do not attribute good and evil to the two gods in the way that Christian Scriptures attribute good and evil to God and Satan. Both ≠Gao N!a and //Gauwa are sometimes helpful and protective to humans, sometimes destructive.

No other supernatural entities that I would categorize as spirits are believed to exist. For instance, animals are not believed to have spirits, and inanimate things like trees or water or stone are not animated by spirits. The sky beings are the important, vital, supernatural entities in present Nyae Nyae !Kung belief.

The earth that the !Kung see and walk upon is small and flat.[1] Except for an occasional mighty baobab tree and a few pans, which become little foot-deep lakes during the short season of the rains, this semidesert land is featureless. It is sparsely covered with clumps of grass, pale gold most of the year, green for only a brief time during the rainy season. Dull gray-green bushes and stunted trees grow here and there. Vegetation looks sparse nearby, but when the horizon is viewed across the expansive flatness, the vegetation merges visually into a dark rim that does not appear to be far away, and the earth seems small.

By contrast, the sky that domes the earth is vast. The whole hemisphere is constantly visible and constantly glorious—at dawn and sunset, in moonlight as bright as day, and on moonless nights, when the blazing stars measure the earth's turning. To human awareness the earth lies still, but there is always action in the sky, from the slow wheeling of the sun, moon, and stars to the violent windstorms and rainstorms, when fearsome thunderheads, streaked with lightning, reach from heaven to earth.

THE CREATION

The !Kung say that the great god, ≠Gao N!a, created himself. He created himself to be omnipotent. He then created //Gauwa, and he gave //Gauwa power, but less power than he had given himself. The great god created wives, one for himself and one for //Gauwa, and the wives bore children to the gods. The great god then created the earth. He made holes in the earth for water, and he created water. He created the sky and the things of the sky—rain, wind, lightning, sun, moon, and stars. Then he created the plants and the animals and gave the animals their many different forms and colorings. Finally he created humans.

THE NAMES OF THE GODS

When ≠Gao N!a created //Gauwa and the divine wives, he named himself, and he gave names also to //Gauwa and the wives and children. He gave himself his names to praise himself. He said, "I am Hishe. I am unknown, a stranger. No one can command me." He praised himself also with the name "!Gara" when he did something against the people, and the people said, "He causes death among the people and causes the rain to thunder." "I am ≠Gaishi≠gai," said the great god. "I am *tshi dole*.[2] I take my own way." He gave himself many names because he was the cause of sickness and death among the people. This was apparently a satisfying reason to the !Kung, who offered no other explanation.

The great god has seven divine names and one earthly name, "≠Gao N!a" (Old ≠Gao). His earthly name can be given to human males, and is a name that we came upon fairly often. I refer to his seven other names as "divine" because they belong only to the gods: Hishe, Huwe, !Kxo (or Xu), !Gara, ≠Gaishi≠gai, Gani ga, and //Gauwa.

Isaac Schapera (1930) states that the name "Hishe" is used by the Nharo and the Auen. He thinks that it may be a corruption of "Heitsi Eibib," the name of a mythical hero of the Nama. Since this name is not reported by Dorothea Bleek, Heinrich Vedder, or Viktor Lebzelter for other !Kung groups, it is possible that it has been borrowed by the Nyae Nyae !Kung from the Auen, who live immediately south of the Nyae Nyae area.

The name "Huwe" was found by Lucy Lloyd among the !Kung from Lake Ngami, by Vedder among the !Kung at Tsumeb, and by S. S. Dornan among the eastern Kalahari group (see Schapera 1930). It was not found among the Auen or the Nharo. Bleek was told that "He [Huwe] was the 'captain' of the men in the north, the Makoba and others. They also said he was the brother of Hishe, while one man called him the 'captain' of the white people" (Schapera 1930:183).

The name "!Kxo" is something of a puzzle. I originally spelled it this way because I thought I heard both the *k* and the velar fricative sound *x*, which would distinguish the name from "Ko." The !Kung told us that "Ko" is the name of a god of other people, not of a Bushman god. They had heard that the name of the white man's god is "Ko." One added that Ko might be the god of the white people but that he could kill anyone—white, black, or Bushman. I now believe that what I heard as "!Kxo" is the name that is spelled "Xu," "Xuwa," and "//Khu" by Lebzelter (see Schapera 1930). Lebzelter's account of Xu given him by the group he calls the Eastern !Kung accords so closely with the Nyae Nyae !Kung's account of the god known as "Hishe," "Huwe," "!Kxo," and "≠Gao N!a" that I feel certain that Xu and !Kxo are conceptually the same being.

The remaining three names—"!Gara," "≠Gaishi≠gai," and "Gani ga"—do not appear in the accounts of Bushman religion that Schapera analyzed. I have struggled to ascertain that they are names rather than terms, titles, or descriptive words. My evidence leads me to consider them names, but I do not have sufficient comparative material to trace their origin or adoption among the several Bushman language groups. The !Kung with whom I spoke had no idea where the names had come from. They could say only that the Old Old People had told them that ≠Gao N!a gave himself these names and that "≠Gao N!a" is the oldest of the names and "!Gara" is the next oldest.

The Names of //Gauwa, the Lesser God

The great god named the lesser god by giving him all of his own divine names but not his earthly name, "≠Gao N!a." Having been named for the great god, the lesser god is the great god's namesake, his *!guma* (*!gu:* "name"; and *ma:* suffix meaning "small" or "younger"), and the great god is the *!gun!a* (*n!a:* suffix meaning "old," "older," or "big"). The concept of namesakes and the relationship between them is an important one in the !Kung kinship system. Namesakes are always of the same sex, because !Kung names are sex-linked. One shares in some mystical way the entity of the person for whom one is named. Behavior between namesakes is as open and free from formal restraints as any in !Kung society; namesakes have the joking relationship (see Marshall 1976:204–8).

The Names of the Wives of the Gods

The Nyae Nyae !Kung believe that ≠Gao N!a gave six of his divine names, with the feminine suffix *di* added, to both the wives: "Hishedi," "Huwedi," "!Kxodi," "!Garadi," "Gani gadi," "≠Gaishi≠gaidi." "≠Gao N!a," the great god's earthly name, is not applied to the wives, because men's names are never given to women. One would say instead, "≠Gao N!a *a tsau*" (≠Gao N!a his wife). Each wife has an earthly name as well. The older one is Khwova N!a (Old Khwova). The younger one is //Gow. (We knew only two women named //Gow but many named Khwova.) Khwova N!a is also called "the mother of the bees." When men go to look for honey, they pray to her.

The wives of the gods may be referred to or addressed by a respect term used only for females, "*kolidi*," which may also be applied to women when one wants to be polite and to honor them. It is used to address a woman "who possesses lots of things," especially if one wants to ask her for a gift. "*Gaoxadi*," the feminine form of one of the respect terms for the gods, may also be used.

The wives of the gods have the same work as their husbands; their work is also strong, we were told.

The Children of the Gods

The !Kung with whom we spoke thought that there are six divine children, three boys and three girls, but they did not know which mother begot which children. The children have names, but I am uncertain of them.

In the ancient tales, but not in the !Kung's current account of their beliefs, ≠Gao N!a has two other sons, who are involved in many strange events with their father. Their names are "Khan//a" and "Kxoma." The !Kung have named two stars in the vertical axis of the Southern Cross for these boys: Alpha Crux is Khan//a, and Gamma Crux is Kxoma.

Dorothea Bleek (a pioneering linguist/anthropologist who worked with several Bushman groups) was told that Hishe was sometimes "followed by children like baboons" (as quoted by Schapera 1930:192). The image that this gives of the divine children leaping and playing and following like young baboons is amusing. However, the image that the Nyae Nyae !Kung have is very different: "The girls are fresh and beautiful, not ugly like Bushmen." Their skin is the color of Bushman skin but at its lightest shade, *gau* (a light yellowish brown). The children are called little *//gauwasi*. The spirits of the dead are also called //gauwasi. The children's special duty is to carry the spirits of mortals when they die from the dead bodies to their "father in the sky." We were told that the little //gauwasi are helpful to mortals. They watch over them and help to prevent their father, ≠Gao N!a, from becoming too angry with them.

Association of the Names

I wondered if some of ≠Gao N!a's names were more closely associated with certain phenomena, such as lightning or rain, or with special functions, such as presiding over childbirth, but the responses to all my inquiries on this theme led me to conclude that the names do not have such associations. There appears to be, however, a vague tendency, though not a strict rule, to associate some names more with benefaction, others more with ill treatment of the people. "Gani ga," which is a very respectful name, seems to come to mind when the !Kung want to thank the god or ask him sweetly to help them. We heard "!Gara" and "≠Gaishi≠gai" spoken in anger; they are "scolding" names. One man used "Huwe" when he spoke of the greatness and power of the god: "Huwe was the tallest of the Bushmen, a great man with many names." "Hishe" was the name used when the creator said, "I am Hishe. I am unknown. No one can command me." "!Kxo" was not often uttered.

Terms of Respect and Disrespect

In addition to the names, the Nyae Nyae !Kung use three terms of respectful address for the gods: *"gaoxa,"* *"n/iha,"* and *"n!au."* "Gaoxa" and "n/iha" are applied to people who are over others, such as Tswana or Herero chiefs or district commissioners. "Gaoxa" is the most exalted term and is commonly applied to the deity. The term "n/iha" is usually used for men. Some of the !Kung feel that to call a man gaoxa is to compare him with the deities, which might anger the gods. Others feel that calling a man goaxa "sounds like a curse." The term pleases ≠Gao N!a, however. When he hears it applied to himself, he knows that the people respect and fear him, and "he has a good feeling about them."

The term "gaoxa" has other applications. The power of the great god, his power to create, is called gaoxa, as is the potent *n/um* that the great god puts into the healers, the *n/um k"xausi* (owners of n/um).

"N!au," among the Nyae Nyae !Kung, is a term of respect for any old man. The !Kung often apply it to their great god, especially when they are addressing him in prayer. We were told that they call the great god n!au "when he is good."

The !Kung often call the great god *ba* (father), especially in supplication, as when pleading that he succor his "children" and give them rain or good fortune in the hunt, take away their sickness, or whatever they may be requesting.

"Nonabe" is a term of great disrespect, a "scolding" term, sometimes used in blasphemy against the gods in the Ritual Healing Dances. When "nonabe" is used for a human being, it is a curse and a terrific insult. A man who felt himself greatly wronged by another would say, in violent anger, of the man who wronged him, "That nonabe!" But one person explained to us that he would not say this to a man's face, for if he did there might be a fight, so great is the insult.

The Fear of the Names

The Nyae Nyae !Kung fear *(koa)* to utter the names of the gods. "Koa" means both "to be afraid of," as one is afraid of a lion, and "to respect and avoid," as one respects one's mother-in-law and avoids speaking to her and saying her name. The !Kung fear the gods' names in both senses. They say that they fear to call the gods' attention to themselves. ≠Gao N!a would hear his name and be displeased. He would say, "Who is calling my name? What does he want?" There seems also to be an element of respectful avoidance in not saying the names. Children must strictly avoid saying them. Old men and women need not avoid them entirely; they may and do say the names, but in soft voices and with discretion.

Throughout our stay with the !Kung, people varied as to the degree of caution with which they spoke the names. Sometimes we talked literally in whispers and usually at least in soft voices, referring to the gods as "the one in the east" or "the one in the west." On one occasion /Ti!kay told me that my questions made him sick. He meant to claim, I ascertained, that he had an actual physical sensation, such as a nervous twinge, in his stomach. The woman who first told me the name of the wife of the great god put her lips to my ear and whispered, barely audibly, "Huwedi." The next day, unfortunately, she had a high fever. She recovered, but the episode put an end to my trying to learn from her about the wives of the gods. When someone was ill at Tsho/ana and !U, the wife of ≠Toma, who was the leader of Band 1, was filled with anxiety and longed to be home at Gautscha, she made me promise not to say the names or ask any more questions about the gods, at least until we were all safely back. The !Kung appear to make a distinction between discussing the gods and addressing them, for in their prayers they sometimes address the gods by name.

≠Gao N!a, the Great God

≠Gao N!a, Protagonist of the Old Tales: The Ancient Image

Through "≠Gao N!a," the oldest name of the great god, the !Kung merge the present, all-powerful sky god with an earthy old ≠Gao N!a who belonged to the past, the protagonist of a cycle of ancient tales.[3] When they are asked, the !Kung say that the ≠Gao N!a of the old tales and the great god are the same being. It would appear, however, that this is a forced and superficial verbal resolution. The two beings could hardly be more different. They belong to two different strata of concepts. The people obviously imagine the two ≠Gao N!as as different and speak of them in different manners. They tell the tales of the old ≠Gao N!a's doings without restraint, say his name aloud, and howl and roll on the ground with laughter at his exploits and humiliations. When they speak of the great one in the eastern sky, they whisper and avoid speaking his name. They offered no explanation for the radical difference of character and function between the two beings. Yet they think that somehow in the rightness of things these two beings must be one, so one they are said to be.

The old ≠Gao N!a, the protagonist in the tales, had magical powers and performed many strange deeds. He could change himself and others into various forms. He could bring the dead back to life. He gave fire to mankind, but he could not be called a great benefactor of mankind. He wanted fire for himself because he liked cooked food and gave the fire to man rather as an afterthought. He was not concerned with man or with man's morals. He was not the life-giver and not the death-giver, nor was he a wrathful punisher. If he took vengeance, it was not a mighty vengeance but only a getting back at those who had tricked him. More often his reason for killing someone was not vengeance but his own hunger. In those days, according to the tales, people often ate one another, parts of one another, or parts of themselves. In appearance and size, the old ≠Gao N!a was manlike. He lived on earth among men. Like man, he was subject to passions, hungers, wrongdoings, stupidities, failures, frustrations, and humiliations, but men imagine his emotions or actions to be on a larger scale and more grotesque than their own. Like the Bushmen of today, he was much concerned with hunger and sex. To the !Kung, the two worst wrongdoings—unthinkable, unspeakable wrongdoings—are cannibalism and incest. ≠Gao N!a committed both without concern. He ate his older brother-in-law and his younger brother-in-law, and he raped his son's wife.

Several of the tales follow. In paraphrasing them, my daughter and I have adhered to the events, the ideas, and the details as they were told to us, and we have attempted to preserve something of the quality of the telling as it came to our ears.

≠Gao N!a, His Tun!ga (the Fat Paouw), and the Pit

The old ≠Gao N!a's wives were sisters. They had a brother who was a paouw [*Choriotis kori kori*, the giant bustard]. They all lived in ancient times, when animals and people lived together and animals could talk. One day ≠Gao N!a, when he was walking about, met the paouw, his *tun!ga* [!Kung kin term for wife's brother older than the speaker]. His tun!ga was very fat. A fat paouw has bags of fat under his wings. ≠Gao N!a and his tun!ga spoke together and parted. ≠Gao N!a was surprised to see so much fat. He said, "Oh, how fat my tun!ga is." A few miles farther on they met again. ≠Gao N!a said, "Look, do you see that veld fire over there?" He pointed with his arm way up. The paouw said, "Do you mean *that* fire?" He pointed, but only with a restricted gesture, keeping his wing to his side. "No," ≠Gao N!a said, "that fire," and he pointed with his arm far up, his whole armpit showing. "I see it," said the paouw, and he stretched his wing far up to point. ≠Gao N!a was standing behind him. He seized the fat from under the paouw's wing and cut it off and ran home. The paouw cursed ≠Gao N!a and shouted at him, "Break your bones and die of a broken back, or die of a broken neck."

≠Gao N!a took the fat home and rubbed his wooden basin with it. His wives came home and found the wooden basin covered with fat, and they asked him what he had eaten that was so fat. ≠Gao N!a said that he had taken the fat from a puff adder. He said that he had beaten the snake with a stick until the fat from the front had gone to the middle and had beaten the tail until the fat there had gone to the middle. Then he had slit the skin and scraped out the fat.

≠Gao N!a now planned how he would get his tun!ga. He slept that night. The next morning he set snares under the tree where the paouw went to eat gum. ≠Gao N!a then met the paouw again. The paouw was wary and wouldn't come near. ≠Gao N!a asked, "Why are you so wary with me? There is a tree with gum on it, but my eyes are not good enough to see the gum. Let's have a contest; we shall see who can see the gum first. The one who sees it first must run and snatch it." So they went to the tree and saw the gum. The paouw ran fast to get it, and ≠Gao N!a ran too, but he did not run as fast. The paouw snatched the gum, and the snare caught him. ≠Gao N!a ran up and clubbed him and carried him home.

≠Gao N!a's wives were out gathering plant foods. He put the fat from one wing into a small pot. When the wing fat was ready, he ate it, and ate and ate, but he ate too much and had diarrhea.

The wives came home and suspected that he had killed their brother. The paouw began to expand in the pot, and he swelled until the pot burst [koah!] and pieces of meat came whizzing out, so ≠Gao N!a had to duck away from them. When all the meat was out, the paouw came back together again and flew away. ≠Gao N!a chased after him, but the wives called to him, "Come back, you forgot your stick." ≠Gao N!a went back, got his stick, and ran after the paouw again. The wives called him, "Come back, you forgot your sandals." ≠Gao N!a went back, got his sandals, and ran after the paouw again, but the paouw was gone by this time. ≠Gao N!a swore at his wives, "You stupid, lazy women, why were you so lazy that you lay down and didn't stir the pot?" The wives were much annoyed that ≠Gao N!a had wanted to eat their brother.

Next day ≠Gao N!a went hunting. While he was away, his wives, because they were very annoyed, turned themselves into k'idwa [*Coccinia sessilifolia* (Sond.) Cogn., a fruit the size and shape of a small cucumber]. When ≠Gao N!a came home, he saw the pile of k'idwa and ate them all. Then he came and sat by the fire. Soon he heard laughing. He looked around, but no one was there. He heard the laughing again and looked around. "What is that?" he said, but he could see nothing. "Where is that laughing coming from?" he said. It was his wives inside him laughing at him, and at this they kicked and kicked until they burst his stomach open and came out and were women again. ≠Gao N!a was very surprised. How had he eaten his wives? he wondered.

/Naru, a dung beetle, then came to sew up ≠Gao N!a's stomach. It was very sore. ≠Gao N!a squirmed and struggled when /Naru pricked him. Then a little *zwa zwa* fly came. He took over the sewing and sewed so gently that it was only like a tickling. ≠Gao N!a was healed and soothed, and he slept.

On the following day ≠Gao N!a went hunting again. He was annoyed with his wives for tricking him into eating them and for laughing in his stomach and bursting him open. Presently he came upon some fruit. He said, "Oh, if only I had my sister or mother to gather food for me!" He turned back and told his wives where the fruit was, and then went on in the other direction. The wives went to gather the fruit, but ≠Gao N!a with his n/um had made the heavy fruit able to fly from the tree and hit the women, so they ran away crying. [The !Kung telling the story made the sounds of the fruit bombarding the women. They slapped themselves, cried like the wives, and rolled over with laughter.]

The wives returned to their *tshu ko* [*tshu:* "shelter"; and *ko:* "place"; hence, "encampment"]. They were sad because their husband had treated them in this way, and they discussed what they would do to get even with him. Next day they went out to gather food again. They came to a place that they decided was right for their plan. They dug a pit. Into it they opened their bowels, and the pit was partially filled with feces. Then they went to their tshu ko and waited for ≠Gao N!a. When he returned, they said, "If only we had our brother, he would go and kill the little eland we saw." ≠Gao N!a said, "My wives, I shall go for you." They said, "We know you are lazy, but our brother would go." But ≠Gao N!a said, "No, my wives, I shall go for you tomorrow." So they slept.

The next day the wives led him to the place where they had supposedly seen the little eland, where they had made the pit. They said, "There it is by that tree. You must go quietly." ≠Gao N!a poised his spear to kill the eland, but the wives said, "You will let all the blood run out. We like the blood to eat. That is what we meant when we said that we wished we had our brother here to kill the little eland." So ≠Gao N!a put his spear away. The wives said, "Right there is where the little eland is; you must jump on it and catch it. We shall go on either side to help you." And when they were near, they said, "Jump and fall on it and catch it." ≠Gao N!a got all set and steadied himself. Then he jumped into the pit, and the wives ran away, laughing and saying how lazy he was.

There he was in the pit. He could not stand up. He slithered around like a snake. [The storytellers were making graphic gestures and shrieking with laughter.] He got up and fell down again; he got up again and fell again, swearing at his wives and cursing them, "These wives are very cruel." [The people imitated his voice, higher than a man's voice and mumbling.] When ≠Gao N!a finally climbed out of the pit, he went to a water hole and washed himself and walked home in the evening, thinking of what he would do to his wives to punish them.

While talking with ≠Toma, Lazy /Qui, and Old Demi one day, I inquired about cannibalism. They laughed a little in an embarrassed way and somewhat hesitantly said that they had heard that Europeans ate people, not other Europeans but other people. Old Demi then said he had been told in his youth that long ago there had been people called */gai da* who ate people. They lived far to the north, beyond the river (the Okavango). Lazy /Qui had never heard this, he said, but he knew an old tale:

Eyes-on-His-Feet

≠Gao N!a's young *tun!gama* [brother-in-law] was named "Eyes-on-His-Feet." His face was smooth, without eyes. He and ≠Gao N!a went together to gather food. They found *//haru* [*Lapeyrousia cyanescens* Bak., a plant food similar to a Jerusalem artichoke]. After a time they came to a place where they wanted to stay, and they made a fire and started to roast the //haru. While they were sitting by the fire, ≠Gao N!a watched his tun!gama's feet and saw what looked like eyes. He tossed a pinch of dust on them, and the eyes blinked. ≠Gao N!a said to himself, "These are really his eyes. His eyes are on his feet." ≠Gao N!a then asked his tun!gama to lean over and press the //haru down into the ashes so that they would be all covered and would roast evenly. Eyes-on-His-Feet stood close to the fire to do so, and ≠Gao N!a took the fire paddle and quickly pushed the coals over his tun!gama's feet. This killed Eyes-on-His-Feet, because his strength was in his eyes and they were burned. ≠Gao N!a then cut up Eyes-on-His-Feet and covered his whole body with the coals and roasted him. While the tun!gama was roasting, there was a sound, *tsi tsi ii tsi ii,* like meat sizzling. It was the tun!gama putting a magic curse on ≠Gao N!a's mouth. Then the sound said, "Come and eat me, and your mouth will be closed." [In another version of the tale it said, "When you eat me, you will become dumb."] When the tun!gama was well roasted, ≠Gao N!a ate all he could of him and put what he could not eat into a bag. He then tried to eat the //haru. He put one up to his mouth, but his mouth would not open. He took another; it fell down to the side. ≠Gao N!a could neither speak nor eat. He put the //haru into the bag with the remainder of the tun!gama and went back to his people in the tshu ko and asked them to make a dance to cure his mouth. He danced and danced with them and treated himself with the Healing Rite. While he was dancing, his wives took his bag and ate what was left of Eyes-on-His-Feet and all the //haru but one. [The tale makes no point of the fact that they were eating their brother, albeit unknowingly, and one senses the omission.] Then they filled the bag with earth and put the remaining //haru on top. Suddenly ≠Gao N!a's mouth was cured. He went to get his bag to finish eating his tun!gama, put in his hand, took some earth, and tossed it into his mouth. He spat and swore at his wives. "You silly women," he said, "what have you done?" And he thought what he would do to them.

Next evening he called for another dance. He was still angry that his wives had eaten all the //haru and the tun!gama and had filled the bag with earth. A woman got up to dance, but ≠Gao N!a said, "No, I want a good singer to dance with me, not you." At last, ≠Tamsa, the wife who had put the earth in the bag, got up to dance. She danced around ≠Gao N!a, he danced around her, and when she came near, he beat her fiercely on the stomach with his stick until her stomach hung down below her groin. She fell unconscious, and the women, crying, carried her away and cared for her until she was healed. This is why Bushmen have stomachs that hang down.

≠Toma and /Qui thought that this was an appalling story. /Qui said that he did not know why ≠Gao N!a had eaten his tun!gama. He thought the reason could not have been mere hunger: after all, /Qui pointed out, ≠Gao N!a had had //haru. There must have been some other reason. Perhaps, /Qui suggested with a laugh, he was very hungry for meat, but ≠Toma said, "≠Gao N!a is evil. Even now he goes about killing people."

In another version of the tale, the awfulness of eating a human being is modified by having Eyes-on-His-Feet come to life again. During the dance, ≠Gao N!a's stomach began to ache and to swell and to make sounds, as with severe constipation. Suddenly it burst open, and Eyes-on-His-Feet sprang out, whole and alive, as the wives had done after their laughter. And ≠Gao N!a's people sewed up his stomach. In still another version, ≠Gao N!a turns his wife ≠Tamsa into a bird called *chu* (a hornbill), one of the birds that the !Kung eat.

My efforts to learn more about the possible identity of Eyes-on-His-Feet availed nothing. He is a man in this tale, but I wondered if he were not originally some plant food, for instance, with a formation that suggested eyes, or an animal turned into a human being or personified, like the paouw, but the !Kung did not know. The Old Old People had not told them.[4]

As usual, when my inquiries suggested to the !Kung that I expected them, possibly, to know something that they did not know, they became embarrassed and defensive. !U said that her mother was lazy and did not tell her stories; that is why she knows so little. Old Xama said that her mother died when she was young, so she had remained ignorant.

Another tale, that of ≠Gao N!a's raping of Te, the pretty young wife of his son Kxoma, is long and detailed and was recounted with great enjoyment and much laughter:

> ≠Gao N!a tried to be away with the women alone while they were gathering plant food. First he changed himself into a baby wildebeest and pretended that he was dead. Te picked him up and tied him to her back to carry him as she would carry any meat. As she carried him along, he slid down her back and tried to rape her. He did not succeed, so he made another plan. Some days later he disguised himself very cleverly as his own sister and went with the women to gather when they planned to stay out overnight. During the night, he raped Te in her sleep. Next morning, when the women discovered who he was, he tried to persuade Te that it was not he but her husband, Kxoma, who had been with her during the night, but Te knew that it was not her husband, and she was very upset. The women decided not to tell Kxoma or Khan//a, because they were afraid that the sons would kill their father, so they all kept quiet when they returned, and they lived in peace.

These tales or segments of them are often mixed together. In another version the pit episode is used again: It is the sons' wives who dig the pit and entice ≠Gao N!a to jump into it in revenge for ≠Gao N!a's "spoiling" Te. The substance in the pit is not feces, but ≠Gao N!a's own semen. The women shape the semen into the form of a young giraffe. When ≠Gao N!a finally climbs out of this pit, he cleans himself by rubbing himself on trees.

≠Gao N!a sometimes prevails in his endeavors, but he has lapses and often appears to be far from clever. In one tale he is both stupid and generous—too generous. This is a very long tale in which Kxoma and Khan//a, his sons, kill an eland. Lions come and kill the sons. With the help of another brother-in-law, Zam Zam—a little tortoise—≠Gao N!a kills the lions by magic and restores his sons to life. The story ends in their all returning to the tshu ko with the eland meat:

≠Gao N!a and His Stupid Generosity

They walked along. They met a man. They gave him gifts of meat. This man quickly hid his meat in a tree; then, dodging along behind some bushes, he ran ahead and met ≠Gao N!a and his party again. The sons and Zam Zam said, "We have already given you some meat," but ≠Gao N!a could not remember and gave again. [Dam and /Qui were speechless with laughter as they acted this out.] For the fifth time the man ran ahead, and ≠Gao N!a did not remember him and gave him his last bundle of meat. ≠Gao N!a would now have to return to his wives without any meat for them, but instead he hit his buttocks very hard. He hit them and hit them until he knocked his insides out. He cut his insides into pieces, like meat, and took them to his tshu ko. Others had meat, but he had none except his own insides. He cooked them for his wives. They said that the meat was too tough to eat and asked, "Why do the others have nice eland meat and you have only this?" He said that it was eland meat but that it had become dry. ≠Gao N!a and his wives went hungry.

The story about ≠Gao N!a's getting fire was told in several versions. In one of them the name "Huwe" was used. That was the only time I heard the protagonist of the tales called by any name other than ≠Gao N!a.

≠Gao N!a and the Fire Sticks

There was a time when no one had fire except one man, whose name was "/Ka /Kani." He had fire, and the name of his fire was "Doro."[5] Doro was made with fire sticks. /Ka /Kani cooked his food with the fire. All other people ate raw food. One day ≠Gao N!a was walking in the veld, and he came upon the place where /Ka /Kani was living. He was not there, but his children were. They were eating cooked //haru. ≠Gao N!a asked for some and found it very good. "Oh, you eat nice cooked food," said ≠Gao N!a. "How do you cook it?" The children said, "Our father has a nice thing, and he always gives us cooked food. He does all the best for us." ≠Gao N!a said, "I shall come back tomorrow and eat this kind of food again."

Next day he went back. As he was walking along, he saw /Ka /Kani and his children digging for food, and he hid himself and watched. When they had gathered enough, they went back to their tshu ko, and /Ka /Kani went and got his fire sticks from the place where he had hidden them. He twirled and twirled and twirled the male stick against the female stick, saying, "Fire will come; fire will come." When the fire was made and the food was cooking, /Ka /Kani hid his fire sticks again. ≠Gao N!a was watching all the time. When the food was dished up, he came out from his hiding place and sat down by the fire, and they all ate together.

After a while ≠Gao N!a said, "Now we must make a game to play," and he made a *djani*, mounting it with a guinea-fowl feather, and weighting it with a *tsi* nut.[6] He tossed it into the air with his stick and, when it floated down, ran and caught it and tossed it up again and again without ever letting it fall to the ground. /Ka /Kani wanted to play. ≠Gao N!a gave him the djani, but /Ka /Kani could not toss it high enough and did not get away from his house in following it. ≠Gao N!a said that the guinea-fowl feather was no good and that they must put a big paouw feather on it. This they did, and the djani flew high. ≠Gao N!a then opened the wind, and the wind blew from the eastern side and blew the djani toward the west. /Ka /Kani followed and followed it, fascinated, each time tossing it higher after catching it. ≠Gao N!a followed /Ka /Kani, and when they reached the place where the fire sticks were hidden, he seized them, and ran with them into the veld. As he ran, he broke them into little pieces and then threw them the whole world over. "All the world is going to have fire now," he said. "Fire, fire, go over the world." Since then there has been fire in every piece of wood, and all men can get it out and cook their food. /Ka /Kani stopped playing and looked at ≠Gao N!a. ≠Gao N!a told him, "It is not right that you alone should have fire. From now on you will not be a person," and he changed /Ka /Kani into a bird named ≠*ore.*

These events were told by the Old Old People. They happened long ago.

The Present Image of ≠Gao N!a, the Creator

In his present image, the image of power, ≠Gao N!a, the creator and controller of all things, is very different from the old trickster protagonist. The !Kung insist, nevertheless, that the old ≠Gao N!a and the great god of the eastern sky are one and the same. Concepts from two strata of beliefs evidently merged. Possibly through the name the two beings became identified as one.

The !Kung did not bring up the question of when or how ≠Gao N!a's nature had changed so greatly from trickster to all-powerful creator. We learned that there is interchange of the gods' names among northern Bushman groups. Doubtless the concepts about the gods were interchanged as well. In all probability, some elements of the present concept came from other groups, and some the !Kung created for themselves. I am sure that the imagination of the people today has worked upon the images of the gods, reinterpreting them, recreating them, and bringing them to their present form, and I have no doubt that the images will continue to evolve by the same means.

≠Gao N!a's present image has many aspects in common with the Hishe, Huwe, and Xu of the other Bushman groups, as well as some differences. The image of Hishe, Huwe, and Xu of other groups is of a creator and a good being. Schapera gives the following accounts: "Vedder . . . speaks of *Huwe* as a 'good being,' to whom the people attribute the creation and maintenance of all things. . . . Lebzelter . . . says that all the groups [of !Kung] investigated by him have the belief in a 'supreme good being.' . . . Among the Eastern Kung this being is termed *Xu*" (Schapera 1930:183). The Western

!Kung of Oschimpoloveld believe that the supreme being "lives in a house in the sky to which the souls of the dead are brought. He is often prayed to, especially for rain and in hunting, as well as in the case of illness, 'because he has made all things and can do everything and knows everything,' and he is given the first offerings of the chase. The rain comes at his command as a mist out of the earth, and then falls down, thereupon making thunder and lightning" (Schapera 1930:184). Schapera notes that Lebzelter also reports that Xu of the Heikum is regarded almost everywhere among them "as the creator of all things, including mankind, and he sends the rain. He is prayed to for rain, in sickness, before and after hunting, and before travel, and by the group at Uukualuthi he is also given the first offerings of the chase, as among the !Kung of the Oschimpoloveld. Almost everywhere he has neither wife nor children; it is only among the Eastern !Kung that mention is made of these. He is regarded everywhere as benevolent and good, but appears to have no connection with the moral life of the people" (Schapera 1930:185).

This old god was not the death-giver. The old //Gauwa held that role. The great god of the Nyae Nyae !Kung, however, is presently believed to be both life-giver and death-giver. I think that the Nyae Nyae !Kung, believing him to be all-powerful, have logically attributed to him ultimate control over sickness and death and hold him ultimately responsible, over and above the lesser god, whose ancient association was with death. First and foremost, however, they conceive of ≠Gao N!a, the great god, as the creator and life-giver, the controller of all things—benefactor as well as destroyer.

The !Kung say that ≠Gao N!a created himself. /Ti!kay claimed that ≠Gao N!a came out of the water, the water in the east, in the place where the sun rises, but others said that they were not told this by their old people. I could discover no established myth of creation that was known to everyone, or any myth or lore that told how ≠Gao N!a created himself. People simply said they did not know. !U turned on me and asked me if I knew. When I said that I did not, she snapped, "How, then, do you expect me to know?"

After creating himself, ≠Gao N!a created the lesser god and then their two wives. Next the great god created the earth and gave it its name, "*kxa.*" In the earth he created holes for water, and he created water. The people were not told how he created these things. Gao Feet explained that ≠Gao N!a has an "iron" of his own with which he works, a *!ka* (literally, "metal"). Some metal tool, a special one, is what he used. The people have never seen it and do not know just what kind of tool it is or what substance he may have worked with, but they do know that he is the creator and the commander of metal.[7]

After he made the earth, ≠Gao N!a made the sky in a dome over the earth, and he made rain *(!ga)*. He made gentle female rain *(!ga di)* and violent male rain *(!ga !go)*.

After the rain he made the sun. The sun is a death-thing. It dries up the plant foods and the water holes and scorches the people. He made the moon and the stars all at the same time. Then he made the wind. He is the creator of all these things, and he commands their movements.

≠Gao N!a created the things that grow from the ground, and he created animals and branded their stripes and markings on them and gave them their names. Then he created human beings. He created animals as animals and human beings as human beings. He commanded them to breathe. Without breath they would not live. In the cryptic account of one old man: "First was woman and then man. The woman had fire. The man asked the woman to give him fire.[8] She did. The woman dug some roots and was eating them. Then the man married the woman."

In an equally cryptic but different account of the creation of people, it was said that man was created before woman and that the question of incest was addressed. According to Short Gao of Band 12:

> After ≠Gao N!a had made the earth and the sky and the animals, he thought and thought. He said, "There must be people. I must make a plan. I am the one who knows everything." He then made a man, and after that he made a woman. He said to the man, "Take this woman and marry her and have children. When the children grow up, they must have children."
>
> First the man and the woman had a boy, and next a girl. When ≠Gao N!a saw the boy and the girl, he said, "They must not marry each other." So he created a husband for the girl and a wife for the boy, and they had children.
>
> "These children must not marry each other," said ≠Gao N!a, so he created a husband and a wife for each, and so on till all the families were made. That is how the people now know that they must marry and have children but that they must not marry their sisters or brothers. Those old people of the first creation died long, long ago.

≠Gao N!a named the first woman "Khwova" for his wife, and he named the first man "≠Gao" for himself. From the beginning ≠Gao N!a created men and women to be mortal. He sends sickness and death to the people, and they die. He takes the spirits that leave the bodies at the time of death and turns them into the spirits of the dead, the //gauwasi. He commands them to live in the sky with him and to be his servants. When he wishes to do so, he orders them to go down to earth, to mortals, carrying sickness or death to them, or he orders them to carry good fortune.

≠Gao N!a has a n/um with which he can renew himself at any time. He also renews all the beings who live in the sky with him. They become old, and he renews them. They do not die. But he has not given human beings that n/um, and, the !Kung say, "We cannot make it." ≠Gao N!a created all n/um, including the n/um he gives to the healers, the n/um k"xausi, and the n/um in the songs of the Healing Dance. He has given those n/umsi to people, but some n/um he keeps for himself alone. He is the great owner of n/um.

≠Gao N!a gave arrows and bows, assagais (metal blades hafted onto long handles), and digging sticks to human beings. He gave men the knowledge of poison for arrows. He taught people how to make all the things that they now make, and he taught them all that they know to do. "If he did not want us to know, he would not have taught us." He commanded human beings to dig for food with their sticks and to hunt with their weapons. From the beginning they have done these things.

≠Gao N!a commanded men and women to marry and live together and have children. He controls the actions of people. If they do good deeds or bad deeds, they do so under his control, for he arranges all things.

The tale that tells how the old ≠Gao N!a gave fire to mankind was not told in the accounts of the creation that the !Kung gave to me. It apparently did not occur to them to tell it in this context. It belongs, evidently, to what I am calling another stratum of beliefs.

Several times in our talks I asked whether the great creator controlled the lives of only the Bushmen or the lives of all the people on earth. It was not surprising that the !Kung's thinking on this point was vague and contradictory. Some said, "He is over all people. He can kill anybody." Others claimed that ≠Gao N!a and the lesser god as well were "only for Bushmen." "White people and black people," they said, "have their own gods."

≠Gao N!a's Appearance and Dwelling Place

Different Bushman groups perceive the god's appearance differently. The /Gwi Bushmen in Botswana visualized Pisiboro, the protagonist of their old tales, as being of supernatural size—enormous. In the tortures of his death throes, his thrashing and writhing limbs gouged out the *omurimbi* (shallow, ancient water courses), the putrefaction of his body became the rivers, and his black hair became the rain clouds. But the !Kung, it seems, always thought of the protagonist of their old tales, the old ≠Gao N!a, as manlike in size and appearance, and ≠Gao N!a, the great god of the eastern sky, also as manlike. He has the power to change himself into the forms of animals or objects, and he sometimes does so, but in his own form he is like a man.

The !Kung say of the great sky god that he is "the tallest of the Bushmen." His bearing, as the people at present imagine him, suggests the bearing of the tall, proud Herero, the Bantu-speaking pastoralists, whom the !Kung see in western Botswana.

But ≠Gao N!a does not look like a Herero. Gao Feet, Gao Beard, Old Demi, ≠Toma, /Qui, and /Ti!kay described from time to time how they imagine ≠Gao N!a. He has a big head. He has black hair, but it is long, not twisted and knotted like the Bushmen's peppercorns. He has a long beard and hair on his chest, not at all like Bushmen, whose beards and other body hair are extremely sparse. Gao Feet thought that ≠Gao N!a's skin is reddish *(!gā)*, like Europeans' skin. (The !Kung called us the "red people." Indeed, we were reddish under the desert sun.) Others claimed that ≠Gao N!a's skin is the color of Bushman skin in its lightest tone. ≠Gao N!a wears European clothes and a hat; his pants and shirt are white. Some said that he possesses a gun. "He is the great god and has power over all these things, so he possesses them."

He has a horse and rides everywhere across the earth and the upper sky. The sound of his horse's hooves can sometimes be heard passing overhead. Especially when it rains, he goes about a great deal, and the tracks of his horse can sometimes be seen. They are like those of the Hereros' horses, not exceptional in size or form. If ≠Gao N!a hears his name spoken in the daytime and is displeased, he will come down on his horse at sunset and beat stiff, dry hides with a stick or snap an eland-hide rein to make a noise like thunder and frighten all the people. How the horse descends to earth from the upper sky is not clearly visualized. Obviously, the concept of ≠Gao N!a wearing white pants and riding a horse has come relatively recently into !Kung belief, with the !Kung imagining what the all-powerful one, the possessor of all things, would want. The concept of the sky beings descending and ascending on cords belongs to the older stratum of beliefs. The !Kung hold the two concepts without worrying about resolving them, vaguely attributing the horse's descents and ascents to the great god's wondrous and mysterious ways.

The majority of the people with whom we spoke held these beliefs about ≠Gao N!a, telling us these details from time to time as we sat in groups. Some, however, held a different view, for instance, that ≠Gao N!a never came to earth. Their old people had told them this, they said.

≠Gao N!a lives in a house at the place where the sun rises in the eastern sky. Near the house is a single great tree.[9] The people fear the house and the tree. The house and the tree are associated with the spirits of the dead. ≠Gao N!a's house has two stories. It is long and made of stone, with a shining roof of corrugated iron. There are big doors on the ends and small doors on the sides. All the //gauwasi are believed to live on the lower floor, and ≠Gao N!a and his wife and children on the upper floor. Although the house differs so much from a Bushman shelter, the !Kung use the same word for it—"tshu." No mortal—not even the greatest of the healers who have ascended to the upper sky—has seen ≠Gao N!a's dwelling place. The Old Old People were told about it, but how they were told is not known.

The image of the great god's house accords with beliefs held by other northern Bushmen: "Among certain of the North-Western Bushmen *Huwe* . . . dwells in a house in the sky where he receives the souls of the dead. This belief is apparently not found at all among the Hottentots. . . . It is also held, however, . . . by the Bergdama" (Schapera 1930:397).

The image of the house also is in accord in several respects with that of the Eastern !Kung, whom Lebzelter describes, except that in the belief of the Eastern !Kung, the spirits of the dead live on the upper floor and ≠Gao N!a on the lower. In Lebzelter's description:

> This "supreme being" *[Huwe or Hu'e or Xu]* is regarded as anthropomorphic, he looks like a Bushman and he also speaks !Kung. He lives in the sky in a house with two storeys, the lower of which is occupied by himself, his wife, whose name is unknown, and many children, while the upper is occupied . . . by the souls of the dead *(xa)*. In appearance this house is similar to the ordinary Bushman hut, although not quite the same, and its exterior is "hairy like a caterpillar." Honey, locusts, fat flies, and butterflies are found here in superabundance, and the "great captain" feeds upon these; the souls of the dead, however, merely sit around and eat nothing. *Xu* summons the magicians to their profession, and gives them supernatural powers; he is the lord over rain and lightning, as well as over the spirits, *//gauab*, and through the chief of the latter he sends good fortune in hunting or in the collection of veldkos. If anybody thinks or speaks evil of him, he punishes the evildoer with lightning; otherwise he takes no interest in the doings of his "Bushman children," except when somebody swears falsely by him, for the !Kung have a regular oath in which they invoke him. He is prayed to by them in fixed form for rain, in case of severe illness, before going out hunting or before undertaking a dangerous journey (as reported in Schapera 1930:184).

Only exceptionally great healers see ≠Gao N!a, not because he is generally invisible but because he comes near only to them. ≠Gao N!a is "wild," as an animal is wild; he keeps his distance. He has such strong n/um in him that he is dangerous. If he came into an encampment, his n/um might destroy it. He never comes near the Ritual Healing Dances, we were told. His strong n/um together with the n/um of the healers and the n/um of the songs would be devastatingly strong. Some of the healers said that ≠Gao N!a would stay at least a hundred yards away, pointing to a tree to illustrate the distance. /Ti!kay, who claimed that he himself had never seen ≠Gao N!a, said that even a great healer is apt to be frightened when he sees ≠Gao N!a for the first time and might say, "What does this man want? He is bad. I don't like him." /Ti!kay continued, saying that even an extremely important healer old in n/um, having seen ≠Gao N!a many times, would still be frightened, but when sickness came and the healer was curing and his n/um was strong, he would keep a "tight heart," take a stick, and rush toward ≠Gao N!a, yelling, "You send a bad sickness. You must take it back." And the sick person would recover. This is how all the healers habitually treat the lesser god and the spirits of the dead, who regularly hover in the shadows at the dances. To shout at ≠Gao N!a himself, even though he was keeping his distance, would indeed require courage.

//Gauwa, the Lesser God

Among the Nyae Nyae !Kung, the word "//gauwa" has three applications: a //gauwa is the spirit of a dead person; the children of the gods are called little //gauwasi; and //Gauwa is the name of the lesser god. It is one of the seven names given him by the great god and the only name we ever heard applied to him.

Among other Bushmen and among the Hottentots, //Gauwa was a being distinct from the one who was variously named Hishe, Huwe, and so forth; //Gauwa did not bear all the other being's names. As I interpret the present belief of the Nyae Nyae !Kung, their lesser god is Old //Gauwa. However, his image has changed, as the image of the old protagonist, ≠Gao N!a, has changed. //Gauwa's name has been attributed to the great god, as the great god's names have been attributed to //Gauwa. The two beings nevertheless remain separate entities and are now in the *!gun!a-!guma* (namesake) relationship.

I interpret the lesser god to be the traditional //Gauwa because so many of his attributes are the same as, or similar to, those of the traditional being and because I did not hear people use any other name for him but "//Gauwa."

Schapera's information indicates that //Gauwa was generally believed to be the destroyer. Vedder reports that the !Kung at Tsumeb expected only evil from him and thought of him as opposed to Huwe (see Schapera 1930:187). But the Eastern !Kung studied by Lebzelter believed that, although he was most frequently the cause of illness, he (//Gauab, //Gaunab, or //Gamab) was good as well as evil and that he helped hunters. Some thought him the creator: "He is everywhere and moves between heaven and earth on cords" (Schapera 1930:188). The Heikum also thought that he was the creator. "The souls of the dead . . . come to live with him, and he eats their hearts" (Schapera 1930:188–89). The Hottentots considered him to be wholly the destroyer, the black chief, opposed to Tsui //Goab, the creator and rain-giver: "It is further said, by the Naman, that '*Tsui //Goab* lives in a beautiful heaven, and *//Gaunab* lives in a dark heaven, quite separated from the heaven of *Tsui //Goab*,' while the Korana told Wuras that Tsui //Goab lived in the Red Sky and //Gaunab in the Black Sky" (Schapera 1930:389). The //Gauwa of the Nyae Nyae !Kung lives where the sun sets.

//Gauwa was more independent in these past concepts than he is in the present Nyae Nyae !Kung concept, but otherwise he preserves the same mingling of characteristics. He does both good and evil deeds from man's point of view but with a distinct emphasis upon death-giving and evil-doing. He has now become subservient to the great god. He should always obey ≠Gao N!a, carry out his master's orders, and do his master's work, but he preserves considerable independence nevertheless and often instigates his own affairs.

One of his works, the Nyae Nyae !Kung said, is to go about to see what is going on. Gao Feet said, "He tells the old man in the east whatever he sees and hears. 'These people are staying well; those are not so well.' He may say to the old man, 'Let us help these people get some food.' Or he may tell him that lightning is killing some people and ask, 'What shall I do?'"

Short Gao of Band 12 told us that one time //Gauwa went to see ≠Gao N!a and asked him for n/um. ≠Gao N!a was annoyed. He said, "The n/um must stay with me. I am bigger than you." //Gauwa went away and did not ask again until some time had passed. Then he went and asked again. ≠Gao N!a said, "You bad, stupid fellow! You think that you are clever, but you are not. I am bigger than you. I have everything. You must come and ask me every time, but this time take the n/um and go and work with your Bushmen." This explains how it is that //Gauwa, as well as ≠Gao N!a, gives n/um to the healers.

//Gauwa is a "small" man, we were told; he has "small" sense, and he makes many mistakes. If someone is sick, when the healers see //Gauwa lurking at the edge of the firelight at the Healing Dances, they rush at him, give him a blow, and shout at him, "Idiot! You have done wrong. You make me ashamed. Go away." And //Gauwa then runs away. Sometimes, after his chastisement, he comes back with healing n/um, and the sick person recovers.

The !Kung associate //Gauwa with whirlwinds, as the other Bushman and Hottentot groups did. The !Kung call a whirlwind *//Gauwa ≠a* (//Gauwa smell). *≠A* is not an ordinary odor that one can actually smell, and a whirlwind is not an ordinary wind *(maa)*. The !Kung believe that a whirlwind is a death-thing, "a fight." //Gauwa walks in the whirlwind; his smell is in it, and death is in it. If the wind passes over a person, the ≠a goes into him, and he will become sick and die. The spirits of the dead, the //gauwasi, also come in the whirlwinds. One cannot see or hear //Gauwa or the //gauwasi in the winds. There are no precautions one can take to protect oneself against them except to try to get away. Little dust devils played around us very frequently in the Kalahari, and huge whirlwinds or tiny tornadoes tended to form in the areas burned by the veld fires. The winds swirled the ashes into awesome black funnels that reached from the earth to the heavens. Sometimes white clouds condensed on their tops, and we believe that we saw pillars of cloud like those the Children of Israel saw: "And the Lord went before them by day in a pillar of a cloud, to lead them the way; and by night in a pillar of fire, to give them light" (Exodus 13:21).

//Gauwa's Dwelling and Appearance

//Gauwa lives in the western sky at the place where the sun sets. /Ti!kay said more than once that the lesser god lived in the east. That was what he remembered being told by the old people, he claimed. However, all the other people with whom I spoke in many different interviews agreed that it was the other way—that the lesser god lived in the *west*—so I take that to be the true !Kung belief.

Some believe that //Gauwa first lived on earth, in a hole. He made the hole, one person told us, by pushing the earth out with his head. The hole was like a springhare hole but very big. There were two entrances, one facing toward the sunrise, the other facing toward the sunset. //Gauwa later made a house in the sky. The house has poles made of iron and is tied together with wire. The house stands in a flat, open space. It is built up off the ground—the ground in the sky—upon the iron poles that are stuck into the ground and rise up into the air. The !Kung said, "When a person is sick with a sore throat, the sickness has been caused by those irons. The old man, ≠Gao N!a, tells //Gauwa the way he must hurt a person." When the healers are in trance, their spirits go to that house. This is how they know what it is like. Their spirits climb up by the cords that hang from the sky.

Near //Gauwa's house are two trees. They have names. Nothing else on the earth or in the sky bears those names, one person told us. The name of the tree that is toward the north is "/Gaie"; the one toward the south is named "!Dua." The names mean nothing; they are "just names." /Gaie and !Dua have smooth bark and large white flowers, no thorns, and no nuts. I thought that they might be like baobabs, which have these characteristics, but I was told that they are not. They are more nearly like the camel thorn (*Acacia giraffae* Burch.), which incidentally has two names, "/gi" (a respect name) and "/ana" (a "rough" name), but they are not exactly like any tree on earth.

The healers frequently see //Gauwa at the Ritual Healing Dances. ≠Gao N!a sends him as his messenger, and the healers become familiar with him. Anyone may see //Gauwa in dreams.

The image of //Gauwa varies. The present image accords with the traditional images in some aspects. Whereas ≠Gao N!a is "the tallest of the Bushmen," //Gauwa is short. He has the form of a man but can appear in other forms. The color yellow is associated with him. Individuals have their own interpretations. I am convinced that some of the healers—Gao Feet for one—really believe that they do see //Gauwa. They may see objects in the shadows among the trees and bushes that they interpret to be //Gauwa, or they may see the light of the veld fires between the branches, or some other such phenomenon, or they may have visions or hallucinations, perhaps while in trance. Some possibly just imagine a form.

Demi, a healer in Band 12, saw //Gauwa the night of a great dance at /Gam, when the members of four bands danced together. Demi was the smallest Bushman we had seen in the region. He was bedecked with many beads and walked with a prance like a bantam cock. He had seen //Gauwa in the darkness, he told us, and had confronted him and driven him off with imprecations and sticks. I asked him to tell me what //Gauwa looked like. //Gauwa is the size of a mouse and has legs like a mouse, he promptly told me, showing me a pipe about four inches long to demonstrate //Gauwa's size. //Gauwa is covered all over with short yellow hairs. This bright, prancing little man had seen a little god. None of the other healers saw //Gauwa as small as this.

Short Gao sees //Gauwa regularly. //Gauwa is like a man in form, but not like an ordinary man. He is about two and a half feet tall. (Gao demonstrated with a stick.) He has yellow hair over his whole body. He does not speak as we speak; he says, "hu hu hu," as the healers do when they are performing the Healing Rite, but softly. Only the healers hear him and understand him.

Another Bushman named Gao said that //Gauwa has the form of a man but is only about a foot tall. He is the color of a warthog.

When Gao Feet is in trance, he often sees //Gauwa. //Gauwa, he says, is a being about the height of a guinea fowl and gray, like the bark of the ubiquitous camel thorn tree. To Gao Feet, //Gauwa is not clearly visible; he is like a mist.

/Ti!kay claimed that he was "young in n/um" and had never seen //Gauwa. This was an engaging torsion of the truth. I myself had many times seen /Ti!kay appear to confront //Gauwa during the Healing Dances. /Ti!kay was to me the most spectacular of all the healers in performing the Healing Rite. He did not fear to scream into the shadows, "Nonabe! You have brought a bad n/um. It is going to kill someone. Take it back." The people, I am sure, did not believe that he was young in n/um and that he did not see //Gauwa when the other healers did.

/Ti!kay, as I think is apparent even in these brief accounts of him, was something of a deviant. I believe that he contradicted others because his nature habitually drove him to oppose others, and that, at the same time, he deliberately and rationally tried to deceive me and lead me astray, first for one reason and then another. He was jealous of our harmonious relations with ≠Toma and Gao Feet. It was clear that we were pleased and grateful to them for working so cooperatively with us, whereas he so often was standoffish and refused to help us. His jealousy seemed to make him spiteful. Also, for reasons I do not know about, he may actually have believed some of the things he said, such as that //Gauwa lives in the east instead of the west. Individuals among the !Kung often hold different versions of their beliefs. We were never certain about /Ti!kay's.

THE //GAUWASI

The Nyae Nyae !Kung believe strongly and vividly in the existence of spirits of the dead, the //gauwasi, who live immortal lives in the upper sky with ≠Gao N!a, doing his bidding. The //gauwasi come to earth and enter into the affairs of men when ≠Gao N!a so commands them, and they come sometimes on their own initiative. The !Kung pray to them to evoke their mercy or sympathy, exhort them in anger, and fear them. The concepts of ancestor worship and of an individual's having special relations with his dead relatives are not a part of !Kung belief.

The spirits of dead people are transmuted into //gauwasi by ≠Gao N!a. When a person dies, //gauwasi soon come to take his spirit *(n/)*. The children of the gods are sometimes the ones who come, we were told, but any of the //gauwasi may do so, either ancestors of the dead person or nonrelated spirits.

The //gauwasi draw the spirit out through the head of the corpse. The spirit that the //gauwasi take, the n/, is distinct from life. The !Kung believe that life *(/xwa)* is another entity existing inside the body of a person or animal, and that it is put there by the creator. It exists in the torso, in all the vital organs, in the abdomen, in the blood, in the heart, lungs, throat, and mouth, and everywhere in the head. It does not exist in the arms or the legs, the !Kung believe, because they know that human beings and animals can be wounded in a limb or even lose one and still not die, whereas a wound in one of the vital parts is likely to kill. The people with whom I spoke thought that life must be especially concentrated in the heart. A wound there is sure to kill. When life dies in the body, it stays there, dead, as the body itself is there but dead. It is the spirit that does not die.

The spirit is like breath or like air. It cannot be seen and cannot be kept by mortals. The //gauwasi draw it out of the person's dead body, and they take the heart and blood of the person as well. The //gauwasi carry these vital parts first into the western sky to the place where //Gauwa lives, but they do not leave them with him. They carry them farther, around by the south to the east, to the place where ≠Gao N!a lives.

≠Gao N!a receives the spirit, heart, and blood of the dead person and transforms these elements into a //gauwa. To do this, he makes a fire under the tree that grows near his house. He sets a pot on the fire, and in it he boils certain n/umsi. Only he has these particular n/umsi. Mortals do not know their names. ≠Gao N!a then hangs the spirit, heart, and blood of the dead person in the tree. The tree itself has strong n/um. That is why the people fear it and why ≠Gao N!a hangs the spirits in it. Smoke rises from the pot, carrying the n/um in its smell. It flows around the dead person's spirit, heart, and blood and transmutes them into a //gauwa. ≠Gao N!a then smears the //gauwa with fat. This fat is not from an animal; it is a special substance that does not exist on earth and belongs only to ≠Gao N!a. It is called *!thu.* ≠Gao N!a then takes the //gauwa to live with him in his house.

The //gauwasi have bodies that resemble those they had on earth except for the hair. Their hair is changed from a Bushman's spirals to hair like ≠Gao N!a's, which is long like a European's but as black as a Bushman's. The //gauwasi are invisible to ordinary people. Only healers old in n/um see them.

≠Gao N!a gives the //gauwasi everlasting life. They grow older, but before they are very old, he rejuvenates them. He has a n/um for this that he does not give to mortals. Children who die remain children.

Life with ≠Gao N!a and his family is not a life of great hardship. The //gauwasi have their own implements, weapons, karosses, and carrying bags. They want nothing from humans, and there is no point in offering them things. The //gauwasi eat food, the same foods that mortals eat—meat and plant food—but they have their own supplies, and they have plenty. They are particularly fond of honey.

The //gauwasi keep their own spouses if they wish, and they live together but do not beget children. No great point was made of this. It was interesting to learn that if a //gauwa tires of his wife and wants another, he may kill a living woman whom he finds attractive; so if a beautiful woman dies, one who is "fresh" and "clean," who wears fine ornaments, a //gauwa could be suspected of having taken her for himself. And a strong young hunter might be killed by a female //gauwa who wanted him. In spite of the power and dominance of the gods, the //gauwasi sometimes seem to take matters into their own hands.

With the exception of those who have died by suicide, the //gauwasi live together in equality, without differentiation of status or function. No distinction is made between a good //gauwa and a bad //gauwa; his personal morality or immorality during life has no bearing on his fate after death. No punishment is imposed. The circumstances surrounding his death make no difference to his state in the afterlife. Burial, for instance, has no effect. Whether a person is buried properly in a deep, round grave, is put into a shallow trench, or is not buried at all and his body is eaten by beasts makes no difference. In some Bushman cultures, a distinction is made between good and bad deaths. For example, Fourie reports that, for the Auen, people who die a good death die easily, without great pain, whereas those who die in agony die a bad death: "People who die a 'good death' are said to go to *!khutse* [a good being], those dying a 'bad death' to *Gaua*. The former have a good time and live in plenty; the latter, on the other hand, often suffer hunger and distress" (Schapera 1930:168).

Among the Nyae Nyae !Kung, only people who commit suicide are believed to be excluded from the afterlife with ≠Gao N!a in the eastern sky. They have immortal life, but they live with //Gauwa in the west. The people with whom I spoke said nothing about hunger and distress; in fact, they had little to say about suicide from any point of view. Suicide is very rare among them (see chapter 8).

The function of the //gauwasi is to carry out orders. They obey ≠Gao N!a primarily but are servants of //Gauwa as well. They are the messengers, whether good or bad fortune is being sent to the people. In that role they interact with mortals in many ways. They move freely in the sky and on earth. All over the sky, fine cords are stretched like the strands of a spider's web, invisible to living humans but strong. Cords also hang between the sky and the earth, which the //gauwasi move about on and use to climb down to earth. In their bodily form they can be seen only by the most powerful of healers, but they can appear to anyone in dreams.

The //gauwasi are associated with evil, particularly with sickness and death. The !Kung believe that when the gods have decided to take a person in death, most often they send the //gauwasi to kill him. The //gauwasi have innumerable ways of doing so. They can lead a buffalo to gore the person, a lion to maul him, or a snake to bite him. Lightning—"rain fire"—is used by the //gauwasi to kill people when the gods so command. Sickness, however, is the greatest tool of the death-bringers, and the most common cause of death. The //gauwasi can bring sickness, death, and other misfortune to mortals at any time, but they are sure to come during the Ritual Healing Dances and lurk in the shadows, watching for their chance to inflict ill on the one or more people whom they have been sent to destroy.

The //gauwasi are mischievous as well as being conveyors of serious evils, and they trick and fool people on their own initiative, often appearing to people in dreams to do so. A man might dream, for instance, that the //gauwasi had come and told him that he would shoot a fat buck if he hunted in a certain direction. If he hunted there and failed to kill anything, he would know that they had tricked him. When ≠Toma was sick, he felt that he was lying on thorns and that the //gauwasi were pressing down on his chest.

The pervading association of the //gauwasi with the infliction of ills has led to an avoidance of speaking of them freely. The !Kung say that to speak of them aloud and freely is a death-thing. It would draw their attention to the speaker. A //gauwa might ask, "Who is this? What goes on here?" His displeasure or anger might be aroused, and he might do something to harm the speaker. The language has a respect term, "/airisi," for use when one wishes to show deference and be ingratiating. Actually, the !Kung seem to speak of the //gauwasi quite often with some discretion but with much less caution than they use when they speak of the gods. I heard them use the respect word only once other than the time when they told me the term.

Although the !Kung associate the //gauwasi primarily with sickness and death and have a pervading fear of both, they do not appear to suffer great fear of the //gauwasi themselves. I think their fear is mitigated by the belief that the //gauwasi are minor characters who can be driven away and that in their own natures they are not wholly evil. Like the mortals they once were and like the gods themselves, they are capable of being good, bad, or indifferent to man. People can plead with them for their favor, and sometimes the //gauwasi feel pity and are helpful.

The Interrelationship of the Gods with Each Other and with Man

The great god said when he praised himself, "I take my own way, and no one can command me. I am a stranger, unknown, unknowable. I am tshi dole." The !Kung evidently imagine him to be as rash as he was in the olden times. However, the ≠Gao N!a of the present is not indifferent to mankind, and even though he lives in the sky, he is not remote. On the contrary, he is deeply involved with mortals, very much aware of what people do. He reacts with pleasure or displeasure, and he favors, punishes, or treats people ill—but according to his whim, not according to any system of man's.

The good and the evil that befall mankind are thus explained by a duality that has its principal source in the omnipotent ≠Gao N!a's own self-oriented nature, his power to bestow good or evil. The scope of this duality is enlarged by the similar duality in the natures of //Gauwa and the //gauwasi. They sometimes do good deeds to man and sometimes bad when they instigate actions on their own initiative, which they do especially, I gather, when ≠Gao N!a is not around. Although ≠Gao N!a is omnipotent, he is not omniscient or omnipresent.

The !Kung sometimes account for evil by saying that the sky beings work at cross-purposes among themselves. For instance, //Gauwa might lead a man to find honey that ≠Gao N!a had intended for someone else, someone he wished to favor. In such a case, ≠Gao N!a might be angry and take revenge upon the man who found the honey. On the other hand, the gods might talk things over and agree. The //gauwasi might want to take a person in death. One god might say, "Go ahead," but the other might say, "No, let us not take him." The first might then change his mind, and the person would be saved. That is how people may be very ill and still be cured, ≠Toma explained.

Punishment

The concept of sin as an offense against the gods is vague among the !Kung. Man's wrongdoing against man is a social matter on the human level. It is not left to ≠Gao N!a's punishment, nor is it considered to be his concern. Man corrects or avenges such wrongdoings himself in his social context. ≠Gao N!a punishes people for his own reasons, which are whimsical and often obscure. It was interesting to see in the examples given by the !Kung how often food is involved.

Burning bees, I learned, displeases ≠Gao N!a intensely. He likes the bees; his wife is the "mother of the bees"; and he is very fond of honey himself. On one occasion two men found honey in a tree. They tried to chop it out, but the bees stung them so badly that they built a fire to drive them away, and many bees were burned. ≠Gao N!a did not like this. He sent a sickness upon the men, causing their bodies to become hot, as though burned by fire, and they died.

≠Gao N!a can change himself into a gemsbok and walk in the veld. A hunter might come along and kill that gemsbok, thinking how lucky he is to have gotten it. He would take the meat home and eat it, and the next day he would be dead. Others, who had had no part in the killing, would not die. ≠Toma, who was telling the story, went on to say that ≠Gao N!a might regret having done such a thing—killing a man who was just hunting to feed his children—and to make amends he might particularly favor that man's son.

If ≠Gao N!a really sets out to kill someone in punishment, ≠Toma told us, one method he might use is to convert himself into honey and place himself in a tree like an ordinary honeycomb. Then he would direct the person he wants to kill to that tree. The person would take the honey home, eat it, and then die.

≠Toma added that ≠Gao N!a might punish a person just a little by giving him a mild sickness, which would be comparable to giving him a thrashing. A good person who had done no wrong at all might also be punished by a mild sickness. ≠Gao N!a's motive, ≠Toma explained, might be to test him or to "break" him.[10] "Why?" we asked, but ≠Toma could not say. Not man's due, but whim and pride in demonstrating supremacy and power would be a reason in keeping with the nature of one who has said, "I am tshi dole."

≠Gao N!a is, fortunately, not a god of mighty wrath and vengeance. "He does not get too angry," ≠Toma remarked. "That is why there are still people living on earth." He and others who were present at our talk went on to point out again ≠Gao N!a's benefactions. They spoke of ≠Gao N!a sometimes helping a hunter by showing him a spoor to follow or, better still, the spoor of a crippled animal, easy to track and kill. Or he might show the man a tree where he would find honey. ≠Gao N!a's greatest benefactions, they said, were the gifts of children, rain, and arrow poison. They elaborated upon the arrow poison, saying that ≠Gao N!a had taught them how to find it and how to put it on their arrows so that they would have meat to eat. They compared ≠Gao N!a's gift of arrow poison with the gift of cattle and the knowledge of growing crops that the god of the black people had given to them. Both gifts make food available so that people can live.

Prayer

The !Kung have no rites in which they seek to placate the gods or to praise or worship them. They make no sacrifices, no offerings. The greatest of their rites, the Ritual Healing Dance, is the one rite that explicitly involves the gods. In this rite, when all the people come together and the healers go into trance and heal the people, the gods are confronted, not worshiped. The !Kung say that they scold the gods.

With the exception of this dance, all the !Kung's communication with the gods is through individual prayer. !Kung society is egalitarian to the utmost. No person or class of people is set apart or exalted above others, and there are no socially defined specialists, such as priests. Anybody may pray directly to the gods or to the other sky beings. People pray frequently and spontaneously at any time or place without assuming a special posture or observing any other formality. They speak to the gods as intimately as if they were talking to another human. Often, but not regularly, they address the great god as "father" and refer to themselves as his "children."

The people say the words of their prayers silently to themselves, or aloud as though thinking aloud, but speaking directly to the gods. They may also speak to each other so as to be overheard by the gods. When men go to look for honey, they may pray to Khwova N!a, the mother of the bees, to give them luck. Demi said, "We talk to ourselves, and she feels pity and leads us to the honey."

The prayers seem very often to be in the form of questions that imply accusation—"Why do you do thus and so?"—but the people mean to plead mildly without displaying anger. The swearing of the healers, customary when they are in trance, does not appear in prayers. People often use the respect terms for the gods, but they also sometimes say the gods' names aloud when they pray. There is no rule about which names to use; people use the second or third person, one as readily as the other. In our many talks about these matters, people told me what they would say to ≠Gao N!a or //Gauwa. I quote:

N!au, excuse this man and make him well.

Sympathize with me, N!au, because you are our Gaoxa. Feel pity for me.

≠Gao N!a, why have you made me grieve so? You gave me this person, why will you take him back? Favor me. Let this person live. If he dies, where shall I go?

!Gara has taken that person while we were still loving him. Why has he taken him?

You have created me and given me power to walk about and hunt. Why do you guide us so that we do not get animals?

≠Gao N!a, when the women are walking in the veld gathering food, let them find a dead animal. Shoot it for them with your bullet. Favor us.

Give rain. Wet the earth. Let there be food to be gathered. We are starving because we have to stay by the water hole where there is no more food to be gathered. You have favored some people with rain. Will you not favor us?

Gani ga, give us coolness.

Give us rain. Give us a chance to rest. Give us food. We have nothing else if you do not give us food. Let food grow.

Please, our father, great man, will you send us rain?

My father [*m'ba*], why is it that you help other people and do not help me to find food? We are all your sons. Help me too. I am the same as your other sons.

Why does ≠Gao N!a send lightning? Why does he destroy our houses with mad rain? Why does the lightning not go and die somewhere and leave us alone and just let a gentle rain give us water?

If someone were struck and killed by lightning, Gao Feet said that he would say:

Hishe, why have you taken this person? Why do you strike us with a storm? You cannot always be good; you keep changing. You created all things and are present in every movement. Why must you do ill?

About another storm Gao Feet said:

It is N!au who makes these things. He is scolding us because we are his children. It is because of our bad ways that we are so punished. We must not complain. This is a good time, the time of rain. We must not complain.

When the people are pleased, they thank ≠Gao N!a: "This is how you must serve your children."

One old man, Tuka N!a, turned a prayer into a song and taught it to his people. The prayer is to //Gauwa. The men sometimes sing it when they are walking along in the veld on hunting trips:

//Gauwa must help us that we kill an animal.
//Gauwa, help us. We are dying of hunger.
//Gauwa does not give us help.
He is cheating. He is bluffing.
//Gauwa will bring something for us to kill tomorrow,
After he himself hunts and has eaten meat,
When he is full and is feeling good.

The song then changes to the past tense. It tells how //Gauwa favored them and gave them luck in the hunt and how afterward the man said to the women:

You sing well.
We are happy now.
Our hearts are shining.
I shall put on my rattles,
And put on my headband,
And put a feather in my hair
To explain to //Gauwa how happy we are
That he has helped us and that we have eaten.
My heart is awake.

When we do not have meat,
My heart is sad from hunger,
Like an old man, sick and slow.
When we have meat, my heart is lively.

The concerns and anxieties of these people are manifest in their prayers. The anxieties about food and about sickness and death—in other words, about survival—become vividly apparent. Their anxieties are mitigated, however, in my opinion, by their belief that they have resources for their protection. They have many traditional rites for the protection of health and for hunting success, and they are active in performing these rites. Furthermore, although they appear to expect more evil than good from the gods, the concept that the gods are not evil incarnate, but that their dual nature makes them capable of pity and helpfulness as well as displeasure, makes their beneficence a possibility. Influenced by the supplication or scolding of the healers and by the prayers of the people, the gods may be diverted from harming people to helping them. This gives the people hope. In the end, however, the people are helpless before their all-powerful, self-willed ≠Gao N!a and must resign themselves to his will.

PART II

RITES FOR THE PROTECTION OF LIFE AND HEALTH

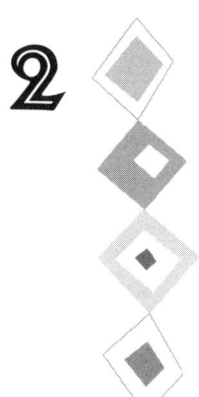

2 Concepts of Sickness and Healing

Staying alive on this earth is the paramount concern of the Nyae Nyae !Kung, if we may judge by their prayers and also by their rituals. By far the most frequently performed rites and informal ritualistic practices are directed toward survival—specifically toward protection of health and protection from starvation. Rites for the protection of health and the curing of sickness are the most numerous, followed by rites for success in the hunt. The rather meager rain rites that are performed have to do with both the protection of health and the inducing of rain to make the food plants grow. The other rituals that the !Kung perform are rites of passage: the Rite of First Kill and *Tshoma* for boys and the Menarcheal Rite for girls. Death and burial are not honored with highly developed rituals among the !Kung, and no formalized rites are performed to venerate or to propitiate the gods or the //gauwasi.

An ardent clinging to life rather than a strong fear of death seems to underlie the many !Kung survival rites. The !Kung, in my opinion, fear death as most humans do at some level of consciousness, but in their culture the fear of death is not intensified or given concrete conception by mythical and religious imagery. In the !Kung cosmos no underworld exists inside the earth, and nowhere on earth or in the sky is there a Hades or a Hell with its devil and eternal torment. In !Kung belief, people are not punished in the afterlife for transgressions committed during their life on earth. The afterlife in the sky with the great god is not fear-inspiring. The //gauwasi live in a house. They have plenty of water and food, including honey. So it seems to me that it is not so much a conscious fear of death that inspires the many !Kung survival rites as an ardent clinging to life.

Foremost among the rites for the protection of life is the great Ritual Healing Dance.[1] It surpasses all other !Kung rites in frequency of performance, in intensity, in the fervent participation of the people. It draws all the people together into concerted action as nothing else does. Led by the healers, the people act together for their mutual good.

Healers have a very special role in !Kung society. They are the major communicating agency between the supernatural and the natural worlds. They are the protectors of the people and the physicians. Healers are called upon to perform the Healing Rite for the sick whenever any individual needs them. They give their services without reward other than gratitude and respect. At the dances the healers not only cure any individual who is manifestly sick but also purge all the people from ills that are not manifest—mysterious ills that people may harbor unknowingly. In trance, with great show of courage, the healers confront //Gauwa and the //gauwasi, who are sent by the great god when he decides to inflict sickness and death upon the people. With yells and shouts and hurled sticks, the healers drive the death-bringers away, demanding that they take with them the sickness and death they brought.

Except for the Ritual Healing Dance (and this is a strong exception), the other rites for survival are performed with little formality, and they may be performed with variation and flexibility. !Kung culture does not give great emphasis to formalization. The !Kung seek the protection and help that the rites are believed to provide, but the rites are performed as an adjunct to life's activities rather than as a primary compelling activity. John Marshall, my son, emphasizes the point that the !Kung are a practical, realistic people. They pray to the gods for help and perform the protective rites, but they actually depend for their lives on their excellent knowledge of their environment, their skills, their vigor, and their efforts.

Concepts of Sickness

Before describing the healers and their Healing Rite, I want to describe some of the !Kung concepts of sickness. I use the word "sickness" in a broad sense to include various kinds of minor ailments, disabilities, and injuries, as well as diseases.

The !Kung had good factual knowledge of human anatomy from cutting up the game the hunters kill and from knowing that human bodies are similar to animal bodies. They understood something of the functions of the stomach, intestines, lungs, bladder, and heart, although the functions of the kidneys, liver, and spleen baffled them. They knew that blood circulates. They observed the difference between dark venous blood and bright arterial blood. They had, however, only scant factual knowledge of sickness and none of modern medical theory. No Western outsiders—no missionaries, doctors, teachers, anthropologists, or government officials—had ever provided them with Western concepts of disease or Western cures. The !Kung concepts of the causes and cures of sickness lay largely in the realm of the supernatural.

Although I speak at length about sickness in this account, I do not want to imply that the !Kung were a sickly people or overly concerned with sickness in daily life. On the contrary, our impression was that they were in good health, and their attention was certainly not morbidly concentrated on sickness.[2] They were all thin but strong, wiry, energetic, and lively, much given to talk and laughter.[3]

Several factors were favorable to health in Nyae Nyae. The desert climate is salubrious. The !Kung diet was a balance of meat and wild vegetables, nuts, and fruits. Botanists have identified more than a hundred plant foods that sustain the !Kung, some common, some rare, all adding to a varied, wholesome diet (Marshall 1976; Lee 1979). The !Kung had no rickets or kwashiorkor. Their remoteness from white people and their limited contact with their Tswana and Herero neighbors over the Botswana border meant that the !Kung had limited contact with the diseases of those peoples. I count the presence of the healers and the healing rituals among the factors favorable to health. The !Kung ritual processes of protection and healing undoubtedly have beneficial psychological effect, which in turn has beneficial physical effect on the people.

Believing as they do that the great god is the creator and controller of all things, the !Kung say that ultimately all sickness must come from him and all injuries are within his control. He may protect a person from disaster or be indifferent to his movements and let him be attacked by a leopard or step on a puff adder. Being logical and consistent, the !Kung verbalize and reiterate that belief, especially when questions are put to them by an anthropologist. At the same time, in what is apparently another stratum of belief, an ancient lore about sickness mingles with the belief that the great god is directly responsible for it.

Sickness of the Sky

In !Kung concept there are two kinds of sickness. One consists of common minor ailments, minor localized pains, boils, injuries, and wounds from visible causes; the other is defined as "sickness of the sky." Minor aches and ailments are not greatly feared. People do not call the healers to treat such conditions. They treat themselves and each other with bleeding, binding, and the application of ointments made from plants that they believe have curative or protective n/um. A sickness of the sky is different. It is a threat to life. It has no visible, earthly cause. The afflicted person feels very hot all over with high fever, suffers a general internal misery, and may have other symptoms as well. Sky sickness is sent directly by the great god. //Gauwa and the

//gauwasi are usually his messengers. They may bring the sickness at any time, but they are very likely to bring it when they come to the Ritual Healing Dances and lurk in the shadows beyond the light of the dance fire.

Sky sickness comes in the form of tiny invisible arrows smeared with deadly n/um. The messengers shoot the arrows with tiny invisible bows into the person who is to be made sick. The arrows of sickness are invisible to ordinary humans. However, the Old Old People must have seen them, because they described them. The !Kung with whom I spoke picked up little sticks to show the size—about two inches long and as thin as a little blade of grass. A person feels nothing when the arrows penetrate him, but in time he falls ill. Sky sickness goes into the blood and is carried into the torso of the body and the vital organs, not the limbs. Hotness and misery are its common symptoms. Severe internal pain, severe diarrhea, and vomiting are also symptoms. Unless the healers with their powerful n/um succeed in drawing the sickness out by performing the Healing Rite, the person dies.

In addition to the arrows that carry the sky sickness, there are believed to be little invisible n/um sticks that can enter the body anywhere. They too are sent by the great god. //Gauwa and the //gauwasi bring them and throw them into the person to be afflicted, causing sharp pain. A n/um stick in the area of the kidneys is especially dangerous. The healers draw the sticks out when they cure.

Some Earthly Causes of Sickness

Other beliefs about sickness appear to belong to a very ancient lore. These beliefs involve causes that are visible and earthly, but that have supernatural attributes. According to the !Kung, they are ultimately under the control of the great god but not directly wielded by him. I mention those I happened to learn about; there are probably more. Except for the sickness called /owha, caused by pythons, each cause does not produce a specific disease or condition; the causes can produce various ailments.

Walking on a grave or passing close to one could make a person sick. The !Kung made a point of telling me that they are especially careful to teach their children to avoid graves. A wind blowing across the grave can carry the sickness. People toss sa powder into the wind to protect themselves.[4]

As noted, little whirlwinds, those we call dust devils, are very common in the Kalahari, and small tornadoes are not uncommon. The !Kung believe that //Gauwa moves in the whirlwinds and that, even if he is not present in the wind at a given time, the wind carries his smell, his ≠a. If the wind blows directly over a person, //Gauwa's smell will go into him and make him sick.

A new fire made ritually by an old man with fire sticks has very strong n/um, so strong that it is dangerous. A new fire must not be kindled near a person who is sick. The strong n/um in the fire could affect the strength of the sickness and cause death.

Mantises in !Kung lore are not personified as /Kaggen was in the myths of the Cape Bushmen. The !Kung give the insects a special status, however, in calling them "the servants of //Gauwa." They believe that //Gauwa protects mantises, and to harm a mantis would attract //Gauwa's attention and displeasure. If a person should throw a mantis into the fire, however inadvertently, that person would become very sick.

When a child is sick, all his ornaments are removed. Other ornaments are given to him when he recovers. If he were to wear the old ones, they might make him sick again.

To drink water from a pool in which a python lives might give a sickness called /owha, which causes violent vomiting and diarrhea. "/Owha" is the word for a green slime that appears on water where a python lives.

If a person should drink water from a water hole in which a lion had urinated, he would become very sick. The urine of any animal that people eat is not harmful, except giraffe urine. Giraffes are so strong that their urine would cause a person with a weak heart to vomit violently. A person with a strong heart would dislike the bitter taste but could withstand the strength of the urine. Some !Kung went on to speak of hyenas, though I had not asked about them. Although hyenas are predators and people do not eat them, their urine in the water hole is harmless. Human urine in the water hole would cause a person who drank the water to have severe stomach pains.

In !Kung culture some foods are avoided at certain times of life and during the observance of some of the rituals. Violation of these avoidances is another believed source of physical ailments and disability. Each avoidance, if violated, is believed to carry its own penalty. Thinness was the penalty for a considerable number. The person who fails to observe the avoidance becomes as thin as a stick. Thinness is a dreaded condition to the !Kung, a death threat. Other penalties, we were told, are severe headaches, tender skin, aching bones, boils, distension and pain in the stomach, diarrhea, nosebleeds, difficult childbirth, madness, weakness, and failure in the hunt.

In what appears to be a fragment of almost forgotten lore, falling stars are associated with sickness and death by the Nyae Nyae !Kung (see chapter 13). A shower of falling stars means that somewhere many people are dying, we were told. Other Bushmen make the same association. Schapera says that among the Eastern !Kung "a shooting star heralds the death of someone" and that shooting stars were "omens of death" to Cape Bushmen (Schapera 1930:193–94).

None of the people with whom we spoke could explain more about these omens of death, but they had another lore about falling stars—to me it seemed a very strange lore—that falling stars are ant lions *(Myrmeleontidae neuroptera)*. They appear as meteors in the sky at night; in the morning they fall to earth (see chapter 13).

Richard Lee (personal communication) tells me that the Dobe !Kung believe in a "bird sickness" *(tsama)*. They believe that the shadow of a hawk, kite, or eagle falling on a young infant could kill it. I wish I knew if the Nyae Nyae !Kung have this belief and for one reason or another did not tell me about it, or if it is an example of divergence of beliefs among the !Kung groups.

The !Kung recognize a few natural, nonmysterious causes of sickness as well as the supernatural causes. They mentioned especially cold, fatigue, and fright. They often said they could die of fright.

Injuries and Wounds

Other earthly causes of "sickness," or let me say other threats to life, are injuries from accidents and wounds from animals. These are visible, understandable, earthly things. If a person is bitten by a mamba, the cause of his death is the mamba, not a sky sickness.

The !Kung are lithe and agile, and we observed not an unwary, ill-coordinated one among them. Few accidents occurred. We had the episode of the broken toe but heard of no broken legs or arms. We were told that, in the past, two men had accidentally fallen from baobab trees and had died. Such a death was appalling to the !Kung, who are as careful as cats. We learned of one accident with a poisoned arrow. A man's bowstring had broken, and the arrow had sprung back and nicked his arm. His life had been saved by his friends' care in sucking the wound.

Injuries from animals in Nyae Nyae could be considered rare statistically, but they are talked about so vividly that they remain in the foreground of memory, charged with horror, and are given great emphasis. Several stories were told of people having been killed by pythons. The story I cannot forget was about a woman bathing with a group of women in Thinthuma Pan. A python swam toward her, only its wide, flat head barely showing above water. She reached out for the head. People said that undoubtedly she thought it was a frog that she would catch to eat. In a flash the python coiled around her and drew her down to her death. The other women had nothing to fight the python with. They could not save their friend. They splashed, screaming and shaking with terror, to the shore. The python was still living in Thinthuma when we visited the Thinthuma Pan.

People speak of hyenas with strong aversion, making their stylized gesture of tapping their lips with their fingers and crying a prolonged "oooooooo" (rhyming with "few"). Hyenas bite off one's nose or one's buttock when one is sleeping, they declared. However, not one !Kung we met lacked a nose or a buttock. We heard of only one actual, relatively recent attack. A hyena dragged off a sleeping child while her family was sitting by their fire a few feet away. The hyena bit through the little girl's ankle. The people drove off the hyena and applied the plant medicine *tami* (unidentified) to the wound. The little girl recovered.

Leopards were considered very dangerous, and I was given several accounts of hunters being killed. Wounds by buffalo were more frequent. Snakes were the greatest menace. Many !Kung have died of snakebites, most often from the sluggish puff adder, which lies still and lets itself be stepped on. Mambas and spitting cobras were also a danger.

Lions have a special place in !Kung thought. The lions of Nyae Nyae were not man-eaters. We were given two accounts of people mauled by lions, the events set elsewhere and in the past, but no accounts of anyone killed by a lion.[5] However, the !Kung had many reports of lions circling their fires at night and graphic descriptions of their terror. They have endowed lions with mystique and fear them in a special way.

Common Treatments and Protections for Minor Ailments

Minor ailments, disabilities, and injuries may be treated by anyone. The healers are not regularly called to perform their Healing Rite for every little pain or scratch or cough. People treat themselves and each other. Only if an ailment turns serious need the healers be called.

The everyday mundane treatments often involved the medicine plants that the !Kung believe have curative properties. The plants are charred in the fire, crushed to powder with mortar and pestle, mixed with fat or marrow to form an ointment, and rubbed on the person's afflicted part—either just on the skin or into little incisions made for bleeding. *//Gwey* (*Ximenia caffra* Sond.), *zao* (*Terminalia sericea* Burch.), and *!qui dam* (unidentified except by the !Kung as "a tree with a medicine root") are regularly used in this way. The use of the plants is a very common practice. Everyone carries bits of the plants among his possessions, whatever he manages to procure. Whoever has an appropriate bit shares it with others when occasions arise.

Binding and massage

The !Kung believe that binding alleviates pain. There are always several people around with their heads, chests, abdomens, or limbs bound with strips of zao bark, which is pliable. It is pressure, not n/um, in this instance that the people are using.

Massage is another common practice. It relieves aching muscles. The !Kung walk everywhere. They go to hunt or to gather, to visit, to move from one fertile area of their territory to another, and back and forth to their permanent water hole, walking hundreds of miles in a year—Richard Lee (1972) estimates about fifteen hundred miles—carrying their possessions, the foods they gather, and their children. They often have sore muscles. Di!ai let me massage her aching shoulders several times when we sat together by her evening fire.

The most picturesque massage I saw was given to ≠Toma. One day when his back ached he instructed a boy of about eight or nine to swing from a low branch of a tree. ≠Toma then lay down under the branch, and the boy, with his weight partly supported by the branch, walked up and down ≠Toma's aching back, kneading the sore muscles with his feet.

Bleeding and sucking

Perhaps the most commonly used treatment for minor ailments and pain is bleeding. In !Kung concept, sickness can be in any organ, including the blood. Pain, they say, is felt in the blood. Bright red blood is healthy; dark blood, they believe, has sickness in it. Bleeding lets the sickness out. A common method of bleeding is to make a row of tiny vertical incisions or a shallow slash over the place where the sickness is thought to be or the pain felt. More often than not, an ointment of a n/um plant is rubbed into the bleeding incisions. In a case of insanity (rare but existing among the !Kung), the people resorted to making a deep slash in the man's forehead to let the bad blood out. The !Kung claim that bleeding is sometimes successful, sometimes not.

The blood is allowed to ooze gently unless a greater flow is necessary, as it would be in a case of snakebite or the rare occasion of an accident with the ever-present deadly poisoned arrows. The !Kung know no antidote to their arrow poison. Sucking is then the usual method used to induce the flow of the contaminated blood. Cupping may also be resorted to. We saw little duiker horns for cupping among the men's possessions, but we never saw them used. Sucking is the common method.

If the snakebite is from a mamba, it is almost certain to be fatal, but for bites of the several other poisonous snakes, including the frequently encountered spitting cobra and puff adder, sucking may save the person's life. The companions of the stricken person quickly slash the wound to let it bleed. They loosely tie a tourniquet above the wound, if it is feasible to do so, and begin to suck vigorously and to massage the area of the wound with strokes directed away from the heart. If they have some available, they give the person powdered root of the zao tree mixed with water to drink. This might make the person vomit, and the !Kung believe that vomiting would increase the chances of his recovery. We learned of several lives saved from snakebites this way and one saved from a poisoned-arrow wound. Of the man wounded by his own poisoned arrow, people said they sucked his wound so hard and so long that he was almost sucked to death. The !Kung laugh at the untoward—and they had a good laugh at the thought of having almost sucked their friend to death.

Apparently there are conventions regarding the exact place to bleed and more lore than we learned. For a severe nosebleed, for instance, in addition to rubbing the person's nose, someone cuts little incisions on the back of the person's neck and rubs in charred, powdered bark of the zao tree. For bites of a certain large, poisonous black spider that lives in the ground (not a tarantula), incisions are made behind the ear of the person bitten and in a vein in his arm. For toothaches, the incisions are made in the cheek or lip over the painful tooth, and when the blood begins to ooze, someone shouts, *"Tsatsabi"* ("snatch"; that is, "snatch out the pain").

Although healers are not regularly called to treat every minor sickness or wound, they may be called at any time for any degree of ailment, mild or severe. It is their custom, with only extremely rare exceptions, to respond readily to any request. They are present to the people, not aloof, and they are definitely the major factor in the protection of health and the curing of sickness. Their curing power is believed to be of another order of magnitude and in another realm of !Kung belief from the mundane cures mentioned above.

THE HEALERS

The healers of the sick and the protectors of health are called n/um k"xausi (owners of n/um). In !Kung belief the n/um specially given to the healers by the great god is the powerful, supernatural force that enables them to heal. It is believed to be inserted into the bodies of the healers. In !Kung metaphor, to be an owner of something means to possess it or, if it is a skill, to be excellent in performing it. A person who sings very well is an "owner of music." The owners of n/um are owners in both senses. They may also be addressed by either of two respect terms, *"n/um n/iha"* and *"n/um gaoxa."*

Men and Women Healers

In the Nyae Nyae area, at the time we were present, all the healers were men. Women healers were not unknown, but healing was not within women's ordinary expected role, and the women healers were regarded as deviant. It is not that women in !Kung culture are totally excluded from healing. Some years later in Botswana, Megan Biesele and Richard Katz found a number of women healers.[6] However, at the time and place of our fieldwork in the Nyae Nyae area, there were no active women healers.

We learned of only two living women who were believed to have n/um and who in the recent past had healed in a minor way. Two or three others, by then dead, were remembered from the more distant past; one of them had become insane. Of the two living women, one was Old N≠isa, an exceptional old woman, whom I describe in chapter 3. She had received two n/um songs from //Gauwa. When we met her and had her tell us about the songs, we did not know that she had healed in the past, when she was younger, and we missed the opportunity of talking with her about that.

The other woman was Old //Khuga of Band 12 at /Gam. The night before we were to leave /Gam to move to Gautscha, we attended a most intense dance at which four bands danced together. Late in the night Old //Khuga fell into trance. She did not dance with the men or perform the Healing Rite, but she experienced what appeared to be genuine trance and sat swaying, her eyes staring, softly uttering the sounds that healers make in performing the rite. Next morning we tried to talk with her, but she looked demolished and was totally unresponsive to us. Others told us that they believed she actually had the healing n/um and that in the past she had performed the Healing Rite on occasion. She also possessed another power, we were told. She dreamed about game and where the animals were to be found. Hunters went to her in the mornings to ask in which direction to start their hunt. Because we had to leave, we had no further opportunity to talk with her about her powers. She was the only old wise woman of this type whom we heard about in the Nyae Nyae area.

Eligibility and Ages of Healers

!Kung healers are not an esoteric or elite group and are not drawn from special families or segments of society. Nothing excluded any man from becoming a healer, and most men did become healers. Even Old /Gaishay, who had never married, had been a healer when he was younger. This Old /Gaishay was the only !Kung man we knew or heard about who had never married. Although he was strong enough, he had never been able to hunt, had never killed a big animal, and had never had the Rite of First Kill, which a boy must have before he may take a wife.[7] Yet he could be a healer.

Among the forty-five men in the bands we worked with most intimately, Bands 1 to 7 and Band 9, thirty-two were active healers, nine were old men who had been healers but no longer attempted to heal, and four were young men who had not yet received n/um.

The motivation to become a healer must have been very strong. Healing, like hunting, was regarded by the Nyae Nyae !Kung of our period as a worthy male activity. While every male was expected to hunt, not every male was expected to heal, but those who did heal were looked to, depended on for protection and healing, and rewarded with esteem and gratitude. It was a respected role and was desired by most !Kung men.

None of the men we knew who had wanted to become healers had failed to do so, but a few claimed that they had not wanted to. One reason was a fear of n/um and the fear of trance. A young man named Gao, from /Gam, spoke frankly of his fear, saying that he had been afraid of n/um since he was a boy; in his heart he did not want it. He liked to dance and would attend the ritual dances but would sit a little apart from the dance circle when the healers were going into trance and performing the Healing Rite over the people. He, along with a few others, was an exception.

Men usually become healers when they are in late adolescence or early adulthood, but there is no regularity or formal requirement about the age. /Gunda began to perform the Healing Rite soon after his marriage to N!ai. He was then about seventeen or eighteen. The most active healers were, as we estimated their ages, in their late twenties, thirties, and early forties. !Kung healers do not necessarily practice their calling all their lives. Old men say that their n/um weakens and they are no longer able to cure, and one sees them dancing at the ritual dances but not going into trance and not performing the rite. At any given time, however, many men are active healers.

In the egalitarian society of the !Kung, the healers are the only category of persons who have a specialized function. They are respected for this function but are not set apart by it in any way. They do all the things that the society expects of men; their healing is an additional function. They are not paid for their services, accorded special privileges, or given more food or worldly goods than the people have in general. The healers are as thin as the rest. They do not mark themselves with special garments, hair arrangements, or scarifications. Though they deal with mysterious n/um, nothing about the healers themselves is wrapped in secrecy. Their ritual proceedings and the medicinal substances they use in healing are known to all.

We were told forcefully and repeatedly that the healers are concerned only with protecting and healing, that their n/um never, as they say, "works against" anyone. Their n/um is "only for healing"; it cannot harm. In other words, the healers are not sorcerers with evil intention.

Among themselves the healers are all of a kind, with no division of function or specialization in treating different conditions. They use the same methods and the same medicinal substances. They tend to combine and cooperate in healing. At the dances and in special curings, it was more usual to see two or three healing together than to see one alone.

The main differentiation among the healers was that some were believed to have stronger n/um than others. The !Kung told of great healers of the past whose n/um was so fabulously strong that they could do miraculous things. One, who had died only two years before, could sit in the fire like a pot and not be burned. A few had such strong n/um that they could go directly into the presence of the great god when their spirits left their bodies during trance. They would climb up to the sky by one of the cords that hang between sky and earth. They would meet the great god, talk with him, and climb back down to earth and enter their bodies again. Others had reputations for having extraordinary power to heal. They knew always where the sickness was and could draw it out; they never healed "on the wrong side." These and other such miraculous doings were not within the province of the present-day healers, who explained that they had no such n/um. They must be content just to do the best they could in their efforts to protect and heal. However, there was a perception among the Nyae Nyae !Kung that some present healers were more potent than others and deserved more respect. They were remembered for having achieved more cures.

When the healing fails and the person dies, people do not blame the healers personally. They say either that the healers' n/um had weakened or simply that the great god was determined to take the person and would not allow him to be healed. To this they must be resigned.

Becoming a Healer

A young man who is preparing to become a healer is already familiar with the proceedings of the Healing Rite. There are no hidden mysteries about it. !Kung children are always present at the ritual dances. The young man has danced with the men throughout his childhood, knows all the n/um songs, and is entirely familiar with the sounds and gestures of the Healing Rite in the trance states, which he has seen and heard countless times since his birth. He has learned which n/um roots a healer keeps in his tortoise shell and which foods a healer must eat and which he should avoid—in the way !Kung children learn everything, not by any formal instruction but by being intimately present in the adult activities and listening to or participating in whatever is going on. On this level he need be taught nothing more.

What must happen is that he must be given n/um and learn to perform the rite as he has seen it performed. There are basically two ways in which n/um is given to a novice. Some young men consciously wanting to become healers ask a healer who they believe has strong n/um to give n/um to them. Others have mystical experiences in which they believe the great god or //Gauwa comes to them and gives them n/um directly. The great god does not come near to ordinary mortals in their waking conscious state. He may, nevertheless, come to them when they are asleep and appear as if in a dream. However, it is more usual, we were told, for him to send //Gauwa with the n/um he intends to bestow.

The !Kung make a distinction between ordinary dreams and the concept of the appearances of the gods. Dreams are puzzling to the !Kung. The great god "allows" them, but they are only illusions, or "lies," as the !Kung call them. You see people in your dreams as if they were actually present, but they are not present. You dream of quarrels that have never occurred, of rain falling when there is no rain. The !Kung we worked with do not believe that dreams foretell or influence events or portend good or evil. Among the people we knew, only Old //Khuga at /Gam, who dreamed about the game, was believed to provide information through her dreams.

When the gods appear to them in their sleep, it is like a dream, people say, but not a dream. They believe that the gods are actually there beside them, that the experience is not a "lie" like other dreams. According to accounts, the gods appear fairly frequently in this way, to anyone, not only to healers. //Gauwa appears much more frequently than the great god. He may come at the great god's bidding to give n/um or a n/um song. Often he comes on his own initiative to speak to men about their hunting. Sometimes he is kindly, saying he pities them because they have killed nothing for many days and promising to lead them to game. Or he might promise to lead them to an animal lying in the veld, killed or wounded by lions. Sometimes the people do find such an animal. But //Gauwa also fools them, they say, and then they find nothing.

Several people described waking encounters with //Gauwa. They described, sincerely I believe, what their culture teaches them to imagine, drawing on mythical imagery and fantasy. Whether or not they had actual hallucinations we have no way of knowing. We have accounts of healers receiving n/um in waking as well as in sleep.

Demi's account

Demi was the prancing little man who told us that he had seen //Gauwa when he was in trance at the very big dance we attended at /Gam. Then four bands danced together, and six or eight healers at a time were in frenzied trance. At that time he had described //Gauwa as being as big as a mouse and covered with yellow hairs. Demi was willing and eager to describe to us how his healer's n/um had been given to him.

He was about nineteen or twenty at the time, as we judged from his pointing to a young man and saying he had been about that age. He had not been thinking of becoming a healer and had done nothing to indicate that he wanted to be given n/um. But quite unexpectedly //Gauwa appeared to him. Demi had been hunting. He was at a place called !Gai, alone, resting at night. Demi said the experience was not a dream; he was awake, he claimed, and it was like meeting a real person. Demi again said that //Gauwa was much smaller than a man but did not say again that he was as small as a mouse and did not again mention yellow hairs. //Gauwa spoke to him, not in words, but softly in the sounds that the healers make in the Healing Rite, sounds that they call *n//hara*, "huh huh huh huh huh," and the high-pitched yelping cry "kai kai." After speaking this way to Demi for a moment, //Gauwa put n/um into his back. Demi could feel it being inserted. //Gauwa also gave him a medicine root. Demi has it to this day and uses it in healing. //Gauwa then stood in front of Demi and made all the gestures of healing, and Demi followed his actions and in this way he learned. Six days later, Demi said, holding up the five fingers of one hand and the little finger of the other, //Gauwa came and gave him n/um again. After the second donation, Demi said, he was strong enough in n/um and was a healer.

Old N!aishi's account

Old N!aishi told us that he had been given n/um many years before. He said that //Gauwa knew he wanted n/um and came to give it to him one night when he was asleep, inserting the n/um into his back. This was painful, and N!aishi cried out. His wife roused up and took a medicine root from her bag and touched his back and chest with it. That soothed him, and he slept on. N!aishi saw //Gauwa as if he were in a dream. He appeared to be a small being, manlike in form. N!aishi pointed from his fingertips to his elbow to show how tall. //Gauwa, he said, was dark gray, the color of a warthog. //Gauwa came to give n/um to N!aishi every other night until he had come five times. Then N!aishi had enough n/um and began to practice the Healing Rite.

Gao's account

When Gao Feet (Gao Medicine) was about the age of his tall son, /Gaishay, whom we thought to be in his late teens, he became concerned because there was no active healer in his family group. Old /Gaishay, Gao's father, had been a powerful healer, but his n/um had weakened. He violated a required food avoidance (see chapter 4) by eating leguaan before he reached the age when the lizard need no longer be avoided by healers. He believed that for that reason he was unable to heal. Aware of this, Gao wanted to become a healer and be able to take care of his family. When Gao told his father of his desire, his father was glad and said that Gao should not delay.

Gao went to /Ti!kay. This was not the /Ti!kay we knew well, who was so spectacular in performing the Healing Rite, but another /Ti!kay, now dead, who lived south of /Gam. He had been given exceptionally strong n/um by //Gauwa, and he agreed to be Gao's mentor and to give n/um to Gao and to several other boys who wanted it at the same time.

/Ti!kay instructed Gao to dig //haru (*Lapeyrousia cyanescens* Bak.). (This root is one of the ordinary plant foods of the Bushmen.) Gao brought the //haru. /Ti!kay then took medicine from his tortoise shell, the little container in which the healers carry their medicines. He mixed it with the //haru and gave it to Gao to drink. He had the plant medicines that healers regularly keep in their tortoise shells, and in addition he had a very special one called *!kaishe*. The plant is called *!kaishe n!oru n!oru* in the Dobe area, according to Richard Lee (personal communication). It has been botanically identified as *Ferraria glutinosa* (Bak.) Rendle (Lee 1979). The Nyae Nyae !Kung attribute supernatural qualities to it. They say it belongs to the gods, and when the great god wishes to favor a healer very much, he sends //Gauwa to him with one of the !kaishe roots. !Kaishe is invisible except to such a healer. //Gauwa urinates into the healer's tortoise shell (see p. 57). The healer then mixes the !kaishe with the urine and the other medicines in the shell. This makes a bitter and potent brew, we were told. When a man drinks it, he may go mad for a while. This was what was given to Gao, who drank it mixed with the earthly //haru. Fortunately he had a "strong heart," we were told, and did not go mad. Some days later /Ti!kay told Gao to get more //haru, and the procedure was repeated. Gao then had n/um enough to practice the Healing Rite.

Another method of inserting n/um

In another method, the healer who is the mentor gives the novice n/um through incisions. The novice should first drink !kaishe. Then the healer who is giving the n/um should heat a knife in the fire. (This was the only context I learned of in which the knife used for ritual incisions was heated.) With it he makes little vertical incisions, like those made for bloodletting and scarification, but only on the novice's right side. (The right side is associated with maleness, the left side with femaleness.) The tiny incisions are made on the chin, throat, thigh, and shin. Into these incisions, as they bleed, the healer rubs the substance from his tortoise shell and his own sweat, best taken from under his arms. The sweat carries his n/um.

Variant Concepts

I believe that the concepts I have described of the methods of putting n/um into a novice were held in general. On two occasions we heard from single individuals of two other concepts, which had not come up in our many other discussions on the subject of healers. One man told us that a healer has, inside his arm, an arrow that is impregnated with n/um. To put n/um into a novice, he shoots this magic arrow into the man's abdomen. Another man claimed that when //Gauwa gave him n/um, it was in the form of little silvery slivers, which looked like streaks of rain. //Gauwa, he said, put these into his abdomen. He draws them out when he wants to use them for healing. They are invisible to everyone except very great healers.

The Healer's N/um and Hunting: The N/um-Meat Rite

When a young novice has received n/um, a rite is performed that fully establishes him as a healer. The rite is a hunting rite and shows a belief that an interplay exists between the healer's n/um, the n/um meat *(!kha n/um)*, and success in the hunt.

The new young healer must dance at the first Ritual Healing Dance that takes place after he has received n/um. He participates as a healer at that dance, performing the Healing Rite as the others do. After the dance he should go hunting and should not give up until he has killed a large animal. Animals such as warthogs, small antelopes, birds, or other small creatures do not provide the required meat. The young man should eat the liver of the animal at the place of the kill and should eat *sha sha* (a root) with it.

When the young man returns to his people with the meat, the rite is performed. It is, in part, like the Rite of First Kill, performed when a boy kills his first large animal—the rite of passage that must be performed before a boy may marry (see chapter 6). In the young healer's Meat Rite, his mentor, if he has one, or some other healer old in n/um, takes certain parts of the animal called n/um meat, makes a broth of some of that meat and chars other bits in the coals. N/um meat consists of the meat from the chest, the front muscle of the foreleg, and a place in the throat called ≠oru. In telling us about this, the !Kung showed on their own throats the place above the collarbone where they could feel a pulse. It is called the "heart's stand place." ≠Oru meat is at the center of the throat beside the pulsing place. The mentor washes the healer's face, chest, and arms with the broth. He then makes lines of tiny vertical incisions on his right arm and rubs the particles of the charred meat into them. This establishes the young man as a healer and also strengthens his powers as a hunter.

The n/um meat should then be eaten by any other young healers present at the rite who are new in n/um and by older healers who want their n/um strengthened. The meat must not be eaten by the young man who killed the animal. All the remaining meat of the animal may be eaten by any men of the group, but the whole animal is totally forbidden to women.

We learned that the men who are healers sometimes perform the Healing Rite over each other before setting out to hunt in order to activate their n/um, and that regularly they rub some of the substance in their tortoise shells on their faces before hunting. This substance, rubbed on their faces, is believed to bring them luck in finding honey as well as success in the hunt.

Foods a Healer Should Eat or Avoid

Food is used as a complex symbol in !Kung culture. The !Kung have many concepts about the effects of food and many regulations about food, and food is an element in many ritual procedures. Some foods must be avoided by certain people at certain times of life, and some foods are believed to be especially beneficial to certain categories of people. The healers should observe all the food regulations that men in general observe (see chapter 4). In addition, a few regulations apply especially to healers.

N/um meat, in addition to being a part of the N/um-Meat Rite, should be eaten by the healers from any kill the hunters bring in; it is beneficial to them and strengthens their n/um. Healers should eat liver and blood at every opportunity. A berry, *n/n* (*Grewia flava* DC.), is believed to have n/um and to strengthen a healer's n/um. The roots of *sha* (*Vigna dinteri* Harms) and //haru are beneficial; they should be eaten with sha sha.

Certain foods must be strictly avoided by healers. A healer must not eat any part of an animal killed by a lion, a leopard, a hyena, or wild dogs. The predators may be driven off their kill by the hunters, or the dead animal may be found and may be taken by the hunters; either way, healers should avoid eating such meat.

Leguaan, puff adder, and a snake called ≠khu must be avoided. (The latter snake was not positively identified, but in all probability it is the nonpoisonous mole snake, *Pseudaspis cana;* see FitzSimons 1962). Mole snake is also avoided by other categories of people. These three reptiles should be avoided until the healer is old and has ceased to perform the Healing Rite. Old /Gaishay, Gao Feet's father, believed that his n/um was made useless because he ate leguaan when he should still have avoided it.

Honey and baby bees are strong in n/um. When a young man has newly received his healer's n/um, he must strictly avoid honey, but only for a few years. The length of time was not specified precisely. A young man who looked to be twenty-one or twenty-two was pointed out as one who still avoided honey.

Some avoidances apply to women. In addition to totally avoiding any of the meat of the animal presented in the new healer's N/um-Meat Rite, women must avoid the n/um meat of any animal killed by a healer. Such meat is especially dangerous to young girls. If they ate this meat, very bad abscesses would form on their throats.

The healer keeps his tortoise shell, which contains his medicine, in a leather carrying bag. When food is also carried in that bag and has been in contact with the tortoise shell, only healers eat it. Such food is especially dangerous to women and children. It would cause them to have severe nosebleeds.

The Healers' N/um and Rain and Lightning

Remarks made by Gao Feet one day suggested that in !Kung belief healers in the past, with their strong healers' n/um, had been able to predict rain and to protect the people from lightning and the dangerous whirlwinds that carry //Gauwa's smell. Lightning is a very real danger in the Kalahari, and we had heard several accounts of people killed by it. Gao Feet was lamenting that his n/um had weakened and the n/um of all his people had weakened:

> Our strength has gone, our n/um is worn out. In the past our n/um was strong. We would dance and go into trance and see everything. The good girls who sang so well for us are dead. When we go hunting, we do not kill anything. In the past, when lightning threatened, we knew where it would strike and could warn the people. We could see where the whirlwinds would go. We were good in n/um. We could tell about rain. Now the lightning and the whirlwinds can come against us. We cannot see when the rain will come. Our strength has gone. We could cure strongly in the past. We could see everything and knew where to cure. Now we can cure sometimes, sometimes not. All the old n/um k"xausi who had strong n/um are dead. We do not know how to get our n/um renewed. Why does //Gauwa not come some night and give us n/um again?

"We could tell about the rain. . . ." The ability to predict or control rain is no longer attributed to the healers. The !Kung healers perhaps never were specialists in rainmaking, like those who drew the rain bulls over the land in the rock paintings of the southern Bushmen, but whatever power may have been attributed to them in the past, it is now believed to be lost.

HEALING

The Healer's Tortoise Shell

The one piece of equipment with which healers supplement their own n/um in healing is their tortoise shell filled with a mixture of n/um plants and marrow or fat. We observed specimens of three species of tortoise used for this purpose: *Geochelone pardalis babcocki* Loveridge, *Pasammobates oculifer,* and another (unidentified).[8]

The men catch young tortoises about three inches by two-and-a-half inches. They clean and dry a shell and plug the bottom with a gum called *toro*. They attach a little thong for a handle and provide a stopper of soft grass, a bit of fur, or the nest of a penduline titmouse. Women use the same kind of little tortoise shells to carry the fragrant sa powder, which they toss onto the healers or onto visitors for their well-being and which they use as a cosmetic to powder themselves.

The plant substances commonly used in the tortoise-shell mixture are the roots of the camel thorn tree, /ana (*Acacia giraffae* Burch.), the stone of the fruit of an evergreen bush, //gwey (*Ximenia caffra* Sond.), and the root of zao//o (unidentified). /Ana, //gwey, and zao//o are not possessed exclusively by healers. They are among the plants generally used by anyone in treating minor ills. However, in combination in the tortoise shell and handled by the healer, they give off potent n/um. Incidentally, zao//o, in addition to its curative n/um, has other powers. Rubbed on a hunter's face, it will bring animals to him. Mixed with mamba fat and rubbed on a person's legs, it will protect the person from being bitten by a mamba.

Four other plants might be used in the tortoise shell if the healers happened to have them, but they are uncommon, and we did not see any of them. Their names are "*!gein,*" "*//doli,*" "*≠keng,*" and "*//kedi*" (all unidentified). Whether any of the plant substances have medicinal value from the material point of view, we do not know. In any case, it is for their believed supernatural properties, their n/um, that the !Kung value them.

The healers combine the plants in any way, using what they happen to have at hand. To prepare the mixture they roast the plants in the coals until they are charred black, pound them to powder with mortar and pestle, and mix them with marrow or fat. The marrow or fat is added for cohesive and inflammable properties as well as for the n/um it may have. The marrow from the foreleg of a giraffe below the knee is preferred, but giraffe marrow is hard to come by, so any marrow may be used. Eland fat is preferred but, again, not always available. (Both giraffe and eland have n/um.) Other fat may be used, but not wildebeest fat, which is unacceptable because of its strong odor and its stickiness.

Three supernatural substances may be added to the tortoise-shell mixture if the gods favor the healer and send them. They are invisible to all but the great healers. One is //Gauwa's urine. The great god tells //Gauwa to go to a healer he wishes to favor. When the man is dancing, holding his tortoise shell in his hand, //Gauwa urinates into it. Another substance that the great god sends by //Gauwa to a favored healer is supernatural giraffe urine. The third is !kaishe, the supernatural plant that resembles the earthly //haru but belongs only to the gods. In Gao Feet's account of receiving n/um as a young novice, we were told that he drank //Gauwa's urine and !kaishe from his mentor's tortoise shell and that it was a potent brew.

When the healer uses his tortoise shell in healing, he drops a glowing coal into the mixture. This produces a medicine smoke, *!go n/um.* The n/um is in the smell and is carried by the smoke. In healing, the healer holds the shell under a person's nose, then he passes the shell around a person's back, abdomen, legs, and head so that the smoke wafts all over the person. The healer may also touch his fingers to the substance in the shell and convey the benefit of the n/um by running his fingers over the person in a prescribed manner. First he touches the feet, then runs his finger up the backs of the legs, up the back, around the eyes, down the nose, across the upper lip, under the chin, down the chest, under the breasts, and down the abdomen.

In another healing practice in which the tortoise shell is used, a healer shaves the top of the sick person's head and rubs the medicine mixture from his tortoise shell onto the shaven place. !U had had her head shaved twice. If a sick person has been very ill and has recovered after a healer's head shaving, the whole band might move to another place and set up a new encampment. The move has ritual significance. After a death or when there has been a long period of failure in the hunt, a band moves. In the new place an old man twirls a new fire with fire sticks, a ritual fire, and the people all start new family fires with brands from the ritual fire. The fires symbolize a new beginning and fresh hope. It is usual for the band to move after a death, but the practice of shaving the head for curing and the band moving was not regularly resorted to.

The healers may rub their faces with the tortoise-shell mixture before starting out to hunt. The zao//o in the mixture is believed to have special power to bring animals to the hunter. The tortoise shell is regularly used when healers in trance treat each other. We learned of nothing specific that the n/um smoke does in healing and assume it is believed to have a general beneficial effect.

The Healing Rite

The Healing Rite is in a different realm of experience from the mundane physical bleeding, binding, rubbing, and application of ointments that comprise the curing practices for minor ailments. The Healing Rite is an intense, heightened, ritualistic experience involving the supernatural. This does not mean that it is in any way uncommon or set apart from ordinary daily life. The rite is the special feature of the Ritual Healing Dance, but it may also be performed anywhere, anytime, without pomp or circumstance. It is very much a part of daily life. The supernatural and the natural were two aspects of one reality in the Healing Rite, as they are in other aspects of !Kung life.

The Healing Rite is regularly performed in three contexts. First, at the great Ritual Healing Dances it is performed in spectacular form over everyone present when the healers go into trance and purge the whole community of known or unknown ills. Second, healers perform the rite with special intensity over each other for the protection of their bodies and their spirits, especially when they are in deep trance at the dances. Third, the rite is performed apart from the dance in what I call "special curings" for individuals who are actually sick. These might be called the "private practice" of the healers as a means of distinguishing them from the communal practice at the dance, but the word "private" cannot be appropriately applied to the !Kung. There is no privacy in !Kung lifestyle. They live in each other's presence without walls. They build little grass shelters but live outside them by a fire. The family fires are clustered only a few feet apart so that their combined light at night holds out the darkness and the prowling beasts. Being near together, able to see and touch each other, is security and comfort to the !Kung.

In the rite at dances or in special curings, the healers extract sickness, real or potential, from the persons they are healing. It is the healers' n/um that enables them to draw sickness out. The !Kung say they "pull" it out. The n/um has been put into them in one way or another, as described in the healers' accounts of receiving n/um. The n/um is believed to go into their backs and stomachs, and some goes into their heads and hair and sweat. For them to heal, the n/um must be activated—"awakened," they say. (The !Kung word is *gam:* "to awaken" and "to get up in the morning.") At the dances the n/um songs awaken the n/um. The heat of the fire and the exertion of dancing also awaken it. The men dance and sing for some time before they begin to heal, and they make a great dramatic play about the fire. They run through it, leap over it, stand in it, kneel in it, throw the coals over themselves, and thrust their heads into the flames to set fire to their hair. At special curings, where the behavior of the healers is always more subdued, the men may only sing and stand by the fire a few minutes, or handle a few coals, or set fire to their hair to activate their n/um. Heat makes their n/um boil, the !Kung say. It boils up through the spinal column into their heads. It is then at its strong state for healing. At the dances the n/um becomes so strong that, as the !Kung believe, it overcomes the healers and they go into trance. Then the word "n/um" should not be spoken. If a word must be used, it should be the respect word "*shibi.*"

No special posture is required in healing. A person who is being healed may stand, sit, or lie on the ground; the healer bends over him. Singing a n/um song, the healer places his hands on the person, usually one hand on the back and the other on the chest. He flutters his hands. In a moment or two he begins to make the indescribable sounds of the rite, the n//hara sounds. They are the sounds that might come from a human being in extreme agony, but they are formalized, a convention of the rite, consistently repeated and having a suggestion of rhythmic pattern.

Leaning over the person he is healing and fluttering his hands on him, the healer begins with rapid, gasping grunts, "gu gu gu gu," which turn into long, intense, high-pitched, formalized cries, "kai di di di, kai di di di," which fall to gasps, "aaaaaaaa-uh, aaaaaaaa-uh." These gasps may trail out into a very rapid expulsion of little coughs, "uh, uh, uh, uh." Or a man may make low, rumbling groans that also end in coughs. As the healer straightens up and throws back his head, his wails become louder and higher pitched. They then turn into long, quavering screams, which the healer emits over and over and over, "waaaaaaaa, waaaaaaaa, waaaaaaaa." Gasps, grunts, wails, and screams climax in yelping shrieks—"kai kai kai"—that the healer utters as he throws his arms up. He may rub his hands together as though brushing something off; he may shake his head. He may stand where he is, shrieking and making violent gestures as though throwing something away.

The !Kung believe that when the healer flutters his hands on a person, he draws the sickness out of that person and into himself through his hands. The groans and screams show that this is "heavy" work and that the sickness is painful to the healer. The men claim it burns them. Once in the healer's body, the sickness goes up his arms into his neck and his head. He ejects it through his neck from a place at the back of his neck called n//au by the violent shakes of the head, through his mouth by his shrieks of "kai kai kai," and through his arms and hands by shaking them and hurling it out.

When healings take place apart from a dance as special curings for individuals who are actually sick, several additional curing practices are performed. These are ordinarily omitted at the dances, where, if no one is manifestly sick, the general protection of the group is emphasized above individual curing. The healers work very earnestly over the sick person at these special curings. The special curings were very moving to see: a healer gently healing his baby in the middle of the night, lying prone on the ground, his forehead against the baby's stomach, his n//hara sounds subdued; or two or three healers working intently and earnestly together over a sick woman, their n//hara sounds at highest volume.

Transmitting some of the healer's n/um into the patient is one of the supplementary practices. The n/um helps to dislodge the sickness and makes it easier to remove. In setting fire to their hair the healers exude n/um. The n/um comes out in the smell of the burning hair and is breathed in by the patient. N/um is exuded also in sweat, the !Kung believe, but not in saliva or other emissions of the body. //Gauwa's urine carries n/um, but that of the healers does not. A healer takes sweat on his hands from the sweaty places of his body—his face, chest, abdomen, backs of knees, and especially his armpits—and rubs it on the patient. When healers are protecting other healers in trance, they give great importance to sweat and fervently rub each other.

Diligent massage is another supplementary practice. The healer rubs the person's feet and legs, back, arms, and abdomen. This rubs the sickness into one place and makes it easier to extract. The smoke from the healer's tortoise shell contributes its n/um and helps to dislodge the sickness. The healers drop glowing coals into the mixture, waft the smoke carefully all over the person they are curing, and have him breathe it in. The smoke, the sweat, the massage are all supplementary elements to the power inherent in the healers' n/um.

Another element in !Kung healing is trance *(!kia)*. At the Healing Dances trance is a convention of the healers. It is common, expected behavior and is induced routinely. At special curings the healers may or may not go into trance. Trance is not essential to healings; it is not a power in itself and does not increase the healer's power. It is believed to occur because the healer's n/um is so strong that it overcomes him. Trance is the result. The strength of the n/um is thus manifest.

Trance is a spectacular feature of the Healing Dances. All the men who are active healers go into trance at the dances, and in that state, when their healing power is believed to be very strong, they heal all the people.

It is not the role of women to trance; it is not expected of them. However, on three occasions we saw women in trance. It seemed that the power of suggestion had overcome them, and they had inadvertently slipped into very light trance. One attempted to dance with the men but was led aside by other women. One just sat with a vacant look and cried "waaaaaa" a few times. The other was Old //Khuga, who softly imitated the n//hara sounds at the large dance at /Gam.

The men induce trance with apparent ease, without the use of material substances such as mushrooms, alcohol, or *Cannabis sativa,* none of which they had.[9] The idea of trance is implanted in earliest childhood. Boys watch and listen to the healers' performances from infancy. As children, they imitate trance when they play Healing Dance, which they often do. When they become young healers, it must be an easy step to imitate the older ones in the familiar actions. The actions and sounds of the rite act, I believe, as powerful suggestions. Also, the loud singing that assails the ears for hours at the dances, the exertion of dancing, the repetitiousness of the rhythms, the expectation that they will trance, the physical nearness to others, and the synchronization of movement with others—all, I believe, help to fortify the power of autosuggestion that induces trance.

Furthermore, although they say it is a frightening experience, the men want to go into trance and are predisposed to do so. Their society values trance as a benefit to all the people. Trance shows that the healing n/um is strong and that the healing power is at its highest. In trance the men make a great display of courage. They rush out to encounter //Gauwa and the //gauwasi and defy them in a frenzied way. In their normal state their behavior toward the sky beings is caution tinged with fear. The more violent the frenzied behavior or the deeper the withdrawal from normal consciousness, the stronger the n/um is believed to be, and the more the trance is valued. Men whose trances are notable are esteemed.

Deep trance rarely occurs apart from a Healing Dance. At special curings the healers go into light trance if they trance at all. However, John Marshall witnessed one special curing at which the behavior of the healers was as frenzied as he had ever seen and at which the healers apparently went deep into unconsciousness at the end. The trances occurred at a time of great tension, which involved the curing of a very sick baby. Two healers, who were believed to have strong n/um, had failed to come to perform a curing rite for the baby when they were asked to do so. (We never learned why they did not come. Ordinarily, healers respond to any request to cure.) Other men cured, but later in the day the baby appeared to die. The parents blamed the two men for having failed to come. Relatives and friends of the parents and those of the two healers began to quarrel among themselves about the curing. People were overwrought, and the arguments set aflame dormant grievances over food and past gifts. A fight ensued. Women rushed to hide the men's weapons in the bushes. One woman kicked another. One man struck another. People shouted in blazing hostility. Suddenly the baby moved and whimpered. The parents snatched it up. Instantly the women began to sing a medicine song in full voice (without a tentative beginning; see chapter 3). Men from both groups began to cure the baby. In minutes two men from the parents' group and one from the other group went abruptly into deep trance and soon fell unconscious. The baby lived.

It appears that trances do occasionally occur in situations that involve no healing matters at all. I observed no instance of this, but the following episode was recounted to me. A little group of two families was making a long journey. They were encamped in the night alone in a vast, flat space. A lion came and prowled around them. The moonlight was bright, and the people could clearly see the lion circling. They were terrified. They took their screaming children into their arms and stood, shifting around to keep the fire between them and the lion, ready to throw burning brands at it. One of the men, Bo, cried out to the lion, "You lazy beast! Why do you not go and kill an animal instead of coming after us? We are not equals." The lion growled and did not go away. Toward morning, one supposes in the long-continued emotional stress, Bo fell into trance. At sunrise the lion left, and the people said that Bo's spirit followed it and chased it far away, and they never saw it again. When Bo's spirit returned to his body and he came out of trance, his nose bled severely.

I believe that trance has been of great value to this society. It is a heightening experience for the men who go into trance and for the people who watch them, especially at the Healing Dances. Although people are well accustomed to the trance behavior and receive the healing with equanimity, there is always an excitement in it that elevates the experience beyond the daily routine.

THE RITUAL HEALING DANCE

The Ritual Healing Dance is called *n/um tshxai,* "n/um dance." When people gather together to dance they say they "dance a song," *tshxani tshxi.*

In comparison with the other ritual dances that the !Kung hold, namely the Eland Dance and the Men's Dance, the Ritual Healing Dance is a frequent occurrence. The Eland Dance is held only on the occasion of a girl's first menstruation; the Men's Dance is part of Tshoma, the initiation rite for boys. In a band of thirty or forty people—the size of the Gautscha bands—the number of girls and boys is not great, so several years may intervene between performances of the Menarcheal Rite or Tshoma. In contrast, the Ritual Healing Dances are frequently held. Also in contrast to the Eland Dance at which most of the men are excluded, and to the Men's Dance, which totally excludes women, the Healing Dance excludes no one. Every man, woman, and child attends.

A Healing Dance is the one activity in !Kung life that draws people together in groups that are of considerable size and are not shaped by family, band, close friendship, or ritual exclusions. Nothing but a Healing Dance assembles all the people present into a wholly concerted activity. During the dance no words divide them. In close configuration they clap, sing, and stamp the dancing steps with such coordination and rhythmic precision that they are like one organic being.

As the dance proceeds, the healers go into spectacular trances and perform the Healing Rite for everyone—including the infants in their mothers' arms, and including the anthropologists. As their trances deepen, the healers with great show of courage confront the //gauwasi, the death-bringers, who lurk in the shadows beyond the firelight, and try to drive them away with shrieks and hurled sticks.

Although the protection of the people's lives is a serious matter, the dance is not pious or solemn. The !Kung take great pleasure in the music and dancing and enjoy the sociability of the occasions. They talk and joke, sometimes insulting each other outrageously in their customary joking relationship behavior, evoking much laughter. In all, the dance gives a lift to the quiet sameness of their days.

Dance Groups and Occasions

During thirteen months in 1952 and 1953, from July to July, thirty-nine Ritual Healing Dances took place where we were present. We attended more dances on later expeditions. In the 1952–1953 year we stayed in three places: at /Gam during July and August; at Gautscha from September through December; at Tsho/ana from January through most of April; and at Gautscha again until the end of July. At /Gam eight dances were held in July and seven in August. At Gautscha three were held in September, three in October, five in November, and none in December. At Tsho/ana four were held in January, four in February, and one in March. Back at Gautscha, one dance was held in April, two in May, one in June, and none in July.

The number of people participating in a dance varies with the size of the groups assembled. One intense and ardent little dance was held by ten people; the ten included my husband and myself. The other dances were large, probably unusually so. At /Gam five bands were encamped within half a mile or so of each other and with a radius of about half a mile to the water hole. It was a time of drought. These bands all had rights, according to their territorial concepts, to drink at the /Gam water hole, which was the one permanent water hole in their area.

A scarcity of food did not limit the desire to dance. The people were poised in delicate balance between water and food. They would go on trips to gather plant foods, carrying as much water as they could in their ostrich-eggshell containers, stay to eat as long as the water permitted, and return to the water hole with whatever food they could manage to acquire and carry. The drought limited hunting also. (Hunting was not good near /Gam.) Food was scarce, but this did not quench the desire to dance. When a dance was started by one band, people from other bands would come to join in, walking in the darkness half a mile or more through the low grass and brush that surrounds /Gam, although they were afraid, and rightly so, of encountering lions or stepping on snakes while walking at night. Sometimes they carried burning sticks to light their way. There is no compulsion for people in neighboring bands to join in each others' dances; those who came, and there were many of them, did so because they wanted to. As many as eighty or ninety people would converge to dance all night long. Twenty or thirty women would be singing at a time, and as many men would be dancing. Ten or twelve of the men would be active healers who would be falling into trance and healing the people.

Our presence had no influence that we were aware of on the dances at /Gam. The !Kung bands were assembled there because they were tethered to the water, not because of us. We camped at a distance and were still strangers to most. When we settled in Gautscha, however, our presence brought many people who would not normally be there. In their curiosity to see us and their desire for our gifts of tobacco, people came from all over the Nyae Nyae region to visit. At any given time seventy or eighty people would be encamped in their several groups around us—plenty of people to dance—and the dance groups, which took in everybody present, were about as big as those at /Gam.

Large groups assembled because of our presence, but I really believe that we did not affect the dance in any other way. We were accepted. We merged with the people; no particular attention was paid us during the dance. The dance took its course, and we were healed along with the rest.

No rule determined when dances were to be held. The decision to dance on any particular night was spontaneous, and the factors that determined or influenced it appeared to be varied.

Sickness is not frequently a reason for holding a Healing Dance. If someone were ill, it would be more likely that a special curing would be performed for him. Only three times that year, to our knowledge, was a dance called for actual illness.

On six occasions at Gautscha, dances followed triumphal hunts. The animals brought in were huge, a giraffe and five elands. Several times during this period, hunting parties had failed completely or brought only small creatures. The sight of so much meat from a triumphal hunt is occasion for rejoicing. A buzz of excitement enlivens the whole encampment, and a Ritual Healing Dance is likely to occur.

A Ritual Healing Dance is not only a response to the satisfaction of having meat; it may be an important factor in dissipating group tension. It is the responsibility of the person whose arrow killed the animal to distribute the meat, satisfying expectations as best he can and at the same time fulfilling his kinship and affinal obligations. He must also bear in mind what gifts he has recently given and received. The hope of every individual is to receive as generous a portion as the system allows, but in many instances opinions differ as to the sharer's responsibilities. Hopes are disappointed, and tensions rise. A dance held at this time can function both to express the people's satisfaction at having meat and to relieve the tensions generated by the meat's distribution. (See Marshall 1976:287–312.)

It appears, however, that a dance does not always follow a successful hunt. Three times large antelope were brought in, twice a gemsbok, and once a kudu, and no dance followed. One dance followed failure in the hunt. Two parties had been away hunting for five days. They returned with nothing. Tired though the men were, a dance was held, as ardent a dance as any we observed, lasting through the night as well as into the following morning. Fear of hunger pervades the lives of the !Kung, whether food is critically scarce or not, and failure in the hunt brings this fear to the fore in their consciousness. It seems very likely that the dance was held in response to this anxiety.

Dances followed arrivals of visiting groups. People who perhaps had never danced together or who had not danced together for a long time would want to do so, we were told, and a dance would be arranged. Two dances preceded departures of visiting groups. One was held with a group that was congenial to the Gautscha band, and the people said that the dance was held so that the departing group would be safe on its journey. The other dance was held with a visiting group whom the Gautscha people had treated with considerable reserve. At the dance, however, the reserve appeared to vanish, and the people mingled without constraint.

!Kung might dance in response to any great emotional stress, I believe. One such dance, one of the most fervent we ever attended, took place in 1955, the night after /Qui Hunter's foot fell off. This was the /Qui who had been bitten by a puff adder. A tourniquet of strips of bark and assiduous sucking of the wound had saved his life, but gangrene had set in and his foot had fallen off. He was, by everyone's account, the best hunter in the area. The people were stricken, and the ardor of the dance appeared to express their emotional response to what was a terrible misfortune, both for /Qui and for the community.[1]

A longing for fun and excitement may induce a dance, and I believe that three of the dances we attended had such origin. Young people in high spirits started them. Twice they petered out after a time—the adults were not in the mood to dance all night—but one developed into an ardent Healing Dance. That night young /Qui of Band 2 had really wanted to dance, and, when he failed to get the women started by asking them to sing, he rounded up the little girls, sat them in a circle, took their hands in his, and set them to clapping. He then sat with them, singing in high falsetto, imitating the women's gestures and glances. In no time the boys were dancing around the group, staggering with laughter, dancing their thundering approach steps toward /Qui as they would toward the circle of women at the beginning of a serious dance. The women came gaily capering into the circle, and the men hurried to tie on their rattles. From this frolicsome beginning, a serious Healing Dance developed.

My impression was that the full moon put people into the mood to dance, but the nights of dancing were not exclusively moonlit; they were of all kinds. I speak of nights of dancing. Most Healing Dances were held at night, but no ritual requirement precludes their being held in the daytime. We attended four daytime dances, which I shall mention later. My memories and my descriptions, however, are mostly of dances held at night.

The Dance Circle

For a dance, an open place is chosen where the ground is free from brush, usually a few yards from the shelters and family fires of the encampment. All the people who are encamped together assemble—men, women, and children. When so much n/um will be concentrated and when the //gauwasi will be lurking in the shadows, no one stays apart from the group. A fire is lighted around which the dance takes place. Families build a few little fires near the dance fire. Old people and children sit around them, and the dancing men rest from time to time beside them.

It is the role of women to sit in a circle around the dance fire to sing the n/um songs and clap a rhythmic accompaniment throughout the dance. At a big dance twenty to thirty women would be seated singing at any given time. Although there is plenty of space around them, the women squeeze together, shoulders and knees touching. When the men begin to dance, they form a single line and dance around the circle of women, close behind them. Their stamping feet scuff up the sandy soil, and soon a groove appears, which deepens with the hours. During the time that a band lives in that encampment, subsequent dances are held in the same place and the groove of the dance circle becomes four or five inches deep. The groove in the sand is called *n≠ebe*. The n≠ebe formed at the big dances, when eighty or ninety people might have assembled, could be as large as fifteen feet in diameter. Smaller groups form smaller circles. Some of the larger circles spread out to ovals.

The motif throughout is the circle: the women's circle, the circle that the dancing men imprint in the sand, the circle of firelight, and the circles of people sitting around the little fires. One is strongly aware also, in that flat, desert land, of the circle of the horizon and, as one sits through the night, of the circling stars. Humans, earth, and stars, an intersection of circles.

The Dance Fire

In some !Kung rites the fire must be lighted ritualistically by an old man with fire sticks, but not the fire of the Healing Dance. Anyone may light it by any means; any wood may be used. Ordinarily one or two women bring burning brands and wood from their family fires to start the dance fire. Anyone may add wood during the night. The fires, like all !Kung fires, are kept fairly small. The !Kung like to draw near their fires without being scorched or driven back by the smoke.

One has only to imagine a dance taking place in darkness to realize how greatly the firelight contributes to the occasion. On dark nights it creates the embracing circle, the space into which the people gather, and the light plays on the dancing figures and lights their way. On moonlit nights its warm glow contrasts with the cold, silvery diffuseness of the moonlight and, as on dark nights, gives focus to the place of dancing.

The fire makes several contributions in addition to giving light. Its heat activates the n/um in the healers, and it is welcome to the women who sit around it through the cold desert nights.

Although a fire is a usual feature at a dance, and although it makes its contribution, a dance fire is not a ritualistic necessity. Healing Dances are sometimes held at which no fire is built. We attended five dances that were without a fire. One, an extraordinarily intense dance of a small group, was held at night; the others were held in daytime. At these dances the men did not have the heat of the fire to warm their n/um, but we assume that they considered the exertion of dancing to have sufficient heating effect. We observed no less fervor in their healing and their trance behavior than we observed when they danced around a fire.

When lurching and staggering about in trance, the healers deliberately throw burning brands around, walk in the fire, and set fire to their hair, and often fall into the fire. Other healers and women who are sitting near are alert to pull the men away and steady them before they burn themselves severely.

We heard claims that the fire does not burn a healer when he is in trance. People told us about a very great healer named Old /Gao who lived south of /Gam at N//o!gau. He had died two years before we arrived. It was said that he could sit in the fire like a pot with the flames leaping up around him higher than his head and not be burned. (It was usual for accounts of such miraculous occurrences to be set at a distance in time or space, or both, among other Bushmen or among people of different races, not among themselves. After all, they do not observe such happenings among themselves.)

Several healers, although not making such fabulous claims, did say that the fire did not burn them when they were in trance, but they were vague about this claim and did not insist much on the point. Among all their beliefs about the supernatural, none is subject to more immediate and irrefutable contradiction by the facts. Although they may not feel them while in trance, the healers get burns all the time, sometimes very bad ones. The contradiction apparently caused them no concern. Without embarrassment they came to us to have us treat their burns with our ointments. One healer after getting an especially bad burn on his knee at a dance went away hunting for several days. He returned with a nasty sore for us to treat. His peers chided him for waiting so long before coming to us.

Garments, Paraphernalia, and Equipment

A !Kung woman has no dress-up garments to wear at dances. Each has only one kaross made from the skin of a large antelope, usually gemsbok, which she wears constantly. To carry an extra kaross in her nomadic way of life would burden her. For a dance, a woman might put on a fine headband, if she had one, or other hair ornaments, and she might wear her best beads, but not necessarily.

Most of the men are naked, as usual, except for their ordinary breechclouts. No special articles of clothing or ornament are required at dances, but some men do possess and wear skin aprons, which are tied around their waists and hang down behind about to their knees. Some carry the tails of animals in their hands (we observed giraffe, eland, and wildebeest tails). The aprons and tails appear only at the dances. If long ago there was some symbolic significance attached to these articles, the !Kung no longer know what it is; they say they are only for adornment. Many men carry their digging sticks or carrying sticks while they dance. One man who had a skin cap always wore it when dancing. Anyone who might happen to have some ostrich feathers would stick them into his hair. The cap and feathers are worn for ordinary dressing up and not exclusively for the dance.

Most of the men possess and wear dance rattles, called */khonisi,* wound around their legs when they dance. The rattles are a musical instrument and will be described with the dance music.

Time and Periods

Although it is usual for the !Kung to hold their Healing Dances at night, dances are also held in the daytime. We attended four. On two occasions we requested that the people dance in daylight so that we could film them. The men went genuinely into trance as usual. (I have not included these two dances in this count of the thirty-nine we attended in 1952 and 1953.) Twice while we were present, people danced by day for their own reasons. Once in Tsho/ana they wanted the healing of an especially revered healer who was visiting only for that day. They held an ardent dance with impressive trances, which even intermittent torrents of rain did not quench. Another time when they were going to dance the Men's Dance at night, they held a Healing Dance in the afternoon. These daytime dances did not have fires.

Dances usually began after people had eaten their evening meal, about nine o'clock or so, sometimes later. A dance occasionally stopped around two or three in the morning, but more often people danced the whole night through. Richard Lee, in a valuable paper on the Bushman dance and trance states, describes a dance held by a group of !Kung at Dobe (in Botswana), which continued all night and on through the next day and into the following night (Lee 1968b:41). Individuals drop out to rest from time to time, men more than women. The whole group of women rest to some extent by singing and clapping with reduced vigor during some periods of the dance. And throughout the night's dancing, there are breaks between the dance periods. Most of the dances we attended went on until eight or nine o'clock in the morning. The Gautscha people said that if they stopped the dance and slept for a few hours they felt tired and dispirited the next day, but if they danced all night and went right on about their daily affairs, they felt fine. Some of the men said they liked to start out to hunt straight away after a dance while their n/um was still hot.

The night's dancing is broken up into periods of ten or fifteen minutes of dancing with short pauses between in which people walk around and chat. To distinguish between the dance as a whole and the ten-minute (or longer) periods of dancing, I shall call the former a dance and the latter a dance period.

No one is a designated leader in starting a new dance period. Any man or woman sings out a line of one of the n/um songs, and if two or three more join in singing it, it becomes the choice for the next dance period. The women soon sing in full chorus. The men gradually begin to dance again one by one, and in a few moments the dancing line is moving, the sound becomes firm and full, the tempo picks up, and a dance period is under way.

In contrast to this gradual start, the end of a dance period has more definition. One or another of the dancing men turns toward the singing women and, holding his arms out over them, stamps a few steps in place. He may call out a signal. I could never observe exactly what happened. Other men follow his lead, turning in their line and stamping. The women clap a formalized cadence, and the singing, clapping, and dancing stop.

During the night the intensity of the dance rises and falls in waves. At a long dance it may crest three or four times: the tempo quickens, the dancing is strong, the singing is loud and sharp. The healers fall into varying degrees of trance and heal ardently. After a time, from fatigue and the natural inability to hold to an emotional peak and pour out energy for long periods, the people ease off. In the easing-off periods, the dancing and music-making become somewhat lackluster. Always at dawn comes a high moment, and sunrise is often the highest point of all. As the sun rises, the people sing the Sun Song. They feel that the n/um is very strong then. If people dance on a few hours more they hold the intensity high. They like to end a dance in a mood of exhilaration.

THE MEN'S DANCING

The Men's Dancing Line

The single line of dancing men moves slowly, in stately fashion, around the circle of seated women. No one line is rigidly maintained. A single individual or a small group may separate from the line; there will then be two or more segments of the line moving around the circle. When the men begin to go into trance and heal, the lines break up even more, but the form is not completely abandoned. Now and then individuals interrupt their healing for spurts of dancing, and at any given time a few men will be dancing in line. They dance close together, and when they are paying attention and dancing well, they coordinate their advancing steps so exactly that the moving legs remind one of millipedes.

Nicholas England took careful note of the direction in which the lines move and is able to state that when the men begin a dance period they consistently start off counterclockwise (England 1995: chap. 4). However, after dancing for a while, they change direction. The line may reverse itself several times within a single dance period with no observable correlation to any particular state of the dance or trance state. Usually, the changes seem to be at the whim of the man who happens to head the line at the moment, but it could be some other who would start the turn. With arms outstretched at shoulder height, the man slowly pivots around in place without interrupting the rhythm of his dancing steps, always turning inward toward the women, his arms passing over them; the other men do the same, and the line moves off in the other direction. The man who was at the end becomes the new leader.

At the beginning of the night's dancing the women are seated in their circle and the line of men dances close behind them, around and around. The men may continue to do so for varying lengths of time, perhaps two or three dance periods or more. At some time, however, one of the men turns and slowly dances into the circle of women, and the line follows passing close to the fire and out the other side of the circle. Sometimes the women between whom the line enters move over barely enough to let the men cut through; at other times the women's circle spreads somewhat more widely, making a bisected oval or two crescentlike forms. Thereafter, the circle remains open at the two points and the men continue to dance through it, but not necessarily every time they pass. They still may circle the whole group without cutting through. In this state it is usual for a figure-eight to develop, the men dancing around first one crescent of women, say counterclockwise, passing through the center and dancing around the other crescent clockwise. If the line has broken into segments by this time, the segments may dance simultaneously in opposite directions.

The Men's Dance Steps

The names of the songs are given to the periods of dancing during which they are sung, and one uses expressions such as, "That was a Rain Dance, the one before was a Giraffe Dance." This does not mean that different steps or a different configuration of the dance go with the different songs. The contrary is true. In a Healing Dance, the dancing is always the same whatever song is being sung. All !Kung men and boys dance in fundamentally the same way using the same basic step or a variation of it. It is this step that a !Kung will use when, spontaneously, on occasions quite unconnected with the Healing Dance, sudden exuberance leads him to dance alone for a moment or two.

One of the most notable characteristics of the dancing is that the movements are so small and controlled. There are never any wild flings or even large free movements of the body apart from outstretched arms on occasion. The dancing movements are designed, I think, for a twofold purpose: to give forward motion to the line of dancing men, which describes the circle around the women, and to reproduce sound—the percussion sounds of thudding feet and swishing rattles, which deepen and elaborate the n/um music.

The men generally move straight forward except when they turn to reverse the line's direction, but occasionally a man dances sideways holding his arms out over the women. Sometimes a dancer will remain stamping on one spot for a short time.

The men dance with knees slightly bent and their bodies held erect or leaning forward bent at the hips. Many of the men move their bodies so little that they are like statues being carried by the dancing legs, but some give variation to the posture by swinging their torsos a little from side to side, and some, when they are dancing very ardently, bend forward until their torsos are at right angles to their thighs. The arms have no fixed positions. They may hang at the men's sides, or be extended at shoulder level, or bend at the elbow. If a man is carrying a stick he sometimes uses it as a walking stick, balancing with it, sometimes holds it out in front of him, and sometimes swings it over the women's heads.

The basic step is a precise, loud stamp. A man lifts his foot two or three inches off the ground, or a little more, and stamps it down with vigor. The basic pattern appears to be a period of four steps; a man stamps with one foot, say his right, then with his left, again with his left, again with his right, with an accented beat on the first and third steps—*right*, left, *left*, right. The steps carry a man forward very little. In stamping the unaccented steps he may move forward no more than an inch or so, or not at all, but on the accented beat he steps forward three or four inches.

The men vary their steps in several ways. When they are tired they may just walk to the rhythm. One sees old men dance this way. Strong dancers may make two stamps to a beat, or very strong young dancers may float a light triplet of stamps onto a beat. A man may hop with both feet on beat one, move one foot forward with a stamp that scuffs up the sand on beat two, hop again on beat three, and scuff his other foot forward on beat four. He may put two stamps or three into the beat after the hop. Individuals keep to no one way of dancing consistently throughout a dance period. They change from moment to moment in response to mood and energy. The !Kung dancing is so expert that it looks easy, as ballet does, until one sees someone dancing who is not practiced in it, with a mischievous young !Kung following him and mimicking his slovenly, ill-timed steps.

The volume of sound made by the dancers varies, falling in slack periods, rising when the intensity rises. At the moments of highest intensity, all the men would be stamping loudly and some young, very vigorous dancers would be bent over in the right-angle position, lifting their feet higher off the ground than is usual and driving them down like pile drivers. Such strenuous dancing occurs only in bursts. Even the young men cannot sustain it long.

The tempo changes as the intensity rises and falls. When a dance period is just beginning, and also when people are tired, the dancing is somewhat lackadaisical. When the dancing is most intense, the tempo quickens.

One man speaking of the Giraffe Songs said, "We sing it for the tail, it begins at the tail, the way he waves it." Another said, "When he (a man) dances the Giraffe Dance he 'becomes giraffe.'" Another said the same of the Honey Dance—he "becomes honey." This suggests some subjective identification on the part of the dancers, which I failed to understand more deeply. It does not indicate that the dance steps and gestures are purposefully imitative. The !Kung can imitate the movements of animals in uncannily expressive gestures. They do so when dancing a form of the Eland Dance, and they often do so for fun, to our enchantment. /Ti!kay imitating a female ostrich, strutting and laying eggs, threw us into paroxysms of laughter. When hunting, the men gesture with their hands and heads to let others know what animals they see without having to make a sound. Although a dancer may occasionally move his head and shoulders, almost imperceptibly, in such a way as to suggest the movement of an animal's head, the dance steps are definitely not intentional pantomime. Their primary function is to produce sound and to move the line forward.

THE WOMEN'S DANCING

Although it is their role to sit and sing and clap, not to dance, custom does not prohibit women from dancing briefly with the men from time to time. If the mood seizes her, a woman will get up during any dance period, dance a few seconds or a few minutes, then return to her place among the singing women. Only a few women make these brief sallies, perhaps three or four women or fewer in an evening. There are two ways in which a woman may dance on these occasions. She may go a little aside from the dance circle and dance her capering step, as at the beginning of the dance before the women have begun to sing and clap. This step consists of two or three small, rapid stamps followed by a sideward fling of a foot, the arms bent at the elbow pumping back and forth. It is the step women regularly use when they dance for fun. Or the woman may enter the line of dancing men. If she does this, her dancing motions are very restrained. Her arms, bent or hanging at her sides, are still. She barely lifts her feet. To each two beats of the men's stamping, she makes two tiny quick shuffles with a minute pause, one-*two*-pause, one-*two*-pause. Her little steps carry her slowly along in the line of moving men, inch by inch as if she were floating.

The man behind her may hold his arms out on each side of her, but he does not touch her. Her eyes are cast down. Her kaross is drawn closely around her. Nevertheless, there is a hint of the erotic in her dignified restraint, or so I imagined. If so, the hint is as delicate as an Ingres drawing, and in extreme contrast to the remarkable shaking of breasts, shivering, and swinging of buttocks seen in the dancing of the women of the neighboring Bantu tribes. We never saw Bushman women (or men either) dance with overtly sexual gestures. Even in the Eland Dance of the Menarcheal Rite, although the women took off their karosses and hung beads from their waists down their bare behinds, their dancing gestures were not overtly sexual.

When a woman is dancing in her capering style outside the line, she may occasionally dance toward a healer with a gesture of praise, encouragement, and appreciation, and she may toss sa powder on him. Sa powder tossed or rubbed lightly on a healer enables him to see more clearly where the sickness is in the person he is healing. The sa cools the healer's n/um if it is "boiling" too strongly, and sa also keeps the healer from feeling excessively tired after a night of dancing.

THE N/UM SONGS

The !Kung believe that the great god, ≠Gao N!a, creates the n/um songs (*n/um ts'isi*) and endows them with n/um. ≠Gao N!a gives the songs to individual people whom he favors. He often sends //Gauwa with the songs. Those who receive the songs give them to others, and the songs pass from group to group.

"Receiving" a song from ≠Gao N!a is what we would call composing it. Everyone sang, and almost everyone played instruments among this music-loving people; but not everyone composed. However, there were a number of composers. Those who were well known for composing charming lyrical songs for the little pluriarc, the //gwashi (a wooden stringed, harplike instrument), or tunes for the hunting bow or the one-string violin were not the same people to whom the n/um songs were attributed. The composers of n/um songs were somehow especially imbued with n/um music as well as being especially gifted musically. The songs were composed by both men and women.

I knew personally three people who had been "given" n/um songs: Old N≠isa from Samangaigai, Gao Feet of Band 1, and Old Demi of Band 6. I was told in some detail about three others: Old /Gao of N//o!gau, the old healer in the fire; /Ti!kay and Be, his wife, from Samangaigai. England learned about three more composers of n/um songs: another /Ti!kay from Otjinini, another /Gao from some place south of Gautscha, and N!ani from Kubi. It seemed that usually people who had been "given" songs found them in their heads after sleep and dreaming or after trance. They may or may not have dreamed that //Gauwa was present.

England learned from Gao Feet that when Gao had received two Buffalo Songs he had been in trance. ≠Toma, Gao's best friend and hunting companion, had been badly gored by a buffalo; he had almost been killed. Everyone was in great distress. Gao prayed to ≠Gao N!a asking him for a song to help him heal ≠Toma. He went into trance, and when he came out two songs were in his head. He taught the songs to the women and proceeded to heal ≠Toma with them (England 1995: chap. 4).

When Old N≠isa from Samangaigai was visiting Gautscha, she told us about //Gauwa coming to her in her sleep. Very full of herself, smiling, pleased with our attention, she said that //Gauwa had come to her in the days when she was "young and fresh." He had appeared beside her while she was sleeping and had said, "You are crying for singing. Why do you not get up and sing?" She did get up, she said, and she sang with him imitating him and learning. He taught her in a kindly way and said, "Now, do not stay quiet as you used to do. Go and sing. Sing for the people as I have taught you." She was glad. When he left, she slept again. In all, he came to her five times in this way, in both the cold time and the hot time of the year. People said they thought she had received this exceptional attention from //Gauwa because she was so extremely good at singing, but when she was young she had been shy and //Gauwa had wanted to encourage her to sing more. Hoping for another image of //Gauwa, I asked N≠isa what //Gauwa looked like and elicited the following answer: "Like a man," she said, adding that he wore pants like a white man (as we had been told the great god did). "He walked away a little distance when he left," she said, "but then rose into the air."

We recorded the songs that were regularly sung at the Healing Dances when we were in the field, among them two Giraffe Songs that had been given to the Gautscha people by Old N≠isa. One must have been the song she learned from //Gauwa in her dreams. As to the other, the !Kung had told us that Old N≠isa had been given a Giraffe Song by Be and /Ti!kay of Samangaigai. I am assuming that it is one of the two we recorded. I had not clarified this information and do not know which is which.

According to the account we heard, when Be of Samangaigai received a Giraffe Song she did not see //Gauwa in a dream. She only awakened in the morning with the song in her head. She sang it to her husband, /Ti!kay, who recognized it as a powerful n/um song. Anyone with sense would know, the !Kung assured us. Be and /Ti!kay gave the song to others, among them Old N≠isa. It passed from person to person in the Nyae Nyae area and into Botswana.

Megan Biesele says that when she was in Botswana in the early 1970s, this song had virtually replaced the earlier Gemsbok Songs for which the Dobe people had been known (Biesele 1993:68). Biesele goes on to say that the several differing accounts she heard about the origin of Be's song illustrated that !Kung beliefs can change greatly as they pass among the people and that varying beliefs can be held simultaneously. Biesele was told not that Be had been asleep when she received the songs, but that she had seen real giraffes running before an approaching thunderstorm. The sound of their hooves and the sound of the rain mingled in her head, and the song came to her. In another version, Be's husband, /Ti!kay, was said to have received the song when he was hunting and heard the sound of giraffe running and the sound of rain (Biesele 1993:68). In yet another version that Biesele heard, the song had been given by the great god to a boy named /Twi, who gave it to his mother who was named Be (Biesele 1993:68).

Richard Lee had still another account of this Giraffe Song, which Biesele gives in her dissertation. In Lee's account, it was told that /Ti!kay had failed in the hunt for three days. On the third night while he slept, //Gauwa came to him and said, "The first day you shot an eland but it fled, the second day you shot a giraffe but it fled. The third day you saw nothing. I will give you three things. I will give you an eland song. I will give you a giraffe song. I will give you a sky and earth song. These things I give you." /Ti!kay, who in this version has two wives, turned to them and said, "Did you hear what //Gauwa said?" The wives said, "We didn't hear anything." Then /Ti!kay said, "I will teach you three songs" (Biesele 1993:68).

Of the old man who could sit in the fire like a pot and not be burned, Old /Gao of N//o!gau, we were told an account in keeping with the miraculous abilities that people attributed to him. He had received a Honey Song. It was daytime, and he was awake when //Gauwa appeared and bid him follow to a tree that had a beehive in it. //Gauwa pushed /Gao into the hole in the tree where the baby bees and the honey were. Bees and honey both have n/um. Thus //Gauwa gave him the n/um of the

Honey Song. //Gauwa then taught /Gao the music of the song. That song had been brought to Gautscha and was regularly sung at the Healing Dances.

A person who receives a song from the gods possesses it and gives it to the group he lives with, then that group possesses it and its n/um. However, just to hear a song and be able to sing it does not constitute possession of it. The song and its n/um must be deliberately given in some way. The Honey Song is an example. When Old /Qui visited Old /Gao at N//o!gau, he heard Old /Gao's Honey Song, learned it, and brought it to Gautscha when he visited his sister Xama. He taught it to her people in Bands 1 and 2. They liked the song very much and sang it at every dance, but they did not really possess it or its n/um, and they did not use it in the special curings. The Gautscha people sang Black Mamba also, but did not possess it or its n/um in the proper way. They did strongly possess the Giraffe Songs and their n/um and were known for them throughout the Nyae Nyae region.

Members of the Marshall expeditions recorded fourteen n/um songs.[2] The order in which they are listed below comes from Nicholas England, and I am indebted to him for several items of information that supplement the material I gathered (England 1995: chap. 4).

1. Giraffe Song Great, ≠*Kowa Ts'i N!a.* [Giraffe I.]
   Composer: unknown.
2. Giraffe Song, ≠*Kowa Ts'i.* [Giraffe II.]
   Composer: Old N≠isa.
3. Giraffe Song, ≠*Kowa Ts'i.* [Giraffe III.]
   Composer: Old N≠isa.
4. Quicken Song, *!Khari Ts'i* or Giraffe Song. ≠*Kowa Ts'i.* [Giraffe IV.]
   Composer: unknown.
5. Honey Song, *Zo Ts'i.*
   Composer: /Gao of N//o!gau.
6. Sun Song, */Kam Ts'i.*
   Composer: unknown.
7. Rain Song, *!Ga Ts'i.*
   Composer: /Ti!kay of Otjinini.

These seven songs were recorded in 1951 or 1952 and were still being sung when a Marshall expedition was last present in the field in 1961. England tells us that numbers 1, 4, 6, and 7 are musically old, and that they are sung by Bushmen of different language groups in different parts of the Kalahari. The !Kung told us that they consider songs 1, 4, 6, and 7 to be their strongest. Rain Song is very strong. Giraffe Song

Great could cure any sickness, they said. The n/um of Sun Song sung at the moment of sunrise reaches a peak of strength.

8. Eland Song Great, *N!i Ts'i N!a.*
   Composer: unknown.

The Rain Song and the Great Eland Song have the distinction of being the only two !Kung musical compositions to be composed in an unusual and probably very old scale, which England calls the Rain-Eland Scale, Scale 4 (England 1995: chap. 4). The Great Eland Song comes from the repertory of the Menarcheal Rite music. Like the Rain Song, it has been incorporated with the Healing Dance music because it is strong and beautiful, we were told. However, at the time we were in the field, it was not sung regularly at the dances as the aforementioned songs were. We heard it at dances only four times.

9. Black Mamba Song, *N≠igu Ts'i.*
   Composer: /Gao from somewhere south of Gautscha.
10. !Gara-little Is Fire, *!Garama ku da.*
   Composer: N!ani of Kubi.

Songs 9 and 10 came into the repertory of the Gautscha people in 1955, brought to them by visitors from Kai Kai. The title of number 10 is obscure. No one could explain it. "!Gara" is one of the seven names of the great god; *ma* means "small." England learned that the title comes from a line of text that the old people had sung to the song (England 1995: chap. 4).

11. Buffalo Song—The Bellowing, */Gau Ts'i—Kxai.*
   Composer: Gao Feet.
12. Buffalo Song—The Weeping, */Gau Ts'i—Tshi.*
   Composer: Gao Feet.

These two songs, the ones received by Gao Feet when ≠Toma was gored, came into the repertory in 1955. The titles obviously refer to the roaring of the buffalo and the laments of ≠Toma's relatives and friends.

13. Aardvark Song, */Kha Ts'i.*
   Composer: unknown.
14. Mourning for the Dead.
   Composer: unknown.

The last two songs were recorded in 1951. I heard Aardvark in 1952, but since then it has not been noted by expedition members. Mourning for the Dead was not noted after 1951. The title suggests that the song might be sung on the occasion of a death, but such a custom was not mentioned in any of my discussions with the !Kung about death and burial. We were told of two songs that the Gautscha people once had, which had been very powerful when the people then middle-aged were young adults. They were another Giraffe Song and a Gemsbok Song (*!Goe Ts'i*). People said that the n/um of the songs had weakened and that they no longer used them. Possibly Aardvark and Mourning for the Dead had also lost their n/um.

The list of fourteen songs does not purport to be a complete list of n/um songs. The !Kung spoke of other songs sung by other groups.

The n/um songs have titles, but few if any words. The !Kung are not given to developing their thoughts into verses and setting them to music. A singer may drop in a word or two that has bearing on the title, or an extraneous word or two about something that apparently happens to come to his mind, often about hunger or hunting, but, for the most part, the singing is in syllables without meaning. The syllables are mostly vowel sounds. One man gave me an example of the way he sang a Giraffe Song. The sounds are not fixed; he might sing them differently another time.

a yéa, yéa, á hoo hoo
a yéa, yéa, hoo hoo, a a
a hóo, hoo á, hí hí
yea á hóo hóo, ≠koa da.

The last utterance in this case happens to be the word *da,* "fire."

I was unable to elicit much clarification about the relationship between the name of a n/um song and the thing or animal of the same name. All the !Kung had to say was that the things or animals and the songs are all strong. This appeared to them so evident and so sufficient an explanation that they could think of nothing more to tell me. However, while all of the songs have n/um, only some of the animals or things do: giraffe, aardvark, sun, rain, and honey have n/um; black mamba and buffalo do not.

THE MUSIC

The !Kung are a music-loving people. Music is their art, their pleasure, and a vehicle for symbolic expression. Much if not most of the time in a !Kung encampment, someone is making music.

The !Kung have several repertories of music: traditional singing games, tunes played on the hunting bow and bows adapted for music-making, and a large repertory of songs of the //gwashi. The //gwashi is a little pluriarc of four or five strings. The songs it accompanies are currently composed by any one of a number of people who has the talent for composing, and there are, therefore, many //gwashi songs. These delightful songs commemorate events and reflect moods.[3]

The most important repertory of !Kung music is the music of the n/um songs. The belief that the songs are given by the great god to their composers, that the songs are charged with powerful n/um, and that they are an essential element in the Ritual Healing Dance does not set them apart as exclusively sacred music. On the contrary, they are very much a part of daily life and are sung anywhere, anytime, by anyone, more than any other music. They beguile leisure hours, enliven tasks and miles of walking, and soothe and delight babies.

The manner of presenting the n/um songs differentiates their two aspects. As daily-life music, the songs are sung by an individual or perhaps by two people together. They are sung simply and relatively softly. At the Healing Dances they are elaborated and given greater magnitude by being sung very loudly in full chorus, with men's and women's voices weaving together, accompanied by an intricate pattern of percussion sounds made by the men's stamping feet and the women's clapping hands, to produce what England calls "a web of polyphony" (England 1995: chap. 4).

Except for the dance rattles, which add a tonal swish to the music, the n/um songs are not accompanied by instruments: the human bodies make the music—the voices, the clapping hands, the stamping feet. The brilliant, shimmering music that the !Kung achieve with their voices, feet, and hands is truly remarkable. It is achieved by structuring the music in contrapuntal form. Two or more rhythmic lines of the women's clapping ripple over the men's stamping patterns. The women in contrapuntal manner sing several lines of melody together with the basic melody of the song. The singing lines are beautifully coordinated with the lines of the clapping and stamping. England says that the music has a heady, floating quality that often seems to "defy . . . Euro-American musical gravity" (England 1995: chap. 4).

The Scales and the Rain Song

Except for dance rattles, the instruments that the !Kung possessed until late in the decade of our fieldwork were strings: musical bows, the //gwashi, and a squeaky one-string violinlike instrument. !Kung musical concepts are based on the sounds of strings.

Apparently the instruments basic to mankind's music, the horn and the drum, have not appealed to the !Kung as they do not produce what the !Kung consider to be musical sound. They do not use horns to make purposeful sounds of any kind, musical or other, nor did they use drums, so common in other African cultures. The Nyae

Nyae !Kung had known about drums at least since Bantu peoples had migrated into their part of the world. Since around 1880 the Nyae Nyae !Kung have had contact with the Tswana, who then began making hunting trips and bringing their cattle for summer grazing to western Botswana (Lee 1979:77). However, the Nyae Nyae !Kung did not adopt drums, to my knowledge, until 1961 when two boys acquired two smallish drums in trade and soon learned to beat them very well. Another ubiquitous African instrument, the thumb piano, had not been adopted by the Nyae Nyae !Kung until 1961.

!Kung music is structured on strings, particularly on the hunting bow played as a mouth bow. A man places one end of the bow in his mouth and plucks the string with his fingers or taps it with a small stick. By changing the size of his mouth cavity, he can produce the tones of the bow tunes. This must be a very ancient way of making music. In other methods of bow playing, a gourd is used as resonator, or, after our arrival, one of our large tin cans. The string is tapped, and the tone is modified by stopping the string.

Men and boys play tunes on their hunting bows a great deal. They play while they are walking—traveling or tracking, and they play while they are at leisure in the encampment. Many of their tunes are composed spontaneously; some are remembered from the past. England says of bow playing, "Casual as it is, then, and inconsequential as its little tunes may seem, the mouth-bow . . . playing cannot be underestimated as a more or less constant influence on the tonal concepts of the Bushmen." And he says further, "For the ju (the !Kung), at least, and most other Bushmen as well, the two fundamentals used in bow playing and their lowest, strongest overtones (partials 2-4) seem to appear constantly in the music as a formative and regulative set of tones for the scale system" (England 1995: chap. 1).

The !Kung have four scales, two of five notes, two of four notes. The scales differ in various ways from the European Equal Tempered Scale or the Natural Scale. The n/um songs are composed in all of the four scales: five songs in Scale 1, four in Scale 2, three in Scale 3, but only two in Scale 4, namely the Rain Song and the Great Eland Song.

Scale 4, the Rain-Eland Scale, is of particular interest. England describes it as a tetratonic scale that is "a most unstable (and most un-European) tri-partitioning of a fifth that itself varies in size, but is usually around 711 Cents—that is, somewhat larger than the natural (702 C.) or tempered (700 C.) fifths" (England 1995: chap. 4).

England believes that the Rain-Eland Scale is very old, perhaps the oldest of Bushman tonal material. It is found in the Great Eland Song in several Bushman language groups; Auen, Nharo, Tsau, and !Ko (England 1995: chap. 6). The scale, however, is not pan-Bushman. England did not find it among the /Gwi or among the northern groups we visited, which included the !Kung of Angola, the Kwengo at Popa Falls, and the Tsexa near the M'Babe Depression in northern Botswana.

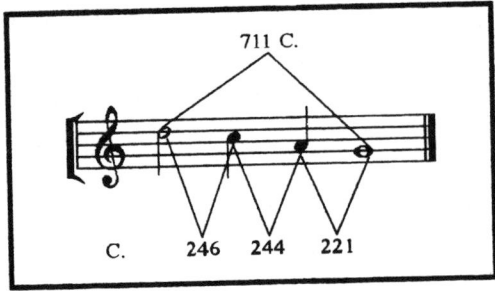

The Rain-Eland Scale

Although England thinks that the Rain Song may be a vestige of an ancient rain-making ceremony (England 1995: chap. 6), it is not now used by the !Kung to induce rain, nor is it a part of their meager rain-controlling procedures. The Rain Song is, however, linked by the Rain-Eland Scale to the Great Eland Song and is a part of a rich symbolism widely held among Bushmen groups, evoking the concept of fertility, plenty, and well-being. Rain evokes the concepts of growth of vegetation, food, water, fertility, and plenty. Eland evokes the concepts of meat, fat, strength, plenty, and, as Patricia Vinnicombe points out (Vinnicombe 1976:163), unaggressive behavior—all life-giving things. Vinnicombe in *People of the Eland* (1976) and David Lewis-Williams in *Believing and Seeing* (1981b)—two superb works on the rock art of the Bushmen in the Drakensberg—trace the eland theme at length in the myths and in the paintings of the southern Bushmen. The symbolic link of the eland with rain is most explicitly expressed in an unpublished myth collected by Bleek and Lloyd, quoted by Lewis-Williams. It begins:

> A very long time ago a man hunted !Khwa, the Rain, as he was grazing, champing the grass quietly. At that time the Rain was like an eland. . . . (Lewis-Williams 1981b:106)

The Percussion Sounds

The stamping steps of the men have been described earlier. The steps are well coordinated and sound in clear basic stamps—*one*, two, *three*, four. When some of the young men stamp their double beat or a triplet of beats onto the basic beat, they fit the embellishments into the pattern and the basic two-four rhythm is clear. The sound is a heavy *thud*; the quicker beats are an overlay of lighter thuds.

Over the thud is the swishing sound of the rattles (/khonisi). The rattles are made of the dried cocoons of either of two moth larvae. One is *Lasciocampid trabala*, the other is unidentified. The two kinds of cocoons are much alike, grayish in color, about 1 3/4 inches long and 3/4 inch wide. The unidentified one is smoother than the other. The cocoons are moistened in wet sand. While they are moist, the larvae are gouged out. Little stones or fragments of broken ostrich eggshell are inserted, and the openings are pressed closed. When the cocoons are dry and hard, two little holes are bored at each end on the underside, and the cocoons are strung on two strands of strong cord made of sansevieria fiber. A long rattle has eighty or ninety cocoons and is fifty or sixty inches long. The dancer winds a pair of these rattles around his legs beginning at the ankle, tying them under the knee. They make a loud swish, which adds considerable volume and texture to the percussive sound of the dancing feet.

The Women's Clapping

Coordinating their clapping with the men's stamping feet, the women contribute a complexity of rhythm, and they also contribute brilliance to the musical sound.

The women clap in such a way that they produce a sharp, high-pitched popping sound, a sharper sound than Europeans make in their way of clapping. !Kung women hold their hands with their fingers straight up, matching finger to finger, thumb to thumb. They spread their fingers apart a little and often bend them slightly back. This brings the rims of the palms together making a small air chamber, smaller than that made in European clapping. This small chamber produces the sharp, high-pitched pop. When the intensity of the dance is high and the women are clapping ardently, they bang their hands together with such force that the sound cracks out. At other times when the intensity is lower, the clapping is less loud, but it is always sharp and rhythmically precise.

The women clap different rhythmic lines. The basic line is called *!gaba;* the others (there may be more than one) are called ≠*ku.* Most of the women at any dance session clap the !gaba line. It provides the basic time unit of the song and the stamping feet.

Interposed with the !gaba line are the ≠ku lines. Only a few women clap them—women who, I believe, are especially skilled in fitting rhythmic patterns together. The ≠ku lines have no standard pattern. With a subtle understanding of the overall structure, women invent them and develop them according to their pleasure, interposing their claps between the claps of the !gaba line.

The women have musical skill and great precision. They watch each other, listen to each other, and feel each other. I mean this quite literally. Sitting so close together, shoulder to shoulder, knee to knee, the women actually feel the rhythm clapped by the others. Some women who clap well deliberately sit next to each other for the enjoyment of weaving their rhythmic composition that England calls a filigree (England 1995: chap. 4). He says, "Their clapping contributes, perhaps more than any other element, to the brilliance of the musical sound" (England 1995: chap. 3).

The Singing

The chorus of women's voices singing the n/um songs is the principal element in the music of the Healing Dances. Men sing with the women while they are in the dancing line or while healing, but singing is not their principal duty and they may sing or not as they wish.

The women sing in high register, and they sing loudly. Many of their voices are piercing. Only some old women whose voices have decreased in range produce a drone-like sound under the higher voices. The men sing less loudly, but they make a very welcome contribution to the music. Many had truly beautiful ringing tenor voices that enriched and deepened the tonal range of the songs.

Two characteristics of Bushman singing are the falsetto and the yodel. The falsetto is used by both men and women. Men softly singing their songs of the //gwashi regularly use falsetto. Women also use it in singing lullabies and //gwashi songs. The most extraordinary characteristic of Bushman singing, however, is the yodel. Both men and women yodel, but women much more than men. Yodeling is the women's specialty. The technique is used consistently when the women are singing loudly at the Healing Dances and in the singing of the menarcheal music—not in the everyday singing of n/um songs or //gwashi songs, when the singing is much softer.

England tells us that Erich M. von Hornbostel in "Die Entstehung des Jodelns" (1924:203–10) considers the overtone of instruments to be the source of the yodel. Alpine yodelers hear the overtones of alphorns, Solomon Island yodelers those of panpipes. Bushmen have no horns, but as England has pointed out, their bows readily produce overtones. So if the overtones in the bow playing have suggested the yodel, the Bushmen have had ample opportunity to receive and respond to such suggestions. Yodeling is not common in Africa. Binga Pygmies yodel, but few other African peoples do (England 1995: chap. 3).

A n/um song has a basic melody, which may be quite simple. When the women sing a song at the Healing Dances, it becomes a complex polyphony. At the beginning, the women sing the basic melody for several minutes. Then those who enjoy embellishing the melody will begin to do so. They invent their own variants; they are accomplished. In England's description, the women insert and elide tones, they shorten and prolong rhythm intervals, they enter a melodic phrase earlier or later than others, and they play their lines off against each other, complementing here, opposing there (England 1995: chap. 4). Sung in clarion tones, accompanied by the clapping hands and stamping feet in their intricate rhythm patterns, a n/um song becomes, as England says, a "soaring complex of sound; it shimmers in the night" (England 1995: chap. 4).

THE DANCE AND THE HEALERS

The first sign of a dance beginning is a woman carrying a burning brand from her fire to the dance circle. Other women bring a few sticks from their night's supply, and a dance fire is started. These women sit down, other women join them, and the singing circle is formed. Gradually everyone assembles.

The adolescents are often the quickest to assemble. All the children are likely to participate in the beginning stage. The babies tied in little leather slings to their mothers' sides or backs under their karosses stare out gravely upon the scene. Some of the little children join in the dancing by holding on to their mothers and bobbing rhythmically up and down. A father, when he begins to dance, may pick up his child and dance for a while with him astride his shoulders. The five- to eight-year-olds hop around and push each other about, but often little boys of that age dance around the circle more or less sedately, imitating their fathers, as do the older boys. Later in the night, when the children are ready to sleep, they lie in their mothers' laps or are wrapped two or three together in bundles in karosses and put down to sleep near people who are sitting aside at their little fires, who can watch them and see that they are not stepped on.

Often at the beginning before they sit down, two or three of the women dance a few rapid capers, the babies jerking contentedly on their mothers' backs, never uttering a cry. The women stop in a moment or two and sit down with the others. The women clap and sing at first in snatches, but they soon settle down to the business of making music. Young men who are strong and lively dancers make an exciting approach. Frequently in pairs, they dance with exceptionally loud, fast, stamping steps across the clearing toward the women, their arms outstretched before them. The other men, perhaps laughing and joking together, tie on their rattles and begin to dance, forming the line of dancing men that will encircle the seated women. Gradually the singing and the dancing become vigorous and concerted, and the intensity begins to rise. It may build up for some time before it reaches a high point. By the time it does, the tone of the dance has become more serious, but it never becomes heavily solemn or pious.

The dance will have been in progress an hour or two before the healers, their n/um heated by the fire and awakened by music, begin to go into trance and to heal. One will show the signs of trance; soon another follows until several are reacting.

In this first stage of trance, the men usually look grave and preoccupied, and then they begin to stare fixedly and to be unsteady on their legs. In this condition they are able to walk without assistance, and although they stagger slightly, sway, and tilt, they move sedately, slowly, and purposefully, singing a n/um song along with the women. They appear to be somewhat withdrawn but aware of what they are doing.

A gradual entering into trance is usual, but a few men whose withdrawal is hardly perceptible and whose movements are still normal will suddenly topple over and appear to lose consciousness for a few moments. They quickly revive.

At this stage they begin to heal the people. One of the healers, perhaps singing in full voice, leans over a woman, places one hand on her back, one on her chest, flutters his hands for a few seconds, then throws back his head and cries out the n//hara sounds in full voice: "gu, gu, gu, gu, kai di di di di, kai di di di di, kai di di di di," he yelps, then gives the screams and shrieks of "waaaaaa, waaaaaa, waaaaaa, kai, kai, kai." He then flutters his hands on the woman's baby, if she has one, and utters his cries again. The babies never ceased to amaze me. They are so accustomed to the healers' behavior that they look serenely up into the faces of the screaming, shrieking men without a sign of fear. The healer may rejoin the line of dancing men for a few moments, then stagger over to someone else and heal again.

More of the healers begin to heal in this way, going from person to person apparently haphazardly. Their laying on of hands is rather brief and perfunctory compared to the more assiduous procedures in special curings. If any one at the dance were actually sick, the healers would go to him or her several times. But at this stage in the dances, they do not perform any of the additional functions of the special curings, and if there is any vagueness in the actual laying on of hands, it is fully compensated for by the exciting sounds of the loud singing, the sharp clapping, and n//hara wails and shrieks.

The dancing, singing, and healing continue. The intensity increases, and some of the healers begin to go into deeper trance. A man may suddenly begin to breathe heavily, open-mouthed. He may stare ahead, tense, unseeing, his face like the mask of tragedy. He may stand trembling and swaying, his eyes closed, or shuddering and heaving his stomach in violent gasps. He may fall down on his knees. He may moan, or throw back his head, yelling, "//Gauwa is killing me." He may stagger around and lurch into the fire, trample on the women, fall headlong into their circle, somersault over them, or crash full-length onto the ground and lie there rigid as a stick. The men say that the strength of their n/um overwhelms them. They lose their senses. Things appear to be smaller than normal and to fly around. The fire appears to be over their heads. Things whir.

Other healers, less deep in trance, try to catch a man when they see the signs of his entering this state. They take charge of him: they drag him to his feet if he has fallen, take his stick away if he has one, and as he staggers about, they hold him, steadying him and keeping him from injuring himself and others. This is a stage in which the healing power is believed to be most intense.

During this stage one or two of the healers rush around the dance circle and out into the darkness to coerce or defy //Gauwa and the //gauwasi. When they run they are usually steady, running with long loping rhythmic strides or in swift sprints. They jump over bushes and occasionally over people sitting by their small fires, and perhaps they leap over the circle of singing women. They may fall headlong during these bursts of action. Other men dash around with them trying to hold onto them, or if they fall, helping them up. In their dashing around, the men in trance pick up sticks or burning brands from the fire and hurl them into the darkness, yelling to the beings there: "You are killing people." "Go away. You are bad." "You are a liar. This man will not die. I'll fight you." "Go away." "Take away the sickness you are bringing." They also shout insults at //Gauwa and the //gauwasi. The !Kung are not as modest and decorous in speech as they are in bearing. The common everyday insults that the men exchange in the joking relationships play principally upon the themes of genital organs, excrement, sexual intercourse, and incest. I do not know of the healers accusing the supernatural beings of improper sexual relations as they do their joking partners, but they do shout slurs at the death-bringers that to the !Kung were insulting, based on the genital organs and excrement. "Uncovered penis," "hyena penis," "lion penis," "thrown-away penis," "filthy face" were epithets shouted by the healers.

After making their sorties against the death-bringers, the men may resume their healing, or they may collapse on the ground or go into paroxysms. Paroxysms occur at any time to men in this stage of trance. Certain men are known for the violence of their seizures. They sink down groaning and gasping. They shudder; sweat pours from them. Sometimes they froth at the mouth. Mucus runs from their noses. (Although nosebleeds are often depicted in dance scenes in the rock art of the Drakensberg and Bo experienced a nosebleed in the lion episode, nosebleeds are not common at the !Kung Healing Dances. I did not observe any.) The men throw back their heads, uttering shriek after shriek. Several at a time reach this state. Others, who may be by then far gone in trance themselves but not in paroxysms—holding the gasping, shrieking men in their arms, three or four clinging together—may lie in a heap or get up and stagger around in a knot.

This is a time for the dramatic play about the fire. One or another of the healers leaps up from his paroxysm or breaks away from the men who are holding him and rushes toward the fire. He may plunge into it or trample it, scattering the coals, or he may kneel in it and thrust his head into it, setting his hair aflame. He may scoop up coals and throw them over himself and over people sitting near. Women are quick to reach out to hold him before he crashes full length into the fire. They pat out the flames in his hair, and men come to lead him away.

Other men, meanwhile, are swearing and throwing sticks at the death-bringers. In the excitement, two or three women may jump up to dance. They might throw sa powder on the healers. Other women continue to clap and to sing in clarion tones. Some of the men still dance and sing. The music soars, the tempo quickens, the intensity crests.

Between their paroxysms and their rushing around, the healers continue to heal, very often in pairs. They believe that two men together bring double n/um and double strength to the healing. A man who is still in control of himself takes hold of one who is not and leads him around by the hand or the arm. Sometimes he plasters the trancing man to his back. The trancing man's eyes would be shut, and his arms would be held tightly around the body of his helper. His feet might drag or shamble weakly, or instead, they might move in precise, uncanny, apparently unconscious coordination with the dancing or walking motion of his helper. Together the two men dance and heal. One man, /Gao Music, used to carry another, the very small Gao from /Gam, on his back. Gao, although he appeared to be almost unconscious, would wrap his legs around /Gao Music's waist and hang on. It did not matter that Gao was too withdrawn to make the healing gestures or the n//hara sounds. The n/um in him was boiling and powerful, the people believed, and he was much respected for the depth of his trances.

In the final stage, which I assume to be the deepest stage of trance, a man falls into apparent unconsciousness. He may fall into this state suddenly and crash down in the midst of a frenzy; or he may slip down more gently, but instead of leaping up in a moment, he remains prone. (When I tried to observe men in this state, and a few times sat beside them and touched them, I noted that their bodies felt sweaty and clammy to the touch.) Some tremble; others are taut and rigid—some so rigid that they can be lifted by the backs of their necks and come up like boards lifted at one end. Their arms may stand out stiffly from their bodies or be clutched to them with clenched fists. Their eyeballs may be rolled back so that only the whites show, or their eyes may be squeezed tightly shut, their eyelids trembling. Some lie limp and still.

This state of apparent unconsciousness, whether the man is rigid, trembling, or relaxed, is what the !Kung call "half-death." In it, they believe, the man's spirit goes out from his body through his head. The !Kung said that in half-death a man's "life," /xwa, remains in his body as before; only the spirit goes out.

The healers believe that when the healer's spirit leaves his body, it goes to encounter //Gauwa and the //gauwasi. Many men claim that when in trance they see these other-world beings on earth. There were great healers in the past whose out-of-body spirits could climb to the upper sky on one of the cords that hang between the sky and the earth, and up there would encounter //Gauwa and the //gauwasi. According to old tales, some very great healers had even met with ≠Gao N!a himself. No one among the !Kung I spoke with knew anyone now living who told of such experiences when in trance. Compared to those great healers of the past, they said, the healers of today were *tsema* (small or young) in n/um.

The !Kung I spoke with may not have been to the upper sky, but other healers had. Megan Biesele and Richard Katz in Botswana heard fabulous accounts of out-of-body journeys in trance and encounters with the sky beings.[4]

When deep in half-death, the healer is believed to be in danger. His spirit might wander away or be taken by the //gauwasi. The women should sing loudly and well at this time. The n/um of the song is protective, and the sound can guide the spirit back. Other healers, often three or four at a time, work ardently over the man in half-death, performing the Healing Rite and calling to his spirit to return. "Where are you? Where are you?" they cry.

When healers work over a healer who is in half-death, their purpose is two-fold. They exhort the spirit to return, calling out, "Where are you? Come back." They take off the man's rattles and shake and pounce them up and down his body to gain the absent spirit's attention and to indicate where the body is. Their other purpose is to care for the man's body; they make the same gestures for his protection that they make when healing the sick, but more ardently. The gestures are definitely more ardent than in the perfunctory general healing of everybody at a dance, and they are even more charged with intensity than in special curings when someone who is really sick is being treated.

The healers may place their unconscious colleague on the ground. If he is face down and not rigid, they carefully rest his head on his arms so that his face is up off the ground and he can breathe easily. Or one man may hold the unconscious one in his arms, propped against his chest. The others bend over him or kneel or lie beside him. They flutter their hands on him and make the n//hara sounds in an impassioned way. As in special curings, they scrape sweat off themselves and rub it on the man. They do this over and over, rubbing hard, and they grind their sweaty foreheads against him. They throw their legs over him—anywhere over his body if he is prone, over one shoulder and then the other if he is propped up. I think this is done to get sweat onto the man directly from the backs of their knees (a sweaty place). In addition to rubbing sweat on him, they massage him lightly—not systematically, but passing their hands over him here and there. They call for water—a woman is likely to bring it—and they pour some over the man to cool him. Some of the men get their tortoise shells, put coals in them, and waft the n/um smoke over the unconscious man, holding the shell under his nose to let him breathe the smoke in. Not to transfer n/um to him but to give him physical care, they flex his feet, tired from dancing; they blow in his ears to clear his senses; they watch his tongue and pull it out and hold it, if need be, to keep it from slipping back into his throat and choking him. When he begins to regain consciousness, they give him water to drink.

A period of this intense care might continue for about twenty minutes or half an hour. (Variations are so common in Bushman behavior that any such measurement is a mere approximation.) During this time, some of the healers who began to care for the unconscious one would be likely themselves to fall unconscious, and to be the recipients rather than the givers of care. On one occasion four lay in a heap; only two swaying, staggering, staring ones were still able to move. They were barely able to hold a tortoise shell and shake a rattle to protect their prostrate friends.

There is considerable variation in the length of time that men remain in trance. Some are unconscious only a few minutes, and when they return to consciousness they get right up and go about their affairs. Some stay unconscious for half an hour, others still longer, perhaps an hour or so. Those who remain unconscious for long periods appear to relax. Their rigidity or trembling ceases, and they lie as if asleep. Perhaps they are, in fact, asleep.

A dance may come to an end after a period of intense trancing and the defying of the death-bringers. More often, however, the dance continues. There would be an easing-off period, the singing less ardent, the dancing a mere shuffle. With the sunrise, the dance would again become intense. The n/um of the Sun Song is very strong at that time, they say. It makes them sing and dance strongly. They end the dance in exhilaration.

In this positive mood, they face the activities of the day. The men usually go off to hunt "while their n/um is hot." The women set out to gather or take up other tasks.

The general concepts about healing, the Healing Rite, and the Healing Dance, I believe, are a great cultural asset to the !Kung. The psychological effect of the Healing Rite on a person who is sick must be beneficial. Believing in the protection and the power of the healer and the performance of the rite would help to allay anxiety and tension, and that, in turn, would help the body to heal itself.

A more manifest benefit is the social cohesion that the dance engenders. Richard Lee makes an insightful statement about !Kung concepts of healing that bears upon this point. He says:

> Bushmen regard healing power as being derived from other living men. Illness and misfortune, however, are brought mainly by the spirits of the dead and by other forces external to the living. In other words, they seek *within* the social body for benevolent powers, but project the blame for malevolence to forces *outside* the social body. Such a conception of health and disease serves to bind together the living in a common front against hostile external forces (Lee 1968b:51).

People bind together subjectively against external forces of evil, and they bind together on an intimate social level. The dance draws everybody together. All the members of the band and all visitors unite and dance together. Whatever their relationship, whatever the state of their feelings, whether they like or dislike each other, whether they are on good terms or bad terms with each other, they become a unit, singing, clapping, moving together in an extraordinary unison of stamping feet and clapping hands, swept along by the music. No words divide them; they act in concert for their spiritual and physical good and do something together that enlivens them and gives them pleasure.

4  FOOD AVOIDANCE AND THE TSHOA RITE

Food is an important element in !Kung ritual observances. The Bushmen are much concerned with food and hunger and make much use of food in their ritual symbolism. Food, either animal or plant food, has a role in most !Kung rites: in Tshoma, the Menarcheal Rite, weddings, the Rite of First Kill and other hunting rites, the Meat Fire, the rite for a novice healer after his first hunt, the rite of a baby's first haircut, and the *Tshoa* Rite. The foods used in these rites are associated with strength, fatness, plenty. The !Kung symbolically associate these desired conditions with themselves by ritually taking in the food. In the various rites, the food is either eaten, rubbed onto a person or inserted into little cuts made in the skin, or the person is washed with broth made with the food.

In another body of !Kung belief, certain regularly eaten foods are believed to have potencies that endanger people at certain times of life or in certain states. These foods are avoided according to a cultural system. I do not consider the practice of a food avoidance to be a ritualistic practice, but some of the avoidances are as strongly required by the society as if they were governed by formalized ritual. The potencies believed to exist in the foods could be called supernatural; they are different, at least, from the natural physical properties of the foods.

In both aspects, the ritual acts of taking in or avoiding food are in support of life. Food is not associated ritually with death. It has no part in !Kung burial practices. No ritual consumption or avoidance of food is required of mourners.

The !Kung appear not to have the concept of eating to acquire a desired characteristic of the thing eaten—as if one would eat lion to acquire the strength and courage of a lion.

There are several animals living in the area that the !Kung do not eat, not because the rules of food avoidance apply to them but because the Old Old People told them not to eat the creatures, or because the very thought of eating them is abhorrent.

Food Avoidance

I use the words "food avoidance" for the systematic abstention from eating certain foods that are regularly a part of the !Kung diet—ordinary wholesome foods commonly eaten except when the !Kung cultural calendar requires their avoidance. The foods are believed to have the potential of causing various ill effects for those who should avoid them. The word for avoidance in this sense is *dzi*.

Food avoidances are required of the following categories of people in !Kung society: all boys and girls and young adults, pregnant women, women in childbirth, parents of newborn babies, hunters, and healers. These people are in their procreative years or in states of life when their functions are vital to the life of the group. Some avoidances are required at the Menarcheal Rite and Tshoma. To end any food avoidance, the Tshoa Rite is performed, and the person resumes eating the food. The rite reintroduces food to the person and makes it safe for him to eat it.

Food avoidances do not give great advantage to one category of people in the social scheme to the disadvantage of others by allowing one category to have more food or the more choice foods. The avoidances favor the old to some extent, but not greatly. They allow the old to have the softer foods, which they welcome because of their poor teeth—foods such as ostrich eggs, intestines, fetus, blood, and the tender and delicious meat of steenbok, duiker, and giant bustard.

Although the foods avoided are appreciable in number, the avoidances seem to me to impose only slight deprivation on any category of people. Most avoidances are required for limited periods in a person's life, some for only very short times. There is considerable variety in the food supply, and some foods are not avoided at all—some of the big game animals, for instance. Only parts of other animals are avoided. Few plant foods are avoided. Several avoided foods are not staples on which the !Kung depend for daily sustenance; they are of minor nutritional importance, either because they are rarely obtained or because they are not very nutritious. Aardvark and kudu hooves, respectively, come to mind as examples. It is the ritualistic and social symbolism of the avoidance, not deprivation of food, that is meaningful.

The Social Value of Food Avoidance

The system of food avoidance has two aspects. The avoidances are practiced for the protection of health, strength, and skills, and at the same time, they serve as a social control.

Mary Douglas says in *Purity and Danger:*

> The analysis of ritual symbolism cannot begin until we recognize ritual
> as an attempt to create and maintain a particular culture, a particular set of
> assumptions by which experience is controlled. . . . The rituals enact the form
> of social relations and in giving these relations visible expression they enable
> people to know their own society (Douglas 1966:128).

Adapting Mary Douglas's statement to the !Kung practice of food avoidance, we
can say that through this practice the !Kung give visible expression and affirmation to
three of their social ideals. One ideal is obedience to social law. A second ideal is self-
control and restraint with respect to food. The third is to take care of oneself. The
!Kung word for taking care of oneself in this context is //gao. One should //gao, that
is, one should do what one can to keep oneself strong and well. Any individual's sickness, injury, or weakness weakens the group. Proper food avoidance is believed to help
a person to avoid illness, loss of strength, loss of skill, and to remain healthy and vigorous in any role—a mother of a healthy baby, a successful hunter, a healer with
strong n/um—all for the good of the group as well as the self.

For a people who lived entirely by hunting and gathering and were on the verge
of hunger much of the time, and for whom starvation was not only a specter of fear
but an actual practical concern, the avoidance of food made a strong symbolic statement. In obeying the rules of the avoidances, a person demonstrates active, personal
support of accepted customs, the social law, and shows that he is not "too fond of
food," not "light-hearted," not lazy or indifferent to taking care of himself, to keeping
himself strong—that he or she is, in all, a proper person.

We may ask more specifically what the group gains through the individual's
observances of the avoidances. One benefit, as I have mentioned, is restraint in eating.
The practice trains the young to curb the impulse to take food freely, reinforcing the
habit of restraint. Restraint toward food is a major virtue among these people whose
food is so often scant and almost always shared.

The meat of the big game animals is shared by the whole band according to a system (Marshall 1976:287–312). Smaller animals, such as duikers, which are not enough
to feed the whole band, are shared by smaller groups. Such groups are usually relatives,
for example, an extended family. The plant foods that a woman gathers are shared
with her immediate family and among other relatives and friends according to her
wishes. Approval rewards those who are generous. Disapproval and reproach fall on
the ungenerous who are said to be "far-hearted," or like "bags without openings." Not
to share as custom dictates is virtually unthinkable to the !Kung. When, for my own
amusement, I suggested the idea of a hunter's hiding his kill from others, to eat alone

or to give only to his wife and children, people screeched and cried, "Ooooo," and declared that lions take food for themselves that way, not humans.

Children are taught from an early age not to take food or to ask for food at other people's fires.

Etiquette demands that people do not appear greedy. If a visitor approaches when people are preparing food or eating, he should sit quietly aside and wait to be offered a portion. He must not be importunate and ask for food. When food is being passed around in a group and there is too little to satisfy everyone's hunger, one observes very modest demeanor. Each virtuously takes a small portion and passes the food to the next. More than once I have seen the first person pass on almost all of a portion of food I had given and only lick his fingers, while the last person got the biggest bite. A person who appeared selfish or greedy would incur severe disapproval. "People would laugh at him," they say.

The !Kung spoke in the following terms of the virtues that are enacted and given visual expression in food avoidance—vigor and willingness to hunt on the part of boys; conformity on the part of the girls. If a young hunter keeps himself strong, people explain, he can run down an eland, go two or three days without eating, survive long periods of thirst, and endure the cold of the desert nights. A young man who obeys the laws of food avoidance demonstrates his desire to keep himself strong and not risk disabling himself. He sets up an image of himself as a vigorous and willing hunter whose heart says to him, "Why am I sitting here in the encampment; why am I not setting out to hunt?"—an image that greatly pleases the !Kung.

By observing the food avoidances, girls demonstrate the same willingness to take care of their health, but people spoke especially of their compliance with the social laws. The !Kung said that if a girl failed to avoid the foods she should avoid, she would be laughed at. People would say that she did not //gao as she should, that she was unfaithful to the social laws, that she showed herself to be lazy and self-indulgent, too fond of food and, in fact, not a good girl. Boys ready to marry would say that she had not done the things proper to her age. A young husband might even divorce such a girl.

When a girl reaches an age at which several of the avoidances may be discontinued, if she has behaved properly and has taken care of herself well, her people wash her with tsi, cut her hair, put red powder on it, rub her with fat (eland fat preferably), and adorn her with bead ornaments. They show that they are pleased with her, and they make her beautiful.

Physical Effects

There are a few foods that are avoided simply because for generations it had been the custom. People no longer know a reason for these particular avoidances. They believe that no physical harm would come from disregarding them. The social disapproval would be mild, if any. The !Kung explained that only people who were especially assiduous in respecting custom would make a point of practicing these particular avoidances.

In a whole other realm of thought is the belief that many of the avoided foods do have the potential to cause physical and mental harm to certain people in certain periods of life. I believe that the !Kung do not conceive the potential ill effects to be symbolic, if that means that those effects do not actually exist or that they are simply devised by the society as a social sanction. They believe, rather, that there are actually potencies in the foods that can cause the ill effect. Each of these avoided foods has its own particular ill effect, and a person who eats a food when he should avoid it risks that effect. Among the ill effects that the food can cause are:

madness[1] (Some foods are believed to convey madness directly. *"Di"* is
the word for madness.);
headaches (The !Kung believe that severe headaches can cause madness.);
nausea (Severe nausea, the !Kung believe, can cause severe headaches,
which might lead to madness.);
thinness (Thinness was the disability risked by disregarding several of the
food avoidances. It was also the penalty for disregarding several
ritual observances.);
distention of the stomach;
boils;
tender skin (subject to sunburn);
bleeding from the nose;
diminished lactation.

The avoided foods are wholesome foods commonly eaten by everyone except during the required periods of avoidance. The !Kung say explicitly that there is "nothing bad in the foods," no poison, nothing defiling. After all, people eat them regularly. What is it about them that makes them dangerous to certain people at certain times of life? The !Kung could only say that the foods are "strong." To the best of my understanding that means that the foods have potencies and that mixing these potencies together with people in critical stages of life—in youth or in childbirth, for instance, could cause harm.

The !Kung say that the Old Old People taught them which foods they should avoid. The Old Old People seem to have gathered together an agglomeration of associations and beliefs, and we are left to our own conjectures as to what analogies; resemblances in shape, textures, or colors; what past events; coincidences; old tales; lost myths; or whatever might have led the ancestors of the !Kung to see specific foods as ones that should be avoided. I wondered about the foods that have n/um in relation to avoidance. The foods that I had been told have n/um are all avoided by one category of persons or another, but n/um is not the only criterion for avoidance. Numerous foods that do not have n/um are avoided.

None of the avoided foods is believed to be sacred or to belong to the gods. No food offerings are made to the gods or to the spirits of the dead. The gods and the other sky beings have no need of human food; they have their own, the !Kung say. The ill effect that follows the eating of a food that should be avoided is not believed to be sent by the gods to punish wrongdoing that displeases them. If they were asked, I am sure the !Kung would say (as they say about n/um) that the great god, being the creator and controller of all things, can control the effects of foods and stop their working, but unless he does so, the effects befall automatically.

In their associations with respect to the foods, the !Kung have sometimes used methods of thought that are common the world over. The concept of contagion lies behind the belief that steenbok are constipated and that the young must not eat them lest they become constipated. The concept that "like produces like" lies behind others. A pregnant woman, for instance, must not eat hooves lest her baby be born with buttocks shaped like hooves. And the !Kung believe that in the rightness of things some elements must be kept apart, such as femaleness and hunting.

I did not find food avoidances based on the concept of ritual or physical uncleanliness. The concept of ritual cleansing does exist among the !Kung. At least in one rite I know of, a widow is washed in the first rain that falls after her husband's death to cleanse her of his death. She should not remarry until she is cleansed. The concept of ritual cleansing, however, is not highly developed; the !Kung are not preoccupied with cleansing.[2]

Some food avoidances involve earth and ashes. It is my notion that earth and ashes are not "dirt" to the !Kung. During her Menarcheal Rite and at her wedding, when a girl must be carried so that her feet do not touch the earth, it is not to keep the girl's feet clean from the earth in a literal, limited sense. Rather, I think, the !Kung believe that both earth and girl have strong potencies that must be controlled. For instance, when earth has gotten into a root that has been accidentally chopped with a digging stick, that food is avoided by the young. I think this avoidance is observed for the same reason—not that earth is dirty but to separate potent forces. Also when certain foods must not be cooked in ashes if they are to be eaten by pregnant women, I think the symbolism of the avoidance is linked with fire and its potency, not with dirt. What these potencies are and whence they come is not put into words in the !Kung system of beliefs. I believe the concepts about the potencies are so taken for granted as eternal truths that a need for explanation does not occur to the !Kung.

Another avoidance involves food splashed by a baby's urine. The babies are naked, and because there is no floor but the sandy earth, nothing is made of their urinating. Their feces, however, are promptly gathered up with grass and carried away, and the baby is wiped with grass. If food should be accidentally splashed with the baby's urine, that food must be avoided by the young even though it is thoroughly washed. The !Kung I spoke with said the avoidance applied to both girls and boys, but their thoughts were only on boys. One might think that avoidance served as a lesson in cleanliness. However, the !Kung had nothing to say about cleanliness. Instead, they said that if a boy or a young man ate that food he would become very thin. People would laugh and point at him and say he had eaten food with a baby's urine on it and that was why he became so thin. The food would also give him bone trouble. Furthermore, he would have accidents walking about; he would step on thorns and sharp sticks and would gash his feet. It is in the nature of things that food with a baby's urine on it would have these effects. Also, incidentally, it is in the nature of things that a baby's feces must not be burned in the fire. If this should happen, the baby would not grow.

Age and the Practice of Avoidance

!Kung society requires most food avoidances from the young. Very few avoidances are required of the old, and eventually old people pass entirely beyond food avoidances. When the !Kung speak of old men, trying to explain why the latter no longer need to avoid foods, they express in double-edged remarks both respect and lack of respect for age. The old men were born long ago, they say; they have seen everything, they know everything, they are the "owners" of knowledge. At the same time people say that old men are useless. Old men give up hunting, they give up healing, they give up hope of being strong and do not try any longer to //gao. The old men say resignedly that it does not matter anymore what happens to them; they do not need to //gao.

Old women also pass beyond the practice of food avoidance, but not so much is said about them. Although the !Kung depend more on the plant foods the women gather than on meat for daily subsistence, women perform a somewhat subdued role compared to men in !Kung society. Women's work—the gathering of roots, nuts, and berries—is less spectacular and exciting than hunting and healing and is less risky and exacting than hunting. Besides, the strength of the wiry old Bushman women remains adequate to their work longer than that of men to hunting. I know only one old woman who was "useless." This was Old N/aoka, the sister of /Goishay, who became blind and dependent on her sister. (N/aoka was the only blind person we met in the Nyae Nyae area).

Food avoidance is practiced mainly in the reproductive years. It centers on young girls and boys as they leave childhood, on girls during their Menarcheal Rite, on boys during Tshoma, and on young adults. Food avoidances are also observed in especially potent states of life, by pregnant women, women in childbirth, parents of newborn babies, and by hunters and healers.

The ages of the young people are not defined in years. The !Kung do not reckon their age in years, but by stages of growth and by physical signs of age. Many of the food avoidances begin at what I took to be the approach of pubescence; none are required of younger children. N!ai and /Gishay became my measure of age because the !Kung we spoke with so often pointed to them as being at the proper ages to begin an avoidance. My guess was that N!ai was around nine or ten judging vaguely from her size and her behavior.[3] /Gishay was a little older than N!ai but had not yet killed his first big animal and had not been in Tshoma.

The age for ending most of the avoidances is marked by the number of babies the person is parent to. Many avoidances end with the birth of a first baby. Others should be continued until a person is parent to two or three babies, a few until a person has five babies—or until a person is old enough to have had five babies. It is not the actual birth of the babies that determines the ending of an avoidance; babies are used metaphorically as a measure of age. !Kung girls marry young but tend to have late menstruation. A girl would be likely to be in her late teens when she had her first baby; her husband would be a few years older. Five babies would place the young people in their late twenties or early thirties.

Infraction

One risks dire effects from violating the avoidance rules. The effects are apparently not believed to occur inevitably. Someone may eat something he should avoid and see no ill effects. The !Kung I questioned had no explanation for this. In any case, they pay more attention to instances that reinforce their beliefs in the dangers—instances in which someone suffers some disability and they look back and remember that the person had eaten something he should have avoided. They believe the dangers are real.

How much infraction actually occurs I do not know. There is considerable latitude and flexibility in the practice, I am sure, and people spoke freely about instances of infraction. Attitudes vary. Some people would practice the food avoidances assiduously to show they were proper people and to have social approval. Others might practice the avoidances primarily for the sake of safeguarding their own health and strength. Others might be "lighthearted," "too fond of food," lazy, indifferent to taking care of themselves, yielding to hunger, or too ready to take chances. Some people have stronger self-control than others with respect to hunger.

The !Kung believe also that the foods vary. Some foods are "stronger" and more "dangerous" than others, and people do really fear the effect of eating them. I doubt if any !Kung would risk eating ostrich eggs until it was considered proper and safe to do so. I have observed people using sand and water to scour a pot in which others had scrambled ostrich eggs in order to avoid even a speck of egg. !Ungka, who was well beyond the age when ostrich eggs are avoided, was still not eating them, saying explicitly that she was afraid of getting a terrible headache. With less dangerous foods, a "lighthearted" person might more readily take a chance.

I have observed other scrupulous observances of the avoidances, but I did not actually see a clear instance of infraction. That does not mean that none occurred. Early in my fieldwork I did not know about food avoidance and was not looking for behavior in avoidance. Detailed information about it came piecemeal. Even after I learned that the custom existed, an infraction might occur before my eyes without my recognizing it. Although I have no observations as to the amount of infraction, I believe that the avoidance laws were obeyed more often than they were disregarded.

Compliance with the avoidance law is a matter of individual responsibility, except when parents guide their children in the avoidances. Neither individuals nor the group, as such, have authority over anyone to require compliance or to punish infraction. However, the influence that the group exerts over an individual through its approval or disapproval is very strong.

Group disapproval is a very powerful sanction among the !Kung. A !Kung has no way to live satisfactorily except in the intimately shared life of his group, a life that offers no privacy, no retreat. Disapproval, even if it is expressed only by side remarks or a song, makes a !Kung feel cast out and alone. A feeling of isolation is unendurable.

Conversely, the proper observation of the avoidances allows a person to enact and give visible expression to his virtuous intent and to show that he is capable of restraint and that he is doing what he can to keep himself strong and well, an asset to his group. I believe the !Kung are motivated by desire for approval and acceptance and that this influences their behavior, as does the negative deterrent of group disapproval.

Creatures Eschewed as Food

Nonfoods

A number of animals, birds, and insects exist in the Nyae Nyae area that the !Kung do not eat. Although there is never a great abundance of food available to the !Kung and although these creatures might be edible, the !Kung do not consider them to be food. I thought their attitude could be compared to that of an American who might declare to an inquiring anthropologist from elsewhere that he never had eaten horse meat and never would do so, but would not think to mention that he did not eat bluejays, cats, or caterpillars, to mention a few American nonfoods.

Creatures that the !Kung eschew with indifference include baboons, night apes (bush babies), gerbils, hyraxes, snails, the rarely seen secretary birds (*Sagittarius serpentarius)*, and the migrating pelicans, gulls, and storks.

Tshi Dole

Unlike the creatures that are not thought of in terms of food are a number of creatures that the !Kung call *tshi dole* (see note 2 on p. 312). The !Kung take a very definite position about them and vehemently declare that these creatures are not to be eaten; they are bad. The !Kung do not have conscious concepts of the reasons. The creatures do not come under the food avoidance rules and are not thought to cause ill effects. Nothing would happen to a person if he did eat them—but to eat them is unthinkable.

The cats

The great predatory cats come to mind first. I opened the subject of predators by asking the !Kung if they ate lions, though I knew full well that they did not. How could I think they would eat a lion, they demanded in a hubbub of protest; I was wasting their time with such talk. Nevertheless they did talk, and they expressed their aversion with their cry of shocked disapproval, the high-pitched, long drawn-out "ooooo," tapping their lips with their fingers. One is reminded of Leviticus 11:27: "And whatsoever goeth upon his paws, among all manner of beasts that go on all four, those are unclean unto you. . . ."

Because of their feet, the !Kung place the cats in a category called *jumhmi.* Unfortunately, they could not say precisely what "jumhmi" signified or on what basis the cats' feet were anomalous and wrong. "Jumhmi" is a plural noun designating the great cats. A silent sign for these animals is a clenched hand held like a paw in a walking position. The verb *"jum"* means to turn oneself into a lion and to walk about stealthily at night, something some healers are believed to be able to do.

It is conceivable that, in !Kung thinking, because the footprints of the great cats in the sand look somewhat like human footprints with visible toe marks (the footprints are especially like footprints of the small Bushmen feet), the horror of eating human flesh is extended to these animals. The !Kung used "jumhmi" not only as the designation for animals with cat feet, but also as a derogatory term for the Herero on the Botswana border—those Herero whom they dislike because they are harsh in trade transactions or harsh to the !Kung who work for them. The Botswana !Kung also refer to the Herero, and sometimes to Tswana and whites as well, as *!xohmi*, a general term for carnivorous animals. More research remains to be done on the relationships among the !Kung's systems of animal and food classifications.

Hyenas

The !Kung cried that no one would eat hyena; they would starve first. They offered no reasons. It was simply unthinkable that anyone should eat hyena.

People declared in talking about hyenas—as though the idea had significance for them—that hyenas do not kill, they eat what other animals kill, animals they find dead, but so do humans, except for healers, who avoid animals found dead. My conjecture is that the repugnance arises from the association of hyenas with the eating of human corpses. It is not an uncommon experience for the !Kung to find that a hyena has uncovered a corpse and devoured it if the corpse had not been buried deeply enough or been otherwise adequately protected.[4]

Wild dogs and domesticated dogs

Wild dogs are among the bad things that no one eats. The !Kung in the Gautscha area had no domestic dogs, but they had seen dogs of their Herero and Tswana neighbors, and dogs that visiting Bushmen sometimes brought with them. They did not express as strong an aversion to either wild or domesticated dogs as they did to hyenas and lions.

Monkeys

Monkeys were mentioned among the animals no one eats, but without strong feeling. What the !Kung had to say about monkeys was that they were utterly "useless." They were uncommon in the area. I saw none.

Vultures

The hubbub of disgust and protest reached its peak when I asked, just to hear the outcry, if the !Kung ate vultures. Some people in the group misunderstood what I said and thought I was saying that they should eat vultures. "Why should they eat vultures?" they cried indignantly. "No one had ever eaten vultures. They smell bad." In the clamor someone said that vultures eat people; others spoke of their scavenging. I believe the very strong aversion comes from the idea of vultures eating corpses, as I think the aversion to hyenas does.

Flamingos

It had not occurred to me to ask about flamingos; they were a nonfood to me. The !Kung, however, announced of their own volition and with vehemence that flamingos are bad, bad, bad. No one would eat them. They are bad, and they taste bad. People also remarked that flamingos make a sound like "hoo hura," a sound the !Kung apparently dislike. They were so created the !Kung said. No further reason was given. To call a man a "flamingo feather" is a shocking insult, we were told.

Chameleons

Chameleons are not to be eaten; they are very bad people said. But in one respect, they are good. If a chameleon walks on a man's bow it will bring him luck in hunting.

Mongooses, meerkats, and squirrels

Mongooses, meerkats, and squirrels are among the bad things that no one eats, but they are in a different category from the other avoided creatures. Whereas the !Kung have strong aversions to lions, hyenas, and their like, animals that "no one would eat," they believe that no physical or mental illness would befall a person who did eat these creatures. But if a person were to eat mongooses, meerkats, or squirrels, that would be different; he would die. No one could say why except that the animals were so created by the great god. The Old Old People had said to throw away any of these animals if they were caught in a snare, and *never* to eat them.

Rats and mice

Rats and mice are in still another category. I had asked about them, having heard that they were part of the diet of some Bushmen. The !Kung said most people did not eat rats and mice because they did not like them or because they were too small to bother with, but that some women used to eat them. However, no one was eating them at the time we were present in the field. This abstention was unique in that it did not spring from their own culture; it sprang from European information about disease. When some of the Gautscha people visited relatives to the north near Tsho/ana, they had met !Kung who had returned from visiting still farther north at Runtu. A European doctor there was passing the word to all the Bushmen he could reach, telling them to tell others not to eat rats and mice because they had a disease or carried one. I do not know what disease he said they had, but he may have feared bubonic plague. Bubonic plague had appeared in Botswana about that time (1953), and a government expedition had been sent to control it. The Gautscha people had evidently been sufficiently impressed by what their friends had told them about the doctor's advice to comply with it.

Jackals and wildcats

It is interesting to note that jackals and wildcats, in spite of one being a scavenger and the other having little cat feet, are not included in the category of tshi dole. They are eaten, however, only by old women.

INDIVIDUALS' VOLUNTARY ABSTENTION FROM CERTAIN FOODS

For personal reasons, individuals sometimes abstain from eating foods that are habitually eaten by others and for which the !Kung customs do not require avoidance. Similarly, individuals sometimes abstain from eating something for a longer period than would be required by the avoidance rules. Many American adults and children reject foods because they dislike their taste or texture—foods such as parsnips or brains, for example. This attitude was not prevalent among !Kung children, who appeared to eat eagerly whatever was given them. Adults spoke very little about the taste of food except to say that bladders, gall bladders, and certain roots were too bitter for anyone to eat. A few !Kung, however, do dislike some foods. /Qui Neanderthal, for example, did not eat python. He told me this just after he had captured a python, cooked it, and given all the meat away, mostly to the children. Another day he was talking with me when the children were playing with an enormous kudu eye. They dropped it into the fire and it burst. /Qui said, like eating python, it made him feel squeamish. It made me feel squeamish too, and it occurred to me that we do not regularly eat eyes. I said this to /Qui, adding that I did not know why. The group of six or seven people I was talking with burst into laughter. /Qui said he was glad I had said that. He had thought many times that I did not understand when they did not have an answer to my constant probing for concepts that explained an act or a custom. He thought I had been disappointed in them and considered them ignorant. Now he believed that I did understand.

More frequently the reason for a personal abstention is not a personal dislike but a definite idea about the protection of physical and mental well-being. If, after eating a food, a person suffers some physical reaction that suggests that the food does not agree with him, he may abstain from eating it.

The thought of allergies crossed our minds, but it was impossible to pursue that question to any conclusion. The !Kung did not exhibit the blotches, rashes, or wheezes that we interpret as allergic reactions, and they did not mention those manifestations as signs that they should not eat something. The usual signs they mentioned were nausea and headache, and they said if they experienced them after eating something, they knew that the food was not good for them.

If people especially dislike the smell of something, they take this as a sign that they should abstain from eating it. They believe that an especially offensive smell makes them vomit and could give them such a bad headache that they would go mad. The smell of decaying meat is not the smell they mean. The smell they fear is the natural smell of the creatures. After smelling ostriches being cut up, I understood what they meant. Individuals mentioned that they voluntarily abstained from eating the following creatures because of their distinctive and strong odors: buffalo, honey badger, mamba, puff adder, ostrich, and zebra.

People spoke of other foods that they did not eat, not because of their odor but for other unexplained reasons: anything red, blood, duiker, jackal, mole snake, pangolin, and python.

Of the animals listed above that are eschewed by personal choice, all but buffalo and zebra are avoided according to the rules of avoidance by some category of persons for a limited time. The person who continues to abstain from eating them after the allotted time of avoidance does so voluntarily.

One more abstinence might be said to be voluntary: women do not eat the plant //geit'ama. It is said to cause flatulence. If a woman ate it and had to expel gas, her husband would complain, and this, we were told, would destroy the love between them.

SPECIFIC FOOD AVOIDANCES

Foods Avoided by the Young

In the following pages I list the foods avoided by both boys and girls and young men and women, and in addition, a few foods avoided by women and girls only, and a few by men and boys only. The avoidances begin when the boys and girls are the ages of /Gishay and N!ai—between seven and ten. Some avoidances end at the birth of a first child. Some continue until the young person has had, or is old enough to have had, two or three children. Some are required until the person is old enough to have had five children. The foods are believed to cause varying disabilities if eaten when they should be avoided. A number of them are believed to cause madness.

Foods that Cause Madness

Ostriches, embryonic ostriches, ostrich eggs, other birds' eggs

The !Kung believe that ostrich eggs, if eaten by the young, would cause headaches so violent they could cause madness. The headaches could be so severe that the person would not only go mad but in his madness would "run away"—the implication being that the person would die alone in the bush. This to the !Kung would be a most terrible fate. People fear ostrich eggs, saying that they are very "strong," and they avoid them scrupulously from the age of N!ai or /Gishay until they are old enough to have had five children.

Ostrich eggs are among the foods believed to have n/um. N/um in food is not a therapeutic, curative, or protective agent; it gives no exceptional positive value to the food. On the contrary, n/um gives the food an extra potency for ill effects and requires strict avoidance. The presence of n/um does not put the foods into a unique category of avoidance; some foods that do not have n/um, leguaan for instance, are avoided with equal strictness and for as long a time or longer.

The !Kung had nothing to say about eggs other than ostrich eggs except that all eggs are strong and should be avoided. They do not often find eggs of other birds in their vast arid land.

Young people avoid ostrich meat as they do ostrich eggs. The !Kung pointed out that ostriches sit on ostrich eggs. The wings, legs, and feet must be strictly avoided by the young because those parts touch the eggs when the birds sit on the nest. The heads too must be avoided, and the internal parts are especially dangerous. Many adults who are old enough to eat ostrich meat avoid it voluntarily because they cannot bear the smell and fear that it will nauseate them.

Occasionally when a clutch of ostrich eggs is brought to the encampment, the eggs are found to have embryonic ostriches in them. This provides a feast for old and young and a concern to those who must avoid ostrich. The pot in which the embryos are cooked and the container from which they are eaten must be vigorously scoured with water and sand to remove every morsel of ostrich before the young people may use them.

Gemsbok heads

The young avoid the heads of both male and female gemsbok. The heads are "mad things," say the !Kung. The reason, we were told, is that gemsbok eat ostrich eggs.

Cow eland heads

Cow eland heads are avoided by the young for the same reason. The !Kung claimed that cow elands eat ostrich eggs although bull elands do not. I question the latter statement but have not been able to verify or disclaim it. John Marshall assures me that antelope do sometimes eat ostrich eggs for the moisture in them.

Udders and milk

The udders of lactating female game animals are a cherished food, though rather rarely obtained. They are cooked, milk and all. Little children and old people may eat them. At the age of N!ai and /Gishay, a strict avoidance begins. Girls observe this avoidance until after their Menarcheal Rite has come to an end; boys observe it for a longer time—until they are old enough to have three children or longer. (This period was not definitely stated.)

If a person failed to observe this avoidance, the !Kung believe his or her bones would ache and he or she would go mad. As I recounted in the chapter on marriage in *The !Kung of Nyae Nyae* (Marshall 1976:260), the madness of /Gunda Legs was attributed to his having drunk the milk of a gemsbok doe. /Gunda Legs did something no one in his right mind would do. He married at the same time both a woman and her daughter by a previous marriage. This amounted to incest, and nothing short of madness could account for it.

Even if the female is not lactating, the young should avoid the udders of certain animals—eland, gemsbok, giraffe, and du!ker. The udders of wildebeest and kudu, however, need not be avoided unless, of course, the animal is lactating. When I asked why this distinction was made, I was told that the Old Old People had not told them why, and the group roared with laughter at the familiar refrain.

Red-crested korhaans

Two kinds of korhaan are found in the Nyae Nyae area: the red-crested korhaan and the white-quilled korhaan. The !Kung call both birds by the same name, "*nam.*"

The !Kung say that korhaans are mad things. The courtship display of the red-crested korhaan certainly makes them seem so. The male flies high into the air and suddenly begins to dive wildly down, fluffing his feathers out, seeming to somersault over and over, clattering his bill, until he is about to crash. Just before he hits the ground he straightens out and glides away. The !Kung imitate the korhaan's clatter.

The !Kung avoid korhaan even longer than they avoid ostrich eggs—past the age at which they can have had five children. People said the young would get exceedingly bad headaches from eating the bird, headaches that would certainly make them mad.

They told about a boy named Garu /Qui who ate korhaan when he should have avoided it. During the Tshoma Rite in which he was participating, at the time when the men wash the boys, he suddenly began to behave strangely. He began to say "kwara, kwara, kwara" over and over. He could say nothing else. *"Kwara"* means "nothing" or "none" in !Kung. *"Kwara-kwara,"* however, is the name for the red-crested korhaan in the language of the neighboring Tswana, something the boy may have heard. Whether there was any connection in his mind between the Tswana or !Kung words and his having eaten korhaan, no one could say. The boy never resumed his normal behavior. The healers tried repeatedly to cure him, but he died not long after. Since that time, !Kung boys who knew about the episode have taken no risk, we were told, and have strictly avoided korhaan.

Giant (or kori) bustards
The giant (or kori) bustard (a flight bird larger than a korhaan but smaller than an ostrich; in Afrikaans, paouw) is avoided. As with korhaan, headaches and madness are said to result from eating it when one is too young. Girls would not only go mad; they would also lack sufficient milk for their babies.

Giant bustards exhibit no such behavior as that of the wildly plummeting male red-crested korhaan. The bustards walk about in stately dignity, and one is left to wonder why the ancestors of the !Kung thought they must be avoided by the young. The meat of these birds is delicious.

Puff adders and savanna leguaans
The deadly poisonous puff adder and the big lizard, the savanna leguaan, are both included in the !Kung diet when they can be found, but both should be avoided scrupulously until a person is old enough to have had five children. They can cause madness and other ills. These are among the food avoidances that the !Kung take most seriously. They tell of Old /Gaishay who lost his power to cure because he ate leguaan when he was too young.

Honey badgers (ratels)
The odor of honey badger is so repellent, the !Kung say, that it can cause nausea. The nausea might, in turn, cause a severe headache, and the headache madness. The young avoid eating honey badger from the age of seven to ten until sometime after their Tshoma or Menarcheal Rite. The precise length of time was not specified.

Foods That Cause Various Disabilities

Steenbok and springhare

Steenbok, we were told, are constipated; furthermore, they are red in coloring. If a young person were to eat them, he or she would have severe nosebleeds and would suffer from distention of the stomach, intestinal disorders, and constipation. The young person might become so constipated that he would die. The !Kung told us that a young person who was "lighthearted" about observing the avoidance might stop avoiding steenbok when he was old enough to have had one child; others, more concerned with taking care of themselves, would continue to avoid steenbok until they were old enough to have had two or even three children.

Springhare are as red and as constipated as steenbok, we were told, and must be avoided as long as steenbok lest the same disabilities befall.

Although the !Kung, talking about these animals, did not explicitly associate the color red with blood, and although they do not systematically avoid all red things, some berries for instance, one assumes that the association is there and that is why these reddish animals are believed to cause nosebleeds.

Throats

The young avoid eating the throats of animals or the skin over the throat. If they did not do so, their throats would have abscesses.

Eyes

Eyes should not be eaten by the young lest their own eyes become sore.

Tails

Girls avoid tails. To eat them would give them boils on their backs. Boys avoid tails because they would cause their arrows to go only into the tails of the animals they hunt and the arrow poison would not kill the animals.

Fetuses

The tender meat of a fetus of one of the great animals is relished by the old people. The young must strictly avoid it—girls until after their Menarcheal Rite, boys for a comparable time.

Foods cooked at a fire of a family with a newborn baby

Such food is avoided by young boys and girls.

Foods splashed by a baby's urine

If food splashed by a baby's urine were not avoided by the young, they would get thin and have bone trouble.

Pounded or chopped sha (Vigna dinteri *Harms*)

Sha, a potatolike plant food, is a favorite food of old and young. The root may be eaten whole and fresh, raw or roasted by the young, but it should be avoided if it has been pounded in a mortar. Pounded sha would give the young a bad odor. This was one of the avoidances that was frequently disregarded, we were told.

Plant foods with earth in them

Sha that has been chopped by a digging stick and has gotten earth into it must be strictly avoided by the young. This avoidance applies to any root with earth in it,[5] but sha was particularly mentioned. Earth in a plant food would cause the young to become very thin.

Foods Avoided by Women and Girls

Blood

When a game animal is slaughtered, the blood is carefully collected into the cavities of the body, dipped out, and poured into a bag, probably one made of the animal's stomach. Blood is a cherished food. Old women with poor teeth are especially grateful if the blood is given to them in the meat distribution. The !Kung cook blood in a pot until it has the consistency of porridge, stirring it constantly with a little forked stick that they twirl between the palms of their hands. They speak of eating rather than drinking blood. Blood is a "strong" food. Girls begin the avoidance at N!ai's age and continue it for varying lengths of time depending on their determination to //gao. Several women who had children eight or ten years old were still avoiding blood. Blood eaten when it should be avoided would cause severe stomach pains and diarrhea. (Boys avoid blood during Tshoma, and blood is involved in a hunting rite.)

Redwing partridges

This bird has n/um. A girl must have two or three children before she may eat it. The !Kung did not say what disability would befall a girl who ate redwing partridge too soon. The partridge's redness may link it with blood and with steenbok and springhare. The disabilities that would result from eating these animals are nosebleeds and intestinal and stomach disorders.

Warthogs

A girl avoids warthog until she has her first baby. If she did not, people would laugh and say that she had eaten something with tusks. The !Kung commented that tusks protrude but did not elucidate that remark. To eat warthog would make a girl's skin tender. Warthog is one of the meats most often brought in by the hunters. This avoidance, in my opinion, causes a certain amount of deprivation for the girls.

Duikers

Duiker, the !Kung say, have tender skin and are easily irritated by heat. Girls avoid eating them to prevent their skin from being easily irritated by the sun—that is, according to Old /Gasa, some girls do. Old /Gasa said the girl in her family held to this avoidance but the other girls in their band had given up avoiding duiker.

Tortoises

Tortoise is avoided but not as scrupulously as leguaan and puff adder. The !Kung we spoke with were vague about tortoise.

Giraffe heads and internal parts

The !Kung gave giraffes' tallness as the reason that girls must avoid eating giraffe heads and internal parts. If a girl ate them, she would have terrible headaches and be in danger of going mad. Tallness is not admired by these small people; it is considered an abnormality.

Eland chests

A girl would not have enough milk for her baby if she ate eland chest before her first baby was born. This is not a strictly obeyed avoidance; some girls disregard it.

Kudu hooves

If a girl were to eat kudu hooves, she would step on thorns and sharp sticks when walking in the bush and would wound her feet. The !Kung thought this was because kudu walk so much in thick brush. Furthermore, her eating kudu hooves might cause her baby to have buttocks in the shape of kudu hooves.

Certain internal organs of all animals: hearts, lungs, intestines, kidneys, spleens, stomachs

We were told that girls must avoid these internal parts of animals until they have had one baby because they are girls, and it is customary and proper for girls to avoid these parts.

Snouts
Girls avoid eating snouts because it is the custom.

Testicles
Young women and girls avoid testicles. To eat them would cause severe stomach disorders. Old women may eat testicles according to the rules, but several, talking to me about food avoidances, said they never would; they dislike the thought of eating testicles.

Flesh sticking to the hide when an animal is skinned
The baby of a girl who fails to observe this avoidance might be born with a caul. The people who told me this said they had been advising the girls not to eat hide freely when there was flesh attached to it, but the girls had not been following their advice. So far, the girls had been fortunate. None of the Gautscha girls had had a baby with a caul, but a baby at Tsho/ana had been born with one. If one should be born among the Gautscha people, they said they would simply take the caul off and scold the girl for disregarding the avoidance; nothing more would happen.

Foods Avoided by Men and Boys

Apart from the numerous food avoidances practiced by men (especially young men) in their roles as hunters and healers, and those avoidances that boys and girls practice because they are young, only a few food avoidances are required of boys and men.

Uterus
Men avoid eating uterus all their lives.

Marrow
Boys avoid marrow until they are old enough to have had three children. This is considered to be an important avoidance and is strictly observed.

Food near old men's heads
Men who have been in Tshoma are believed to have strong n/um in their heads. If an old man who had Tshoma n/um in his head were lying on the ground with his head near some food, that food should be avoided by boys and young men. One who ate it would become sick and would bleed severely from the nose, so severely that he might die. We were told that the whole of such an old man's head is "poisonous death," an emphatic, metaphorical way of saying that the Tshoma n/um in his head is very strong.

Although some associations made in the !Kung system of food avoidances are unfathomable, some are easily comprehended given the concepts of contagion, and that like produces like, and the !Kung idea that certain "strong" things should be kept apart. Another concept, as I see it, on which some food avoidances may be based is anomalousness. I believe that korhaans, giant bustards, ostriches, and leguaans are anomalous creatures to the !Kung, outside the proper nature of things, and for that reason may be associated with madness and avoided by the young with special care. The korhaan's strange courtship flight is unlike the behavior of proper birds and suggests madness. The handsome giant bustard, walking about in stately dignity, alert and confident, gives no suggestion of madness, but because it so seldom flies, I believe the !Kung see it as anomalous. Dr. O. P. M. Prozesky in *A Field Guide to the Birds of Southern Africa* (1970:103) says of this heavy bird that it can fly but is reluctant to do so. Ostriches, whose eggs are so strictly avoided, never fly. To the !Kung, birds are "owners" of flying; for a bird not to fly is strange. Leguaans are even more anomalous. They have four legs like the many mammals the !Kung hunt, but they are hairless, they hiss, and they lay eggs—like snakes.

THE TSHOA RITE

When a person comes to the end of a food avoidance and is ready to resume eating the avoided food, the Tshoa Rite must be performed. "Tshoa" is a verb that means simply "to perform the rite." One may say, "I tshoa tsi," for example, or, "Mother (or someone) tshoas me for tsi." The rite is performed once for each kind of food the first time it is eaten after the avoidance has ended; for each kind of meat, for each kind of plant food.

A Tshoa Rite is informal. No special place or prescribed time is required. A fire is needed but not a ritually kindled new fire; any fire will do. Anyone may attend a Tshoa Rite. The person who performs the rite must be one who no longer avoids the food he or she is "tshoaing." An older man tshoas a boy or young man; an older woman tshoas a girl or young woman. Their kinship relationship imposes no restriction. For all its informality, the rite is taken very seriously by the !Kung.

The rite is performed in connection with other rituals in addition to ending a food avoidance. It has a part in hunting rituals, in Tshoma, and in the Menarcheal Rite. In the latter, the act of gathering and the act of cooking on a fire are "tshoaed" as well as the food and the girl. In Tshoma, the act of hunting is tshoaed as well as the eating of the previously avoided foods.

In still another context, young girls from the age of N!ai are tshoaed each year for certain plant foods the first time they eat them, when these plant foods are in their new growth after the rains. Each of these foods need to be tshoaed only once each year; then the girl may eat that food until the next rains bring new growth. Girls continue this practice of annual tshoaing until their first menstruation.

The rite is performed in essentially the same way each time and has the same purpose in all contexts—to protect a person from the potency of the foods that, in !Kung belief, could cause harm when the person is in certain life states. The rite is not believed to influence the food plants—to make them more plentiful, for instance.

The rite I observed was performed for Baú, daughter of N/aoka and /Ti!kay, when she was about to eat tsi for the first time that season.

There are four plant foods that the girls tshoa annually. Dr. Robert Story (1958) identified them as:

tsi	*Bauhinia esculenta* Burch. The edible part is the seed. The plant grows in open grassland. The seeds are borne in pods on vines that run along the ground. In Namibia, tsi is popularly called "eland bean." It is an important food to the !Kung, delicious, satisfying, nutritious, more so than the fibrous roots and dry berries that comprise much of their diet.
//k'a	*Ricinodendron rautanenii* Schinz. The edible part is the nut of the tree. In Namibia the tree and the nut are popularly called mangetti, a name derived from the Herero name "*omungete.*" In Botswana the Tswana name "*mongongo*" is popularly used. Like tsi, //k'a is a nutritious, highly desired food. It is not regularly available to the Nyae Nyae !Kung we lived with, who have no //k'a growing in their territory. They have //k'a only when visitors bring presents of the nuts or when they go to visit relatives who have //k'a available to them.
tshu	*Walleria nutans* Kirk. Tshu is the storage organ of a small plant, which is about six inches high with paired grasslike leaves. The storage organ is about the size of a golf ball. The leaves of the plant are among the first to turn green at the time of the little rains, like /gam grass and sha sha. Tshu is the first plant food to be eaten in its new growth. When the bulbs become dry in the winter months of May and June, girls must avoid them until the plant is freshened again by the next rains.

n/n   *Grewia flava* DC. The edible part is a berry with a large seed and little pulp. It is important in the !Kung food supply because it is widespread. When hunting, for instance, men may find n/n when they can find nothing else to eat.

I wondered what was common to these four foods—a seed, a nut, a bulblike storage organ, and a berry—that young girls must be tshoaed for them. Or what was common to the running vine, the tree, the little plant, and the berry bush that produce edible parts? What was their potency and their meaning to the !Kung? Why had the ancestors believed they should be tshoaed? I was convinced that important foods in new growth after the rains and young girls performing a rite over them had something to do with fertility, either in the girls or in the food plants or both. If so, that specific aspect of belief is lost to !Kung memory. The Old Old People had said nothing about fertility. They had said that it was proper for girls to be tshoaed for these foods and that the girls must be faithful to the law.

Two agents that provide the protection in the Tshoa Rite are two medicine plants, sha sha and ≠*khali.* ≠Khali is used only by men and boys in the Tshoma Rite. To my regret I do not have an identification of ≠khali. Sha sha is used in all other Tshoa Rites by boys and girls, men and women.

The occasion for performing the rite for Baú was the arrival at Gautscha of a visitor who had brought with him a big bag of fresh tsi to give to relatives and friends. N/aoka had received a share and took the opportunity to tshoa her daughter and another girl of about the same age.

The girls sat down by N/aoka's fire, which had burned down to coals and ashes. N/aoka had a tortoise shell about five or six inches in diameter, which she valued highly as a bowl. She filled it with tsi and dumped the tsi into the coals. She then bit off and chewed a sliver of the sha sha root she wore hanging from her bead necklace. With the sha sha in her mouth, she placed Baú's hands on the fire paddle, her hands over Baú's, and blew vigorously up and down the fire paddle and Baú's hands and arms. Still holding the fire paddle together, the mother and daughter scraped hot coals and ashes over the tsi and let them roast. When the tsi seeds were cooked, N/aoka scraped them out of the ashes and shelled them. She took another bite of the sha sha and some of the tsi into her mouth, chewed them together, spat the material into her hand and rubbed it vigorously with a downward motion onto Baú's throat, chest, abdomen, and arms, pausing to hold Baú's throat, and rubbing her arms especially vigorously. N/aoka repeated the chewing and rubbing three or four times. That ended the rite.

With its protection Baú could now eat tsi the rest of the year without its harming her. N/aoka explained that when she pressed her hand against Baú's throat it was to press the girl's heart where a pulse is felt. This pressure hardens the heart and makes it strong so that the girl would be strong to keep the food avoidance, to show restraint in eating, and to endure hunger. Her people would say that she was faithful to the law, that she had taken care of herself as she should, and that she had shown herself to be a good and proper girl.

After N/aoka had tshoaed the other girl, I joined the group in eating the remaining tsi, not as part of the ritual, just eating together.

5  Concepts of Childbirth and Rites for the Protection of Children

Concepts of Pregnancy

The !Kung believe that in conception the woman's menstrual blood unites with the man's semen to form the embryo. Menstrual blood is believed to be a unique substance, different from the blood that flows in veins and arteries. The child at first is blood, the !Kung believe. It is a little thing. Gradually it grows and becomes a child. The woman can feel it move. The gestation period is believed to be about five moons.

Except for a few additional food avoidances, which I shall mention, no rituals attend pregnancy, and little attention, if any, is given to prenatal care. I learned only that the man and wife should not have frequent sexual intercourse. The women laughed merrily in telling me this. They said they should wait many nights. Sexual intercourse is believed to be weakening to men and women and in excess would make the woman's bones sore and affect a hunter's powers. After the baby is born the parents should strictly refrain from intercourse for three moons.

Food Avoidance Observed by Pregnant Women

A few food avoidances are required of pregnant women in addition to those required of all young women. During pregnancy a woman might be more assiduous in observing all her avoidances, and less likely to make an exception.

Throats and entrails
A pregnant woman must assiduously avoid eating throats and entrails, not for the protection of herself or her baby, but for the protection of the hunter who killed the animal. Should a pregnant woman eat these parts of the animal, the hunter would lose his luck.

Steenbok, hooves, and sha with holes in it

These foods are avoided by all girls and young women. In pregnancy, the avoidance must be strictly observed. If the pregnant woman ate steenbok, her baby would be very small. If she ate hooves, the baby's buttocks would have the shape of hooves. If she ate a root of sha that had holes in it, the baby's buttocks would have cavities.

Food that has lain on the ground

Food that a pregnant woman is to eat should not be left lying on the ground in the encampment. It is usual for nuts or roots brought in by the gatherers to be left in piles beside the shelters. A pregnant woman should keep her food off the ground. If this precaution were not taken, the woman would get thin.

Three foods cooked on the coals and in hot ashes

The women teaching me about food avoidances listed three foods that must be avoided by a pregnant woman if the foods are cooked on coals or in hot ashes. These foods may be eaten if they are cooked in a pot. The foods are redwing partridge and two roots— /ama (*Ceropegia pygmaea* Shinz) and !ama (*Ceropegia tentaculata* N.E. Br.). If these avoidances were disregarded, the baby would get thin. To me this was one of the most obscure groups of avoidances. Why just these three foods must not be cooked on coals or in ashes, I wondered. The women could not say why but warned me that I should remember what they taught me and not eat anything I should avoid, so that my children would be strong.

Eating from the pot of an unrelated person

A pregnant woman should not eat from the pot of a person who is not a kinsman or affine. No disability would befall her or her child, but the Old Old People had said this was a custom to be followed. It suggests the cultural tendency toward caution with respect to strangers. In the !Kung language, "bad" and "strange" are one word—*dole*. The women told me that this custom was dying out. Only women exceptionally assiduous in observing avoidances would observe this one.

CHILDBIRTH

When a !Kung girl is about to give birth for the first time, her mother goes with her to teach her what to do and to help her overcome her fear. If the mother is not present, another experienced woman attends the girl. After the first birth, it is usual for a woman to give birth alone, although a mother or sister or someone close to her might accompany the young woman if she wished.

The !Kung have no midwives, no women who specialize in helping at a birth, and the men healers do not attend a normal birth. Only if the birth were prolonged and very difficult would the healers be called. They would perform the Healing Rite as they would over any sick person. Healers do not aid in a birth in any other way, such as turning the baby, for instance. The !Kung believe that no one should touch the baby for fear of stretching it and deforming it. John Marshall was present when a Healing Rite was performed for a girl who had a very difficult, prolonged labor. The girl lived, the baby was stillborn. That was the one occasion any of us knew about when a healer was called. My impression is that healers are seldom called. !Kung women generally give birth alone and relatively easily.

At her first giving birth, the girl learns how to handle the umbilical cord and the placenta and, as the women told me, she must learn not to scream or cry out in pain. They mimed for me the gestures they make, squirming, wincing, grimacing, in their effort to bear the pain in silence. If they cried out, the women said, they would die. There may actually be some old lore about women dying in childbirth if they scream, but I think no one takes this lore literally now. The saying acts as a figure of speech. It indicates that a social rule or ideal is held to be very important or admirable, and that failure to conform is reprehensible. It is admirable that a woman demonstrates the courage, willingness, and strength to bear the pain in childbirth. The !Kung admire such a woman. They would laugh at a woman who failed to do so.

When a woman's labor begins, she goes to a discreet distance from the encampment where she is hidden from view behind bushes. She must be well away from men and boys, who must not see the childbirth because they must not see the placenta. Young girls are also excluded from seeing a birth, lest witnessing a birth would cause them to fear and dread childbirth unduly.

A girl in first childbirth takes off her ornaments. She does so, the women explained, because she is afraid. She wonders if she may fail in some way, and she wants to be free from the ornaments. If the birth goes well, she would not be so afraid next time and would not feel the need to take off her ornaments. No one explained why she should feel the need to take off her ornaments. I remembered that ornaments are taken off a sick child, but the significance of removing ornaments was never made clear. The women said that some women take off their earrings, head ornaments, and necklaces at any birth, not just the first, because the ornaments jingling might frighten the new baby. That was a reason I could understand.

The woman in labor preparing for the birth gathers an armload of tall grass and lays it on the ground. Most of the women I talked with said they sit on the grass with their legs spread wide apart. One spoke of squatting. The baby may lie on the grass but must not touch the ground. If he did he would not flourish; he would be thin. The woman cuts the umbilical cord with a small stick, any stick she picks up, split so that it has a sharp edge. She leaves about seven inches of the cord protruding from the baby's navel. The mother wipes the baby with soft //galli grass, which she has brought with her. Whereas the baby must not touch the ground, the uterine fluid and blood are allowed to flow freely through the grass onto the ground. !Kung believe that at the instant the uterine fluid touches the ground, the force called n!ow is produced in the baby, the force that has to do with weather—with rain and seasonal dryness and cold. (See chap. 7.)

The woman's next act is to dispose of the placenta in such a way that no man could ever see it or inadvertently step on it. Most of the women I talked with said they buried the placenta under a bush close to the stalk using a stick they pick up for the digging, not a digging stick. They must not contaminate their digging sticks. The bush must be marked. The stick the woman used is left under it, and a bundle of grass is wedged into the branches. This warns men not to go close to the bush. The placenta is a n/um thing, exceedingly dangerous to men. If a man were to see or touch a placenta, he would become thin, weak, and excessively tired. His skill and ability to hunt would be nullified.

The grass the woman has been sitting on, though it may have a trace of blood and uterine fluid on it, is not dangerous to men. No special care is taken in disposing of it.

When a woman has attended to all the necessities, she nurses her baby briefly, then carries him back to the encampment.

To my disappointment, I did not witness the birth of a child. In the whole time in the field, only one child was born where we were present. The child was !Ungka Norna, the daughter of !U and ≠Toma of Band 1. She was named for her father's sister, !Ungka, and for me. The !Kung do not have the L sound in their language, so Lorna became Norna. Although she had the two names, she was ordinarily called Norna, and is to this day. Although I had asked !U to allow me to go with her when she gave birth, she had not agreed to do so, and did not let me know when the time came. Her labor began during the morning. John was filming the making of a carrying net at Gao Feet's fire about ten feet away. !U told no one and lay quietly by her fire giving no sign of her labor. About ten o'clock she slipped away into the bushes alone. No one took special notice. Half an hour later she walked back smiling radiantly, carrying a tiny pink baby in her arms. John was breathless with surprise and excitement, and so was I when he ran to tell me.

!U remained perfectly calm. First she nursed the baby for a few minutes. Then she asked for someone to bring water, and she washed the blood off her legs with a sponge of grass. She then lay down under a kaross in her shelter and gave her attention to nursing the baby. Her young son, /Gaishay, leaned over the baby, touched her gently, and then began to cook a root for his mother. ≠Toma, the father, sat on his heels nearby and smiled. He would go hunting the next day to get meat for a broth for !U. Broth makes a mother's milk flow well. The great concern is the mother's milk.

A newborn !Kung baby is like a little marsupial held to the mother's body, skin to skin, the breast at the baby's mouth ready for nursing at any time. All day !U lay with Norna held close and warm at her side, covered from the sun and the September winds by !U's kaross. The two dozed and wakened through the afternoon in serenity. Norna did not cry at all. When she said "ah," !U put her nipple into her mouth and Norna would nurse a moment and sleep again. My thoughts turned to the contrast between the experience of a !Kung baby at birth and that of an American baby in a hospital, especially during the 1930s when my babies were born. The procedures in childbirth were less enlightened in the United States than they are today. In those days the mother would probably be under anesthesia. The newborn baby would be held by the heels upside down and slapped by the doctor, then bathed, dressed, put away alone in the nursery crib, and not nursed for hours.

!U spent the next three days resting beside her baby giving full attention to nursing. Her breasts became full and dripping. !U's sister brought her food. On the fifth day after the birth, !U went gathering with her sister and cousin, the baby tied to her side in her soft little leather sling. If the umbilical cord bleeds at the time of birth or later and the bleeding does not stop with gentle pressure, the mother stops the bleeding by making a paste of very finely scraped dry wood well moistened with her saliva. She scrapes little slivers off her digging stick or fire paddle, pestle, or a wooden bowl—any wood that has been used a long time and is thoroughly dry. She plasters the bleeding place of the cord with this paste. Wood from a growing bush or tree would not be used; it would not stop the bleeding, the women said. This is a pharmaceutical procedure, not a ritual.

Norna's cord did not bleed. On the third day, dried and shriveled, it fell off. !U placed it in a small leather bag, which she had made for the purpose. The cord is kept as a safeguard for the child's health. !U would keep the cord carefully among her possessions until Norna was about four years old. Then the cord would be ritually disposed of.

AVOIDANCES AFTER CHILDBIRTH

After a birth, certain avoidances are observed for the protection of the baby, his parents, and other children of the family. The !Kung say that the father and mother must abstain from sexual intercourse for three moons. !U told me she took additional precaution and abstained for five moons. The !Kung believe that if they did not practice this restraint, the mother's milk would be deficient, or might stop altogether, and the baby would get thin and might die. The !Kung did not make a connection between pregnancy and lactation when they talked of this matter. In other words, they did not say that intercourse might result in pregnancy, and because of pregnancy the milk might stop. Their belief is that intercourse per se would endanger the mother's lactation.

Avoidances are observed involving the gathering of plant foods and cooking. These avoidances are observed only after the birth of the first boy and the first girl. Even if the first child dies, the avoidance is not required again for the next baby of the same sex. After the birth of a first boy or first girl, the mother and the father of the baby and other children of these parents, if any, avoid eating any plant food the mother gathers. The mother is not restricted from gathering food; she gathers with the other women and does her share of the work, but she must give what she gathers to an older woman and receive in return plant food that woman has gathered. If the mother of the new baby is living with her own mother, the latter would ordinarily be the woman with whom she would make the exchange of plant food, but no particular relationships are required in this avoidance. If this avoidance were not observed, the father, the mother, the newborn baby, and the other children would get thin.

The food gathered by the new mother may be eaten only by men and women in middle life or older; it must be strictly avoided by the young, especially young girls. The !Kung neglected to say and I neglected to ask, but I assume the !Kung believe that if the young ate this food, they too, as well as the family of the newborn, would get thin.

Another avoidance, observed after the birth of a first boy or first girl, requires that the mother does not cook. As to her fire, she may fetch wood, build her family fire, be beside it, handle it freely, but she must not cook on it, nor must anyone else cook on her fire. Ordinarily in this situation, the husband cooks for the family on a cooking fire that he builds at a little distance from the family fire. Or if there are children old enough, they may cook for themselves on the cooking fire. Alternatively, the father of the newborn baby may cook on the fires of relatives or a relative could cook for the family. The cooking avoidance is observed for three or four months. The penalty for failing to observe it is the same as for the gathering avoidance—the family of the newborn and the newborn would get thin. Remembering that a pregnant woman must not eat from the pot of an unrelated person, I asked if the avoidance strictly required that only related persons should cook for the family of the newborn baby. !U did not answer the question directly, but she stated that only a related person would cook for them. Bushmen are not kindly, she claimed; they are "far-hearted."

This avoidance of cooking applies in a special way to meat. The family of the newborn baby may accept meat in the meat distribution or as a gift from persons in any relationship to the parents, but the meat must be raw. The father of the newborn should cook it himself. This avoidance protects the newborn from having diarrhea.

Meat cooked by visitors must be strictly avoided by the woman and her family. Just as the women had advised me to avoid redwing partridge cooked on coals or in ashes, at this point they earnestly advised me about my daughter. When she had children of her own she must not disregard the avoidance of eating meat cooked by visitors. I must teach her to obey the law.

This particular avoidance of the mother's eating meat cooked by visitors was unusual, even unique, as far as I know, in that the necessity for it could be removed by a ritualistic practice other than the Tshoa Rite. While Norna was still a new baby, visitors came to Gautscha. They had a duiker the man had killed. !U knew the people and went to visit them at their fire while they were cooking the duiker in a pot. The man scraped off some of the carbon that builds up on the outside of a pot set always on an open fire. He then rubbed his hands on his armpits to take sweat from them and mixed the sweat with the carbon from the pot. This mixture he rubbed on Norna's head and stomach. With the baby thus protected from diarrhea, !U could enjoy a piece of duiker meat with her friends. The man was a healer. Presumably he was taking his n/um onto his hands, for a healer's n/um exudes with sweat. I do not know whether a man who was not a healer could provide the protective substance with his sweat and the carbon without a healer's n/um.

The avoidance that I have been describing should be observed, !U said, until the baby can laugh; someone else said, until the baby begins to say "ba, ba" (father, father) and *"tai, tai"* (mother, mother). ≠Toma remarked that the first word !Kung children say is "ba." They think a baby begins to laugh and to say "ba, ba" at about five months old.

When the time comes for the woman to stop practicing these avoidances, an older woman performs the Tshoa Rite with her. They tshoa whatever plant foods they can gather at the time. The Tshoa Rite absolves the mother and her family from the avoidance of eating the plant foods she gathers and absolves her from the avoidance of cooking. The baby's age frees her from avoiding presents of meat that are not raw and meat cooked by visitors.

One more avoidance associated with women at the time of childbirth came to my attention. I had not known to ask about it, but I heard that a woman with a newborn baby must not step over her husband's legs. These people use no stools, they always sit on the ground. It would be usual for a man to sit by his fire with his legs stretched out and for his wife to step over them, if it were convenient to do so, as she moved around the fire. When I asked the women about this avoidance, I was surprised by the vehemence of their replies. Of course, a woman must not step over her husband's legs. Only a mad woman would do that. It would make the man so thin and weak and tired he would be unable to walk, to say nothing of hunting. I must warn my daughter and tell her never, never to do such a thing.

Protection of the Child

The Umbilical Cord

For the protection of the child, the umbilical cord must be carefully kept for three to four years. !U explained that this was a very old custom, so old that no one knows anymore why it must be observed. They know, however, it is very important in safeguarding the child.

!Kung women make little leather bags decorated with beads in which to keep the cords. They wear the bags as ornaments hung from thongs around their necks.

When the mother thinks the child is old enough, at about four, she and the child dispose of the cord in a little rite. The child must be old enough to obey instructions. The mother gives the cord to the child, and together they look for a bush suitable in size, a little distance from the encampment where people are not apt to walk. The child must be able to crawl under the bush for he must bury the cord against the stem in a little hollow, or stuff it well away among the stalks where it will stay safely. It must not be stepped on or blow away. If harm should come to the cord, harm would come to the child. Before he places the cord under the bush, he should lay it on the ground and jump over it.

My talking with the women about the cord put the idea into //Kushay's mind that Little ≠Gao, her son, was old enough to bury his cord. She said she would show me what they do. It was as unceremonious a little rite as could be imagined. //Kushay took the cord out of its bag and handed it to Little ≠Gao. She picked up two axes, took Little ≠Gao by the hand, and we three walked away from the encampment. About fifty or sixty feet away, //Kushay pointed out a bush to Little ≠Gao. Disregarding the detail of jumping over the cord, the boy crawled under the bush and, without any apparent concern for carefully hiding the cord, he stuck it among some twigs at the base of the bush. It was not hidden, but it was very inconspicuous—like a twig itself. Little ≠Gao then asked his mother for a drink of milk. Both standing, she leaned over and he had his drink from her breast. Then I found what the axes were for. The two had planned to gather wood, and, each carrying an axe, they set forth.

Washing in New Rain

In !Kung belief, a baby must be carefully covered and protected from rain until a rite has been performed for him. The !Kung say that if rain were to touch the baby before he had been ritually prepared, he might die. The rite is called "Washing in New Rain." It ritually introduces both rain and food to the baby.

Rain is dangerous to a new baby, but not because rain is believed to have harmful qualities such as the sun's. The sun, the !Kung say, is death-giving. They do not know its function in plant growth and believe it only dries up the vegetation and the people. Rain by contrast is life-giving. It provides water to drink and makes plants grow—the food plants on which their lives depend directly and the vegetation that nourishes the game. The !Kung praise the rain and explain that a baby must be protected from it not because it is itself harmful but because the rain is "strong." The !Kung say that in this rite the rain is "shown" (introduced) to the baby. Food is also "shown" to the baby. The baby does not know the world, he has not eaten adult food, so it must be "shown" to him as food is "shown" in the Tshoa Rite. In performing the rain rite, people say they tshoa the baby.

The rain rite is performed when the baby is old enough to say "ba, ba." A baby born during the rainy season (a variable season of about three months) would not be old enough to be washed that season: the parents would wait until the next year's rains began. They need not perform the rite during the first rains, but would do so early in the season. Indeed the earliest rains of the season, the "little rains," might not provide enough rainwater for the bathing. Meanwhile they must cover the baby very carefully when rain is falling so that not a drop touches him.

A vitally important ritual requirement is that the rainwater used for the bath must not have touched the earth. Water from the water hole must not be used. When five months old, Norna was washed in new rain in Tsho/ana. ≠Toma borrowed a good-sized piece of canvas from our camp supplies and tied it to the branches of a tree so that it formed an effective receptacle to catch the rain. He could have rigged a kaross in the same way, but he preferred that our canvas should get soaking wet rather than his kaross.

A second ritual requirement is that some food should be boiled in the rainwater to introduce the baby to food other than mother's milk. Any plant food or meat may be used in this rite. ≠Toma's family had kudu meat on hand when they decided to wash Norna. As the rite was described to me, when the meat had boiled for a time, the participants took it out and ate it while they waited for the broth to cool. In many rites, eating is a part of the ritual, but in this one the eating is incidental.

If the !gun!a of the baby, the person the baby is named for, is present, he or she must wash the baby. Otherwise, some relative, man or woman, will wash him. The washing is believed to establish or enhance a bond of affection between the child and the person who washes him. The !Kung told me that it is crucial that the parents not perform the act of washing. They spoke especially about the mother. If she washed the baby, they said, the baby would love only her. Such exclusive affection would restrict affectionate responses from other relatives, and the child, as he grew up, might not have the broad base of warm, supportive relationships that the !Kung so want for their children.

When Norna was washed, her !gun!a was not present. Only two families of Band 1 were in the encampment at the time, the family of ≠Toma and !U, Norna's parents, and that of /Qui and //Kushay. /Qui and //Kushay together washed Norna, I was told. We were away, and to my disappointment I did not see the washing.

I tried to learn what concepts lay behind the belief that the rainwater must not touch the earth, remembering that the feet of a bride and a menstruating girl also must not touch the earth. "It is natural that the rainwater must not touch the earth," the !Kung said. The Old Old People had not told them why.

The Milk Teeth

The early appearance of the permanent teeth is considered to be the good state, the desirable state, as early walking is desirable. If the permanent teeth appear early, the child is said to ≠*gani a !gu,* to give honor to his name; if the teeth appear late, he is said to *//ghui a !gu,* to derogate his name.

When a child loses his milk teeth, !Kung belief requires that he must take each tooth as it falls out and push it into the ground among the roots of /gam grass, saying as he does so, "My tooth come soon." In this little rite the grass is critical. It must be /gam grass, the grass that is the first to put forth green shoots in the spring. Before a drop of rain has fallen, obeying an inner signal, tiny green shoots appear among the dry, golden stems. As the new /gam grass comes early, so the new teeth should come early, the !Kung say.

A Child's Haircut

In !Kung culture much attention is given to haircutting. The !Kung all wear their hair short. Women wear theirs cropped close to their heads with a few long strands left from which to hang ornaments. Men often shave their heads leaving tufts or stripes in a variety of designs. The designs are not related to status in society, to show the married or the unmarried status, or to show that a man is a healer, for instance; the hairstyles are designed for adornment. The dull, gray-brown leather garments of the !Kung have no variety; only in their haircuts and ornaments can the !Kung obtain a bit of individuality and adornment. Relatives and friends cut each others' hair in friendly sociability.

Hair is also cut ritually. The design of the haircut is not a factor in this ritual practice. The head is shaved, or partially shaved, and the hair that is cut off is given protection. The purpose in protecting the hair is to prevent sickness, to protect health. The Old Old People had not explained how cutting off one's hair prevents sickness, but the concept is firmly established in !Kung culture.

Hair is cut ritually in four situations. A healer might shave the top of a person's head and apply medicine in a case of severe illness. A boy's hair is cut as a part of the Tshoma Rite (see chap. 10). The two other ritual haircuts are a haircut given girls in their teens to protect their health, and a baby's first haircut.

When a child takes his first steps alone he is old enough for his first haircut, which I consider to be a little rite of passage. As is usual in !Kung affairs, this rite is performed without pomp but with a little more circumstance than attends the other rites of childhood. The time is planned; a relative is especially chosen and invited to perform the rite. He or she may make a long journey to attend. The relative brings a gift to the child. In addition to protecting the child from sickness, the rite is believed to have a twofold beneficence. It introduces the child to a larger world than he has yet known and again "shows" the child adult food. This rite is believed also to insure and enhance the love that the relatives feel for the child. The rite is performed several times in early childhood as the child's hair grows. Each time different relatives are invited to perform it.

The rite involves a ritual washing as well as the haircutting. Ideally, the first time the rite is performed, the !gun!a should wash the child. If the !gun!a were dead or unable to be present, another relative would be invited to take his or her place—a grandparent or an aunt or uncle. The parents must not give the child this bath. As the rite is repeated, the relatives asked to perform it should be first from one side of the family, then from the other, so that both the father's and the mother's relatives are involved in the child's well-being and their love for the child is ritually captured. Thus a supportive web of relationships is woven for the child.

Should a child fall ill after the rite has been performed or even have a slight ailment, such as the commonly seen inflammation of the eyelids, or even if the child should cry very hard during the haircutting, that would be a sign that the relative who had performed the rite was somehow not suitable and next time a relative from the other side of the family would be asked.

The haircutting is actually a head shaving. Only a tuft of hair is left over the fontanelle to protect it. Though the haircutting is as important an element in the rite as the washing, anyone may perform this act—anyone, that is, who is adroit at shaving the head of a squirming child. The !Kung say that they invariably ask a woman to do this because women are better at haircutting or head shaving than men, not because femaleness has ritual significance in this instance. The mother herself, who is restricted from washing the child, may be the one to shave him.

A new fire is built at a little distance from the cluster of family fires that form the encampment. This fire may be lighted with a brand from any family fire. The fire must be new and must be used for nothing else; when the rite is finished, the fire is allowed to burn itself out.

Fresh water must be brought directly from the water hole and set to boil in a pot. Some food, either plant food or meat, is added to make a broth. Tsi is the preferred food for this rite. Tsi is especially associated in !Kung minds with pleasure of taste and satisfaction of hunger. But tsi is a seasonal food and is extremely localized. More often than not, it is not available so other foods are used, such as mangetti nuts. ≠Toma spoke of using guinea fowl and korhaan on two recent occasions when the rite was performed. Other meat could be used.

Norna was ten months old when she began to walk. Among all the !Kung I know, Norna is the only one whose age I knew exactly. Norna had eight little teeth at ten months, four upper and four lower. She had been sitting up alone for some time. !Kung babies are encouraged to sit up and to walk at an early age. Adults hold the babies in a standing position and pass them from one person to another. The babies make tentative little steps to everyone's pride and pleasure. Norna was quite accustomed to play that game and had for some time been pulling herself up to her feet holding on to someone. (She did not go through a creeping stage.) Suddenly one day she stood straight up alone. She did not know how to sit down, she could only plop, but that did not dismay her. She would stand up again and soon was taking herself to where she wanted to be with little steps. This was the stage when the haircutting rite should be performed.

Norna's !gun!a, ≠Toma's sister, !Ungka, had come from /Gam especially for the rite. The others present were !Ungka's little daughter, Sa≠gai; Norna's mother, !U; Old Gaú's daughter, !Ungka; and little N!ai, Norna's cousin. Four boys watched from under a bush. Men are not excluded, but the men were all away hunting, except one who sat nearby working on his arrows. He paid no attention to the rite.

To begin, Norna's !gun!a placed an exceedingly fine necklace of ostrich-eggshell beads around Norna's neck. It was an old necklace of many strands of creamy white beads, a magnificent gift from !Ungka to her !guma. Another gift from !Ungka was a bag of tsi seeds that she had saved for the occasion from the previous season.

While !U fetched wood and N!ai fetched water, the two !Ungkas roasted the tsi in the coals and hot ashes of one of the family fires. They then cracked the hard shells, pounded the kernels in a mortar, and finally set them to boil in a pot on the ritual fire. The tsi seeds were cooked to a porridge.

When the tsi porridge had cooled, !U spread a kaross on the ground. She took off Norna's fine necklace and her few other ornaments and held the naked child in a standing position on the kaross while !Ungka smeared the child all over with the tsi porridge—her head and face, her entire little body, behind her ears, between her toes and fingers. Then using a downward motion, !Ungka began to rub the tsi off, letting the material fall onto the kaross. The !Kung call this material the child's "dirt." Norna expressed her enjoyment of the rubbing with smiles and little crows of pleasure. When the rubbing was finished, !U and !Ungka carefully gathered up every crumb of the "dirt" and placed it in a little leather bag that !U had made for the purpose. Like the little bags made for the umbilical cord, the bag was decorated with beads and provided with a cord to be hung around the neck of the wearer. According to the tradition of the rite, the bag was first hung on Norna's neck. She wore it for two or three days and then !Ungka took it to wear as an ornament for an indefinite time. This, the !Kung told us, insures that the !gun!a's love for the child will not fail. Bags of "dirt" eventually lose their specific significance and are passed along in the stream of gift-giving like any ornament.

After the washing, !U carefully and slowly shaved Norna's head with a razor blade we had given her. Norna was a serene baby; she endured the shaving with equanimity. When the shaving was finished, !U gathered up every strand and put the hair into another small bag.

She would keep the hair until Norna was about three years old. Then another rite would be performed. At that age a child's hair is buried in a hole under a tree or under /gam grass. If the mother were lactating at that time, she would squeeze some milk on the hair before giving it to the child to bury. If the mother is not lactating, nothing is substituted. One group of women told me they might wait until they were lactating again before burying the hair. No one could explain the significance of the milk. The mother may dig the hole close to the tree trunk or under the grass roots, but the child himself must place the hair in the hole and cover it up. The purpose of burying the hair is to protect it from being blown away or burned. The !Kung say that if the hair should blow away, the child's wits would blow away and he would not be able to find his way in the bush. If the hair should be burned, the child would die— an echo again of a belief in sorcery, I thought.

As a last ritual act in Norna's rite, !Ungka took a pinch of "dirt" from the little "dirt" bag, walked to her sleeping place and sprinkled the "dirt" on the pile of soft grass that was her bed. By this act a !gun!a's love for his or her namesake is enhanced as well as insured.

The Burning Arch

The Rite of the Burning Arch is performed for children to cure an infection of the mouth called /atata. The !Kung said that the infection produces blisters and excessive saliva. The tongue becomes very red and looks as though it had been burned. The !Kung believe that the infection is caused by the introduction of metal, any metal, into the child's mouth. If the child should put a metal spoon in his mouth, or if he should lick some metal implement, such as an adze blade, for instance, he might contract the infection. People say they must watch their children and prevent them from putting metal in their mouths. If the symptoms appear, people perform the Rite of the Burning Arch to cure the infection.

The rite was performed for Norna on one occasion when we were present. The relationship between the child and the persons who perform the rite is not ritually restricted as it is in many rites; the mother or anyone else may perform it. !Ungka and //Kushay, daughters of Old Gaú, were with !U and Norna one cold July afternoon when the women decided the rite was necessary and immediately made preparations.

First the women powdered themselves with a sweet smelling powder called *!gai*, especially under their arms and around their necks. !Ungka then went off to find the necessary wood—two saplings about seven feet tall. She dug little holes about three feet apart, tamped the saplings into them, bent their tops, and wove their twigs together so that they formed an arch. This was exactly the same process that she would use in starting to build the frame of a shelter, and she called the arch the /atata shelter, the /atata tshu. The arch faced roughly northwest and southeast. On the top of the arch !Ungka laid a bundle of dry grass. When all was ready, !Ungka took Norna in her arms. //Kushay brought a brand from a nearby fire—no special fire is required. She set the bundle of grass aflame, and while it burned !Ungka ran under it with the baby in her arms. She ran through four times, from east to west and from west to east, from south to north and from north to south. That was the rite.

As always my questioning about the significance of the ritual elements was tantalizing if not downright frustrating. As usual it was clear that the people no longer know the origins of the beliefs involved or the reasons for them. I was interested by the concept that metal, so highly valued in arrowpoints, knives, assagais, and adze blades, could have a disease-giving quality, but only to children.

The !Kung told us their grandfathers as young men had begun to make metal arrowpoints. Had the concept of the /atata disease come with the metal, I wondered, or was it perhaps part of a general fear of Bantu? I began my probing for the significance of the several elements of the rite by asking about the powder. I had seen women powder themselves countless times with sa. On this occasion, I expected to find that the powdering with !gai had some relation to the rite, but the powder was only used incidentally as a cosmetic. As to the background of the belief that metal causes the mouth disease in children and the significance of the burning arch and the running under it in four directions carrying the child, the women could tell me nothing. "It is our custom," they said as they had so many times before, and that was that.

Norna's mouth infection healed itself in a day or so. Daily life went on in all its usual wonders.

Ritual Healing Dance. It surpasses all other !Kung rites in frequency of performance and intensity. Led by the healers, the group acts together for the mutual good. Here, the dance group is viewed from the top of the expedition truck as it circles around the seated group of mostly women and children.

While Old !Naishi dances in the center, /Gunda holds a stick over people's heads, a characteristic gesture of medicine men. The Ritual Healing Dance is an activity in !Kung life that draws people together in groups of considerable size. Men, women, and children all participate.

Ngani in a trance, attended by /Qui Neanderthal, who is in a partial trance. Trance is a special feature of the Healing Dances, and it is believed to allow the healers to contact the gods on behalf of those who are ill.

/Gunda in a trance, with the dance group closed in around him.

/Gunda in a trance, attended by Gao Feet (Gao Medicine).

Medicine men in a trance. While in a trance, the healers confront //Gauwa and the //gauwasi, who are sent by the great god when he decides to inflict sickness and death. With yells and shouts, the healers drive the death bringers away. Here, other healers care for those in a trance. Note the main group resting under the tree during a pause in the dancing.

A group of women, broken off from the main group, have begun singing and clapping in their own dance circle. Here, two women dance vigorously.

The Healing Rite is very much a part of everyday life. The healers' n/um enables them to extract sickness. The !Kung believe that when a healer flutters his hands on a person, he draws the sickness out. Here, /Ti!kay cures a very sick girl.

The Tshoa Rite occurs on the transition of a young girl into womanhood and is marked by the reintroduction of a variety of foods that had been avoided during this time. Here, N/aoka (on the left) performs the ceremony for her daughter, Baú, while (left to right) N!ai and Ghia look on.

PART III

RITES FOR SUBSISTENCE

6 HUNTING RITES

Among the !Kung, in the vital endeavor to procure food, hunting is the province of men. The gathering of the wild plant foods is the province of women. All men are expected to hunt; all women are expected to gather. The reader will remember that up to 1959 these people depended entirely on hunting and gathering. They had no agriculture, no gardens, no domesticated animals. Men are not excluded from gathering. No social or ritual concepts restrict them. They may and they do gather by themselves, or with the women, and are always with the women on their long trips to the mangetti forest or to the area where the tsi beans grow, to help gather and to carry the heavy loads. By contrast, !Kung women never hunt. They may pick up small creatures, a tortoise, a lizard, a snake, for instance—they say they "gather" the creatures—but !Kung women are totally excluded from hunting.

In another contrast, several rituals are performed that relate to the hunt, but no rituals are performed for gathering plant foods. Previous accounts describe avoidances with respect to eating plant foods and the plant foods that are an element in several rituals, but no rituals are directed to gathering per se. I can only think that the lack of such ritual means the !Kung do not believe that chance or luck are factors in gathering. The people know where the plants grow, and they plan their lives around the predictable seasonal availability of the plants. Moreover, plants do not run away. As to the fertility of the food plants, the people know that the plants depend on rain, and they pray to the gods for rain.

Hunting is difficult and exceedingly uncertain in the Nyae Nyae region. In the difficulties and uncertainties, the !Kung look to the supernatural for help. They pray to the gods and, as they say, "talk" to the //gauwasi, the spirits of the dead, pleading for their help. They also practice various ritualistic procedures and avoidances to bring them success. The ritual procedures are directed to finding animals, to controlling the behavior of the animals during the hunt, to insuring the willingness, vigor, and skill of the hunters, and to insuring the effectiveness of the hunting equipment. The concepts found in many cultures—that animals have spirits that can be ritually addressed, that animals must be ritually appeased, or the killing atoned for—are lacking among the !Kung.

Aspects of the Hunt

The uncertainties, difficulties, and the hardships of !Kung hunting will be better understood if some relevant aspects of the hunt are described briefly. !Kung hunters set out from the encampment in voluntarily and informally arranged parties, usually of two to four men who like to hunt together. The parties may be larger, but in their terrain it is more advantageous for several parties to search for game in different directions than for a larger number of men to combine.

The principal game animals of the !Kung in the interior of the Nyae Nyae region are the great antelopes: eland, gemsbok, kudu, wildebeest, hartebeest, springbok. Ostrich, buffalo, and giraffe are also regularly hunted. These animals are not numerous. The large herds that we have seen and read about in other parts of Africa do not exist in the Nyae Nyae area. The small herds and single animals range widely. They do not have migration routes through the area. They are not closely dependent on the few water holes. Lions must come to water regularly, but the big game animals can go for long periods without drinking, and they move anywhere in the vast, arid land. To find them is the great endeavor of !Kung hunters. The hunters set out to look for spoor and follow any that is fresh enough to give them hope, and, if all goes well, they catch up with the animal and make their kill. They gladly take smaller game if they happen upon it—warthog, duiker, porcupine, springhare, paouw, leguaan, tortoise, python, and even honey badger, which some people eschew because of the smell of the meat. However, the hunters give their purposeful hunting time to the search for the big animals that feed the whole band of people who live together. The eyes of the girls, the wives, the mothers-in-law, the mothers, aunts, and grandmothers, and the eyes of the old men are all upon the strong virile hunters. "They must feed us," the people say, "they must bring us meat."

The most important rite in a !Kung boy's life is the Rite of First Kill. He must have killed a big game animal and had this rite performed before he may marry. A !Kung boy becomes a hunter gradually. He plays with toy bows and arrows in childhood, practices shooting birds, beetles, and other small creatures at an early age, and begins to go on short hunts with his father when the father feels he is ready. !Kung fathers also conduct hunting schools, taking their boys hunting in groups to teach them and let them practice stalking, shooting, and tracking together. The boys watch the men and imitate them. When they are big enough and strong enough, they join the men in their serious hunting parties.

A hunting party that sets out from the encampment in the morning may return the same day with game; or the men may return with nothing and set out again within a day or so; or a party may return after several days with game or with nothing.

Countless variables determine the men's plans and decisions, water being a very important variable. Typically, hunters search for a day or two before finding the fresh spoor of big game; they may follow the track for another day or so. When they find the animal and must stalk it, their utmost skill is challenged. The country is flat and open, covered with low grass, sparse bushes, and a few stunted trees. It provides little cover for the hunters, and their greatest difficulty is to approach near enough to shoot their little poisoned arrows, hardly larger than darts, into the animal. (Their range is about twenty yards.) One technique in the stalk is for one man or for two close together, one behind the other, to bend at the hips to make their backs look like an animal's back, to move forward when the animal lowers its head to graze, to remain perfectly still when the animal peers at them, and, when they are within range, to let fly the little arrows as swiftly as they can.

The impact of the little arrows and the tiny wounds they inflict do not kill the great game animals. It is the deadly poison smeared on the foreshaft behind the arrowpoint that kills. Powerful as the poison is, it can take days to kill the big game animals—perhaps two or three days for a kudu or a wildebeest, probably longer for an eland or giraffe. The hunters must track the animal until it dies.

The men follow at a discreet distance to avoid frightening the animal and driving it on. They track it with skills that challenge comprehension, knowing which minute signs are significant, concentrating their highly developed powers of observation on them. They follow, hoping that the arrow is well placed in the body and that the poison that has penetrated is sufficient to kill. They hope that the poison has not become weak and dry with age—"cold," they say. They hope that the animal will not run far. They hope that should it fall and die in the night, lions or hyenas or jackals will not devour it.

During the tracking stage, the men suffer the greatest hardships. They may sleep wherever night overtakes them. They do not carry karosses when they hunt, and they sleep uncovered on the ground by little fires. Desert nights can be bitterly cold. The men may have neither food nor water. They mind the discomforts and they mind being away from their people, and so, if it is feasible for them to return to the encampment to sleep, they do so. Sometimes the animal does not run far and is standing about nearby, sick from the poison but not yet dying. Sometimes the animal has traveled in a great circle and the men are near their starting point. In any case, the hunters return to their encampment if they can, often walking a considerable distance to do so, and in the morning going back to take up the spoor where they left it. When the animal is so weakened by the poison that the hunters' approach will not drive it on, the hunters close in on it. If it is still living, they give it the coup de grâce with their assagais.

The last stage of a hunt is the skinning and cutting up of the animal and bringing the meat and the people together. If the hunters cannot carry all the meat, one may return to the encampment and enlist several men to help carry it. Or, if the animal is very large and the problem of water can be solved, the whole group who are living together may pick up their belongings and move to the meat.

The Opposition Between Hunting and Femaleness

A particular set of avoidances is regarded by the !Kung to be of special importance in influencing the success of the hunters. The practices I refer to are those required by the !Kung's perceived opposition between femaleness and hunting. Femaleness "spoils" hunting, according to !Kung belief—at least certain aspects of femaleness are believed to do so. In another metaphor, the !Kung say femaleness is "poisonous" or is "poisonous death" to hunting. Although I strove to understand precisely how the !Kung perceive this concept, I am still uncertain about some aspects of it. One thing is clear, however: the !Kung do not conceive of any aspects of femaleness, even menstrual blood, as being unclean and defiling, a concept held in many cultures. The word the !Kung use in speaking of femaleness is "strong." It would seem that femaleness has potency that is believed to somehow nullify the potency of hunters and the effectiveness of hunting equipment.

As I understand it, the female potency is believed to be especially strong in certain specific manifestations of female sexuality and fertility—in the sexual act, in menstrual blood, and in women's milk. These are the manifestations of femaleness most assiduously avoided by the hunters. But femaleness in a more general sense also "spoils" hunting. Women must not be present at the performance of the important hunting rites. I, as a woman, was asked by ≠Toma, my mentor, not to try to learn about hunting by talking to young hunters and not to talk about sex with any men. I was to talk about sex only with women and about hunting only with old men. It was thought that in my ignorance I would be especially liable to violate the rules and I would be a danger to the success of the hunters. Actually, although they were not older than early middle age, and although ≠Toma jokingly protested that they should not do so, ≠Toma, Gao Feet, and /Qui Neanderthal did join my talks with the older men.

We honored that rule in the breach, but not the rule that forbade my talking about sex with men. We were all careful about that.

Women should not touch hunting equipment, especially arrows. The equipment would be rendered useless, the poison on the arrows would weaken. In this one avoidance practice, should there be any infraction, the men have a remedy. A certain root, called *gaogaona,* may be rubbed over the men's hands and arms as they handle the weapons. It negates the female influence.

I was glad to know this. One day Little ≠Gao, then about five years old we guessed, was displeased with me for holding him against his will while I applied ointment to his inflamed eyelids. Once released, he ran to get his father's assagai and took after me, holding the weapon in the throwing position exactly as he had seen his father hold it. His mother did not hesitate to grab it from him. Fortunately, no harm had come to me, and the female touch on the assagai could be negated.

The night before the hunt, a man should avoid having intercourse with his wife. The !Kung believe that a man's strength can be drained by having intercourse too frequently. Particularly before a hunt, he must conserve his strength by abstinence. Furthermore, the abstinence places the man squarely on the side of maleness in the hunting-female opposition.

The front apron that covers the women's genitals is a symbol of female sexuality. A man should not touch the apron, and, in a strictly observed avoidance, he must not say aloud the word for front apron. If a man said the word, the meat of the animal he killed would taste very bad and rot quickly. If he touched the apron, he would become lazy and loll about in the camp instead of setting out to hunt—which is totally unacceptable social behavior for men in hunting age.

Women's buttocks as well as front aprons are strongly associated with sex. In sexual intercourse among the !Kung, the man's position is usually at the back of the woman. Buttocks are kept as modestly covered as the woman's genitals. John, my son, told me of a little episode that illustrated the belief about femaleness spoiling hunting. One late afternoon when a returning hunting party was approaching the camp, Khuan//a, a beautiful girl who was, as John said, a tease, ran to meet the men. She danced a few steps before them in exuberant greeting. As she turned a breeze caught her back apron and flipped it up. John says she deliberately assisted the breeze. The men saw her buttocks. John says they later talked and laughed about being sexually aroused. Next morning when they tracked the wildebeest they had shot, they found it had been totally devoured by hyenas, and they attributed this misfortune to their having seen Khuan//a's buttocks.

When a man has shot an animal and is waiting for the arrow poison to work, he may return to his camp at night and resume tracking the animal the next day. He avoids intercourse. If his wife has a baby and is lactating, the hunter must not touch his wife or his baby. He must take special care not to let the milk touch him. Mother's milk is extremely potent in negating hunting strengths. The very smell of the milk weakens the poison on the arrow.

Female potency is especially strong in menstrual blood. Hunters must strictly avoid saying the word for menstruation. If young hunters are sitting by a family fire when a menstruating woman is present, she must protect them by burning slivers of sha sha in the fire.

A hunter is believed to be at a disadvantage if he hunts while his wife is menstruating. Men do hunt under this circumstance, but other hunters prefer not to have them in their hunting parties. Misfortune is apt to follow them. If a man misses his shot or loses the spoor of the animal he is tracking, or if an accident occurs, this is attributed to his wife's menstruation. We were told of a man being killed by an elephant. Whereas he knew he should not engage in such a dangerous hunt when his wife was menstruating, he did so and was killed.

Before a Hunt

On the morning of a hunt, before the men start out, they may resort to several practices to bring them luck. These are not required ritual practices but are performed by choice if the men are seeking to change bad luck to good. I have no data on the frequency of these practices.

Foremost among their practices is prayer. The men told me what they would say before they set out and at any time during the hunt. I noticed that the prayers most frequently asked for help in finding animals:

> You have created me and given me power to hunt.
> Why do you guide me the wrong way so that I see
> no animals?

> I wish to have good luck and see animals.
> Let me find a dead animal today.

> //Gauwa, help us that we find an animal.
> //Gauwa, help us.
> We are dying of hunger.

The wives of the hunters also pray for their husbands' success, and, as they said, ask //Gauwa to have pity and lead the hunters to find an animal to kill.

The !Kung believe that the substances in the healers' tortoise shells, being strong and salutary, can work for success in the hunt as well as in curing sickness. Before a hunt, the men may activate the medicine, as they do in the Healing Rite, by dropping a glowing coal into the tortoise shell. They let the smoke blow over them and inhale some of it through their mouths. A man may take some of the mixture on his finger and rub it onto his forehead and nose, and as /Qui told us, say something like, "Why do I not kill a gemsbok today? Send a gemsbok to me. Let me see a gemsbok." The men may sing the music of the Giraffe Song as they anoint themselves. The Giraffe Song is strong and may have a favorable influence on the hunt.

The roots of two plants are believed to have potency that is helpful to hunters, *mai* and *zau*. Neither of these plants was identified, and they are not to be confused with a plant and a tree of similar names, the fruit plant, mai (*Dichapetalum cymosum* [Hook.] Engl.) and the tree, zao (*Terminalia sericea* Burch.).

Both mai and zau are found only in the vicinity of Samangaigai. Both are rare. One of the most cherished gifts one man can give another is a zau or mai root. Both roots have strong n/um. They are used as curative medicines: zau cures sore eyes, headaches, and stomachaches; mai is rubbed on sore arms or legs. Their special potencies, however, are favorable to hunting.

A mai root is so strong it must be treated ritualistically before it is safe to use. Gao Feet had been given a root by his friend //Ao from Samangaigai. He showed me what they did when //Ao first gave the root. The men heated it in the fire and pressed it against Gao's belly. Gao sucked in his breath, arched himself over the root, and the men pulled his skin over around it to enfold it as best they could. The root was pressed onto the back of Gao's neck and into the small of his back and again Gao arched himself over it as much as he could. This procedure was repeated a second time. If they did not treat the root in this manner, a man receiving the root would have sharp burning pains in his neck and back. His back would break, and he would have to crawl on hands and knees. Once treated, the root was safe. Gao's little son (about four years old) wore it for several weeks as an ornament hanging from a thong around his neck.

When the hunters make use of the mai root's potency before a hunt, they may merely rub their hands over it and then rub their faces. Or, they may pound slivers of the root to a powder and rub the powder onto their foreheads and noses and take some of it into their mouths. If they happened to have a bit of marrow at hand, they would mix it with the powdered mai—as an adhesive, not as an additional ritualistic element. The root, the men said, is "made for hunting." It brings animals to them. After applying it, they will not go far before seeing an animal and, if the mai is at its full strength, the hunters will shoot the animal before the animal sees them.

Zau has the power to make a man aim accurately, to pull the bow strongly, and to shoot far. It also brings game to the hunters. We were told that in the Samangaigai area, the mai root is used as a curing medicine. It is powdered and rubbed into little incisions made over the places where the pain is or the sickness is thought to be. The Nyae Nyae people have no firsthand experience with mai's curing properties and said I must ask the Samangaigai people about it.

A hunter who has been having especially bad luck, for instance one who has lost two or three animals while tracking them after shooting, can seek to change his luck through a procedure that is rather seldom resorted to. I had the impression that the hunters thought it a bit too risky. A man asks a fellow hunter to help him. The men take the outside cocoon off a poison beetle larva and char it in the fire. The fellow hunter makes little incisions in his friend's arm and rubs the charred cocoon into them. The cocoon itself is not poisonous, but it has been in contact with the deadly poisonous larva and might have a speck of the larva clinging to it.

During a Hunt

While hunters are out on a hunt, they should avoid saying aloud the words for lion, leopard, and mamba. Avoiding these words lessens the threat of danger from these animals. Hunters avoid saying the word for wind (maa), so that the wind will not give the scent of the men to the animal. Instead, hunters use a respect word for wind, /doh.

While tracking an animal, the men may see a place where the animal has urinated. If so, they stick the end of a bow into the spot. This will prevent the animal from urinating freely. Urine washes out the poison.

If the hunters are waiting for an animal to die and return to their encampment to sleep, the hunter whose arrow is in the animal must behave in a certain way and observe several avoidances. If the animal is a big one—a giraffe, eland, gemsbok, kudu, or wildebeest, for instance—the hunter whose arrow is in the animal enters the encampment in a subdued manner. He does not speak but sits down in silence, his knees up, his arms around his knees, and his head bowed. People will know he has an arrow in a big animal, and they will not ask him about it. He especially avoids saying the name of the animal. If the name were uttered, the !Kung believe that the animal's tracks would fade away and the animal would never be found. If the hunter remains subdued and quiet, the animal will lie down and be quiet, and the poison will work.

A hunter must not touch his fire to add wood or stir it up, and he must not cook on his own fire. No one should stir up a hunter's fire. The fire flaring up and burning brightly would give the animal strength to run far.

Throughout the encampment people should avoid roasting tsi or mangetti nuts while the hunter has an arrow in an animal. Tsi and mangettis burst with a bang that might startle the animal wherever it might be. It would jump up as fast as the bang and run so far the hunter would never find it.

I have mentioned before that the hunter must not have intercourse with his wife while he has an arrow in an animal, and that he must assiduously avoid touching her apron, or touching her, their baby, or her milk if she is lactating. If he failed in this observance, his strength would seep away and he would become lazy.

In the morning when the hunter tells the fellow hunters about the hunt, especially if the animal he has shot is one of the great ones, a giraffe or eland, the hunter will make light of it saying he has shot some little thing. The fellow hunters will understand and, without saying the animal's name, will prepare to go with the hunter in a tracking party.

THE MEAT FIRE

If the hunters have been unsuccessful for a long time, say a month or more, they may decide to try to change their luck by performing the rite of the Meat Fire *(!kha da)*.

A Meat Fire must be made afresh with fire sticks, not lighted by brands from an old fire. We gave the !Kung gifts of matches, which they gladly used to light ordinary family fires, but we were told that matches must not be used for a Meat Fire or a new fire made ritually in a new encampment. Such fires must be made only with fire sticks, and they must be made by an old man, preferably the oldest in the group. The reason given was that an old man was born long ago and has "seen everything"; that is why an old man must make the fire.

A Meat Fire may be made at a distance from the band's encampment, but if the hunters' luck has been very bad and they want to avail themselves of the full potency of the rite, the whole band moves to a new encampment as they do when there has been a death.

We were told that in another way of performing the rite, the whole group would not move, but would extinguish their family fires, and after the rite of the Meat Fire was finished, make a new ritual fire in the encampment and light new family fires from it.

We observed a third, more simple way of performing the rite of the Meat Fire. The band did not move and the family fires were not extinguished, but the rite was performed in the midafternoon when the family fires are only smoldering before being built up for the evening meal and the night. Perhaps the fires were of less importance in that state.

Old Gaú, the oldest man in Band 1, performed the rite. While the people sat quietly in the encampment—the boys having been told not to rush about or make a noise—Old Gaú went away alone about a hundred feet from the encampment. He allowed me, woman though I am, to sit watching him from about twenty feet away.

Old Gaú had his fire sticks, a few small pieces of wood, and a few tsi beans. He sat down and quickly twirled his fire. When the first thread of smoke curled up from the ignited tinder, he began to "talk to the fire," through it addressing the spirits of the dead, the //gauwasi. The smoke would carry his words up to them. He used the respect word, /airisi, for the //gauwasi. This word pleases the //gauwasi, he said. Old Gaú prayed the same prayers the hunters utter at any time, pleading with the //gauwasi to feel pity and help the hunters:

Let me see an animal and shoot it.

Why are you not giving us good fortune?
What is wrong with the hunters that they do not find an animal to kill?
What is wrong with the women? Let the women find a dead animal.
Let a snake kill an animal, and let the hunters find it dead.

We are starving. This is a Meat Fire.
Let meat come for us to eat.

Old Gaú then roasted some tsi briefly in the fire and solemnly cracked and ate them. The old man's eating some plant food (any kind, we were told) cooked on the Meat Fire is an essential element of the rite. After sitting quietly looking at the fire a few moments more, Old Gaú extinguished the fire, spreading out the brands and coals, covering them with sand so that not a spark gleamed from them. He then returned to his place in the encampment.

A rite of the Meat Fire is simple to see, but the potency of it is very great in !Kung belief. The fire is so strong, the !Kung say, it is dangerous. A Meat Fire must never be made where anyone is ill. The strength of the sickness would increase in the presence of the strength of the fire, and the person would die.

The !Kung say that the //gauwasi take notice of a Meat Fire and feel honored by it. This makes them feel disposed toward the people so they may help the hunters.

"LET THE SUN BE BLIND"

If a hunter has success and brings back an animal from the first hunt after a Meat Fire, an additional rite is performed. It should be performed before any of the meat is eaten by the group. The old man who made the Meat Fire performs it, presumably at a family fire, since no mention was made of a ritual fire.

The old man cuts pieces of meat from the chest and foreleg of the animal, the meat called n/um meat *(n/um !kha),* and puts them in a pot to boil. He cuts another piece from the top of the foreleg and roasts it in the fire. This piece is called //Gauwa's meat. Together with the other old men in the band, if there are any present, the old man eats some of the roasted meat. He then washes the hunter with the broth in which the other meat has boiled, washing his face, arms, and chest. Next the old man pinches up a bit of skin on the hunter's forehead, over his nose, and, using a sharpened knife, makes several tiny, vertical cuts, very close together. He takes some blood from the cuts onto his fingers and throws the blood to the east, saying loudly, "Let the sun be blind." Again, he takes blood from the hunter's forehead and this time he throws it to the west, saying, "Let the sun that is setting be blind." He then drinks some of the broth. If there are other old men present, he shares the broth with them. He pours a little of it onto the fire, bringing the rite to an end.

The !Kung I spoke with said that the pouring of the broth into the fire makes the hunter feel strong and gives him willingness to go out to hunt, not to laze about in the encampment—but they cannot say why this is so, or why the certain pieces of meat are called //Gauwa meat and n/um meat, or why the old man cooks and eats a plant food when he makes a Meat Fire. They could, however, explain a little about the figure of speech about the sun, which they gravely did. They say "Let the sun be blind" not because they think of the sun as having eyes like a person and losing its sight, nor because they think that the sun caused the misfortune. They say this because the sun has shone on many days that were unfortunate days when the hunters failed. They say they mean, "Let the sun that has seen misfortune not look upon this day; let this day change to one of good fortune, let it be a meat day. There has been bad luck upon the hunters. Let the bad luck be removed."

THE RITE OF FIRST KILL

The Rite of First Kill is performed on the occasion of a boy's killing his first big meat animal of each sex, the first male and the first female. The animals must be large enough to provide meat for the group of people who live together—an antelope or a buffalo. Animals the size of warthogs, springbok, or duikers are not used.

I have called the rite "The Rite of First Kill." John Marshall made a film of it and entitled it "A Rite of Passage." The !Kung call the rite *n!amma ko !kha*, which means "to be cut with meat." The word "n!amma," translated "to be cut" in *A Bushman Dictionary* (Bleek 1956:486), means to have scarifications cut in one's skin.

The rite is one of passage. It is vitally important in !Kung culture. A boy may not marry until he has killed a big meat animal and had the rite performed. The rite marks the change of state from boyhood to that of hunter, which in !Kung culture is equated with manhood. The rite in every detail is directed to strengthening the boy's ability as a hunter.

The principal element in the rite is the scarification of the boy. The purpose of this is to put into the boy's body, through little cuts in his skin, substances that, in !Kung belief, will make him a successful hunter. The scarifications remain visible on the skin for a lifetime; they show that the man has been "cut with meat."

The scarifications are lines of little vertical incisions. The man who scarifies the boy pinches up a fold of skin in the proper place on the boy's body and makes the little vertical cuts in a horizontal line along the skin fold with a knife or a well-cleaned arrowpoint. Each cut is about an eighth of an inch long. The cuts are between a sixteenth to an eighth of an inch apart. They are deep enough to bleed a little. While they are bleeding, the man who is scarifying the boy rubs the required substances into them.

The rite we witnessed was performed at Gautscha for a boy named /Ti!kay who, we thought, was about thirteen. His father was Khan//a. Khan//a and /Ti!kay lived at Kai Kai. They were on their way to visit relatives and friends in Gautscha when they came upon a wildebeest and /Ti!kay succeeded in shooting it with an arrow his father had given him. They hurried on to Gautscha, and a party of hunters promptly set out with them to track the wildebeest. The shot had been effective, the poison had worked, and the wildebeest had traveled only about five miles after it was shot. The trackers found it before the predators did, an altogether satisfactory situation. The wildebeest was a female.

Once the meat was brought to the Gautscha encampment, preparations for the rite began. The meat belonged to /Ti!kay as owner of the arrow that killed the animal. He gave the meat to his relative, /Qui, who would make the final distribution of it. /Ti!kay must not touch the animal at any time or eat any of the meat. If he ate the meat, he would never succeed in the hunt again.

Women are excluded from the rite. The men need not remove themselves entirely out of sight of the women as they must do in Tshoma, but there must be a definite separation showing that women are not participating. I was allowed to watch the proceedings from a distance of about twenty feet. All the other women had gone gathering. Only mature men, men old enough to have three children, should attend the proceeding. Six of them did attend in a group near the fire.

Khan//a had built a special fire near /Qui's shelter and had lighted it, not formally with fire sticks but with a tuft of grass ignited at the coals of /Qui's fire. He brought a flat stone that he borrowed from someone. /Ti!kay brought a pot of water and set it on the fire to boil. Khan//a and Crooked /Qui set themselves to cutting special pieces of meat from the chest and the foreleg of the animal, the n/um meat. Khan//a put a piece of the raw meat on the stone and put the rest in the pot to cook. Other parts of the animal were added to the pot: a part of the eye to make the boy see well, a part of the ear to make him hear well, and a piece of meat from the back of the neck. The neck keeps the animals from turning to look around and see the hunter.

When the meat had boiled for a short time, Khan//a prepared two mixtures, one black and one red, that would be rubbed into the boy's scarification. Using the shell of a baobab fruit for a scoop, he took some of the thick froth and some small piece of meat from the pot, and, using the blunt end of his knife handle, he pounded them on the stone together with some powdered zau root that had been charred black. The second mixture was composed of blood pressed from the pieces of raw meat and mixed with another scoop of the froth from the pot.

/Ti!kay had been sitting quietly and passively at a little distance. He now came to sit close to his father as his father sharpened an unpoisoned arrowpoint on the edge of the stone.

Khan//a began the scarification process by eating a piece of the meat from the pot "to give the boy a good heart for hunting." He held the arrowpoint in the steam of the boiling pot for a moment and was ready to make the cuts. The cuts would be on the boy's left side because the animal was female. The first line of cuts was made on /Ti!kay's left upper arm near the elbow. /Qui and Khan//a together held up a horizontal pinch of skin and Khan//a quickly and deftly cut nineteen tiny vertical cuts in it, making a horizontal line about an inch and a half long. /Ti!kay gave no sign of fear or pain. Khan//a dipped his finger into the black mixture and rubbed it on the cuts, then the red mixture. As the cuts bled, he rubbed the mixtures on them again.

Merely to rub the mixtures on the surface of the skin, I was told later, would not "wake up" a boy's heart. The mixtures must be rubbed into the boy through the cuts. The meat of the animal's "arm" (foreleg) in the mixture strengthens the boy's arm for pulling the bow. (Arm and foreleg are one word in !Kung, "≠ha.") The zau powder makes the boy able to shoot far and accurately. The chest meat makes him say to himself as he sits in the encampment, "Why am I sitting here? Why am I not out looking for meat?" The blood in the second mixture also gives the boy the will to hunt.

In all, seven scarifications were made with varying numbers of cuts. The second scarification of twenty-five cuts was about an inch and a half above the first. The third was near the shoulder. These have the same purpose as the first arm scarification. Two scarifications were made on the left side of the boy's chest. These insure his willingness to hunt; he must not become lazy. A sixth line was made on the back of his left shoulder. This scarification would keep the animal quiet when the boy was stalking it. The seventh scarification of twenty-six cuts was a horizontal line on the forehead, a little above the eyebrows. It enables the boy to see well and, furthermore, to find an animal quickly when he starts to hunt.

When Khan//a finished the scarification, he scraped what was left of the red and black mixtures off the stone into the baobab fruit shell and put the shell under a bush where it would not be stepped on.

/Qui then began to portion out the meat and broth among the men who were attending the rite. Each had brought a bowl. Two of the men shared their portions with their sons. Khan//a and /Ti!kay ate nothing. When the men had finished eating, the group dispersed. (An excellent description of this rite, as it is performed by the Dobe !Kung, is given by Richard Lee [Lee 1979:238–40].)

THE BLOOD RITE

Another rite is performed for this boy, the Blood Rite. It must be performed for the first three animals of either sex that he kills after his Rite of First Kill. A boy would die, we were told, if he drank the blood of those animals without being prepared by the Blood Rite. The Blood Rite is similar to the Tshoa Rite.

The oldest man of the group performs the Blood Rite. Again the !Kung explained that an old man performs it because he was born long ago, has seen everything, and because he himself is free to drink blood—he is an "owner" of blood. The old man makes a ritual fire with fire sticks and takes the boy to it. He has some of the blood of the animal that the boy has killed and he puts sha sha into it. Sitting by the fire, he and the boy both drink the blood, and the old man rubs some of it onto the back of the young man's neck, and onto his feet, legs, abdomen, and throat.

FOOD AVOIDANCES RELATED TO HUNTING

!Kung hunters observe a number of food avoidances. The avoidances are required mainly of young hunters from the time they begin to hunt until they are old enough to have had one, two, or three children. A few avoidances are required for even longer periods. As the time approaches when a man may properly expect to stop avoiding a food, he will experiment by eating it, and if he has luck in his next hunt and the animal dies, he will know that he may stop that avoidance; if the animal does not die, he knows he should continue the avoidance for a while longer. Opinions vary as to when it is suitable to end the avoidance. The !Kung explained that those with stout hearts maintain //gao longer, taking more pains to insure their strength and their luck than those who are more self-indulgent and too fond of food.

The reasons given for the avoidances are expressed in negative terms. A young hunter does not eat a specific food so that he will not lose his luck in finding animals, or fail in shooting them; so that the animal will not be warned by smell or sound, or be given strength to go far; and so that the poison will not get "cold" or be diluted so the animal will not die.

Avoidances that Affect the Animal's Behavior

Large intestine of eland
A young hunter avoids eating the large intestine of elands. If he failed to practice this avoidance when he was stalking the eland, its anus would itch and the eland would run away. Furthermore, when the eland defecated, the excrement would hang on a clump of grass and not fall to the ground. This would make the eland's spoor less visible to the hunter.

Snouts
If a young hunter ate a snout, the animal he hunted would smell him, be warned, and run away.

Stomachs
The !Kung believe that if a young hunter ate the stomach of an animal, it would make sounds within his stomach. This would startle the animal that the man was stalking, and it would run away.

Tsi and mangetti (//k'a)
Tsi and mangetti nuts are temporarily avoided before each hunt. Young hunters would not eat tsi or mangetti at their evening meal or later in the night if they were to start on a hunt the next morning. The animals would smell them, we were told, and the hunters would never get near enough to shoot.

After the hunter has successfully shot an arrow into an animal, while he is tracking it and waiting for the poison to kill it, he does not roast tsi or mangetti nuts in the fire. The shells might burst with a bang. However far away the animal was, the sound would reach it and make it run far.

Drinking from ostrich-eggshell water containers

A young hunter must pour the water from an ostrich eggshell into some other container; he must not drink directly from the shell. Ostrich eggs have very strong n/um. If the hunter drank from the shell, strength would go into the animal; it would walk very far, so far that its spoor would be lost and the hunters would never find it.

Avoidances that Preserve the Strength of the Arrow Poison

Tails

Young hunters avoid eating tails. If they disregarded this avoidance their arrows would go into the tails of the animals, the arrow poison would not circulate well through the animal's bloodstream, and the animal would not die.

Fat

When a hunter has shot an animal and is waiting for it to die, he avoids eating fat. The fat would loosen and weaken the poison in the animal, and it might survive.

Honey

Honey eaten by a hunter would neutralize the poison on his arrows. Honey also has very strong n/um. Even if the arrow were well placed, the honey would weaken the poison and strengthen the animal, which would recover from the shot.

//Haru

//Haru (*Lapeyrousia cyanescens* Bak.) should be avoided by a hunter when he has an arrow in an animal. //Haru would make the poison "cold."

Baobab fruit and tshu

Baobab fruit (≠m, *Adansonia digitata* L.) and tshu (*Walleria nutans* Kirk) are avoided by hunters because they stick to the teeth. This would make the poison stick to the arrow and not circulate in the animal's blood. I have eaten baobab fruit and know what the !Kung meant about it sticking to the teeth. Uncooked tshu is said to be as pasty as baobab fruit.

!Xwa, tsha, and huru

!Xwa (*Fockea* sp.), *tsha* (gemsbok cucumber, *Citrullus naudinianus* [Sond.] Hook. f.), and *huru* (*Cucumis* sp.) are avoided by hunters when they are about to start a hunt or when they are on a hunt. The juiciness of these plant foods would cause the animal to have much urine, and the urine would carry away the poison. The succulence also dilutes the poison. Furthermore, gemsbok cucumber has an odor, which animals can detect and be warned to run away.

Avoidances that Affect the Hunter

Certain internal organs

A boy must not eat the intestines, spleens, livers, or hearts of the first five animals he kills after he has had the Rite of First Kill. He must give these parts to an old man, preferably to his grandfather if his grandfather is present in the band. If not to his grandfather, he should give these parts to some old man whom he addresses by the term "!gun!a." This is the kinship term applied to men in several relationships—the grandfather, the man for whom the boy is named, and others. The term carries the joking relationship (see Marshall 1976: chap. 6). If the boy ate these internal organs when he should have avoided them, he would lose his luck in finding animals, or his arrow would miss entirely or not be placed effectively, and the animals would not die.

Marrow

Boys avoid eating marrow from the age of /Gishay, and as young hunters they continue to avoid it for many years. /Gao Music, whose son, /Qui, must have been about eight, was still avoiding it. ≠Toma could eat it. An opportunity presented itself for a member of our expedition to observe a clear instance of avoidance. One day some young hunters, accompanied by John Marshall with his motion picture camera, happened to come upon the carcass of a wildebeest, which had been killed and half eaten by lions not long before. The men prepared to take the head, what was left of the meat and skin, and the marrow bones back to the encampment. Before setting forth, they paused to eat a marrow bone. John, not knowing about the rule of avoiding marrow, asked to take a picture of the cracking and eating. The young man who obliged held the cracked bone up to his mouth but did not actually eat a bite. When John asked why, he was told, "He is too young." This must have required great restraint on the part of the young man. Marrow is a cherished morsel, but the !Kung say that if a boy ate marrow he would lose his skill and luck in shooting; his arrows would miss.

Red-crested korhaan, giant (or kori) bustard, and savanna leguaan

All young people, until they are old enough to have five children, avoid these three creatures. Hunters, talking about the foods they must most assiduously avoid, gave special emphasis to these. To eat them would cause madness.

Avoidances Observed by Women in Relation to Hunting

Hearts, lungs, intestines, stomachs, livers, and throats

If a young hunter has killed the animal, these parts must be avoided by menstruating or pregnant women. The young man might lose his luck if the women did not obey this rule.

A bone at the base of an animal's spine

This particular bone must be avoided by girls if a young hunter has killed the animal. If a girl eats this bone from a young man's kill, the next time the young man stalked an animal, the animal's bones would twitch. This would startle and warn the animal and it would run away. Animals are very sensitive, Old Gaú explained.

The account of the rituals and of the avoidance practices in relation to hunting gives an impression of the difficulties and anxieties that attend the hunt, but nothing of the triumph, the satisfaction, and the esteem for the hunters that the people feel when a hunt has been successful. In *The !Kung of Nyae Nyae,* I describe the arrival of meat:

> Women bring most of the daily food that sustains the life of the people, but the roots and berries that are the principal plant foods of the Nyae Nyae !Kung are apt to be tasteless, harsh, and not very satisfying. People crave meat. Furthermore, there is only drudgery in digging roots, picking berries, and trudging back to the encampment with the heavy loads and babies sagging in the pouches of the karosses; there is no splendid excitement and triumph in returning with vegetables. The return of the hunters from a successful hunt is vastly different. The intense craving for meat, the uncertainty and anxiety that attend the hunt, the deep excitement of the kill, and, finally, the eating and the satisfaction engage powerful emotions in the people.
>
> One time when the people had been many days without meat and were anxious about the hunters' success, an eland was killed, and the hunters were sighted moving toward the encampment in a dark, lumpy, bobbing line in the golden grass, their carrying sticks loaded with meat. We heard the sound of

voices in the encampment rising in volume and pitch like the hum of excited bees. Some people ran toward the hunters, others crowded together at the edge of the encampment, some danced up and down, children squealed and ran about, the boys grappled and tussled together. I think also of the time the women danced a dance of praise for Short /Qui and his ostrich. I venture to say no women have been greeted in this manner when they returned with vegetables, and I believe that the value put on hunting and the satisfaction in its success accrue to the enhancement of men's position in !Kung society. Men, the !Kung say, are "masters of meat," "owners of hunting." (Marshall 1976:177–78.)

7  RAIN RITES AND N!OW

The big rains of the Kalahari are seasonal summer events coming mostly in December, January, and February. The season is called *bara*. Through the winter months of June, July, and August, when the cold south winds blow and the midwinter nights are freezing, no rain falls. Spring brings a rapid change in temperature from winter winds to exhausting, scorching heat during September, October, and November. A relentless sun blazes in a metallic sky. However, in these months, beginning usually in late September, a few thin cirrus clouds appear. They are called "male" clouds by the !Kung. A "male" cloud gives no rain. Then occasional great white cumulus "female" clouds begin to form. From time to time they spatter a few big polka dot drops on the sandy soil or give an occasional brief light shower. The slightly dampened earth has an exquisite fragrance. These are the little rains.

The spatterings of the little rains do not relieve the heat or appreciably moisten the earth. The above-ground food plants shrivel. The roots that are the mainstay of !Kung diet lose their identifying above-ground parts and are hard to find. Furthermore, quickened by the tantalizing drops of the little rains or just because it is spring, they give up their juices to the first stirrings of new growth and become pithy and bitter. Many of the nonpermanent water holes dry. The people must live at their few permanent water holes. The fertile areas of plant foods that they can reach become depleted. The !Kung say that spring is the time of starvation. They blame the scorching sun for the heat, the dryness, and the famine, saying the sun is death-giving. They await the big rains.

The big rains come from great "female" clouds *(!ga kwe disi)*. Female clouds give two forms of rain: gentle or more-or-less gentle rain called female rain *(!ga di)*, and the fierce rains of the thunderstorms called male rain *(!ga !go)*.

As I remember our Kalahari summer experiences, the gentle rains were rare; the storms were more frequent. Of course one tends to remember the more dramatic events. Every day the winds herded the monstrous gray thunderclouds around the sky. They could be seen at a distance with curtains of rain hanging from them called "rain's hair" by the !Kung. The !Kung call these clouds "horses" *(/dwesi)* because, although a person may think the cloud is far away, it comes as swiftly as a horse runs and is suddenly upon him. Lightning streaked through the clouds from heaven to earth. The earsplitting thunder was fearsome. The rain fell in torrents that I felt could knock a person down. There was no runoff in the flat, sandy land, and the sand sucked the rain into itself with a strange low hiss. The rain often turned suddenly into hail. Sometimes, the hailstones were dangerously big. The !Kung call these violent storms "mad rain" (!ga !go) and say the storms are a "fight."

During a bad storm we would struggle to hold up our tents, bracing our backs against the canvas. The !Kung, drenched and chilled, huddled in their little grass shelters that are more a symbol of shelter than actual shelter. They say they fear they will perish in the storms, and sometimes they do perish. They told of a man killed by hailstones when he was walking where there was no refuge, and we were told of several people killed by lightning. Not knowing the danger, the !Kung take refuge under trees. The highest things in the sparse landscape, the trees, standing separately, are often struck.

However violent the storms, the !Kung praise rain. They well know that rain is life-giving. They know that the growth of the plants depends on rain. Furthermore, rain fills the small water holes and pans and hollow trees. This frees the people to leave their permanent water holes and to move over the land to their various fertile areas where plant foods grow, and to visit distant relatives and friends.

Although the !Kung say they do not conceive of rain as animate, they nevertheless talk to it. Gao Feet told us he would praise a gentle rain "as though it were a person," saying, "You are doing very well, rain. This is what we want. Keep on wetting the ground. Make the plants grow. Cool us." To a thunderstorm, he might say, "You seem to be angry. Do not destroy us. Do not make such a noise. Let the rain fall quietly." To lightning, he would plead, "Do not come against me. Go to the other side. Let me live."

If a storm is in progress one must never say the word for rain, "!ga," aloud; one must use the respect word, *"n/oi,"* lest the storm become even more violent.

CONCEPTS ABOUT RAIN

The !Kung believe that the great god created rain after he created earth and sky, but before he created the sun. He controls rain directly. He made thunder and lightning as well. What ancient lore the !Kung may have had in the past to explain thunder, we do not know. Their present belief is that the great god comes riding on his horse carrying a long whip, which he cracks against the ground, making the sound of thunder. He does this to call the rain. The !Kung believe that the great god makes the lightning, also, but lightning remains a complete mystery to them. It looks like fire and they call it god's fire. They remarked that thunder and lightning go together like a fire burning: you see the flame and hear the crackling sound at the same time. However, lightning is not fire. The !Kung fear it and call it a death-thing; they say it spears the people. They do not use the wood of a tree struck by lightning for firewood. They avoid even touching the wood.

We found no great interest in rainbows among the !Kung. The !Kung think of them as a natural phenomenon, like the stars, things of the sky made by the great god. They do not expect to understand them. They believe that rainbows appear when the rain is stopping.

Rainfall is ultimately controlled by the great god. If the expected seasonal rains do not come, or if the thunderclouds pass them by and pour rain on another area, the people become very anxious. They turn to the great god and plead with him in prayer to send them rain.

Our father (m'ba), great one (gaoxa),
will you send us rain?

Give rain. Wet the earth. Give us food.
We are starving because we must stay by water holes
when there is no more food to gather.

≠Gao N!a has favored some people with rain.
Will he not favor us?

Gani ga, give us coolness.

Gaoxa, give us your water. Give us food.
Give us a chance to rest. We have nothing
if you do not give us food. Let food grow.

Why does ≠Gao N!a send lightning? Why does
he destroy our shelters with mad rain?

Combined with the belief that the all-powerful sky god created rain and ultimately controls it, the !Kung have beliefs about what I call supernatural forces that have to do with rain. I think the concepts of these forces are ancient, as I think the concept of n/um is ancient, and that they antedate the currently held concept of an all-powerful anthropomorphic sky god who rides a horse. The !Kung say, as they say about n/um, that the great god made the forces and can control them if he chooses to do so. However, as with n/um, he apparently does not exert that control. The forces are spoken of as though they were fully autonomous.

The most clearly conceived force believed to have an influence on rain is the force called n!ow (see. p. 168). Other magical potencies that the !Kung believe can influence rain exist in horns, in lightning teeth (see description of fulgurite below), in paouw feathers, and in the zao and /ana trees.

It seemed to us that, although the !Kung believe that the forces exist, they do not consider them to be strong or effective. As the forces are put to use to call or stop the rain, they may sometimes seem to succeed, but often they seem to have no effect. No formal rain rites are performed using them, nothing to compare with the rites for health and hunting. The strong Rain Song, which may in the past have been used in a rite to call the rain, has been taken into the healing music repertory. I think the !Kung have long since concluded that humans and their ritual and magic practices have little influence on the Kalahari rains.

To Bring the Rain: The Rain Horn

The !Kung have no rainmakers, no specialists who call the rain, and no structured rain-making rite. Gao Feet told me that in the past some of the great healers had power to "know about" the rain and to know where lightning would strike and could protect the people. They were not rainmakers, however, like the rainmakers of the southern Bushmen who drew a rain animal over the land to bring the rain, as seen in the rock paintings of the Drakensberg. Gao Feet also said that the healers of today had even lost the power to know where lightning would strike. The !Kung tend to be a humble people. They readily think that their own powers are ineffectual or that their n/um is weak.

The !Kung do have, however, a rainmaking artifact and a vestige of rainmaking procedure that must come from the distant past—the rain horn. Anyone may possess a rain horn, either man or woman. None of the women had a rain horn, however, and few men had one. We were told the horn is rarely resorted to. My impression was that people did not consider it very effective.

A duiker horn is used for a rain horn. The !Kung said a springbok horn might be used, but they consider a duiker horn to be the really proper horn. The horn is securely capped with the scrotum of some animal of the right size. In the horn is placed a mixture of lightning teeth (called also rain teeth or rainstones), some of the red heartwood of the /ana tree (*Acacia giraffae* Burch.), both pounded to powder, and the juice of *gwe,* the very succulent storage organ of *Raphionacme burkei* N.E. Br. If no gwe were available, another succulent root, !xwa (*Fockea* sp.) could be used. The heartwood of the /ana tree provides redness to the mixture—an essential ingredient. Gwe or !xwa provides moisture. Some water might also be added.

Lightning teeth are fulgurite, the crystalline substance produced by the fusion of sand or rock caused by lightning. The !Kung find this substance under the many trees that have been struck by lightning. A fairly large lump of the substance they call a rainstone; smaller lumps they call lightning teeth or rain teeth. They splinter this substance and add it to the rain horn mixture.

If the !Kung had been long without rain when the rains were expected and had become very anxious, the people might decide to try to call the rain with the rain horn, if anyone among them had one, even if they had no great hope of success. The owner of the horn, without any formalities, would sprinkle some of the rain medicine from the horn onto a spot of bare ground where no shade ever falls, and then toss the horn onto that spot and talk to the rain. The horn would be left lying in the sun for a few days.

Old Gaú had a rain horn. He showed me how he would toss it on the ground in a sunny spot and, as he did so, he dramatically called the rain: "Where are you, rain? Why do you not come to us? We will starve if you do not come." I wanted to see lightning teeth but had to wait until after sundown. The sun must not shine on rain medicine. The "teeth" looked like splintered glass.

One more practice was mentioned. If a death should occur when the people were anxious for rain, they would sprinkle rain medicine on the person's grave and hang the rain horn on a stick thrust into the ground over the grave. The rain horn would be left there for an indefinite time, but not permanently. The !Kung said that this practice might influence the rains of the next year as well as those of the present season.

A Rite that Gives Protection from Lightning

The rain medicine in a rain horn is used in a ritual practice that protects people from lightning. We were told that women especially need this protection, for much of their life is spent digging roots and gathering berries in the open plains where they are often overtaken by storms. Although women were especially mentioned, it was made clear that the protection is given to everyone and that the !Kung believe it to be efficacious.

While the rite is being performed, the people involved must not look at clouds. A broth is prepared containing a boiled piece of rainstone and some food, preferably tsi, mangetti nuts, or meat. The food may be eaten. The liquid is used to wash the person. One person washes another by splashing handfuls of the liquid over the person's body and rubbing it around. The nest of a penduline titmouse would be used as a sponge, if anyone had a nest at hand.

After the washing, the person is anointed with the rain medicine in the duiker horn. The rain medicine must include the red heartwood of the /ana tree as well as lightning teeth. No substitute may be used in place of these elements.

One person anoints another. A line is drawn across the person's forehead, curving down the temples to the cheeks in a pattern like the one drawn on the face of a girl at marriage. The feet are also anointed. A man, in addition, has a mark made with the red liquid on his upper arm so his arrow will go straight, and he may have a small shallow vertical cut made in his forehead into which the mixture is rubbed so he will see well. The main purpose of applying the rain medicine, however, is to protect from lightning.

To Stop the Rain: The Paouw Feather and the Zao or /Ana Trees

In addition to praying to the great god, pleading directly with the rain, or getting a person with a "cold" n!ow (see definition below) to urinate in the fire or burn some of his hair to stop the rain, someone might resort to burning a kori bustard (paouw) feather in the fire, that is, if the fires had not all been quenched in the deluge, and if anyone happened to have a kori bustard feather about him. No one we knew had ever done this, but the !Kung had been told by their forebears that kori bustard feathers had that power.

People would be more likely to burn a green branch of the /ana or the zao trees. Both of these trees are believed to have n/um. They have various uses. /Ana is one of the ingredients in the healer's tortoise shell. Zao bark has an offensive odor, to lions at least. We were told that a green branch of one of these trees burned in the fire could influence rain to stop, though not infallibly.

N!ow

N!ow[1] is the force that, in !Kung belief, interacts with and influences weather most strongly. N!ow exists in all human beings and in certain large animals. The !Kung could tell us nothing about the nature of n!ow itself or how it influences the weather. They know of its existence, they say, by observing its effects. The !Kung would say that their great god created n!ow as he created all things and, theoretically, could control it. He does not control it, however, and people have no control over their own n!ow. N!ow acts autonomously as does n/um.

There are two kinds of n!ow—good n!ow and bad n!ow. A person possesses one kind or the other. Good n!ow brings rain, bad n!ow brings cold and dryness. Rain and cold are polar opposites to the !Kung, because the Kalahari rains are seasonal summer rains.

In winter no rain falls; thus, winter cold is associated with dryness and with the hardships dryness imposes on these people. Hence, cold n!ow is bad n!ow. Although dryness continues through the hot months of September, October, and November, and the hardships are most severe in these months, the association of bad n!ow with cold persists in the language; the association with dryness is implicit.

All human beings have n!ow and, we were told, the following animals have n!ow: giraffe, eland, gemsbok, kudu, hartebeest, and wildebeest. These are the animals regularly hunted in the Nyae Nyae area, the good benign animals whose meat gives life to the !Kung. The dangerous buffaloes, also hunted in the area, do not have n!ow, nor do the predators.

Small animals do not have n!ow. We wanted to learn why, but the !Kung could only tell us that small animals were so created by the great god. Of the middle-sized meat animals, steenbok have positively no n!ow at all. Some !Kung claimed that duikers had none, others were uncertain. They thought that duikers had some n!ow, but that it was possibly weak or undeveloped. The !Kung were also uncertain about springbok. Springbok are rare in the area, and they killed them so seldom that they had not observed whether they had n!ow. Possibly other large animals would be found to have n!ow if the question were further pursued. The !Kung I spoke with were certain that no other things have n!ow—not earth itself, nor vegetation; not water, clouds, rain, thunder, nor lightning; not the heavenly bodies, not the two gods themselves, nor the other sky beings.

No one could say how or when n!ow comes into an animal, but everyone knew that n!ow comes into a human being at the time of birth while the fetus is still in the womb, at the moment the mother's uterine fluid flows onto the ground. The !Kung say the mother's uterine fluid makes the n!ow at this moment, either the good n!ow, which brings rain, or the bad n!ow, which brings cold and dryness. The mother has no control over the kind of n!ow her child receives, nor has anyone else. Inheritance plays no part, and there is nothing in !Kung belief like magic or a ritual procedure that could cause one or the other kind to come into the child.

Two verbs were used in connection with n!ow: ≠*gani* and //*ghui*. The verbs denote a favorable or an unfavorable interaction. The !Kung say a mother has "≠ganied" her child if the child gets a good rain-bringing n!ow, or she has "//ghuied" the child if he gets a n!ow that brings cold and dryness. If a hunter is lucky with the animal he kills and good weather follows, he has ≠ganied the animal. If he is unlucky with the animal and cold and dryness follow, he has //ghuied the animal. No one has any control over these interactions.

The words are used in some other contexts as well; I happen to know only one. A child is said to have ≠ganied his teeth if they come early. He has //ghuied his teeth if they are unusually late.

The kind of n!ow a child has is discovered by observing the weather at the time of his birth or soon after. If rain falls, the people believe the n!ow of the child has brought the rain and they are sure his n!ow is good-rain n!ow. If water should freeze when the child was born or soon after, the child's n!ow would be known to be a bad, cold, dry n!ow. Should the weather continue in its normal seasonal course and no great extreme or notable change occur, the child's n!ow will be thought of according to the weather that prevailed at the time. However, if the weather is extreme at the time of the birth, there is a feeling of certainty about the kind of n!ow the child has acquired.

At death as well as at birth, the n!ow of a human being affects the weather. A man told us that his n!ow had brought heavy rain when he was born and that everyone knew he had a rain-bringing n!ow. He said his mother, who at the time lived at some distance from him, regularly took notice of the weather, and if rain came at an unusual time or was extremely heavy, she feared he had died and that his n!ow was causing the rain.

N!ow is said to exist in the bodies of human beings, presumably everywhere in them, although particularly in hair and urine.

Hair is associated with clouds by the /Gwi Bushmen in Botswana with whom we worked in 1955. They have a myth, told to us by Old Ukwane, which says that god, whose name there is Pisiboro and who is their one god, tore the black, black hair from his head and threw it into the sky to make the rain clouds.

In *Specimens of Bushman Folklore*, W. H. I. Bleek and Lucy Lloyd record a belief about death, collected in 1875 in the Katkop dialect from Dia!kwain, which refers to hair and clouds:

> The hair of our head will resemble clouds, when we die, when we in this manner make clouds. These things are those which resemble clouds; and we think that (they) are clouds. We, who do not know, we are those who think in this manner, that (they) are clouds. We who know, when we see that they are like this, we know that (they) are a person's clouds; (that they) are the hair of his head. We, who know, we are those who think thus, while we feel that we seeing recognize the clouds, how the clouds do in this manner form themselves (Bleek and Lloyd 1911:399–401).

We do not know what connection there may be between the concept of n!ow held by the !Kung of Nyae Nyae and the /Gwi myth of Pisiboro's hair making the rain clouds, or the hair of the dead resembling clouds and becoming the dead person's clouds, as Dia!kwain told Dr. Bleek. What the !Kung believe now, Demi told us, is that there is nothing about hair itself that affects the weather. It is the n!ow of the person that the hair "gives." As we understand it, some of the person's n!ow is in the hair. When hair is burned in the fire, the n!ow is released into the air in the smell. It goes into the sky and, Demi said, the rain "fears" or "respects" it and pays attention to it.

If the big rains were unusually late and the people were suffering from the dryness, if the rainstorms were so frequent and torrential that the people had great trouble hunting and gathering plant foods, or if a storm were especially frightening, they might try to influence the weather. To influence the rain to come, a person known with certainty to have a rain-bringing n!ow might be asked either to urinate in the fire or to burn some of his hair. The smell of his urine or hair would go up into the sky and influence the rain to come. A person with a cold-dryness n!ow could be asked to do the same to stop a violent rainstorm if this were wanted. No ritual procedure attends the act.

An animal's n!ow interacts with the weather at the time the animal is killed by a hunter. A n!ow animal, as well as a human, has either a good or a bad n!ow. Good or bad n!ow is not correlated with one sex or one species. One giraffe, for example, either male or female, may have the rain-bringing kind, another the cold-bringing kind.

It seems that long or short horns may have something to do with good or bad n!ow, not the long-hornedness of gemsbok as compared with the short-hornedness of giraffes, but the comparative length of horn within the species. But one kind of n!ow is not inherent in short-hornedness nor is the other kind in long-hornedness. It is not as simple as that.

When a hunter kills a n!ow animal, he either "≠ganies" or "//ghuies" it. Like the mother who ≠ganies or //ghuies her child at birth, the hunter has no control over this and cannot tell which he has done unless the effect is observed in the weather. A hunter with good or bad n!ow may ≠gani or //ghui an animal, which has either good or bad n!ow and long or short horns. The precise nature of the interaction remains obscure, but hunters took an interest in telling me about the kind of n!ow they thought they had and gave instances of observing the effects of it in their killing various types of animals. If a man should kill a female kudu with short horns, and water should freeze that night, it would be evident that he had //ghuied the animal. He would expect to continue to //ghui short-horned female kudus. However, although a man's n!ow remains constant throughout his life, the way it interacts with other factors may change, and after a time a man who //ghuied short-horned, female kudus may find he has begun to ≠gani them. We think the !Kung were perplexed at our stupidity in finding these well-known truths obscure and complicated, and they tired of our probing for explanations.

One day in late September, the sun was blazing. The heat beat down upon us. A party of men had gone hunting toward the west. John was with them. In the afternoon there appeared in the western sky three little white clouds like three powder puffs in a neat row. They were the first clouds to be seen since the big rains had ended in March. We ran to each other exclaiming and pointing to them. People felt happy. In the evening when the hunters returned, ≠Toma came at once to me, before he put down his bow and quiver, and said that I could see for myself what it meant to ≠gani an animal. John had ≠ganied the wildebeest he shot, and the clouds appeared immediately above them. ≠Toma said this was what he had been trying all along to explain to me.

If a hunter knows with certainty that he has ≠ganied or //ghuied an animal, as it was known when John ≠ganied the wildebeest, he may take the horns, the scalp, and the forehead bone of that animal and hang them in a tree, remembering where they were hung and whether they had been ≠ganied or //ghuied. If need should arise to call rain or to stop it, and he had appropriate horns, he would make a little rite with them. He would build a ritual fire away from the cooking fires and would burn the horns in this fire. While they were burning, he would take one of the smoking horns, point it to the sky saying, *"goichi goichi goichi n!ow kwi."* This, we were told, is "speaking n!ow." The incantation defied translation. We wondered if it was an archaic spell. The !Kung were emphatic in saying that both the horns must be entirely consumed by the fire.[2]

A hunter has another way of controlling the weather. To bring rain he would cut the throat of an animal he had reason to believe he habitually ≠ganies, or to stop rain, one he habitually //ghuies. The blood, which is ordinarily saved and eaten, would be allowed to flow onto the ground. A giraffe is the best animal for bloodletting. The forms and colors of the clouds are like giraffes' markings, the !Kung remarked. We asked if human beings cut themselves and used their blood to start or stop rain, as they do their urine or hair. The !Kung said, no, they did not. That would be unnecessarily painful.

Except for the demonstrations of the rain horn, we did not see any rain-controlling practices actually performed. While we were in the field there were periods of weather that were comfortable, but also there were periods of extremes, or so they seemed to us. I sincerely believe that some of the thunderstorms we experienced could not have been more violent. The heat of October was beyond any we had ever known before in our long lives. In the winter, although the actual temperatures were not as low as we were accustomed to in New England, we were living without the shelter of a house, and we found the freezing south winds very uncomfortable. So did the !Kung. However, they did not complain about heat or cold or violent storms. Drought was their concern, and that we did not experience. One year when we were in the field, there was a very severe drought to the south of us, but in the Gautscha area the rains came when they were due.

≠Toma said he had never experienced a rainy season when no rain fell, but there had been seasons with so little rain that people feared starvation and wondered if the great god was thinking of killing them all and destroying the world. In such circumstances, they might try throwing down a rain horn or having someone burn his rainy n!ow hair, but with little hope that these procedures would bring rain. Their hope is in the great god. They plead with him to have pity and to give them rain. Gao Feet said, "When bara comes and the rains do not fall, we pray and wait."

PART IV

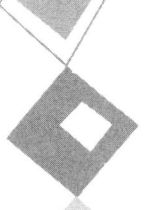

RITES OF PASSAGE

8 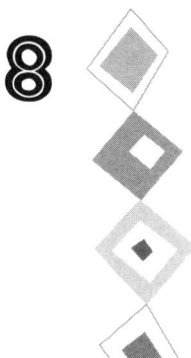 DEATH AND BURIAL

The rites that I have been describing, rites for the curing of sickness, for the protection of health, for success in the hunt, and the rite of the rain horn are all directed toward survival on this earth. We did not find highly developed rites performed for death or burial among the !Kung.

DEATH

On the whole, my impression is that the !Kung accept death in a matter-of-fact way with a considerable degree of resignation, and without great fear. They consider it as much a part of the scheme of things as life itself. Nevertheless, they cling strongly to life, and they seek to preserve it by prayer and ritual, by their social behavior (in keeping the peace, for instance), and by giving most of their vital energies to procuring food.

In !Kung concept, life (/xwa) and spirit (n/) are two different entities. While in the body, n/ is like breath or air. It exists in the body while the person is alive. When the person dies, the spirit does not die. It is taken out of the body through the head by the messengers of the gods and, along with the person's heart and blood, is carried to the great god in the eastern sky. There he transmutes the n/ into an immortal //gauwa (see chap. 1). When death occurs, /xwa dies in the body.

We found no images of death personified and conventionally depicted, comparable to our image of an old man with a scythe. I should not say, however, that death is never personified symbolically among the !Kung. At least one !Kung personified death, not in pictorial image but in poetic metaphor. N!ai sang in her bitter lament:

Death is ruining me.
Death is stealing from me.
Death is dancing me ragged.

Death mocks me.
Death dances with me.[1]

Burial

During my five trips into the field to live with the Bushmen, no death occurred where I was present. John, my son, saw the death of three children at various times. Three old people I knew died while I was in the field, but at a distance from where I was staying. My information on burial procedures was gathered from the !Kung I questioned. I have not observed what people actually do at a burial, but in note 2, with her kind permission, I give Polly Wiessner's description of a burial she attended in the Dobe area in Botswana. The procedures of the Botswana !Kung may not be exactly the same as those of the Nyae Nyae !Kung, but they are likely to be similar.[2]

The !Kung stated that their purpose in burying the dead was to keep carnivores from eating the corpse and to cover the smell of decaying flesh. The procedures of burial that they described to me showed considerable variation. When burials differ it is due to the circumstance or the choice of the people performing the burial, or possibly to the condition of the soil, which might be sandy or very hard, not to regulations based on the status of the dead person or to the manner of the person's death.

In several Bushman cultures, a distinction is made between a "good" or a "bad" death, and burial procedures differ accordingly. Among the Nyae Nyae !Kung, a death by suicide,[3] or an unnatural death caused by arrow poison, lightning, snakebite, a fall from a baobab tree, or by goring by a buffalo is said to be a bad death. Such deaths are outside the normal course of life ending in death, to which one must be resigned. Among the !Kung, however, there are no differences in the burial procedures whether a person dies a good or bad death. Furthermore, they do not believe, as the Auen and Nharo are reported by Schapera to believe, that a bad death makes a difference in the afterlife of the spirit (Schapera 1930:168).

Members of the family prepare the body for burial; anyone may assist. Ideally, the body should be bound in a flexed position, knees drawn up, hands to shoulders. The !Kung with whom I was talking one day offered to demonstrate the binding procedure. Old N!aishi was chosen, with his amused consent. A very jolly affair this was, the binding of Old N!aishi. He assumed the posture of the body, his knees drawn up to his chest, ankles crossed, his arms bent at the elbows, right hand to right shoulder, left hand to left shoulder. Someone had run to fetch some cord. The cord used may be a heavy one made of sansevieria fibers or a light but very strong one made from the fibers of a carrotlike root. A young man undertook the binding. Amid howls of laughter from the group, he passed the cord across the back of the old man's neck, around his left shoulder, across his chest and hands, and around his back. Four times the cord was passed around the old man in this manner, each turn below the last. The last two turns bound his legs. A final higher turn brought the ends of the cord together. They were tied, and the laughing group declared that the old man was so strongly trussed they would never be able to unbind him and would have to bury him.

When the laughter subsided and Old N!aishi was unbound and saved from the grave, the group showed me another binding. It is simply a single turn of cord around the back of the neck, down one side of the flexed arms and knees, under the two great toes, and up the other side of the body, with the ends tied at the neck.

The body may be rubbed with fat "to make it look nice." This is not a ritual procedure and may be omitted. The eyes, nose, and ears must be protected. An old leather bag may be put over the head, or if none is available, the eyes are covered and the ears and nose plugged with some fibrous substance, such as the nest of the penduline titmouse. The protection of the eyes, nose, and ears of the corpse from flies transfers to the living, the !Kung say, and their eyes, noses, and ears are protected by this procedure.

The commonly worn bracelets, under-knee ornaments, and small hair ornaments would be left on the body. More important ornaments are kept and distributed among relatives. A woman's body is wrapped head and all in a kaross. Women's bodies must be especially well wrapped, we were told. I believe a woman's body is covered in modesty as it is in life. A man's body might be covered with a small, old kaross, or a mat thrown into the grave might suffice.

A grave may be placed anywhere—near an encampment or at some distance from it. The people move away from the place after a death. If a person dies far from his encampment, when traveling for instance, he could be buried where he died. !Kung graves may be round or oblong. The Nyae Nyae !Kung said that the ideal grave is a round hole "as deep as a Bushman is tall," or at least deep enough to completely contain a flexed body. In such a grave the flexed body might be placed in a sitting position or on its side. Some Nyae Nyae !Kung said a body should face in the direction of the person's birthplace. Others claimed that the direction in which the body faced was of no significance. Facing the body to one or another point of the compass was not a practice of the Nyae Nyae !Kung.

The grave is dug by male relatives; a father or a husband, a brother or a son would be responsible. The relatives would be aided by any men present. !Kung women do not participate in the digging or in lowering the body into the grave.

When the grave is filled and the earth firmly tamped down, thorny branches are piled on it for protection from the carnivores. Branches of the tree !ei (*Ochna pulchra* Hook.) and the plant mai (*Dichapetalum cymosum* [Hook.] Engl.) would be added if they were available. Their odor deters the carnivores. Then the oldest of the relatives present would sprinkle sa powder over the grave and speak to the spirit, begging the spirit not to make people sick, just to give them good luck and help them to find animals to hunt or dead animals they could eat.

Building a fire at the grave was known as a custom but was not always practiced at the time we were present. A few !Kung said, however, it was still a custom in their groups. A discussion on the value of keeping the old customs had several of these !Kung wagging their heads together in approval of doing so. Withered Old /Gasa and Gao Feet piously stated that it is always best to hold to the old customs. If a fire is built, the bark of zao, which gives off an unpleasant odor when burning, may be sprinkled on the fire to further deter carnivores. The bark of !ei may also be burned. The purpose of the fire itself is to keep carnivores away.

The dead person's shelter is torn down and its branches and grass are thrown onto the grave. These add to the pile of protective branches, but, we were told, the real reason for destroying the shelter is that people do not want to see it. It reminds them too strongly of their loss. A man's bow and quiver are hung on a stick beside the grave. The arrows are broken and thrown on the grave. The arrows are said to be "dead" as the man is dead. They would not be wanted by other men.

If the rains have been disappointing during the previous rainy season, some rain medicine from the rain horn might be sprinkled on the grave and the rain horn hung for a time over the grave in the hope of its bringing better rains next season. This seemed to be a mere vestige of a ritual practice. No one could tell me what beliefs lay behind the association of a rain horn with graves, and the !Kung I spoke with said this practice was rarely resorted to in these times.

A grave is finally marked with a few stones so that people passing by would know that the spot was a grave. ≠Toma said they would not want to walk on a grave, and if a wind were blowing over the grave toward them, they would want to toss sa powder into the wind. Wind over a grave might carry sickness.

After a burial the fires in the old encampment are extinguished and covered with sand with more care than might ordinarily be given. The band moves to a new encampment. There a new fire must be made with fire sticks by the oldest man, who might be assisted by a younger man in twirling the fire sticks. Each family would take a brand from that ritually made new fire to light its family fire.

Several times people in our discussions had remarked that children would be buried with special care. A little shelter is built over a child's grave. John Marshall was present when a baby died. He described the burial as follows:

> N//ami's baby by his younger wife, Khwo//o, died in the midafternoon. They had been expecting the death, although hope had been briefly aroused by our coming and our medicines. Khwo//o, exhausted, wept quietly and bitterly for a while, then slept as if drugged. Before nightfall, N//ami started to build a little shelter in the middle of the encampment. It was a queer little shelter, more like a tiny kraal, tall, with small diameter, made of branches. It was completed in the morning. The baby was buried in the sand beneath it. Everyone sat for a while near the death shelter, then they moved to another place about a hundred yards away and made a new encampment.

When a grave is protected from the carnivores as best it can be, people then stay away from it. The spirits of the dead do not regularly haunt their graves, as I understand from our discussions with the !Kung, but if a mortal should linger at a grave or visit it often, the spirit of the dead might take notice and wonder why that person was there. The spirit might become suspicious or displeased and do something harmful to the person. It is always best not to call the attention of the //gauwasi to oneself.

Variations in Burial

Among the Nyae Nyae !Kung, an ideal grave is deep enough to receive a flexed body. Ideal graves, however, are not always achieved; a shallow trench-shaped grave might be made instead. It might be very shallow, more a symbol of a grave than an actual excavation, or, without even a symbol of a grave, the body might be stretched out on the ground and covered with thorny branches to protect it from the carnivores.

The !Kung discussed such a burial, or lack of burial, at length. They explained that they might have to resort to such a practice if a death occurred when they were traveling. At a proper encampment, they would manage a proper burial. If they were traveling they might be on ground so hard they could not dig a deep grave with their digging sticks. Or there might be no one present at the death strong enough to dig a grave, as when poor Old /Gaishay was unable to bury his sister properly when she died while the two old people were traveling alone after the influenza epidemic at Gautscha.

Disturbing thoughts came to people's minds of bodies inadequately protected in such burials. They knew of one old woman whose body had been eaten by lions, and they had a chilling account of another old woman who had been left unburied and barely protected with branches, not because the ground was too hard to dig or because no one was strong enough to dig a grave, but because she was so disliked that no one would bother to attend to her body properly. The !Kung did not know, but they presumed she was eaten. She must have had no close relatives in the band. I do not believe that among the Nyae Nyae !Kung I knew close relatives would leave an old person's body so poorly protected, however unpleasant the old person might have been. Family relationships are very strong. /Qui brought up the question again of a child's burial. He said they would never leave a child or a very young adult unburied.

One shallow burial proved to be lifesaving for a man named ≠Gao. He was buried unbound in a very shallow trench, and his group moved on. He must have been barely covered. In this case it was because the ground on a limestone ridge was too hard to dig. It so happened that the man was not dead. He had lost consciousness, and the people thought he was dead. When his consciousness returned, he had risen up and followed the footprints of his people to their next encampment. This had happened about three years before. He had fully recovered from whatever had caused his loss of consciousness. He remained well and lived with his band as usual.

A person who has had this experience is called a ≠*twi*. "≠Twi" means something outlandish, against the natural order, or an omen or portent. (My thanks to Richard Lee for this definition, given in personal communication.) The !Kung do not feel that a ≠twi is supernatural, nor do they attribute special powers, functions, or status to one. They did not understand what happened to ≠Gao or what could have caused his loss of consciousness. They said it was merely a mistake, that his life—his /xwa—had not died although his people thought it had. ≠Toma, however, thought that perhaps his spirit had gone to the sky world and met the spirits of his dead parents, who decided that he should not die yet and had sent him back to take care of his wife and children.

We met the ≠twi when he came to visit relatives at Gautscha. I was exasperated that I had not learned until after he left that there was such a thing as a ≠twi, and that he was one, and that I had missed the chance of talking with him and learning more about his experience.

ABANDONMENT

I have read in Schapera's book that old people are sometimes abandoned. "When drought and scarcity force the Bushmen to a long hurried march, some old man or woman may be too feeble to keep up with them" (Schapera 1930:162). The old person might be screened around with brush and abandoned. The people with whom I talked claimed that they would never do that. They plan better, they said. They do not make "forced hurried marches." I suggested their being at the mangetti forest, their water supply very low, the long trek back to Gautscha ahead of them, and some older person falling ill. They do not take old people on the long trek to the mangetti forest, they replied. Old people stay at their water hole, someone would stay with them; others would go and return.

A situation had occurred in which the water hole of Band 5 at Deboragu had almost dried up. We were told that you could see no water but if you dug a hole in the sand and waited, a little would ooze up. It was not enough to support the band and most had left to visit relatives at other, better water holes. The old leader of Band 5, Old N!aishi, was very sick at the time and too feeble to go with them. His two sons had remained with him until he died and had buried him properly.

The Gautscha !Kung, however, had heard an account of an old woman having been abandoned. They said she was still breathing, but she was unconscious and, as they said, her body was "dead." She could not move; she stank. The people of her group did not wait for her last breath. They tore her shelter apart, piled the branches and grass over her and left her. Her body was found eaten by hyenas.

We were told of another instance, not of deliberate abandonment but of an old man dying alone. The old man had a painful burn on his leg. Traveling with his group he walked slowly and fell behind. Night overtook them. His people did not return in the darkness to find him. His body was found next day eaten by hyenas.

The people I talked with did not know how his death had occurred. They talked among themselves wondering about it. The old man had not seemed to be gravely ill, and he had his fire sticks. A man is never without his fire sticks, they said. Why had he not built a fire? With brands from a fire he could have driven hyenas away. They thought that his people would probably have expected that he had a fire and that he was all right.

The !Kung were disturbed by these accounts. /Qui, shaking his head and staring with unseeing eyes as he imagined the scenes, said with a shudder that he hoped the old people were "finished" before the hyenas came.

Again the question of nearness of relationship arises. In *The !Kung of Nyae Nyae* (Marshall 1976:288), I speak of an instance of callous indifference and lack of care for an old aunt on the part of some young relatives when the old woman's sister, who had taken care of her, died. At the same time I speak of instances of relatives in close family relationships carrying sick relatives. John Marshall on his 1978 field trip heard of a woman who had leprosy and was carried by her relatives for several years. Life in its complexity does not permit sweeping generalities about Bushmen or any other people.

Avoidance of Names of the Dead

The !Kung avoid speaking of a dead person by name, making a distinction between speaking of the person by name and saying the person's name. When they gave me genealogical information, they did not hesitate to say the names of their dead relatives but would frame their replies so that they were talking about the relatives' name. Speaking of his father a !Kung would say, "My father's name was 'Tsamgao,'" but he would not say, "Tsamgao was my father."

One may use the word "dead" (*!khi*) in reference, saying, for instance, "m'ba !khi," "my father is dead." However, it is more respectful to avoid the word "!khi." One may refer to a dead person as *!kwa ju.* "Ju" is "person"; we could not translate "!kwa." Our interpreter, Kernel Ledimo, said it seemed to be a word the !Kung use to avoid saying "dead" as the English use "late" in the "late Mr. so-and-so." Megan Biesele tells me that "!kwa" is also used as part of a respectful reference to a dead person's relatives. One !Kung woman at !Goshe in Botswana was routinely referred to as *!kwajumatai,* which means the "late" baby's mother. Another way to refer respectfully to a dead person, Biesele tells me, is to append *!khisi* (not translated) to his name, as in Khan//a !khisi. The avoidance of the name of the dead shows respect and avoids drawing the attention of the //gauwasi to the speaker.

Mourning

The !Kung make no outward sign of mourning, such as change in dress, painting the face or body, or cutting hair in a special way. !Kung mourners do not have conventions of mourning such as wailing. We did hear one woman wail, however, in what appeared to be genuine grief. She was a visitor at Gautscha. Other visitors from her family came from a distance to tell her that her nephew had been bitten by a puff adder and had died. She rose and began to wail, pacing back and forth, back and forth, near where she had been sitting by her fire. The wail was a loud, high, prolonged cry of the word "mother," "*aieya, aieya, aieya,*" a heart-rending sound. Over and over she gave her cry, walking back and forth with tears in her eyes. As we listened to her, Gao Beard said to me that since there were so many, many white people, it perhaps was not so devastating to us if one died, and we would not grieve so bitterly, but to a Bushman the death of a relative was a terrible loss.

POSSESSIONS OF THE DEAD

The concept of providing the dead with grave goods for use in the afterlife is not held by the !Kung. They believe that the //gauwasi have whatever artifacts they need in the sky and want none from earth.

The !Kung have two ways of disposing of a dead person's possessions: they throw some on the grave, others are distributed among relatives. As noted, a man's quiver and his arrows are left by the grave, and the person's shelter is torn down and thrown among the thorny branches that cover the grave. Other objects thrown on the grave would be common objects of daily use made of the materials that are in abundance, such as a digging stick, a carrying stick, a fire paddle, a wooden bowl, the bags women wear containing powders. People said that the relatives would not want to keep those objects, especially those the dead person had made for himself. Such familiar intimate possessions would continually remind the relatives too sadly of the death and of their loss.

No fixed pattern establishes which valuables are saved and which distributed. In general, those distributed would include fine ornaments, such as an ostrich-eggshell bead necklace of many strands, or a fine headband. Others might be dance rattles, a //gwashi, a strong new carrying bag or net, a new kaross, a mortar and pestle, sandals—things that have required skill and time to make, things that would be expected to be given as gifts in the gift-giving process.

Other valuables to be distributed would be the things obtained in trade with the !Kung's Bantu neighbors. They would include knives and assagai blades. ≠Toma told us that the wooden handles of the assagais would be taken off and thrown on the grave. Only the metal blades would be saved, because the wooden handles would probably have been made by the owner, or, if not made by him, continually used by him. These would be intimately associated with him in people's memory; to use the handles would remind the new owner of the death. Other trade items that would be given might include a pot, a pipe, an enamel basin, a cup, a spoon.

While there is considerable flexibility as to who would conduct the distribution and who would receive the objects, one rule prevails: a woman's possessions should go to her relatives, a man's possessions to his relatives. It would be very bad, people said, for a husband to give his dead wife's possessions to his family or for a wife to give her husband's possessions to her family. No one recalled any instance of that happening.

Depending on who was present, the relatives who are expected to make the distribution would be a husband or wife, a father or mother, a son or daughter. As to exactly which relatives should receive the objects, there are no rules, but I imagine that everyone present would have a sense of appropriateness in the distribution. Nearness of relationship would be an element in the decision. The history of the object in the gift-giving system might influence a decision. Everyone would know the history of the objects and what was appropriate.

The sorrow in being too vividly reminded of the dead person was mentioned again in this context. Someone said it might be too hard for a daughter to have her mother's things. Instead, the mother's sister might take them or even the dead woman's mother. "She is old and could bear the sorrow."

Some relatives might covet a specific object, such as an assagai blade or a beaded headband, but on the whole the !Kung are not avid for possessions. Describing the system of gift-giving in *The !Kung of Nyae Nyae* (Marshall 1976:308), I made several points that are applicable to the acquiring of a dead person's possessions. One is that the !Kung have no great need to acquire possessions; they have their own.

Except for food and water (important exceptions), the !Kung live in a kind of material plenty. They make the tools for their living and replace them as needed from materials that are in abundance around them, free for all to take, or sufficient to satisfy most needs—wood, reeds, bone for weapons and implements, fiber for cordage, branches and grass for shelters, hides for clothes and bags, ostrich eggshells for water containers and beads. The materials used in trade are sufficient for every man to have obtained a knife, an assagai blade, and malleable metal for arrowpoints, and for several people in any band to have a pot.

One must remember also that every time these people move from one area in their territory to another where their plant foods grow, they carry all their possessions as well as their young children. This puts a limit to the number of possessions one wants to possess. Much borrowing and lending fills any lack. I think of pots and musical instruments as being especially portable. So the disposition of a dead person's possessions usually causes no great stress.

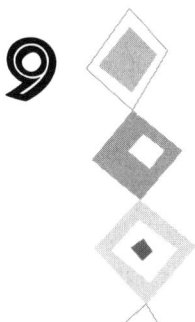

9 ◆ THE MENARCHEAL RITE

The first menstruation and the Menarcheal Rite are given great importance in !Kung culture. Some of the most strictly followed ritual procedures attend this rite. The girl who is menstruating for the first time must be secluded and she must submit to various restraints and avoidances. They are the restraints and avoidances that are common to Menarcheal Rites in many cultures; the !Kung put their own emphasis upon them. The Menarcheal Rite is performed for each young girl at the time of her first menstruation. No girl had her first menstruation while I was present, and I did not see an actual Menarcheal Rite. However, the women of two !Kung bands were willing to tell me about the ritual procedures, to act them out, and to dance the Eland Dance, which is part of the ritual. Those !Kung bands were Band 1 at Gautscha in the Nyae Nyae area in Namibia (in 1952) and Band 28 in Botswana (in 1961). On a third occasion, a Nharo band at !Go Tsao in Botswana (in 1959) danced their Eland Dance for us. My description of the rite is that of the !Kung as described and acted out for us by the !Kung women of Bands 1 and 28.[1]

The !Kung rite makes aspects of approved behavior manifest and develops the girl's willingness and strength to comply. The !Kung believe that it protects the girl from potential harm, especially from becoming thin, and protects her while in this potent state from causing harm to others, especially from negating hunting and from adversely affecting the elements. The rite celebrates the girl's coming into womanhood and links her with health, strength, and fertility through the symbols of rain and the eland. The rite also affirms and celebrates femaleness.

During subsequent menstrual periods no formalities are observed and a woman's restraints are few. For example, she may gather plant foods and she may handle fire and cook for herself and her family, all of which she must avoid during first menstruation. She observes the avoidance required of all women regarding hunting, but when menstruating she must be especially assiduous in these avoidances. She is "poisonous-death" to hunting.

Menstrual blood is not believed to be unclean or to defile, as it is thought in some cultures. Instead, the !Kung say it is strong—a vital, powerful life substance. They believe that in conception menstrual blood unites with male semen and together those substances become the child. Menstrual blood is believed to have exceedingly strong n/um. The verb to menstruate is "*kuru.*" This verb also means "to make" and "to build." *A Bushman Dictionary* (Bleek 1956:107) gives in addition the translation "to work" and "to do." "Kuru" is a strong word, the !Kung say. The respect word for kuru is "*n/aba.*" The !Kung told us that women prefer not to have either of those words used. They prefer to refer to women's menstruation as *tsau n/um* (woman n/um). Another way to avoid the verb "kuru" is to use the euphemism "*ho n!ui,*" "to see the moon." The saying "to see the moon" might imply that the !Kung believe there is some mystical connection between the moon and women and women's monthly cycle. The !Kung may have held some such belief in the past, but those we were with did not make that association.

A Girl's First Menstruation

A !Kung girl is given no formal instruction in preparation for the beginning of menstruation. Girls learn about customs and the behavior expected of them as !Kung children learn in general—by being in constant contact with their families and the whole group of people who live together. The children, always present, hear what is said, watch what is done, and participate in every way they can in all the group's activities. Long before her first menstruation, a girl would be well aware of the beliefs and customs about menstruation and know what was expected of her.

When a girl becomes aware that her first menstruation has begun, she must stay where she is, crouched down in silence, covered closely with her kaross, eyes downcast, until a woman mentor comes to care for her. The girl's mother is in charge of the situation, but she herself must not be the one to care for the girl. When I asked why the mother must not be the mentor, the women were astounded at my ignorance. Vehemently they stated what they had thought everyone knew—that the mother had given birth to the girl and obviously that is why she must not touch her daughter while the girl's first menstrual blood is flowing. They could not understand how I had missed knowing such an important fact of life. They could explain no more, and I was left to think about the mystery of blood—to use Eliade's phrase (Eliade 1958)—and wonder if the blood of childbirth and that of first menstruation are mystically connected in !Kung belief and if their exceedingly strong n/umsi must be kept apart.

As soon as the flow stops, it is the mother who ritually bathes the girl. Other women would help or would conduct the ritual bath if the mother were not present. Meanwhile, during the flow a mentor cares for the girl.

If the woman for whom the girl is named (her !gun!a) is present and able-bodied enough, she becomes the mentor. In many instances this would be the girl's grandmother. If the namesake is not present, another woman becomes the mentor. She should be a woman with whom the girl has the joking relationship, whom the girl addresses with the kinship term *"tun,"* or she might be the girl's older sister, her *!kwi,* with whom the girl also has the joking relationship. I asked what they would do if the family were traveling alone and no other woman were present except the girl's mother who does not have the joking relationship with her daughter. The !Kung women again showed their flexibility and practicality in observing rituals. Of course the mother would take care of the girl, the women said. She would have to do so to protect the girl and to protect the husband and the boys of the family from losing their hunting powers.

The mentor must be strong enough to carry the girl on her back to the place where the seclusion shelter will be built. The ritual requires that the girl's feet must not touch the ground. Two women demonstrated the carrying for our mutual amusement. One bent forward so far that the girl lay horizontally on her back, her feet hanging down but not touching the ground. The other carried the girl more nearly upright in piggyback fashion and held the girl's legs up at her sides. Strong little women that they are, they are barely able to trudge steadily ahead under the weight of the girls.

In an actual Menarcheal Rite, the women build the seclusion shelter at a little distance from the cluster of family fires and shelters that comprise a !Kung encampment. The !Kung like to be near together. Wherever they camp, their shelters and fires are only a few feet apart. !Kung ritual requirements are not observed in extreme or severe form, and they do not require that the menstruating girl be withdrawn to any great distance. Twenty feet would be enough to express her required separation from the group.

The women build a shelter in about forty-five minutes. It may be a little smaller than the usual family shelter and slightly more rounded, with a smaller than usual opening. It is closely thatched with grass, and a mat of grass is laid on the ground inside.

When the shelter is ready, the mentor carries the girl into it, seats her on the grass mat facing inward, her kaross drawn up over her head. The girl sits there in silence. She must not look at the sky. The sun must not shine upon her. She must not look at people, especially men or boys; her gaze would destroy their power to hunt. In such a position the girl spends the days of her flow. After sunset as darkness comes, the mentor carries the girl to her own fire and sleeping place in the encampment where they sleep together. Before sunrise the mentor carries the girl back to the seclusion shelter.

Each day the mentor builds a fire near the entrance of the shelter and keeps it burning all day. The fire has a ritual purpose; the mentor does not cook on it, she cooks on another little fire built a little distance from the shelter. The girl does not cook and must strictly avoid both fires.

The mentor attends to the girl's needs. She brings her food and water. She carries her out to urinate and defecate, keeping the girl's head covered, keeping her feet from touching the ground. A place must be chosen that will not accidentally be stepped on by hunters. A hunter's strength and skill would be nullified by such a contact.

At some time during the first day in the shelter, the girl is bathed by the mentor. This is the first of two ritual baths. In this first bath only the upper half of the girl's body is bathed. The mentor roasts some plant food in the ritual fire before the shelter. The rich, nourishing tsi seeds are the preferred plant food for this ritual bath; mangetti nuts and n≠wara (*Trochomeria debilis* [Sond.] Hook.) are also desirable for the rite. Gwe (*Raphionacme burkei* N.E. Br.), prized for its succulence, might be used. If none of these particularly desirable foods are available, the mentor would make do with whatever plant food she could obtain. When the plant food is cooked, it is pounded to a paste and mixed with fat and sha sha. The girl stands or sits on a mat of grass wearing only her front apron. The mentor rubs the plant food over the upper half of the girl's body, then vigorously rubs it off. The material rubbed off the girl is gathered up and carefully disposed of under a bush where it will not be stepped on. The symbolism of the bath seems not to be to cleanse the girl but to associate her with plant food, hence, with plenty and well-being. A second bath is given at the end of the girl's menstrual flow.

Every day, while the girl is in her seclusion shelter, the women assemble to celebrate by dancing the Eland Dance around her.

THE AVOIDANCES

The girl strictly observes several avoidances during the period of first menstruation. The avoidances have several functions. Some are observed to strengthen the girl's character so that she can bear hunger bravely and so that she will be gentle and amenable in her behavior within the group. Some are observed to protect the girl from sickness, injury, and disability. The !Kung give special emphasis to protecting the girl from getting thin. Some of the avoidances protect the hunters and hunting equipment from the girl's strong tsau n/um. Others have to do with the interplay between the girl and the elements.

The sun and sky

The sun must not shine upon the menstruating girl and she must strictly avoid looking at the sun. Just as strictly she must avoid looking at clouds or the sky itself. The sun is conceived to be devastating—a "death thing." The !Kung say it scorches the people and dries the water sources. The sun is dangerous at any time, but should the girl in first menstruation look at it with her n/um in its most powerful state, the sun would become still hotter and destroy the plant foods. If the girl looked at the clouds they would give no rain. Her looking at the sky would open the world to misfortune.

Some /Gwi, describing their beliefs, which are very similar to those of the !Kung, said not only would the girl's looking at the sky open the world to potential unspecified misfortune, she would cause the dangerous things to come forth. They began to list the dangerous things that would come forth and mentioned lions, leopards, scorpions, and sharp sticks that the hunters might step on. The girl herself would be especially subject to injury at this time and is protected by her seclusion and covering.

It is interesting to remember that a !Kung bride on her wedding day must also be protected from the sun. The bride spends the whole day before the wedding covered from the sun; the wedding takes place after sundown. (See Marshall 1976:278.)

The earth

The feet of the girl in first menstruation must not touch the earth. She is carried by her mentor. A bride's feet must not touch the earth either. When she makes her formal approach to her wedding shelter, she is carried by a young female relative. If a girl at her wedding failed to observe this, she would become "as thin as a bone," as would the menstruating girl.

The women told me that this had happened to Khuan//a. She had become very thin, and the women believed it was because she had walked on the earth when her first menstrual flow began. She had not realized what it was and she walked to the encampment from where she had been gathering. She soon became alarmingly thin. Although she had not violated the avoidance law intentionally, she had violated it, and the women believed she had suffered the consequence. By the time we saw her she had recovered and was a beautiful, healthy, vigorous girl, the "teaser."

Not only must the menstruating girl's feet not touch the earth, she must avoid the earth in another way. She must not convey food to her mouth with her hands but must use a stick instead. Among the /Gwi the sticks are whittled and shaped by old men who give them as gifts to the girls. For some time before their first menstruation the girls wear them as ornaments. Among the !Kung any suitable-sized stick may be picked up and used, but it must be well cleaned. The girl uses it because she must avoid earth. The girl's hands might be dirty, people say, and a particle of earth from her hands might get into the girl's mouth. If she ate the smallest particle she would become very, very thin.

Rain and drinking water

If a girl's first menstruation should occur during the first rain of the season, the girl must be carefully protected so that not a drop of rain touches her. Rain has n/um, and the first rain has exceedingly strong n/um. In !Kung belief, if the first rain were to fall freely on the girl, this would cause the rain to leave her people's place, to go around it and not fall on it again for a very long time. Also, first rain touching the girl would cause her skin, which is especially tender at this time, to erupt in sores. The girl would become thin and might even become seriously ill and die. If her first menstruation occurs later in the season of the rains, the girl must drink rainwater with sha sha in it at her first opportunity. Then rain falling on her will cause no harm.

Throughout the period of her first menstruation, the girl may drink either rainwater or water from the water hole. Sha sha would be added to either. A most stringent rule, however, requires that, like a young hunter, she must not drink water from an ostrich eggshell. Other water containers that the !Kung use are bags made from the stomachs of animals and wooden bowls. The girl may drink water from either of these containers.

Hunting and the hunters

At first menstruation, because a woman's n/um is at its very strongest, a girl is most dangerous to hunting. For her to touch a hunter would be unthinkable among the !Kung. She must not even look at men or boys. They would lose their courage and energy as well as their hunting powers. They would not be able to find spoor to follow or to see animals. Instead, the animals would see them from afar and run away. All women must avoid touching hunting equipment, the girl in first menstruation especially. Her touch would totally and permanently destroy the efficacy of the equipment and the power of the arrow poison.

When I was beginning to make a study of the Menarcheal Rite, ≠Toma, who had observed my method of interrogation for some time by then, asked me not to try to talk to any young men about the hunting avoidances in connection with menstruation. Men should not speak to a woman about menstruation, especially young hunters. To do so would make them weak and lazy.

Restraints on cooking and eating

The girl strictly avoids fire, and she avoids cooking. The mentor cooks or otherwise prepares the girl's food and serves it to her. A very important symbolic act required of the girl is that, whatever amount of food she has been served, she must leave some of it. The mentor eats what the girl leaves. This exercise in restraint strengthens the girl's self-control and her ability to endure hunger. Such ability is held a virtue among the !Kung. Lack of self-restraint or a show of greed are met with strong social disapproval among these people. They would "laugh at" a girl who could or would not restrain excessive expression of hunger.

Animal foods

Meat was the first to be mentioned when the women began to tell me what foods the girl must avoid during her Menarcheal Rite. With the exception of pounded sha, forked sha, and roots chopped with a digging stick with earth in them, all the food avoidances required of the young (both boys and girls) and of women and girls are animal foods; certain animals, certain parts of animals, milk, and eggs. The avoidances required of the girl in her Menarcheal Rite go further; she must avoid all animal foods. The meat of all the animals the hunters bring, all birds and eggs, all snakes, lizards, tortoises, baby bees, and honey are included in the avoidance. The women mentioned hides as well. Hides, well-scraped and dried to a crisp, are pounded to a meal and regularly eaten by the !Kung. The girl must strictly avoid this food.

Although all young people avoid eating birds' eggs and avoid ostrich eggs most strictly, the women talked about this avoidance as though it had special significance during the Menarcheal Rite. They emphatically stated that the girl must not eat ostrich eggs or drink water that has been in an ostrich-eggshell container. If she failed to observe these avoidances she would go mad.

Plant foods

Telling me about the plant foods that the girl may or may not eat while she is in seclusion, the women talked at length among themselves, aiding each other's memories, and settled on a list of fifteen foods that the girl should avoid and three that are good for her to eat. Those that are proper and good for her are:

n≠a	berry	*Ziziphus mucronata* Willd.
//ore	tuber	*Brachystelma* sp.
sha	root	*Vigna dinteri* Harms

The women told us that sha is especially favored because it grows in soft sand. However, sha sometimes occurs as a double root, forked, and such a one must be avoided by all young girls. A forked !xwa must also be avoided. No one could explain the significance of the soft sand and the forked roots.

Plant foods that should be avoided:

Tubers or bulbs

!ama	tuber	*Ceropegia tentaculata* N.E. Br.
!ga	tuber	*Coccinia rehmanii* Cogn.
!goro	bulb	*Dipcadi* sp.
n!umshe	bulb	*Dipcadi* sp.
*!xwa	storage organ	*Fockea* sp.
*//haru	corm	*Lapeyrousia cyanescens* Bak.
†tshu	storage organ	*Walleria nutans* Kirk

Berries

†n/n	berry	*Grewia flava* DC.
!gwa	berry	*Grewia retinervis* Burret

Nuts and Seeds

*†//k'a	mangetti nut	*Ricinodendron rautanenii* Schinz
*†tsi	seed	*Bauhinia esculenta* Burch.

Fruit

*≠m	baobab fruit	*Adansonia digitata* L.
mai	fruit	*Dichapetalum cymosum* [Hook.] Engl.
n!oshu	fruit	*Pentarrhinum insipidum* E. Mey.

Melon

tsha	melon	*Citrullus naudinianus* [Sond.] Hook. f.

*Avoided by hunters before a hunt
†"Tshoaed" by girls every spring

If the girl failed to observe these avoidances, she would become as thin as a bone.

One wonders whether food avoidances impose too much hardship on the girl who must avoid all animal foods and fifteen plant foods as well. In *The !Kung of Nyae Nyae* (Marshall 1976: chap. 3), describing plant foods and gathering, I list sixty-five plant foods, counting all kinds—tubers, roots, berries, fruits, melons, nuts, seeds, leaves, and gums. Not all of them are available to any one group at any one time, but still there would be enough to provide something for the menstruating girl to eat. Of a list of twelve that were the most important plant foods in the diet of the Gautscha people, only three must be avoided during the Menarcheal Rite.

THE ELAND SONGS AND THE ELAND DANCE

The Menarcheal Rite has aspects other than restrictions and avoidances—affirmative ones rather than restrictive ones. It ushers the girl into womanhood and it evokes concepts of health, strength, plenty, and well-being. Through the association of ideas established in Bushman cultures over the ages, the eland is a symbol of these good things. Eland symbolism is specifically brought into association with the !Kung Menarcheal Rite by the naming of the songs—the Eland Songs—and by the dance of the women—the Eland Dance. In this dance the women represent female elands. They take off their karosses and back aprons, hang strings of beads down their bare buttocks to represent eland tails, and, naked except for their front aprons, they sing the Eland Songs and dance around and around the girl in her shelter.

The Eland Songs

The principal song of the Menarcheal music is the Great Eland Song *(N!i Ts'i N!a)*; the several other songs of this repertory are called Small Eland Songs *(N!i Ts'isi Ma)*. Nicholas England gives a splendidly detailed description and analysis of this music in his work on !Kung music, *Music Among the Zū'/'wā-si and Related Peoples of Namibia, Botswana, and Angola* (1995: chap. 6). I take much information about the music from him.

The Great Eland Song is found among the Bushmen of several language groups. In addition to finding it among the Nyae Nyae !Kung and the !Kung at /Gwia, we found it among the Nharo, Tsau, and !Ko, all south of the !Kung. We did not find the Great Eland Song or eland symbolism associated with the Menarcheal Rite among the /Gwi[2] or among the more northern Bushman groups we visited, namely, the Kxoe (Kwengo) at Popa Falls in Namibia, the Tsexa near the M'Babe Depression in Botswana, or the !Kung at Tshimbaranda in Angola.

The Great Eland Song is truly traditional. The !Kung have no memory or lore about its origins except to say that it came from the Old Old People. The fact that it is sung by several language groups testifies to its age.

The Small Eland Songs differ from one another in the several groups. The songs are composed in different scales, none in the scale of the Great Eland Song.

The scale of the Great Eland Song is the one that England calls the Rain-Eland Scale (England 1995: chaps. 4, 6). The Rain Song *(!Ga Ts'i),* which has now been taken into the Healing Dance repertory, and the Great Eland Song of the Menarcheal Rite are composed in this scale. In all the musical repertories of these musical people, only these two songs are composed in the Rain-Eland Scale. England thinks it may represent "the oldest layer of Bushman tonal materials" (England 1995: chap. 6). The scale associating life-giving rain and the eland with the girl in the Menarcheal Rite reinforces the symbolism of plenty and well-being.[3]

The menarcheal music is sung by the women when they gather around the seclusion shelter to dance the Eland Dance. Some of the women stand in a group to sing and clap the rhythmic beat. One of them clinks two adze blades together to represent the sound of eland footfalls. The other women dance, singing as they dance but not clapping. They stop from time to time, and some of the dancers change places with some of the women in the singing-clapping chorus.

The singing is like that of the Ritual Healing Dance chorus in many respects. The songs are without words. The women sing in contrapuntal lines. They sing loudly, and they yodel. In singing the menarcheal music, however, the women employ what England calls a special technique that sets the menarcheal music apart from the music of the Healing Dance. It is, in England's words, "a continuous elevation of the general pitch level of the entire polyphonic complex. . . . The rise is ever so slight (microtonal) with each few successive beats; but it is inexorably steady" (England 1995: chap. 6). The pitch rise covers a whole octave. The voices then drop to the original level and begin the rise once more. This occurs time and time again throughout the performance. England knows of no other music in which the pitch rise is so extensive and consistent. He says, "the technique brings to the Eland Songs of Nyae Nyae an extremely dynamic quality, further enhanced by the shimmering sounds of the tonal elements upon which the vocal polyphony is composed" (England 1995: chap. 6).

The women clap an intricate rhythmic pattern. The pattern has the same metric lines that the Healing Dance music has, the lines called !gaba and ≠ku. The !gaba line in the Eland music is a steady two-pulse beat, the same beat that is struck by the women's dance steps. The beat represents the slow trot of the eland. One of the ≠ku lines is basic to the metric pattern. England says these lines organize the !gaba line into metric groups of four (England 1995: chap. 6). In all !Kung music, this rhythmic pattern is found only in the ritual music of the Menarcheal Rite and Tshoma. The women may clap other ≠ku lines as variations, but the pattern of !gaba and ≠ku lines mentioned above is basic to this music and is always in evidence (England 1995: chap. 6).

In the Great Eland Song, the melodies that the women sing, built on the tones of the Rain-Eland Scale, are formed into three melodic lines that England calls A, B, and C. A and B constitute the main theme, B is what England calls an imitative answer to A. Line C is used for additional musical interest and is not essential to the main theme. The women sing the lines in counterpoint. Some will begin with the A line, others come in with the B line. After these lines are well established, some may add a C line, weaving it in and out (England 1995: chap. 6).

The women manage to produce many variations within the basic framework. In the metric lines, the women may put a triplet of three pulses into a two-pulse space. They hold back or push ahead a pulse in the ≠ku line against the steady, driving two-pulse beat of the !gaba line. They may sing in the octave that suits their voices, above or below the main statement of the line. They create individual variation to the melodic themes. England describes women standing close together in the chorus "bouncing off" two variants one against the other and against the main statement of lines A and B, taking obvious pleasure in the "thematic duels" (England 1995: chap. 6). With the continuous rising pitch and the yodel in the high reaches, this is indeed vibrant music.

The Eland Dance

The women's dancing accompanies the singing as an integral part of the rite. In referring to it, the women might say "we are dancing eland," but they do not give a title to the dance per se as they do to the songs. The dance is a special dance nevertheless, and needing to refer to it, I, with other writers, have called it the Eland Dance.

In the literature on Bushmen, the dance has been called the Eland Bull Dance by several writers, among them Siegfried Passarge (Passarge 1907:102), Dorothea Bleek (Bleek 1928:23), Isaac Schapera (Schapera 1930:119), and J. D. Lewis-Williams (Lewis-Williams 1981b:43ff). The !Kung we worked with did not use "bull" or "male" in the titles of their songs or in reference to the dance. Although the male eland is specifically represented in the Eland Dance, the male role is given much less prominence than the female role. Male participation in the dance is not absolutely essential to the ritual; it may be omitted. To call the dance the Eland Bull Dance seemed inappropriate.

Among the !Kung, all men and boys are excluded and must remain at a distance, except for one or two old men who portray the bulls. They wear sticks on their heads to represent eland horns. The men must be old, well beyond hunting age, and they must have the joking relationship with the menstruating girl. If no such old man happens to be present, the eland bull role is omitted. To my disappointment, no old men appeared when the !Kung women danced at Gautscha and at /Gwia, so we do not know how they play their role.

Among the Nharo, any number of men representing eland bulls dance from time to time with the women. When the Nharo group at !Go Tsao danced for us, five men danced. One man had sticks shaped like eland horns tied to his head; the others held branched sticks against their heads representing horns. With delightful pantomime they imitated bull elands approaching the females, sidling up to them, following close behind, and turning and brandishing their horns at other men to ward off rivals. The dancing women made no playful response to the men's playfulness. Intent upon their own role, they danced earnestly onward, around and around the girl.

Among the !Kung, when the mentor has carried the girl each morning into the seclusion shelter, all the women gather to sing and dance around the shelter. Young girls who have not yet menstruated attend but do not take part in the singing or dancing. Sometimes the women dance at night, as well, around the mentor and the girl at the mentor's fire in the encampment. The morning dance is more usual among the !Kung.

The morning dance is early. By pointing to the sky to show where the sun would be (the way the !Kung customarily indicate time of day), the women indicated that they would dance from shortly after sunrise to midmorning. They then go off to gather or perform other daily tasks, and the girl and her mentor spend the remainder of the day quietly together.

On the morning of the dance at /Gwia, a young girl was chosen to represent the menstruating girl. A mentor was chosen for her, a woman who, as the actual ritual required, had the joking relationship with the girl. The mentor's shelter was used for the seclusion shelter. All the women of the band gathered near the shelter laughing and talking in a lively mood. As was ritually required, the men and boys withdrew, but only to the far end of the encampment where they sat behind a shelter and peered around it from time to time to have a look at whatever was going on. The exclusion of men in the Menarcheal Rite is evidently not as strict a ritual exclusion as that required at Tshoma when women must be totally excluded. At /Gwia an exception was made for Nicholas England. Young though he was, the obliging /Gwia women allowed him to stay and record the music.

The girl's mother had been pounding the red heartwood of a dead Rhodesian teak tree into a powder *(n≠n)*. She mixed the powder with fat, and she and the mentor rubbed the mixture lightly over the girl's body. We had been told that the menstruating girl should sit on a mat of grass in her shelter facing inward. In this demonstration the mentor and another woman wrapped the girl, head and all, in a big kaross and laid her down on grass in the shelter. There she lay while the women danced.

At this point the women took off their karosses and their back aprons and stood naked except for their front aprons and ornaments. Several hung long strings of ostrich-eggshell beads down their bare buttocks to represent cow eland tails. They divided themselves into two groups. Some stood clustered together to clap and sing. One woman made the sound of eland footfalls by clinking two metal ankle ornaments together. We were told that this sound not only represented eland footfalls, but would make the menstruating girl "hear nicely," so that when the girl would be asked to do something, such as to fetch water from the water hole, she would obey and respond cheerfully.

The other women formed a line and began to dance around the shelter, first in one direction, then the other, singing but not clapping. The dancing line might make a simple circle or an ellipse, we were told, but this lively group made a figure eight, dancing counterclockwise halfway around the shelter, then making a large clockwise circle, then encircling the shelter again counterclockwise.

After dancing for some time, the women stopped. Laughing and chatting, some of the dancers changed places with those in the singing, clapping group and soon the dancing line started again.

Only the dance step itself was not what we might call lively. It was entirely different from the quick little rhythmic steps that the women use at the Ritual Healing Dance. The Eland Dance step was a straightforward heavy, flat-footed running step that produced a dull thud. The step did suggest the gait and rhythm of a heavy eland in a slow trot. However, the steps were not plodding. The women danced with precision, vigor, and with apparent intense concentration, singing loudly all the while, their naked bodies gleaming in the morning sunshine.

The nakedness, the clarion singing, and the intensity of the dance lifted it entirely out of ordinary daily experience. It made a powerful statement. Its meaning is to bring to the girl the goodness that the Rain-Eland Scale stands for: strength, health, fatness, plenty, well-being. One woman said to me, "We dance eland because the eland is a happy thing." I thought, looking at those vigorous women, that the Eland Dance was indeed a "happy thing" and that it also made a vivid affirmation of femaleness.

The End of the Menarcheal Rite

The mood of the dance continues for a time after the dancing ends, and when the girl's menstrual flow has stopped, she comes out of her shelter. It is in that mood that the girl is given her second bath. The mother may now touch her daughter, and if she is present, she gives the second bath. If she were not present, the mentor or some other woman would bathe the girl. I had seen N!ai bathed by her mother the morning after her wedding night, and I was told that the menstruating girl's bath is given the same way. "Bathe" is the word I was given, but "anoint" would be a more precise word to describe the process. The girl stands near the ritual fire wearing only her front apron. The woman bathing the girl has prepared the plant food paste, preferably made with tsi, with sha sha in it, as for the girl's first bath. She rubs the paste over the girl's whole body and rubs it off with special care. She then anoints the girl all over with fat. Eland fat is preferred, of course, but if none is available, the woman uses whatever fat she has.

The girl is then marked with ritual markings. If tsi is available, it would be used. If the tsi season is past and none is available, crushed hematite is used. The tsi, roasted in the n/um fire, or the hematite is made into a paste with fat. The mother or the other woman who has bathed the girl takes this substance onto her finger and draws a line with it down the girl's throat, chest, and abdomen, thickly covering the umbilicus with the paste. She draws a similar line down the girl's back. We were told that the line over the abdomen makes the girl's heart strong to bear hunger so that she will not greedily ask for food. The paste on the umbilicus makes the girl grow fat.

A design is then painted on the girl's face. The design is red. It is the same design that is painted on the face of a bride at the time of her wedding. A line about a quarter of an inch wide is drawn across her forehead curving down each cheek to the nose. No one could tell us about the origin of the design or its possible symbolic associations, but we were told that it keeps sickness away.

The girl is then adorned with hair ornaments, earrings, necklaces, bracelets, and anklets. Relatives give or lend her many ornaments at this time so that she will be beautiful in celebration of her new womanhood.

The Girl's Husband

Many girls are married before their first menstruation. N!ai, whose wedding we attended in 1952, did not menstruate until 1959. If the girl has a husband when her first menstruation occurs, he must be ritually protected. Without this protection his wife's menstruation would cause him to be weak and tired and to have pains in his bones. Furthermore, he would have bad luck in hunting and be liable to serious injury. To prevent all this, he is given a ritual bath by his wife's mentor. He stands wearing his breechclout, as always, and is sloshed all over with water that has sha sha in it. A design is then painted on his body with a paste made of marrow, if available, or fat, mixed with n/um plants. The plants used in this ritual are those the healers keep in their tortoise shells: //gwey and !gein were mentioned. The plants are charred, and the paste is black. The mentor draws lines with it up the backs of the young man's legs, over his buttocks, up his back and across his shoulders, on his upper arms, down his chest, abdomen, the fronts of his legs, and over his feet. Circles are drawn around his eyes. Thus striped in black, he looks beautiful, we were told, and his legs would be strong for running and his arms strong for shooting, and the poison on his arrows would be strong to kill the game. His strength and skills ritually protected, he brings strength to his group.

THE TSHOA RITE

In her new state, the girl is reunited with the world of food in the Tshoa Rite, which she and her mentor perform together. First they tshoa fire and the cooking of plant foods. The mentor builds a special fire for the purpose and brings whatever plant food she has at hand. When the fire has burned down, the mentor places some of the plant food on the coals and takes some sha sha in her mouth. She and the girl together grasp the fire paddle, the mentor's hands over the girl's hands. The mentor blows her sha sha breath on the girl's hands, and as she does so, they cover the plant food with coals and ashes.

When the food is cooked, the girl takes some of it into her mouth with some sha sha. The mentor, again with sha sha in her mouth, blows on the girl's face and at the same time rubs the back of the girl's neck, her throat, cheeks, breasts, and abdomen. The mentor does this so that food will not give the girl pains in her stomach. This procedure also protects the girl from the strength of the fire. If she touched the fire before being protected in this way, she would get thin. The Tshoa Rite keeps her healthy and fat.

The next procedure is to tshoa the girl's gathering. She and the mentor go gathering together. When they find a root, the mentor places her hands over the girl's hands on the digging stick, blows sha sha breath on their hands, and together they dig the root. Throughout that day, each time they find a different plant food—berry, fruit, root, anything—they gather it with their hands together, the mentor blowing on their hands with sha sha in her mouth.

That day's procedure concludes the performance of the Tshoa Rite for the act of gathering, but the girl continues to tshoa the eating of the plant foods. Each plant food, whoever has gathered it, must be "tshoaed" the first time the girl eats it after her Menarcheal Rite has ended.

10 Tshoma

Tshoma is a rite of passage that brings the boys into manhood. The rite came to the Nyae Nyae !Kung from the south, we were told. A !Kung man married to a Nharo woman had learned Tshoma from her people and brought it to the !Kung. Old Demi, who we judged was in his seventies at the time, said that Tshoma had come when his father was a young man. Old Demi pointed to a young man of comparable age whom we guessed to be in his early twenties. That would place the coming of Tshoma to the Nyae Nyae !Kung around the turn of the century. Since then it has been regularly practiced among them.

Tshoma was not held while any of our expedition members were in the field. The information we gathered about it was obtained by talking with the !Kung and by our observation of one practice session of the Tshoma dance, the *Tshxai !Go* (Men's Dance), held at Gautscha. Although Tshoma is said to have secret aspects that must not be spoken of with the uninitiated, the !Kung were at liberty to talk about many aspects with us and did so. Whatever aspects they chose not to talk about remained their secret. I turned my inquiries about Tshoma mainly to the old men with whom I was on very friendly terms—Old Demi, Old Gaú, Old N!aishi, and Old ≠Toma. I have used the notes gathered by my daughter, Elizabeth, and my son, John, as well as my own. I have also drawn freely on observations of Nicholas England and Megan Biesele, all with their kind permission. England made a study of Tshoma music among the Nyae Nyae !Kung, which he presents in *Music Among the Zū'/'wā-si and Related Peoples of Namibia, Botswana, and Angola* (1995).[1] Biesele worked with !Kung in Botswana in the 1970s and has information on Tshoma from them, which she has shared with me in personal communication. I know of no eyewitness account in the anthropological literature of the performance of the actual rite; Biesele bears me out. Hans-Joachim Heinz was taken into Tshoma by the !Ko and describes some aspects of the preliminary procedures in *Namkwa* (Heinz and Lee 1979:106ff), but he has kept a vow of secrecy about the rite itself.

The distribution of Tshoma among Bushman language groups has not been thoroughly studied, as far as I know. I can report that in the groups with whom we had contact, England recorded Tshoma music among Auen, Nharo, !Ko, and Tsau (all to the south of the !Kung). He did not find the music among the Angola !Kung or the !Xu of Popa Falls. When he brought up the subject, these people emphatically denied having Tshoma. England was not entirely convinced, however, that they were not keeping the rite a secret (England 1995: chap. 5).

The question arises as to whether Tshoma came originally to Bushmen from the Bantu-speaking peoples. Schapera points out that there is no definite record of a puberty rite for boys among the southern Bushmen (Schapera 1930:125). The above-mentioned groups who do have Tshoma live in a central geographic area between latitudes 19°S and 23 1/2°S, with links existing between the groups. There has been direct contact between at least some of these groups with the Tswana, since the Tswana began to bring their herds for summer grazing to western Botswana in the 1880s (Lee 1965:57). The fact that no record exists of the southern Bushmen having a boy's puberty rite suggests that the concept of the rite may have come to the Bushmen from the Tswana when the Tswana became their neighbors. Schapera leaves the question open (Schapera 1930:126).

England heard the Nharo claim that they had Tshoma long ago; "their fathers' fathers owned it" (England 1995: chap. 5). He thinks they indeed may have been the first among Bushman groups to have the rite. He does not venture a guess as to whether the Nharo were the originators or early adopters of the rite. Wherever the concept came from originally, the rite has spread from Bushman group to Bushman group. Each group has adapted it to its own group culture, which has resulted in considerable divergence in the details of the practices.

Aspects of Tshoma

As the rite is now practiced by the Nyae Nyae !Kung, most of the ritual elements are precisely those found in other !Kung rites—scarifications, ritual baths, food avoidance, and the Tshoa Rite, for instance. One element, however, does seem to come from the Bantu—the bull-roarer *(n≠abbi)*. The scrapings of the bull-roarer are used with the scarification aspects of the Tshoma Rite, and it is not used in any other Nyae Nyae !Kung ritual. It is, therefore, kept secret and hidden between Tshoma celebrations.

Tshoma and the Rite of First Kill

The relatively recently acquired Tshoma did not replace the other Nyae Nyae !Kung rite of passage, the Rite of First Kill, which continues to be a major ritual requirement in the culture. Before they may marry, boys must prove themselves to be hunters by having killed a large game animal and having had the Rite of First Kill performed.

The two rites are independent of each other. Each has a different emphasis. The Rite of First Kill is compulsory in !Kung culture; Tshoma is not. (This suggests to me a foreign origin for Tshoma.) Most boys do participate in Tshoma, but if a boy chooses not to do so, he is not penalized. The older men who had not been in Tshoma were not discriminated against either. The Rite of First Kill is quietly and simply performed by each boy. Tshoma involves groups—all the initiated men who are called Tshoma owners *(Tshoma k"xausi)* and all the boys of proper age. Tshoma has a little pomp and circumstance; the Rite of First Kill has none. The Rite of First Kill celebrates, affirms, and enhances the power of the young man to hunt. In the Tshoma Rite, *Tshoma n/um* (male n/um) is recognized and celebrated as such, and is given to the boys, bringing them into manhood. Tshoma n/um also enhances the power to hunt. Both rites are important in !Kung culture.

Tshoma and Healers

We found a difference of opinion or a change in belief among the Nyae Nyae !Kung with respect to the relationship of Tshoma to healers. In the belief of the !Kung I worked with, the n/um of the healers was not believed to be the same as Tshoma n/um and Tshoma was definitely not a prerequisite to becoming a healer. My daughter, Elizabeth, however, was told by younger people that a boy must have been through Tshoma before he could become a healer (field note, 1/15/1953, p. 3). England heard both beliefs expressed, that Tshoma is a prerequisite to healing and that it is not.

The age of each !Kung with whom I spoke could account for some of the divergences that were expressed—this one in particular. The older men knew healers who had not been in Tshoma, whereas the young man talking with Elizabeth had possibly not known a healer who was not also a Tshoma owner.

Women and Tshoma N/um

Women are strictly excluded from the Tshoma Rite itself, and they must avoid saying the name "Tshoma": they refer to the rite by the name of one of the dances, the Tshxai !Go.

The Tshoma Rite takes place in a space defined by a brush fence at some distance from the encampment. The space is called the Tshoma encampment (*Tshoma tshu !ko*). I call it the Tshoma site. While the rite is in progress, women must not see the Tshoma site even from a distance. In the ritual proceedings concerning hunting, we learned that women avoid touching hunting equipment because, in !Kung belief, their strong female n/um negates male hunting powers and the strength of the arrow poison. In the beliefs about Tshoma, it is the male Tshoma n/um that is so strong it would bring harm to women. A woman who looked at the Tshoma site would die.

Old Demi and Old Gaú told me of a woman who had died from seeing a Tshoma site. She came from a distance on her way to visit relatives and had unwittingly walked up to the site while the rite was in progress. She died a short time later, and those two old men firmly believed that her death had been caused by her having seen a Tshoma site, albeit by accident. Megan Biesele was also told of a woman who died from seeing a Tshoma site in Botswana (personal communication). Old Demi and Old Gaú told me they had decided not to hold Tshoma while I was present in the area, lest it be a danger to me. A Tshoma was due that year, but they would wait until our group had left. They liked me, they said, and wanted no harm to come to me. I hoped that they believed I would not deliberately violate their rules; I hoped they only thought that with all my probing into their customs and because of my ignorance I might somehow stumble into Tshoma.

Another belief exemplifies the !Kung concept of the strength of Tshoma n/um and its possible ill effect upon women. Once a boy has received the Tshoma n/um, he must never point at his mother with his right arm.

Despite their strict avoidance of the Tshoma site, women have a part in the Tshoma proceedings. Before the boys are secluded in the Tshoma site, their mothers give them the ritual Tshoma haircut. Women provide all the food during the rite. They gather the plant foods that the boys are allowed to eat, prepare them, and present them to the old Tshoma owners, who come in the late afternoons during the rite to fetch the food for themselves and the boys and take it to the Tshoma site.

The Purpose of the Tshoma Rite

Among the Nyae Nyae !Kung, the purpose of the Tshoma Rite, we were told, is to put the Tshoma n/um into the boys and to bring the boys into the state of manhood by giving them "sense" (*≠in*), strengthening them physically, and increasing their endurance.

The Tshoma n/um, the strong male power, is called *n/um n!a n!a* (big, big n/um). It is said to be concentrated in the heads of the men who possess it, the Tshoma owners. They give it to the boys during the rite in some way not described.

Tshoma n/um contributes to the boys' hunting ability. One of its contributions is to make them "see well"—that is, to see animals when they are hunting.

To give them "sense," the boys are taught the importance of the !Kung social principles, and they are taught about hunting, although exactly what social principles and what aspects of hunting are emphasized we were not told.

The boys are strengthened by physical exercise and by the endurance of hardships. The physical exercise consists of long hours of dancing. The hardships that strengthen the boys are cold, fatigue, and hunger. These are real hardships, and they are endured by the boys, cold especially. The Tshoma owners who are sponsors to the boys must put the boys through the hardships, but their attitude is not harsh. It is not their purpose to drive the boys to their limits, to cause them pain, or to frighten them badly. The attitude we found among the men we talked with was one of consideration and protection.

Tshoma Assemblages

Tshoma is held at intervals of several years. We judged some of the intervals to be five or six years. Lee records intervals of from four to ten years among the !Kung he worked with (Lee 1979:365). One !Kung explained to us that it takes several years to "grow" enough boys. The group of boys to be initiated would be drawn from several neighboring bands—the bands at Gautscha, Deboragu, Nam Tshoha, Gura, and possibly Kaitsa and Kautsa. No one band has enough boys of the appropriate age at any given time to hold a proper Tshoma alone. Combined, they could gather groups of about ten to fifteen boys. At one point, just as a matter of interest, I counted twelve boys of a proper age for Tshoma in four of these bands.

When the Tshoma owners have decided that a Tshoma should be held in a certain year, they plan among themselves at which water hole the rite will take place. I have no past history of Tshoma, but I imagine that Gautscha was usually, or at least often, the choice because Gautscha had the best water hole, and Tshoma is held in the dry winter season when many water holes are low. The men watch the younger boys to decide which are strong enough to participate and which should wait until the next Tshoma is celebrated. The exact age of the boy is not definitely fixed. The youngest boy to participate might be fourteen or fifteen, the oldest, who might have just missed the previous Tshoma, might be nineteen or twenty. A boy may already be married when he participates, having already had the Rite of First Kill.

When it has been decided that Tshoma will be held, the participating groups each conduct preliminary practice dances to teach the boys the dance steps and the songs. The dancing and singing are a very important part of the rite.

The Tshoma Site

The time for Tshoma is signaled by the rising of the Pleiades about two hours before sunrise in mid-June, the coldest time of year. The participating groups agree upon a certain day for the rite and assemble two or three days in advance.

It is the duty of the Tshoma owners to prepare the Tshoma site. The site should be 400 or 500 yards from the encampment, and it must be directly east. The men take bearings from the sun. To prepare the site, they first clear the ground in a space that might be thirty or forty feet, perhaps more, in diameter. The site will be large enough to contain a space for dancing *(n!ai)*, a shelter for the boys to sleep in, and a fire that is distinctly distant from the n!ai and the shelter. The men eventually enclose that space with a low brush fence, leaving a narrow opening for an entrance facing west toward the encampment, and they clear a path from the Tshoma site to the encampment. Their next task is to cut small trees or branches to build the Tshoma shelter *(//kem)*. They choose trees with leaves for shade. The boys sleep in the shelter during the day. England gives us the information that the men tshoa the trees as they cut them. They take ≠khali into their mouths, chew it, and spew it out, or blow their breath on the trees (England 1995: chap. 5). The trees or branches are tamped into a circle of holes dug to receive them, their tips not woven together as they would be on a regular shelter. The ground inside the shelter is covered with grass; it is the boys' bed. We were told that //Gauwa comes the night the shelter is built and pours a magical substance on the grass around the shelter and on the grass inside.

The Boys' Activities

While the Tshoma owners prepare the site, the assembled boys spend the days quietly in the encampment. The women prepare food, and they also prepare a thin porridge of tsi or mangettis, preferably tsi. Knowing that a Tshoma was pending, they would have tried to save some tsi for this purpose. If there were no tsi or mangettis, they could substitute ≠oa (an unidentified medicine plant with some of the qualities of sha sha).

Just after sunset, the first ritual event takes place; the boys are given a haircut by their mothers or by some other female relative if the mother is not present. This is a very important aspect of the rite. I was told that the haircut must be given after sunset because Tshoma is a "night thing." The boys' heads are shaved except for a bunch of hair at the back of the neck. The hair that has been cut is gathered up and placed carefully under bushes to keep it from blowing away and causing the boys to lose their sense of direction. After they have given the boys their haircut, the women have nothing more to do with them until the end of the rite.

The Tshoma owners then take charge. Each boy has a sponsor. We were told that the sponsor is usually the boy's father but could be another male relative. The sponsor and the boy may or may not have the joking relationship. Occasionally a man will sponsor more than one boy. The boys must give their sponsors deference and complete, unquestioning obedience. They must not speak until they are spoken to and do nothing that they are not told to do.

After the haircut, each boy is given a ritual bath with the porridge that the women have prepared. Although the father may be the boy's sponsor, the father does not bathe his own son (as the mother does not bathe her daughter in the Menarcheal Rite). Another Tshoma owner bathes the boy. All ornaments are removed from the boy—earrings, strings of beads, arm bracelets, and under-knee bracelets. Dance rattles are not worn at Tshoma dances so the under-knee bracelets to which the rattles are attached are not needed. The man bathing the boy rubs handfuls of porridge over the boy and vigorously rubs it off. The boy's whole body is carefully bathed except for his genitals. The boys continue to wear their breechclouts.

When the bath is finished, the men and boys walk to the Tshoma site. As they approach the enclosure, the sponsors take their boys on their backs, or most of them do. Some big boys walk closely behind their sponsors. The boys close their eyes and put their faces against the backs of the sponsors' necks and in that position they enter the Tshoma site, and a new state in their lives.

The Procedures of Tshoma

During the boys' seclusion at the Tshoma site, several ritual practices take place. (Circumcision is not one of them; the !Kung do not circumcise.) The dancing and singing are in every way the most important. The men and boys dance every night from dusk until sunrise. As in the Healing Dances, they dance in periods of about ten or fifteen minutes with a short interval between the periods.

During the days the boys sleep lying on the grass in the shelter. They sleep without covering themselves with karosses or blankets, enduring cold. However, unless a south wind is blowing, the sunny days are not extremely cold, not as cold as the frigid nights when ice forms in the water bags.

Toward the end of the day, the boys are given a meager meal. A number of food avoidances are required, including a strict avoidance of all meat and several plant foods. However small the amount served them, the boys leave a little of what has been offered them, to symbolize restraint and to practice self-control. They must endure hunger.

Water is also given in moderate amounts, but frequently enough to prevent the boys from suffering severe thirst.

Each day the boys' heads are anointed with //gwey. The stone of the fruit of this evergreen bush is used. Story describes it as rich in oil and very pungent (Story 1958:19). The !Kung believe that the stone has very strong n/um. The stone is commonly used as a medicine for various ailments. Charred, pounded to a powder, and mixed with fat, it is rubbed over the affected part. //Gwey is one of the ingredients kept in the healers' tortoise shells.

An important procedure during Tshoma is the scarification of the boys. The scarifications are made in the same way as those of the Rite of First Kill. The man scarifying the boy pinches up a fold of skin where the mark is to be made and makes a line of tiny vertical cuts with a sharp knife or an unpoisoned arrowpoint. Two men together may hold up the fold of skin while one makes the cuts.

A black substance rubbed into the cuts as they bleed makes the scarification permanently dark when the cuts heal. The black substance used in the Tshoma scarification is charred bull-roarer. At the end of a Tshoma rite one of the Tshoma owners takes charge of the bull-roarer that has been used in the rite. It must be kept safe and must be kept out of sight of women and uninitiated men and boys. It might be hidden in a tree. When the boys of the next Tshoma are to be scarified, the wooden blade of the old bull-roarer is carefully charred in the fire, and this charred substance is rubbed into the Tshoma scarifications.

The special tshoma scarification is a vertical line about one and a half inches long in the center of the forehead, beginning at the level of the eyebrows. The line is composed of about twenty-four or twenty-five tiny horizontal cuts, each about one-eighth or three-sixteenths of an inch long, between one-sixteenth and one-eighth of an inch apart. This scarification marks the boy as a Tshoma owner.

Similar scarifications in horizontal lines are made on the boys' upper arms and under their shoulder blades to make them shoot their arrows well.

At some point in the procedures, the boys are given the Tshoma n/um. Like the healers' n/um, it is believed to be exuded in sweat. It would probably be in the intervals between the dance periods, when the men are sweating from the exertion of the strenuous dancing, that they would rub their sweat onto the boys, transferring the n/um.

I wish that we knew more about the teachings that the Tshoma owners impart to their charges. !Kung children as they grow up are not taught in any formalized way. They learn by being constantly with their elders, participating as they can in the activities of the group, hearing everything that is said. I imagine that the boys in Tshoma, particularly the elder ones, would already know much of what their sponsors would be talking about in their teaching. However, hearing the social rules and the hunting wisdom expounded in the charged atmosphere of Tshoma, they would probably listen as never before.

THE TSHXAI !GO (THE MEN'S DANCE)

The Tshxai !Go is in every way the most important part of the Tshoma Rite. Every night the men and boys dance the whole night through. The dance in the cold winter nights is the principal factor in strengthening the boys and increasing their endurance. Furthermore, it is at the dance, insofar as we know, that the boys receive the Tshoma n/um from their sponsors and become owners of the Tshoma songs.

Sometime before the actual rite takes place, the boys will have several practice dances at their own encampments to teach them the songs and the dance steps. One of these practice dances was held when we were present at Gautscha. It was held especially to include John Marshall. He was on very friendly terms with the young men with whom he hunted and with a number of the older men. Had a Tshoma been held when he was present, he might have been fully initiated. As it was, he was moved and honored to be included in a practice dance. //Ao Wildebeest was his sponsor.

The dance took place on a cold clear night in late May 1953 in the light of a quarter moon. The dancers grouped themselves at a little distance from the family fires of the encampment. Women are not excluded from a practice dance. Elizabeth and I and the !Kung women stood aside from the men, but not very far away. The women could easily run a few steps forward and throw sa powder on the men.

A group of ten or twelve men from Bands 1 and 2 assembled; the group of boys also numbered ten or twelve, including John. The boys quietly clustered themselves together. The men walked around joking and laughing. There was no solemnity at all. After a few minutes the men formed a circle around the boys, the men facing inward, the boys in their cluster facing outward. As the men moved into the circle, they shouted the sounds that animals make in a loud hubbub. Someone said, "One sings like a jackal, one like a hyena, one like a leopard, one like a lion," and so forth. John said of the animal sounds, "My friend //Ao told me that they were making special animal sounds so I would 'know' the animals. I thought it was some kind of spiritual 'knowing' or awareness that would help me know what to do when I met the animal and what the animal might be intending to do. My friend may have been hinting at the kind of knowledge or spiritual resource that would be given me in a real Tshoma."

The shouting of the animal sounds made a lively but brief interval. Soon one man began to sing, and the others joined him in a chorus. The boys stood in their cluster and did not sing. When the song ended, the men tramped around again for a few minutes, shouting to the boys to listen well and learn the song. They repeated the song twice more, and then one man turned to his right, others followed, and a dancing line was formed, which began to circle the boys in a counterclockwise direction. When the men began to dance, their singing changed to a chant of gasped vocables. The boys began to chant and dance also, their cluster slowly turning in the direction of the men's dancing line.

For a few minutes the men danced closely around the boys until one of the men shouted, "Come out!" Then the line began to spread as each boy danced out to join his sponsor. Together, with the sponsor holding the boy by the arm or shoulder, they formed a double dancing line—all without missing a beat of the dance rhythm.

One or another of the men seemed to take a position of leadership during a dance. At his signal to turn, the line changed directions from counterclockwise to clockwise and back to counterclockwise, and at his signal the dancers stopped abruptly.

At the Healing Dances, when I watched the dancing line moving in precise synchronization I used to think of millipedes. Although the line in the Tshxai !Go was less precisely formed—with men and boys together it had looked rather lumpy—I felt as I did when watching the Healing Dances that the synchronized movement in exact rhythmic precision melded the participants together. It was as though men and boys became one entity.

An interval followed the dance in which the boys returned to their cluster. The men tramped around shouting to the boys that they must pay attention and learn what was being taught to them. They talked and laughed as they had at the beginning, with no solemnity. Two or three of the women ran up to the men and tossed sa powder on them and two women danced their ecstatic little caper that they often dance at the Healing Dances. Two men picked up their karosses and wrapped themselves comfortably. Others slapped their arms around themselves in the cold. The boys stood shivering in their cluster, shifting their feet, looking very grave, even awed.

The dance was repeated five times that night with intervals between the dance periods. I do not have precise measurement of time, but my impression is that the periods of singing and dancing were perhaps about ten or twelve minutes, the intervals ten minutes. We have an hour and a half of sound recordings of that night.

The practice dance was what I shall refer to as a circle dance. It was typical of the actual Tshoma proceedings for that part of the Tshxai !Go. There is another dance that none of us has seen. My information comes from England (England 1995: chap. 5). Sometime during the night, the chanting men and boys dance out of the Tshoma site down the path toward the encampment. They go about three quarters of the way, not right up to the people's shelters and fires. This dance has the title of *"Tshoma Ts'i*

N!a" (Big Tshoma Song). The men and boys form a triple line, the boys in the middle, a line of men on each side of them. Two places along the path are established as places for a circle dance. One is about one-third of the way to the encampment, the other two-thirds of the way, where the line turns to dance back to the Tshoma site. When the dancing line reaches these places, it moves into them and dances around in a circle for a short time. From the second dance place, the line dances directly back to the Tshoma site. England has estimated that the Tshoma Ts'i N!a takes about thirty minutes. It is a long and strenuous dance.

The Music

The title "Tshxai !Go" means Men's Dance, but the actual dancing is only one of its elements—the songs and the chanting are equal parts. The title applies to the three elements and to the event as a whole.

England has given a detailed description of the recorded music of the 1953 practice dance (1995: chap. 5). I take the following information about the music from him.

In describing the fact that a song begins with one man singing out the first phase and the other men joining in a chorus, England calls the first singer a precentor and the singing of the chorus a responsory, playfully, but I think rightly, suggesting that the songs have the quality of a liturgy. There may be more than one precentor.

The principal songs sung at the practice dance were entitled "≠Kowa Ts'i N!a" (Big Giraffe Song), and "!Ga Ts'i" (Rain Song). "Giraffe" was repeated six times, "Rain" twice. Two other songs were sung briefly, "/Kam" (Sun) and "Zo" (Honey).

The musical material of two of the songs, "Giraffe" and "Rain," is that of the n/um songs of the Healing Dance repertory, sung in a very different manner. The women at the Healing Dances sing in counterpoint. When the men sing the Tshoma music, they all sing the same melodic line, but each may add his own embellishments, and as England says, "the rendition is a heterophonic one, often extremely heterophonic" (England 1995: chap. 5).

A responsory is usually repeated three times before the men begin to dance. Sometimes, however, three different songs may be sung at this time. There may be one or more precentor. With each rendition, the pitch is raised. It may only be raised a semi-tone higher or it may be a third or a fourth higher than before. Once established, it remains the same throughout the song (England 1995: chap. 5). The rising pitch is a feature also in the music of the Menarcheal Rite, in which the rise is much greater. It can be a whole octave, and it is continuous throughout the song (England 1995: chap. 6). It is interesting that the two rites of passage use this same technique. England says that to his knowledge it is unique with the Bushmen (1995: chap. 6).

The Chant

While the men dance they chant. The chant is unlike any other Bushman vocal expression that we heard or learned about: the men gasp or grunt a pattern of vocables. Dorothea Bleek, who heard the chant among the Nharo, rendered the sounds as "honk a honk" (Bleek 1928:34) and as "hanko, hankoho" (Bleek 1956:613) under the item //nai. England says of the vocables, "The vocal tone production in the chant is best described as a simultaneous sudden pressure from the diaphragm combined with tension of the vocal folds, and sometimes (but not always) a glottal release. The result is a forceful vocal sforzando effect" (1995: chap. 5).

England found four dance chants in the repertory. They are entitled "Tshoma T'si N!a" (Big Tshoma Song), "≠Kowa" (Giraffe), "!U" (Long-eared Fox), and "/Gwi Ta" (Hyena Penis) (England 1995: chap. 5).

The Dance Steps

In the Men's Dance, the body position is the same as the usual position in the Healing Dances—torso slightly bent forward, knees slightly bent, arms held any way but usually at the side bent at the elbow.

The dance steps are strong, driving stamps and forward-moving steps, which are lighter stamps. The dancers dance with great vigor, driving their legs forcibly down in the strong stamps. They dance in unison without the variations and light triplets of the Healing Dance steps.

At the beginning of the step the two feet are close together. On beat one, the right foot makes a little hop. The left foot quickly shares the body's weight and, still beside the right foot, makes a driving stamp on beat two. On beats three and four, the right foot makes two lighter stamping steps, moving forward several inches with each stamp. On beats five through eight, the pattern is repeated with the left foot making the little hop and the forward-moving stamps. The line of dancing men moves forward with this step. The boys dance in place until it is time for them to dance out.

The Bull-Roarer (N≠abbi)

At some time during the night of dancing, or perhaps more than once, one of the older men sounds the bull-roarer. The boys do not see the man. The sound comes from a distance. I was told emphatically that a bull-roarer must never be near the Tshoma fire, but no one could tell me what would happen to the bull-roarer, to the fire, or to the men and boys if this Tshoma rule were broken. When a Tshoma session ends, the bull-roarer is hidden from sight until the next Tshoma is celebrated, and a new bull-roarer is made.

England made the following sketch of a n≠abbi. He says, "To judge from descriptions given by several informants, the bull-roarer is probably something like the following sketch:

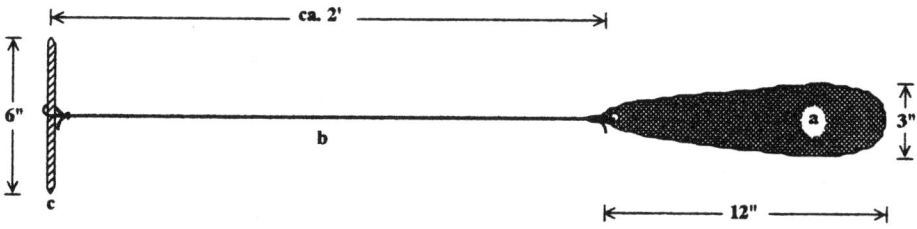

The blade (a) must be made of /ana wood (*Acacia giraffae* Burch.). It is teardrop in shape, pointed at the end by which it is attached to the string, and whittled very thin. The string (b) is of sinew, *(tso)*. The handle (c), called simply stick or wood, may be made of any wood. To play the n≠abbi, a man closes his right-hand fingers around the handle so that the string comes out between his first (fore-) finger and the second. He twirls the instrument out to his right side, the plane of its orbit being roughly vertical to the ground (England 1995:244).

THE AVOIDANCES

The food avoidances required of all young people and those required of men and boys remain in effect during Tshoma. During the rite more avoidances are observed.

Meat

The most emphasized avoidance is the total avoidance of meat. In preparation for the Tshoma ritual, the boys avoid a few small animals and some reptiles and birds, namely: steenbok, springhare, honey badger, ostrich, korhaan, kori bustard, leguaan, and puff adder. They also avoid marrow, eggs, milk, and some parts of animals. However, they do not avoid the meat of the great antelope or giraffe that the hunters bring in. At Tshoma, like the girls in the Menarcheal Rite, the boys avoid all meat. This is a real deprivation.

Salt, termites, and ants

Boys in Tshoma avoid salt *(!gaa)*. Salt is a rare item in the diet of the Nyae Nyae !Kung. The people at Gautscha get a little from a deposit at the edge of the pan, but it is more sand than salt and few people bother with it. When we gave gifts of salt, people were delighted and ate it like candy.

The termites (Isoptera, species not identified), called *guriku gum* by the !Kung and "white ants" by Europeans, must be common in the area judging from the many anthills they build. Common though they are, their nuptial flights occur in areas where people are present only on rare occasions. We experienced one such flight. As the hundreds of termites fell to the ground, the !Kung picked them up and ate them with excitement and relish. Termites are sweet to the taste, they say. To have a nuptial flight occur at a Tshoma site during the rite would be rare in the extreme, but should it happen, the boys must refrain from the delight of eating termites.

Like the termites, ants *(!kxon)* are said to be sweet to the taste. They are eaten only if someone happens to pick one up occasionally as a tasty little morsel.

Salt, termites, and ants have no importance in the !Kung diet. Their avoidance deprives the boys only of a pleasant, rare taste. If deprivation is the symbolic meaning of these avoidances, this deprivation is a very mild one.

Aardvark, redwing partridge, blood, and honey

These foods have very strong n/um. The boys' avoidance of them begins with the Tshoma rite and continues for about a year. They are "death-things"; their n/um should not be combined with the strong new Tshoma n/um in the boys. These foods could cause such severe stomach pains and diarrhea that the boys might die.

Plant foods

Up to the Tshoma, the only plant foods boys avoid are pounded sha, forked sha, and plants that have earth in them from having been chopped with a digging stick. During Tshoma, boys avoid twelve plant foods, nine of them the same as those avoided by girls during their Menarcheal Rite:

Underground parts

!ama	tuber
n!wi	tuber
*sha	root
tshu	storage organ
!xwa	storage organ

Berries

!gwa

n/n

Fruit

≠m

n!oshu

Nuts

//k'a

Seed

tsi

Pod

*/gwi

*Avoided only by boys

Drinking water from an ostrich-eggshell container

Although I do not find this avoidance mentioned in my notes on Tshoma, it must be one of the Tshoma avoidances. When young hunters avoid contact with the exceedingly strong n/um of ostrich eggs, and girls in their Menarcheal Rite do also, how could boys with the strong new Tshoma n/um in them be exempted? I believe I neglected to ask specifically about ostrich-eggshell containers, and the !Kung considered it something everyone knows.

Earth

All young people avoid eating roots that have been chopped with a digging stick and have particles of earth in them. At Tshoma boys take further precautions against eating earth. Like girls in their Menarcheal Rite, they do not put food into their mouth with their hands; they use a clean stick. Furthermore, during Tshoma, foods that the boys are going to eat should not be placed on the ground. Ordinarily, when women return to the encampment with roots they have dug or with mangetti nuts or tsi beans, they dump them in piles on the ground near their shelters or fires. However, the plant foods that are going to be given to the boys in Tshoma should be placed on a pile of grass or on a kaross, not touching the ground.

Rain

The !Kung believe that all rain has n/um and that the first rain of the season, "new rain," has exceedingly strong n/um. The rain's n/um and the strong Tshoma n/um in the boys should be kept apart, as should the rain and girls' strong n/um during the Menarcheal Rite. If new rain touched the boys or the girls, the rains of the next season would not fall on their people; the rains would "go around them."

THE END OF TSHOMA AND THE TSHOA RITE

On the last evening of the Tshoma Rite, the participants prepare to return to the encampment and to their normal lives. The sponsors feed the boys their supper. At the end of the supper, one of the old men tshoas the fire by putting slivers of ≠khali into it. After dancing for a short time in the Tshoma site, they all dance down the path to the encampment. They are greeted with excitement; the women throw sa powder on them in celebration.

Any married boys among them would go to their own fires. The other boys gather at the place where the unmarried boys sleep *(≠kao)*. One of the old Tshoma owners builds a special fire for them by taking a brand from each family fire. They tshoa the fire with ≠khali, and there beside the fire, the boys symbolically rejoin all their people. Nothing more is required of them that night.

During the next days the boys in their new state are ritually bathed and then reintroduced through the Tshoa Rite to the acts of hunting and gathering and to each food they have avoided during Tshoma. The Tshoa Rite is given great importance. Without it, we were told, the boys might die of stomach trouble and constipation, so strongly does the new Tshoma n/um in them react with the foods.

Two protective agents are used to tshoa the boys, sha sha and ≠khali. The boys tshoa the act of gathering and eating plant foods with the familiar sha sha; they tshoa hunting and meat with ≠khali.

≠Khali is used only in Tshoma and is essential to Tshoma; nothing may be substituted. The root of this plant is used; it is believed to have powerful n/um. Before a Tshoma Rite takes place, the sponsors and the boys go especially to dig a supply of the ≠khali roots, which they will use in the rite. We were told they would not hold a Tshoma Rite until they had ≠khali at hand. The men know where the plants grow. They take only the approximate number of roots they will need in the rite and do not keep them among their possessions after the rite. Women must avoid ≠khali; they avoid touching the root and they avoid saying the name "≠khali." I hoped that the friendly old men would show me a ≠khali plant or root. I promised not to touch it, but they refused. They said ≠khali was dangerous to women.

To dig for ≠khali, the sponsor places his hands over the boy's hands on the digging stick, and the two dig together. When the root is first revealed, the sponsor cuts a sliver of it, takes a piece into his mouth and puts a piece into the boy's mouth. The boy must not touch the root with his hands. They dig for a moment or two in this manner. Then the sponsor lets the boy finish the digging alone. At the end of this procedure, they eat the sliver of the ≠khali they have held in their mouths.

The ritual bath is given early in the morning following the ending of the Tshoma Rite. The boys are bathed with a broth in which meat or tsi, or both if available, have been boiled. The sponsor sloshes the broth over the boy, and as he sloshes, he rubs down each part of the boy's body, except his genitals; the boy keeps his breechclout on.

The bath finished, the sponsors take their boys to hunt or to gather. Each boy, now full of strong new Tshoma n/um, must be reintroduced to both those vital activities by having the Tshoa Rite performed over him. This is done preferably during the first two days after Tshoma, in whichever order the sponsors and boys choose.

For hunting, the act that is tshoaed is the shooting of the arrow. I do not know if the boy must shoot a meat animal or if shooting any animal satisfies the ritual requirement.

The boy and his sponser set forth alone. When the boy prepares to shoot his arrow, we were told, the sponsor and he take slivers of ≠khali into their mouths. The sponsor places his hands over the boy's hands on the bow and arrow, they both blow their ≠khali-laden breath on the boy's hands, and the boy shoots. If the arrow should kill something the !Kung eat, the meat would be taken back to the encampment and tshoaed as the boy ate it.

The act of gathering that is tshoaed is the act of digging a root. As far as I know, the !Kung do not tshoa the picking of berries or fruit or the gathering of melons. The sponsor and the boy go alone to tshoa the digging. They stay well away from any women who are gathering. When they find a root they choose to dig, they proceed as they do when digging ≠khali—the sponsor's hands over the boy's hands on the digging stick. For digging the root they have sha sha in their mouths, and they blow sha sha-laden breath on their hands.

With the tshoaing of hunting and gathering, the procedures of the Tshoma Rite come to an end, but the tshoaing of food continues for some time. Each animal and each plant food that a boy has avoided during Tshoma must be tshoaed the first time the boy eats it.

The meat that the boy is to tshoa is cooked by the sponsor or some old Tshoma owner. Slivers of ≠khali are scraped over it, and the boy takes a sliver of ≠khali into his mouth. The sponsor feeds the boy pieces of the meat with a sharp stick. The boy must not touch the meat with his hands. As the boy chews, the old man rubs his own armpits for the n/um that exudes in perspiration and rubs it over the boy's throat and abdomen.

To tshoa plant foods or salt, the sponsor or some other Tshoma owner and the boy, with sha sha in their mouths, take mouthfuls of the food. The boy chews and eats his mouthful. The sponsor takes the food from his mouth and rubs it over the boy. He may need to use several mouthfuls to complete the rubbing. Old Gaú, demonstrating the procedure with /Gunda as a model, showed how the sponsor would carefully rub the boy's head, face, throat, abdomen, arms, underarms, back, hips, buttock, and legs, but not the feet. I asked why the feet were not anointed and was given one of the answers with which I had become so familiar, an answer full of meaning to the !Kung but not to me. The answer was, "because he walks with his feet."

Between celebrations of the Tshoma Rite, the Tshoma owners, old or new, have no formal solidarity. They do not associate together as Tshoma owners or group themselves for any of their daily activities, or for any ritual observance. Although no Tshoma observances are made between the celebrations of the rite, Tshoma is of continuing importance in the men's lives. They believe that their Tshoma n/um continues to strengthen them and empower their hunting.

/Ti!kay

N≠isa, *heavily ornamented*

Gao Feet (Gao Medicine)

≠Toma

A wedding party by the wedding skerm. The bride, N!ai, is at the left entrance while /Gunda, the bridegroom, sits to the right. The younger boy on the far right is playing the //gwashi, a wooden stringed instrument.

Dance rattles, /khonisi, hanging in a tree. These are wrapped around men's ankles and calves to enhance the stamping of feet during the Healing Dance. The rattles are made of dried cocoons of moth larvae, filled with small pebbles or bits of ostrich eggshell.

A close-up of tortoise-shell ornaments and an apron with a variety of objects hanging from it. Healers fill their tortoise shells with a mixture of n/um plants and marrow or fat. Women use tortoise shells to carry the fragrant sa powder, which they toss onto the healers or onto visitors for their well-being.

A poisonous root from which arrow poison is made by boiling it and pounding it into paste.

Gao Medicine (Gao Feet) poisoning arrows. He is stirring the poison in a little bone dish made from an animal knee joint.

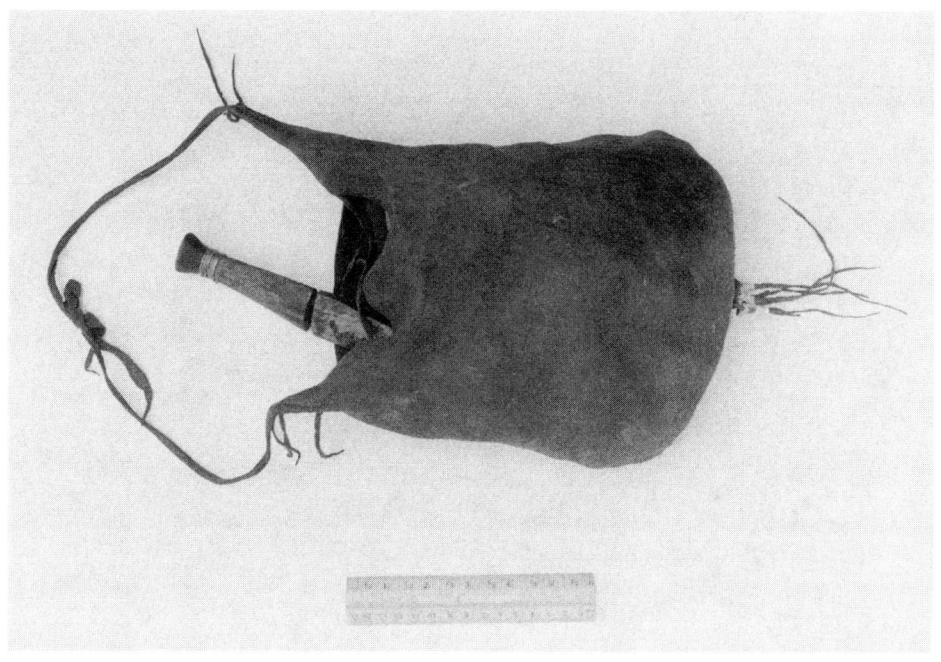

A leather bag used by the !Kung to carry everyday necessities such as knives, tobacco, etc.

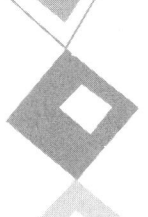

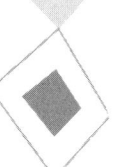

SORCERY AND
OTHER MYSTIQUES

11 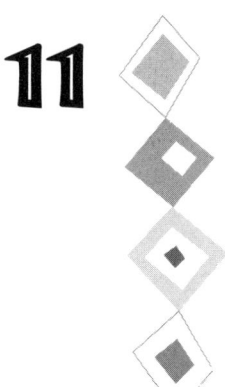 Sorcery

Among !Kung beliefs is one that harm and death can be caused by supernatural means in what I am calling a practice of sorcery. The beliefs in sorcery seem to lie in a different stratum from those described in earlier chapters about the sky gods sending sickness and death and about the healers and the n/um that enables them to heal. Those beliefs are clear and strong in !Kung thinking and are acted upon every day; the Healing Dance, for instance, is a vital element in !Kung culture.

Sorcery, by contrast, was not a structured social element and was of minor importance in the culture. No sorcerers or witches, male or female, were in the service of others. Divination, for instance, was not a function of sorcery among the !Kung.[1] There were only a few individuals who were believed to have an inner occult force that they used to kill or harm others, in their own personal hatred, jealousy, revenge, or anger.

The deaths they caused were deplored; the killings were considered evil deeds. The people who perpetrated the deaths were considered to be bad people. They were relatively few, however, and they had no large social effect. Sorcery seemed to be practiced infrequently and was not greatly feared.

Of course, there is always the possibility that matters of sorcery and magic are shrouded in secrecy. Indeed, there may be beliefs and practices that were kept secret, or that I, for one reason or another, failed to observe, about which we learned nothing. The information that I do have, however, seemed to be in no way secret. The !Kung gave it freely, volunteering much of it. I give the information as it was given to me.

In the course of our discussion on sorcery, I gathered accounts of ten deaths that were believed to have been caused by sorcery. They had occurred over the years within the memory span of the !Kung I spoke with. Seven had occurred in the Nyae Nyae area, two far to the west, and one at Kai Kai; none had occurred at Gautscha. I do not consider this number a definite count; there may have been more that I did not hear about.

The !Kung believe that death or harm can be brought about by humans using supernatural means in two ways. Some substances are believed to have a magic in them that can be manipulated and used to kill. With the exception of /Ka /Kani's fire (see next section), which can be made only by men, anyone, man or woman, who can obtain the substances can use them. In another aspect of the beliefs, some persons are believed to have an occult force within themselves that they can use to kill or harm others. I call it an inner force. This force is given by //Gauwa. Of the ten deaths we heard about, six were said to have been caused by persons using the substances and four by persons using their inner force.

THE SUBSTANCES THAT HAVE MAGIC

/Ka /Kani's fire

I first learned about /Ka /Kani's fire when I was talking to !U about her genealogy. She told me she had a younger sister, Zuma, who had been killed by /Ka /Kani's fire. The !Kung have the belief, held in many cultures, that a person's hair trimmings and fingernail and toenail parings continue to be a part of the person's body, and treated in some magic way by someone of ill intent, they can be used to kill the person. In the !Kung version of the belief, a man who wanted to kill another could get hold of his hair trimmings and/or nail parings, wrap the material in grass, and burn it. The burning substance makes /Ka /Kani's fire, which goes into the victim who will then sicken and die. /Ka /Kani's fire can also cause blindness.

Someone went on to say that if a man making /Ka /Kani's fire were "strong" at making it the victim would be sure to die, but if the man were "weak" at making it the healers might be able to put the fire out and save the person. A very, very strong healer could tell who had secretly made the fire. But, !U told me, the old men who were very, very strong healers were all dead now.

/Ka /Kani's fire is in the male realm; women cannot make it. I assume that femaleness would nullify the magic of the fire as femaleness nullifies the efficacy of hunting equipment and arrow poison.

/Ka /Kani was the man who first had fire sticks, kept them in secret, and made fire to cook his family's food. ≠Gao N!a took /Ka /Kani's fire sticks, broke them into bits, and threw them over the whole world, so now there is fire in all wood and all mankind can get it out with fire sticks (Marshall 1976:348). Here /Ka /Kani's name is given to a lethal magic fire that kills. His name embraces both aspects of fire—fire that destroys and fire that, for Bushmen, establishes a home, gives them light and warmth, cooks their food, and protects them from prowling animals.

!U's sister, Zuma, had married a young man from a place far to the west, in the region near the farmlands of the white people. Zuma and her husband had gone there to live with his people. The young husband loved Zuma very much, !U told us. He was a good hunter and gave his young wife many karosses. She kept them to give to her own people when she should return to visit them at Gautscha. This made her husband's people furiously jealous and resentful, and one of them made /Ka /Kani's fire. Zuma was pregnant. The fire went into her abdomen, and she and the child died in childbirth. This had happened far from Gautscha. The Gautscha people never learned precisely who had made the fire. We were told of two other people who were killed by /Ka /Kani's fire; a woman named N/aoka and a man who was a relative of Old Debe. I did not learn more about them.

The hair of a corpse

The Old Old People had told of another way to use hair to kill. The hair of a corpse can be cut off, rolled into a little bundle of grass, burned, and the ashes placed in a person's shelter while he is absent. When the person returns to his shelter, the magic force from the hair of the dead will go into him and cause sickness or death. The Old Old People had said this could be done, but no one we spoke with had ever heard of anyone trying it.

Discussing these matters, people said that hair trimmings should be carefully buried in holes among roots of bushes or trees where they could not be easily found by someone of evil intent. We saw the hair in the baby's first haircut ritually protected, but we never observed !Kung adults protecting their hair carefully. They would gather up the trimmings after a haircut, roll them into a bunch, stuff them casually among grass stems or the twigs of a bush. They said they wanted to prevent the wind from blowing their hair about because that would cause their wits to swirl about and they would lose their way as they walked in their vast land. They made no effort to conceal the hair, apparently feeling perfectly secure within their group. One man commented that in the group "they lived together in peace."

Lightning teeth

Lightning teeth (fulgurite) placed in the rain horn calls the rain. Lightning teeth can also call lightning. A man who wanted to kill another could secretly take one of the branches that form the frame of that person's shelter. He could place the branch together with lightning teeth on the coals. When the branch was well charred, he would bury a piece of it with the lightning teeth in the ground under the shelter. Lightning would then strike and kill the owner of the shelter. The !Kung believed that this could happen, but none had known of an instance of death caused in this way.

A magic force in tobacco smoke

To the west of the Nyae Nyae area live the !Kung of Karakuwisa. Unlike the !Kung-speaking Bushmen in western Botswana, they have no close ties through intermarriage or visiting with the Nyae Nyae !Kung. It would seem that the Karakuwisa !Kung are exceptionally touchy. If a person speaks angrily to them or if they take offense for any reason, they mix a magic substance with tobacco and give it to the person to smoke. The person gradually becomes as thin as a string and before long he dies. Tuka, a relative of /Qui's, was killed in this way.

The black paste

In /Gam a man named //Ao had acquired a magic substance that was previously unknown to the Nyae Nyae !Kung. The substance had come from some place farther to the south. The !Kung did not know if it had come originally from other Bushmen or from black or white people. The substance was a black paste. It was in a shallow round tin. I thought from the description the tin might be a shoe-polish tin of European origin. We were told that the substance was so powerful that if one merely looked at it one would die. When /Gao Music and his wife , N≠isa, were visiting relatives at /Gam, //Ao, who for some reason the others did not understand must have hated N≠isa, took the lid off his tin and showed her the paste. Her heart jumped violently with fright. She and /Gao left /Gam at once and traveled toward Gautscha. On the way N≠isa died. She had been sick before, I was told, and had recovered. After she saw the black paste she became very sick again and died. /Gao had wanted to go back and kill //Ao, but /Gao's people persuaded him not to because, they argued, it would be dangerous for him to do so and would cause more trouble.

We heard of one other person killed by the black paste in the tin but have no further information.

THE INNER FORCE

The !Kung believe that the inner force to kill or harm is given by //Gauwa. I did not learn how they believe he gives it or on what basis he gives it to some people and not others. I assume that the belief is very old, and in it //Gauwa is in his ancient role as the evil being.

The inner force is like the healers' n/um in some ways, but it is not that n/um. The !Kung made clear that the healers' n/um is only for healing; it could not harm anyone. The inner force resembles n/um in that it is immaterial. The !Kung explained that "it does not come from roots" (like sha sha); "it is not a poison" (like snake poison); "it is not something you can carry in a bag or a tortoise shell," "it is inside a person's heart and body" (like the n/um in the healers). The person who has it "curses" *(xi)* it into another person and that person will then sicken and die. Fortunately few people have it.

A man named /Gaishay !Koa (/Gaishay Knee) who lived at Kai Kai was one of those few. The story about him was told to me by a group of women with whom I was well acquainted, !U, //Kushay, N!ai, and Ghia. I was inquiring about women healers and our talk rambled as usual. We spoke of Old //Khuga who saw in her dreams where the animals were and would tell the hunters in which direction to start their hunt. We spoke of Old N≠isa who had received the two Giraffe Songs from //Gauwa and who had healed in the past. I asked if N≠isa had the ability like //Khuga to help the hunters. The women said she did not, but in her own way she would try to help a hunter by curing him if he were sick. She would say, "Why do you keep on being sick? You must be cured so you can get us meat that we can eat." Thinking more about N≠isa's powers, I asked if she had the force in herself to harm a person. The women thought possibly she did, but said that if she had it she did not use it. She was a good woman, they said; they liked her.

They went on to talk about people who had the inner force that could kill or harm others. Of the four deaths that these !Kung attributed to the use of the inner force, women were accused of having caused three; a man was accused of one. The accounts of the women's killings were given without detail. When a baby died in a family in which the in-laws had been quarreling, an old woman on the husband's side of the family was believed to have caused the death. Another old woman was suspected of having been the cause of the death of an in-law whom she hated. A woman in Kai Kai was believed to have killed her rival. Her husband had fallen in love with another woman—a woman named //Gao, whom we could identify; she was the sister of !Kham, the lame man. The wife was fiercely jealous. When !Kham's sister suddenly fell sick and died, people were certain that the wife had killed her with inner force.

The account of /Gaishay !Koa was quite another story. As !U told it:

> /Gaishay !Koa had a son, Khan//a, whose wife was //Kushay. A young man named Gao lured //Kushay away from Khan//a and married her. /Gaishay !Koa's heart was hurt by this: he was very angry. He put a curse on Gao and Gao got pains in his chest. A healer named Sao Blackperson, a distant relative of !U's, began to cure young Gao. /Gaishay !Koa was then furious with Sao also and said to him, "You think you are a healer. You tried to cure Gao. Now I curse you. You will die." Sao was very upset. He said, "What will happen to my life? I have done nothing wrong. I only tried to cure the boy. Am I wrong in doing that?" Next morning Sao went to gather mangetti nuts. When he returned he took a drink of water and felt he had swallowed

something hard and sharp. He said, "I feel that I have swallowed something bad. I am choking." Sao was sick for two days and on the third day he died.

The women said that /Gaishay !Koa was a wicked man. I learned later that he had died not long after Sao. The Gautscha people believed that one of Sao's relatives had cursed him.

Healers in the Form of Flying Lions

In the accounts of exceptional old healers who had miraculous powers to sit in the fire or make out-of-body journeys, the old healers had not used their powers to harm others. The !Kung believe, however, that malevolent healers do exist, though they are very few. They can take the form of lions and fly through the air. (The verb for this action is *jum.*) In that form they can kill and otherwise cause harm. The !Kung said that even to see such a lion could cause a person to die of fright. The belief seemed not to be integrated with the current concepts of healers and their healing n/um, but to be in a different, perhaps older, stratum of concepts of the supernatural.

Megan Biesele, Richard Katz, and Richard Lee found the belief among the Botswana !Kung as well. Lee says of it:

> The Bushmen believe that a few of the very powerful curers in the past had the ability to transform themselves into lions and to stalk the desert in search of human prey. Lions ordinarily do not attack man and the Bushman hunters occasionally drive lions off fresh kills in order to scavenge the meat. On the several occasions when a lion has attacked a man, the Bushmen attribute the attack to a human curer-turned-lion. Since such incidents occur perhaps once or twice in a decade, there is little reinforcement for belief in the malevolence of trance performers. (It is instructive that apart from this belief, all of the !Kung folk beliefs about trance performers assign to them a benevolent, positive, and socially constructive role.) (Lee 1968:46)

!U and her son, Tsamgao, had seen a lion appear to jump out of a tree. !U knew it was a man in the form of a lion because it acted in such a strange way. !U told me that the lion came down as though from a branch of the tree, but it was not actually on the tree. It came down toward them, then went up again, but it did not seem to be climbing; it passed them as though flying. !U thought the flying lion was /Gaishay !Koa who, she believed, had the power to jum. She and Tsamgao were terrified. They stayed awake and made noises all night to drive him away.

THE MAGIC BOW

We had, of course, heard of the little bows and arrows that have magic power to kill. They are famous in Bushman lore and have been called "Bushman revolvers." In the lore it is claimed that their magic is exceedingly strong. A man using the bow need only shoot the little arrow in the direction of a person he wanted to kill and even though the arrow did not touch the person, the person would die.

L. Fourie in "The Bushmen of South West Africa" records a folktale found among the Auen and Naron, which tells of //Gauwa giving the magic of the bow to a man named Tji-tji:

> Tji-tji had killed a gemsbuck. Gaua arrived on the scene and said, "I have come to you; you need not be afraid; both of us can sleep here." After having consumed the animal and slept Tji-tji remarked to Gaua "Give me that stuff (//ai)." The latter replied, "If I give you the //ai, what will you pay me?" Tji-tji answered, "I will give you the horns." Gaua then took the horns, made the little arrows out of them, invested them with //ai and before departing taught Tji-tji the //ai dance. From that time the Bushmen have known how to use magic (Fourie 1928:104).

When we asked the Nyae Nyae !Kung about the little magic bows and arrows, the men said they no longer had them. Their old people had had them, but they claimed they no longer knew how to make them. Whether it was true that no one among them had a magic bow, I do not know. Someone could have kept a bow in secret, or the custom might have actually waned. In any case I believed Gao Feet when he said he did not have one.

He told me that his father had possessed a magic bow and arrows. Gao Feet had seen them when he was young. They had been burned with other belongings when their shelter had burned down. Gao described their size by using little sticks and my pencil for comparison. He indicated that the bow was about as long as my pencil, 7 inches; the arrows were 5 1/2 to 6 inches overall; the quiver was about 6 inches. I mentioned that I had heard that the arrows could kill if shot in the direction of the person aimed at. Gao said that the only ones he knew about had to actually strike a person to be effective, but that the arrows were so small and flew through the air so fast they could not be seen to strike. Gao went on to say that he could make a little bow and the arrows easily enough, but he did not know how to get the magic force. Arrow poison was not used on the little arrows.

I have two miniature bows with their arrows and quivers, which were given to me when we were visiting in the Ghanzi area by our kind host, Mr. Bert Ramsden, from his collection of Nharo artifacts. The two sets are of different sizes. Schapera described magic bows of the two sizes similar to mine (Schapera 1930:199).

Of the smaller set, the little leather quiver is 4 1/2 inches long, 1 1/2 inches wide, and ornamented at the top with a row of tiny white, black, red, and yellow European beads. The bow is 4 1/4 inches, and the arrows are 3 1/2 to 4 inches, some as slender as the lead in a pencil, some a little wider.

The larger quiver is 6 1/8 inches long, 1 1/2 inches wide, and ornamented at the top with the little white European (not ostrich-eggshell) beads, and it has a little over-the-shoulder strap like a real hunting quiver. The bowstring is broken off at one end. Straightened out, the bow is 8 1/2 inches long. The arrows are 5 1/2 to 7 inches in length and are as slender as the other little arrows.

The arrows in the two miniature sets are different in size and proportion, but the same in structure. They have two segments, a shaft of hollow reed and a point of wood. One end of the shaft is bound with sinew. Into that end is thrust one end of the point, tapered to needle sharpness. The protruding end of the point is blunt. The arrows are said to be shot blunt end foremost (Schapera 1930:199). In the smaller set, the shafts are about 3 inches long, the points, rather crudely whittled, are about 1 inch. They are firmly set in the shaft, not detachable like the hunting arrows. The arrows of the larger set vary in proportions, the shaft from 2 1/2 to 3 1/2 inches long, the points from 2 to 3 1/2 inches. A number of points of the larger set are exquisitely bound with sinew in a crisscross pattern. Some of these points are detachable, some firmly set in. Possibly they are all supposed to be firmly set in, and some have come loose over time. All the arrowpoints are blackened. What the black substance is or what function is attributed to it, I do not know. I am certain it is not the arrow poison we observed the hunters using.

The magic bows and arrows I describe were from the Ghanzi area. It is safe to assume that those of the Nyae Nyae area were similar.

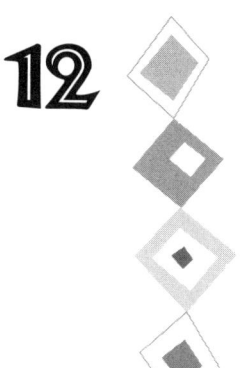

12 MILLIPEDES, THE MANTIS RELIGIOSA, AND THE SUPERNATURAL PEOPLES

In !Kung beliefs, millipedes and the *Mantis religiosa* (praying mantises) have been endowed with qualities and abilities beyond the natural.

MILLIPEDES

Millipedes are believed to be able to harm people, even to kill them. The !Kung fear them very much. I first observed their fear when I was sitting with a group of women in the shade one afternoon. A mischievous teenage boy suddenly ran toward the group and threw a big, live millipede into our midst. The women leaped up shrieking and ran off in all directions. Explaining their behavior afterward, they said that "even men are afraid of millipedes." If one gets on you, the shock of fright you might feel could kill you. The !Kung say that millipedes belong to //Gauwa and work for him. He rears them. He might send them at night when you are asleep to eat your nose.

I was told, furthermore, that if a millipede were thrown on the fire when the n/n berries (*Grewia flava* DC.) were still green, the berries would not ripen properly and would not be sweet. This piece of lore was unconnected with anything else we knew, and no explanation of the association of millipedes and n/n berries could be elicited.

Among the Naron and the Auen, also, millipedes have special significance. Schapera writes: "The millipede, said to belong to Hishe, is only touched by them (the magicians): they dry it and use it powdered as medicine" (Schapera 1930:197).

Silberbauer says of /Gwi beliefs: "The /Gwi share with many Khoikhoi . . . the belief that millipedes have the habit of entering the ears of sleeping people and boring through to the brain to kill the sleepers. Nevertheless, millipedes found wandering around a shelter during the day are simply thrown away; only those that are seen at night are killed in the fire" (Silberbauer 1981:75).

The *Mantis Religiosa*

The praying mantis *(Mantis religiosa)* is believed to touch upon the supernatural in several ways. The insect itself is not conceived to be a supernatural being in animal form. However, as an insect, it has supernatural abilities.

Among the white people of South Africa, the *Mantis religiosa* has been called the Hottentots' god, and a belief that Hottentots and Bushmen worship the insect and pray to it has been widely held. This idea is attributed to an early traveler among the Hottentots, Peter Kolb, in 1719 (Schmidt 1973:109). Although the idea that the insect was actually worshiped as a god may have been a misconception from the beginning, it has been perpetuated nonetheless.

S. A. Brown in an article entitled "Exploding the Myth of the Bushmen's God" (*Cape Times Weekend Magazine,* 9/13/69) says that the belief is so widespread it is "even printed in encyclopedias." He says also that if (South African) school children know nothing else about Bushmen, they know that the mantis is the Bushman's god. He refers to the belief as a "ridiculous mantis myth."

Father Martin Gusinde was of the opinion that the idea of the Hottentot god was deliberately fostered by white settlers and became entrenched because Europeans used it as evidence that Bushmen were abysmally backward and stupid to pray to an insect; that they were nearer to being animals than humans, in order to justify exterminating them (Gusinde 1966:74).

Although not worshiped as a deity, the insect has been associated with the deity in many Khoisan cultures by having been given the same name as the deity or highest being. Sigrid Schmidt in her interesting, detailed study of the mantis in Khoisan beliefs entitled "Die Mantis religiosa in den Glaubenvorstellungen der Khoesan-Völker" (Schmidt 1973:103–4) lists more than a score of examples. A few follow:

Khoisan People	Name of Deity Name of Mantis	References
/Xam	/kaggen	Bleek 1956:296
Auen	!na-m	Bleek 1956:355
!Khu	haishe	Bleek 1956:57
!Khu	hase, hise	Gusinde 1966:71
Nama	//gaunab	Hahn 1882:42
Dama	//gamab	Vedder 1938:424

The Nyae Nyae !Kung differ. Instead of giving the mantis the name of their deity, they call it the messenger of //Gauwa (//Gauwa /koa !a) or the servant of //Gauwa (//Gauwa !kasi).

The best known example of the highest being having the same name as the insect is, of course, /Kaggen, the trickster of the rich folklore of the /Xam Bushmen collected by the Bleek family. /Kaggen is the /Xam word for mantis. In this instance the insect's name has been given to the highest being instead of the highest being's name having been given to the insect.

There has been discussion as to /Kaggen's identification with the insect mantis. In the /Xam folktales, although he sometimes "gets feathers" or "remembers that he has wings" and flies, he does not take the form of a mantis. In one tale, however, he says that in the future he will become "a little green thing"—presumably a mantis. Readers of the folktales will remember that the tale is "The Mantis Takes Away the Tick's Sheep," in *The Mantis and His Friends* (Bleek 1923:30).

In this tale, /Kaggen went to the place where the ticks live. Instead of inviting him to sit by their fire and giving him food as would be expected of proper people, the ticks fell upon him and beat him severely. /Kaggen escaped them and limped slowly home. There Ichneumon told him he should never have gone to the ticks in the first place. "Nobody goes to them," Ichneumon said, "because they drink blood, they are black people, they are bloody-handed. Their houses are always black, because they are angry folk" (Bleek 1923:32). /Kaggen replied, "O Ichneumon, you ought not to teach me, for I am old," and he lay down to sleep, covering his aching head with his kaross. While asleep, he dreamed that all the possessions of the ticks—fires, huts, karosses, pots, knives, sheep, everything—rose up into the air and came to the place where /Kaggen and his family live.

When morning came and the people awoke, there were the ticks' possessions, bleating sheep and all, as /Kaggen had dreamed they would be. /Kaggen then, speaking to his wife, Dasse, predicted the future:

> The Dasse got up; she said to the Mantis: "O Mantis, why did you take away the people's Sheep?" The Mantis answered her as he lay: "It seemed right to me, because those people attacked me; they wanted to kill me in their anger. Then I felt that I wished yonder angry folk should no longer warm themselves at a fire, because they fought me at their fire. They shall now drink raw blood because they lack a fire, they cannot make a fire; they cannot cook, they also cannot roast meat to feed themselves. For they walk about in their flesh. In these pots here the Flat Bushmen shall some day cook, because they shall have a fire. We who are here shall then also be as the Ticks are. We shall eat different things, because we too shall lack fire. You, the Ichneumon, shall then go to dwell in the hills with your mother. She shall truly become a Porcupine, she shall live in a hole, while Grandmother Dasse shall live in a mountain den, for

her name is really "Dasse." I shall have wings, I shall fly when I am green, I shall be a little green thing. You, the Ichneumon, shall eat honey, because you will be living on the hill. Then you shall marry a She-Ichneumon" (Bleek 1923:33).

In Sigrid Schmidt's understanding, although /Kaggen said he would become "a little green thing," he is seen throughout the tales in his trickster character, which is not identified with the mantis. In the other Khoisan materials that she studied, although the deity's name is given to the mantis, in none does she find that the mantis and the deity are conceived to be identical.

Although the mantis having the same name as the deity is a common feature in Khoisan cultures, the concepts about the mantis and the attitude toward the insect differ greatly. Sigrid Schmidt summarizes several. In some of the cultures the mantis is believed to bring good fortune. It is welcomed and protected. For a mantis to creep on a person is especially propitious for that person. A mantis must not be killed or in any way harmed. Some believe that if a person should eat a mantis he would die. In other Khoisan cultures the mantis is a bad thing, a harbinger of misfortune. Especially if it comes out of its own environment and enters a hut, it is much feared and is believed to be a warning of misfortune, or in some instances, specifically a warning that sickness is approaching. In these cultures the insect must be killed. A third attitude is one of indifference. The Hukwe and the Gannekwe with whom Father Gusinde worked are examples of Khoisan peoples who pay no special attention to the mantis. They say it is a useless thing, too thin to eat (Schmidt 1973:107–10; Gusinde 1966:70).

As an oracle the mantis may be asked if stock has wandered off and in which direction it has gone. The turn of the mantis's head would indicate the direction. Mostly the mantis would be asked about rain. It was thought to predict rain if it stretched its arms high or to predict drought if it held its arms down. Sigrid Schmidt points out that the mantis is not the only creature that is believed to have oracular power; quite generally among Khoisan peoples the chameleon is also believed to have it (Schmidt 1973:112–15).

In the beliefs of the Nyae Nyae !Kung, the mantis is seen as the servant or messenger of //Gauwa, and in this it has special meaning to the !Kung. They say that mantises are bad (tshi dole) not because the insects harm people—they only tickle and prick—but because they belong to //Gauwa and people are afraid of their owner. If anyone should injure a mantis that happened to alight on him, or step on one, or especially if anyone should throw one into the fire, //Gauwa would see this, say his servant was being ill-treated, and punish the person with sickness.

The fear of //Gauwa's displeasure did not keep !Kung boys from handling mantises, however. Occasionally they did so, but for no special reason—just because one happened to alight near them. The boys showed no sign of respect or fear or the fascination I felt when watching the eerie creatures.

At Gautscha I shared my office tent with a *Mantis religiosa* for some time. She was an enormous female with her small consort attached to her. Together they must have measured six or seven inches in length. She was a welcome guest, keeping the tent free of less enchanting insects. When I was working on notes at night with a lamp lighted, she would make a slow and stately march around the upper wall of the tent staring fixedly down at me, never blinking, seeming never to take her eyes off me. Fascinated, and with a tingle of gooseflesh, I stared back into her eyes. From that experience I felt that I knew why the mantis is regarded as something other than an ordinary insect; it is because of the way the creature turns its head and looks at you. Among all insects, the mantis is the only one that turns its head to such an angle that it can stare at you with both eyes.[1] To have one of the creatures stop, uplift its arms, and stare like that gives one pause.

The Supernatural Peoples

The Gemsbok People

According to !Kung lore, people who have the form of gemsbok live in the south of the Nyae Nyae area. The Gemsbok People look exactly like animal gemsbok (*!gwe*), we were told. The similarity of their feet was especially mentioned; one cannot distinguish the spoor of one from the other. Gemsbok People can talk. They are reticent, however, and do not approach humans. Their place is far to the south; but they wander, feeding in the veld as the animals do, and one could encounter them anywhere. The Old Old People could recognize them and knew not to hunt them, but present-day hunters might mistake them for animal gemsbok. If a hunter did kill one, however inadvertently, he would die.

Megan Biesele found that the !Kung in Botswana knew the Gemsbok People by the name "*!Xonsi.*" The !Xonsi are gemsboks in the bush and people in camp, according to some she spoke with. Others said that the Gemsbok People have the heads of gemsboks on people's bodies. Some pointed out that the !Xonsi lived in the southwest—that is, in Namibia, not in Botswana. They claimed that Gemsbok People were strange and terrible people. They drank ostrich urine, and the men did not wear breechclouts (personal communication).

The Gemsbok People were benefactors to humans in one respect, according to Nyae Nyae !Kung belief. They originated the art of making ostrich-eggshell beads; they bore the holes in the beads with their long horns. We were told that long ago a group of Bushmen went to visit the Gemsbok People to ask for some beads; they stayed five days. The Gemsbok People were hospitable and generous. They gave the Bushmen water and meat and tsi seeds, and not only gave them ostrich eggshells but taught them how to make the beads. According to the !Kung we spoke with, although the Gemsbok People are aloof with humans today, they are not hostile or harmful.

The Wildebeest People

The Wildebeest People are not well established in the beliefs of the Nyae Nyae !Kung. We heard about them only once, from a visitor, a man named /Qui from /Gam. I did not take time to pursue the concept of the Wildebeest People and do not know from which Bushman group the belief comes—the !Kung at /Gam, or possibly from people farther south. According to /Qui, the Wildebeest People are similar to the Gemsbok People in that they look like the animals. /Qui gave no details about them except that they have wildebeest horns and feet and that their spoor is indistinguishable from animal wildebeest spoor. What interests me now is that /Qui went right on to tell a story about a man named !Gai Goro—a story that could be applied equally well to the Gemsbok People. It supports the !Kung prohibition of cannibalism:

> A man named !Gai Goro went to the place where the Wildebeest People live. When he got there he saw spoor. It was exactly like wildebeest spoor and !Gai Goro said this is wildebeest spoor. He followed it thinking he would get an animal for meat. As he followed the spoor, !Gai Goro saw a big tree and a very old man sitting by it. The old man said to !Gai Goro, "I am an old old man. Go on following the spoor. You will find your friends there." !Gai Goro replied, "No. I have heard what you told me. The spoor is of a Wildebeest Person. I shall go back." !Gai Goro thought in his heart, "I thought this was wildebeest spoor. Now I find it is people's spoor. Do I want to kill people like myself?" As he turned away through the bushes, he looked back. The old man had disappeared. !Gai Goro went straight back to his own people. When he got there he said, "Oh, I nearly killed myself. I was following the spoor of a wildebeest. I thought it was an animal wildebeest. All the time it was the spoor of a person."

/Qui ended the story with the remark that if a person killed one of the Wildebeest People he would surely die.

The Knee Knee None

The Knee Knee None or the People Who Eat the Sun are known also as "those who sleep standing up." They have human form but are not ordinary humans; they are n/um people, we were told. They look like Bushmen except that their feet are as thin as grass blades, and they have no joints in their knees.[2] The !Kung usually call them !Koa !Koa Kwara (Knee Knee None).[3]

The Knee Knee None have hip joints, but it is so hard for them to sit down or lie down without knee joints that they always stand. When they sleep they lean against trees, or, if they can, they wedge themselves into crotches in the trees. When they eat, they lift the food from the fire up to their mouths with long, sharp sticks.

These people regularly eat the sun.[4] The sun is their *//hara.* (The !Kung explained that //hara is a main source of food; the plant foods that the people gather are the //hara of the Bushmen.) Every evening the sun comes down to earth and turns into an elephant. (In another version, the sun becomes a giraffe.) The Knee Knee None kill it, and when we see it round and fiery red at sunset, it is the meat we see. The people then dance the Sun Dance. When the meat is cooked, the adults tell the children to run away and play. (One version of the account says they chase the children away.) The adults then eat the meat. When the children come back, the adults pick their teeth and give the bits of meat that have stuck in them to the children for their supper. (To chase children away and to withhold food from them is the most unBushmenlike behavior that could be imagined.)

When they have finished, one of the men takes the elephant's clavicle bone and throws it across the sky to the east. There it falls into water. By morning, it has grown to be the sun again. It comes out of the water, dries itself in a tree, and bright yellow once more, begins its daily journey. The sun has its own n/um, which makes this happen. The !Kung told us that sometimes they hear the clavicle bone passing over them at night. It makes a humming sound like a wind. They think if a short man throws it they hear it, but if a tall man throws it, it passes so high over them that they hear nothing.

≠Toma, our mentor, said his father's younger brother had told him of meeting a group of Knee Knee None one time when he was traveling in the west with several other men. The Knee Knee None were also a group of men, the uncle had told ≠Toma. They had left their wives and children where they live, far to the west. They spoke courteously to ≠Toma's uncle and his group saying, "We are Knee Knee None." ≠Toma said that, although they are a n/um people, they are not harmful to humans, at least not generally so.

≠Toma's uncle and his companions were uneasy at meeting these strange men despite the courtesy of their greeting, but they were also extremely curious and decided to camp nearby and watch the Knee Knee None to see how they slept. As the uncle told ≠Toma, the Knee Knee None made a big fire, and standing beside it, they cooked some meat in a pot they had brought with them. They ate the meat, spearing the pieces with long pointed sticks and lifting them to their mouths, as people had said they did. And late that evening, each one went to a tree and leaned against it to sleep.

This account has the sound of an actual experience. Whether it was ≠Toma himself who had so vividly imagined the affair or whether the uncle had told it so convincingly, I did not ascertain. If I had to guess I would guess it was ≠Toma. He was a very good storyteller.

PART VI

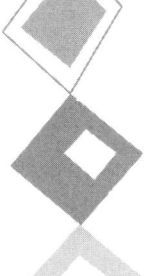

STAR LORE

13  $TAR LORE

The Nyae Nyae !Kung accounts of the creation tell that ≠Gao N!a created the sun, moon, and stars but tell nothing of the nature of the celestial bodies. The !Kung do not know what their substance is or how to explain their movements. They think of them as distant "things of the sky," beyond man's knowledge.

The !Kung do not worship the moon or stars as some Bushmen of other language groups have done (cf. Schapera 1930:173ff), nor do the !Kung pray to the moon or stars for rain or success in the hunt. In !Kung belief the celestial bodies (with minor exceptions to be mentioned) do not influence the affairs of man or affect the weather, the growth of vegetation, or other conditions of the earth. The celestial bodies, these "things of the sky," are in a realm of their own, apart from the earth and man.

Perhaps because of that attitude the !Kung have not applied to the celestial bodies their remarkable powers of observation, which are so highly developed as to seem uncanny when the hunters are tracking an animal or when the women are searching among the grasses for the hairlike vine stems that show the presence of an edible root. Stars do not affect the food supply so they are not of pressing concern. These people recognize the spectacular celestial objects that no one could fail to recognize—the Milky Way, the Clouds of Magellan, the Pleiades, the Southern Cross. They have names for a number of other stars and recognize them if they see them in certain positions, especially if one is associated with some bit of lore or some seasonal significance. However, when such a star is out of that certain position they may not recognize it. If a planet comes near to a star that is significant to them and outshines it, they may transfer the name of the star to the planet without concern.

Such explanation as the !Kung have about celestial bodies comes from an ancient lore that seems unrelated to their current accounts of the creation. The lore is not assiduously or systematically taught. Children only learn it as they happen to hear old people telling it. The lore as I gathered it follows.

THE SUN

The Nyae Nyae !Kung think of the sun in terms of searing heat, thirst, hunger, and exhaustion. N/aoka, the wife of /Ti!kay, angrily claimed that the sun is bad, a "death-thing." Fortunately it is far away, she said, otherwise it would burn people to cinders. As it is, it scorches people when they travel. It withers the roots and berries and turns them bitter. It dries the small water holes and holds the people at their few permanent water holes, where the plant foods within traveling distance may all be consumed before the rains renew them, and the people fear starvation. N/aoka blamed the sun for all this.

The !Kung do not know the effect of sunlight on vegetation, and they give the sun no credit for that. Rain, N/aoka claimed, makes the plant foods grow. She did admit that the light of the sun was good but did not mention the sun's welcome warmth on a freezing morning in June, or the fact that people make good use of the sun in orienting themselves when they travel and when measuring time.

Highly observant as they are, the !Kung have not noticed the solstices. Doubtless this is because their land is so flat, and no permanent roof peak or kraal post fixes a spot on the horizon for these nomadic people. Though they return through the seasons to the same places—the same water holes and the fertile areas where the plant foods grow—the !Kung always choose a fresh place on the ground on which to cluster their family fires and build their little grass shelters in the encampment. They make new fires where there are no signs of old, abandoned fires of former camps. So not even the occasional baobab tree near the water hole is seen time after time from the same angle against the horizon, as a fixed point that could call attention to the sun's apparent movement.

Among the other Bushmen groups we visited, only the Nharo who live near Okwa in Botswana observed the solstices. They mentioned the sun's changing position along the horizon in its yearly motion. They spoke of the longer nights of winter, but like the !Kung, without recognition of the sun's position as the cause. Believing that night per se creates cold, they think that the long nights account for winter cold.

The sun's rising in the east and setting in the west are explained by the !Kung of Nyae Nyae and the !Ko in the lore of the People Who Eat the Sun (or, the Knee Knee None; see chap. 12). The Tshimbaranda !Kung, the Nharo, and the //Gana can only say that the great god takes the sun back across the sky; they do not know how.

The /Gwi say that the sun falls to the ground when it sets, and during the night it somehow returns to the east under its own power. The great god made this to be so. Ukwane, an old /Gwi who was most knowledgeable and cooperative in sharing his knowledge, had heard from the old people that the sun moves around the edge of the earth at the horizon. It goes from the west through the south to the place of sunrise in the east. Ukwane stood up and carefully pointed the direction for us.

While we were talking about the sun, Ukwane, who enjoyed telling me tales, told me how the sun had been created. We found this lore only among the /Gwi.

How N!iriba Created the Sun

N!iriba, whose other name is Pisiboro, is the great god of the /Gwi, creator of all things on earth and in the heavens. Ukwane began telling me about the creation of the sun by sending a little boy to pick a twig and a leaf from a nearby tree. Ukwane bound the leaf to the twig at a certain angle with a little strand of cord and began to show by gesturing how the leaf should be shaped. I suddenly realized that he was making a djani toy. I had watched !Kung boys play with the djani almost every afternoon for a year at Gautscha in Nyae Nyae.

Ukwane went on to tell me that before the sun was made there was only night, no day. To make the sun, N!iriba made a *zini* toy. As he was showing me, Ukwane said that N!iriba took a korhaan feather and shaped it into a nice, evenly curved shape by burning its edges with a coal. N!iriba tied it to a reed with a cord and tied a glowing coal to the reed in the position of the weight. Then he tossed the zini up with his stick. It fell back. He tossed it again, it fell again. The third time he tossed it very high, and it stayed in the sky and became the sun. It cut the night, Ukwane said, and made the day and the night. Thus N!iriba had light.

When there was light N!iriba went hunting. He saw an eland, and to stalk it he crawled on his hands and knees. The sun had made the earth so hot that N!iriba's knees were badly burned. N!iriba shouted and cried out with pain for a long time. While he was shouting, a tree sprang up. This was the first tree that sprang from the ground. (Trees of the same kind exist today, we were told. They have edible berries and thorns that grow in pairs.) N!iriba stood in the shade, and while he was resting there other trees sprang up. N!iriba slept that night, and in the morning there were trees everywhere. That is how people find trees to give them shade.

THE MOON

The moon, unlike the sun, is not thought to be destructive or dangerous. Its light is especially welcomed. In the clear atmosphere of the Kalahari, the moonlight is very bright. It makes rainbows in the clouds. One can easily read by it. The full moon seems always to put Bushmen into the mood to dance.

The moon is not worshiped, revered, or prayed to by any of the Bushmen groups we visited as it had been by Cape Bushmen (Schapera 1930:172). No rituals are performed with respect to it. In one man's words, the moon is a "useless thing" in that it does not affect the weather or vegetation or cause ill or good in man's affairs—with the important exception that it gives its welcome light at night.

In only one bit of Nyae Nyae !Kung lore, the moon is said to reflect (not cause) an event on earth. When the moon is very red, the redness is said to be caused by the blood of a person who has died, or by the blood of some big animal that a hunter has killed.

In Nharo lore when the crescent moon slopes downward, it is said to be looking into a grave and to be a sign that many people will die in that season. A crescent pointing upward is a favorable sign. The round full moon is a sign of satisfaction: people will find plenty of food. To the /Gwi, a ring around the moon is a sign that food will be plentiful.

The !Kung observe five phases of the moon, but have no idea or lore to explain what causes them. The moon in crescent phases with sharp points is said to be male; the full round moon is said to be female by all the groups we visited except the !Ko. All understood the appellations to be figures of speech. The phases are called small new moon, older small moon, female moon or big moon, male moon, and waning moon. When the moon wanes it is said to die. ≠Toma was at pains to tell me that these statements are "just words," meaning they are figures of speech. The !Kung did not mean that the moon is actually male or female or that it dies. ≠Toma said they do not know about the moon; it is a thing of the sky. They do not know what it is, why it changes shape, how it moves, or why it disappears. ≠Toma thought it looked like stone.

According to !Kung lore, the moon falls onto the earth as the sun does when it sets. Somehow the moon rises up and crosses the sky to the east during the day. The !Kung point out that it can sometimes be seen in daylight making the crossing. The !Kung simply say the great god made it to move as it does.

According to Old /Gani, the Nharo say that the moon falls to the ground when it sets and that it turns into an eland. The same people who eat the sun eat the moon. They throw the clavicle bone back as they throw the sun's bone back. No one else told us of this concept, and since we did not have time to search for more information, we have no confirmation of the lore.

Only the /Gwi lore tells of the creation of the moon, as it tells of the creation of the sun. We were given an exceedingly cryptic account:

> Pisiboro dug up a //ha root one day. [//Ha, unidentified, is one of the roots the /Gwi depend on for food. It has a climbing vine.] Pisiboro cut away the bottom part of the root and ate it. A thin piece of the root was left. Pisiboro threw it into the sky. It hung there. It is the moon.

The Moon and the Hare

The Nyae Nyae and the Tshimbaranda !Kung know the myth of the moon and the hare in essentially the same version as given below. The old Nharo, /Gani, had a very different version. The !Ko and /Gwi groups we visited did not know the myth.

The Nyae Nyae !Kung version

This version describes how death came into the world. The moon and the hare lived together. One day they had a talk. The moon, who wanted all creatures to live forever, said to the hare, "We must die, but then we shall come to life again." But the hare answered, "No. When a creature is dead, it is rotten and stinks, and it should stay dead and be buried." (Another teller of the myth had said: "If a person is dead and rotten, he stinks very badly and could not come to life again.") The talk came to a quarrel. The moon was angry and took an axe to fight the hare. The moon clipped the hare's lip so to this day the hare has a cleft lip. The hare scratched the moon's face with his claws. The marks can still be seen. The moon said to the hare, "You have made this choice. You say a person must die and stay dead forever, and you and all living creatures will do so. But when I die I shall come to life again." They parted. This is why the moon dies each night and comes alive again to be seen night after night. But when the hare dies, he is dead forever.

Old Xama added a sequel. The hare died soon after the fight with the moon. He went away after the quarrel and tried to make fire to warm himself; but the moon had put "mouth medicine" (a curse) on the fire sticks, and the hare had no success. Failing to get warm, he fell over dead. That is why one sometimes finds a dead hare in the veld. Old Xama added that people would die also if they failed to make fire.

The Nharo version

Old /Gani gave us the following Nharo version of the quarrel between the moon and the hare. In this version the quarrel is not about death coming to mankind; it is about one person assuming superiority over another—one claims to be cleaner than the other. The person who assumes superiority is brought down in the quarrel; and the quarrel is then put aside, and peaceful relations are resumed. This myth admirably fits the Bushman way of life as we experienced it among the !Kung. For a person to set himself above others was unacceptable social behavior. People wanted peaceful relations and, in by far the majority of instances, succeeded in putting aside their quarrels.

The hunters killed an eland and brought the meat to the people's encampment. The moon and the hare went to the omuramba where their water hole was to fill their ostrich-eggshell water containers, to drink, and to wash their faces. After they washed, the hare's face was still not clean. The moon asked the hare to look at her face (the moon's face) to see that it was clean enough and then told the hare that her face was still dirty. To think that the moon considered herself cleaner than she angered the hare so much that she took up a handful of mud and threw it onto the moon's face. The hare then pushed the moon into the water. Having done so, she filled all the ostrich eggshells with water, her own shells and the moon's, and carried them to the encampment. When the hare returned without the moon, the moon's husband went to the water hole and saw the moon's light in the water. The people slept that night and in the morning they went to get the moon. They washed her and cleaned her and brought her home, and they all lived together in peace again.

A Partial Eclipse

In August 1952, when we were sitting beside our evening campfire at /Gam, we saw a partial eclipse of the moon. We had been without contact with the outside world for some time, and none of us knew that an eclipse would occur. We were excited and hoped the !Kung would explain the event with some lore or myth, like the lion putting his paw over the moon to darken the night so he could have better hunting. However, the !Kung disappointed us. Next day when we talked with them about the eclipse, they showed no special interest. It was only a cloud, they said. These !Kung do have the lore of the lion's paw. Presumably our eclipse was not of sufficient magnitude to impress them, for they told us that when the lion's paw covers the moon they are frightened and hit their digging sticks together to scare the lion away.

We later heard that these !Kung had experienced an eclipse of the sun some years before. They had been terrified, thinking that the sun was "going blind" and that they would all die in darkness.

THE MILKY WAY

The Nyae Nyae !Kung's name for the Milky Way is "Backbone of Night." The !Kung said the whiteness was like the white belly of a steenbok, but went on to say that the Backbone of Night was not like an actual animal. It is a thing of the sky, with its own substance, shape, and motion. They do not know what the Milky Way is; they have no lore that explains it.

Other !Kung groups, the Tshimbaranda !Kung, the Nharo, and the !Ko, also call the Milky Way the Backbone of Night. The Nharo say the Backbone of Night separates the daylight from the darkness. "God's Path" was the name a //Gana visitor gave to the Milky Way. A man whose origins we did not determine said that he had been taught to call it the Middle of the Night, middle being the waistline, clearly indicated by his gestures, where one's belt is worn.

The /Gwi had no name for the Milky Way. Ukwane said it reminded him of the smoke of bush fires. That reminded me that the Cape Bushmen had a myth that tells of a girl of an early race throwing wood ashes into the sky and thus making the Milky Way (Bleek and Lloyd 1911:73ff).

The Coal Sack (the dark cloud in the Milky Way) to the Nyae Nyae !Kung is the Old Bag of Night, old in the sense of being worn out. The Tshimbaranda !Kung, the Nharo, the !Ko, and the /Gwi have no name for it. The Tshimbaranda !Kung think it is a spot in the sky where no stars exist. The //Gana visitor called the Coal Sack "God's Patch."

THE STARS

The nature of the stars and their movement is a puzzlement to all the Bushmen whom we studied and visited. They think of stars as "things of the sky" and do not hope to understand them. However, they are very much aware of them, and they wonder about them.

In the belief of some now-extinct southern Bushmen, stars were said to be the eyes of the dead. In other groups, stars were said to be the hearth fires of the dead. I asked my Nyae Nyae !Kung friends whether they had heard of these concepts. They had not, but since they do not know what stars are, they began to consider the possibility of the stars being eyes of the dead. They said among themselves that the great god had made the sky long ago and that many people had died within that time. This would account for there being so many stars. Visualizing the concept further, they said that the spirits of the dead, the //gauwasi, would all have to be leaning forward looking down. This did not seem plausible, and it was the consensus that stars are stars, not something else, and that people do not know their nature.

I asked different groups of Nyae Nyae !Kung what happened to stars in the daytime. No one claimed to know with certainty, but three concepts were brought forward. Some !Kung thought that stars remain in the sky during the day, as in the night, and that the sun is so bright we cannot see them. This is what ≠Toma believed. Others thought the stars fall to earth wherever they are at dawn and rise up into the sky again at night. How this feat is accomplished, the !Kung do not know. Still others thought that the stars move across the sky and fall to earth in the west, as the sun and moon are believed to fall. No lore explains how they return to their places in the night sky.

!Kung lore does tell that one celestial object remains in the sky with the sun during the day—the morning star.

The Morning Star

The Nyae Nyae !Kung believe that the morning star crosses the sky with the sun during the day. It is said to "herd" the sun. People do not see it after sunrise because the sun's light is so bright. The !Kung pity the star. They think that when the sun scorches the people far away on the earth, the morning star, so close to the sun, must suffer painfully from the heat. Di//khao pointed out that people can carry branches to shade themselves, but that the star has no branches.

The morning star has two names. Before the sun rises, it is called Old Star. When it begins to "herd" the sun, it is called Kuli //Gashay. An exact translation of the latter name eluded us. The idea expressed in the name is that the star tries to save itself; it tries to escape the sun's heat.

The !Kung bestow these names just as we bestow the name "morning star" upon whichever planet appears near the sun in the first light of the sunrise. They believe that they see the same object again in the western sky at sunset where we see the evening star. Kuli //Gashay appears to the !Kung, therefore, to precede the sun in the morning and to follow the sun in the evening. Evidently the !Kung have no traditional explanation for this apparent phenomenon. They talked about it among themselves one day when we were discussing stars. Gao of Band 2 came up with the idea that Kuli //Gashay stops at the zenith, steps aside, and waits for the sun to pass. Someone else said it hides until the sun passes it, but ≠Toma said it could not do that; there is no place to hide in the sky. He insisted that Kuli //Gashay always follows the sun across the sky, letting the fact that it appears, at least briefly, to precede the sun at sunrise remain unexplained. No consensus was reached.

The Nharo, the !Ko, and the //Gana call the planet Morning Star, as we do.

Meteors: "Stars" that Are Not Stars

The Nyae Nyae !Kung star lore holds two different concepts about meteors. We call meteors falling stars; they call them moving stars and say that moving stars appear to be stars but are not stars. In one concept, moving stars are seen as fiery objects with fiery tails that have powerful n/um. They can kill people, and at the times of the meteor showers when many are moving about and falling, the sky is very bad. People know that somewhere many people are dying.

The other belief about the moving stars is that they are ant lions (*Myrmeleontidae neuroptera*). From where they are in the sky looking down, their big eyes shining, the moving stars see ants. If they are hungry and want to eat the ants, they fall to earth. In another version, all the ant lions are said to fall to earth each morning and to go up into the sky again each night. We see them on earth as the insects. They are common in the Gautscha area, spurting out grains of sand as they dig their little holes in which they catch their ants.

The !Kung lore holds an additional concept about the creatures in their insect form; if an ant lion bites a person, that person will die. The !Kung were vague about this concept. Some said the person would die next day, others said within the year. /Qui had been the first to tell us about ant lions. He thought they were puzzling creatures. He pointed out that they appear to move backward, to have horns on their tails, to catch ants with their horns, and to bite them with their tails. He was puzzled by the fact that he saw so few moving stars in the sky compared to so very many ant lions on the ground. He rubbed his head to show that the insects were as numerous as the hairs on his head. /Qui was still more puzzled by the fact that he had been bitten by an ant lion and no harm had come to him. He did not know what to believe about them.

The Tshimbaranda !Kung, the Nharo, and the !Ko gave us no lore about falling stars being signs or causes of death or being eaters of ants. The /Gwi, however, do have a lore about stars eating ants, lore that varies in several details from that of the !Kung.

Old Ukwane claimed that falling stars are not different from other stars and that all stars eat ants. They are up there in the sky watching for ants, and when they see some and want to eat them, they fall to earth.

The stars are little things, Ukwane said. As one sees them on earth, they look like tiny porcupines. They have little legs, ears, and teeth, and are covered with tiny spines. They could easily be killed by a snake or a scorpion, or they might just die after a time. The skin of the dead star, looking like a little porcupine skin, would then lie on the ground. If a person should step on it, a sickness from it would go into him, a sickness for which the skin itself provides a cure. A healer, curing the afflicted person, would take a star skin, pull out some of the spines, make a little bundle of them, and scratch himself with them on the chest, shoulders, and tip of the tongue. This would empower the healer to suck out the star sickness and cure the person.

I remembered that Canopus was called Bushman Rice Star by the Cape Bushmen (Bleek 1929a:307; Schapera 1930:173). "Bushman Rice" is the eggs of white ants. Ukwane had never heard that of Canopus. He remarked, furthermore, that he had never heard of people eating ant eggs.

Canopus, Sirius, Achernar, Altair, Vega, and Spica

Canopus is included in a constellation with the Pleiades by the Nyae Nyae !Kung. Canopus is called Big Star by the Tshimbaranda !Kung, the Nharo, and the //Gana. The /Gwi call it simply Star, which perhaps honors it the most of all, implying it is the star of stars. Sirius is Hipbone to the Nyae Nyae !Kung, Thigh to the Nharo, Water Star to the !Ko, and Side Star to the /Gwi, who refer to it as being by the side of Canopus. Hottentots also call Sirius Side Star (Schapera 1930:415).

The //Gana make a constellation of Canopus, Sirius, and the Pleiades, saying the Pleiades are the wives of the two stars. Achernar is Younger Brother, namely, younger brother of Canopus and Sirius. Spica is called Pig by the //Gana.

The /Gwi pair Altair and Vega together and call them the Steenboks. Vega is the male, Altair the female.

Finish Fire

Da Toa Toa (Fire Finish Finish) is the Nyae Nyae !Kung name for a star that the !Kung associate with firewood and with the fires around which each family sleeps at night. The star is a clock that tells them how much of the night has passed and enables them to know on cold winter nights whether they have enough wood to keep their fires burning until morning. One could, of course, use any star for a clock, and the !Kung may do so, but there is a particular one that bears the name that I changed to Finish Fire. By a combination of mischances, Finish Fire was not identified by the Nyae Nyae.

Describing the star, they said that in winter it rises in the evening and sets in the morning, when the firewood gathered for the night is burned to embers or is gone. The star seems to be alone in an open space in the sky, they said. When they waken at night, they can recognize it easily and know how much of the night remains.

Arcturus is the Finish Fire of the !Ko, the /Gwi, and the //Gana—at least I believe it is. The star was clearly pointed out as Finish Fire by our respected interpreter, /Gishay, who is half /Gwi and half //Gana. It could be the Finish Fire of the !Kung as well. It fits their description: rising in the evening in the winter, setting in the early morning, and appearing to be in an open space in the sky. /Gishay called the star Fire Coal Finish Finish.

A complication arose when on two separate occasions Saturn was identified as Finish Fire by a !Ko and by our //Gana visitor. Saturn was in Libra, relatively near Arcturus. For some time before, the slow-moving planet had been in Virgo, also near Arcturus. I believe that the brilliant Saturn captured the eye of our !Ko and //Gana observers and that they had unwittingly transferred the name that belonged to Arcturus to the glorious planet.

The Nharo Finish Fire is comprised of two stars that, we were told, are a mother and son. These stars were not identified. We were told that they rise in the evening in the cold nights of winter and set in the early morning. They are especially bright on very cold nights. Often the people do not have enough wood, and their fires burn down to embers, to which they say the stars give their light. The mother star, the Nharo said, is red like the embers.

Possibly Antares, a Scorpii, is the Nharo Finish Fire. Antares is red like embers and rises in the evening in June culminating at midnight. Any one of several stars in Scorpius could be Antares's son.

Stars of the Southern Cross

Kalidi is the !Kung name for two pairs of stars in the constellations of the Southern Cross and Centaurus. We could not clarify the meaning of Kalidi but were assured that it is what the old people said to call them. Both pairs of stars bear men's names. The two in the long axis of the Cross are Kxoma (*a* Crucis) and Khan//a (*y* Crucis). The two Pointers are ≠Toma (*a* Centauri) and /Gaishay (*b* Centauri).

The latter two names, those of the Pointers, are common names of men. One feels there should be a myth or a tale about a man named ≠Toma and a man named /Gaishay to explain the naming of the stars, but none of the !Kung we spoke with knew of such a myth or tale.

The two stars in the Cross are named for two sons of ≠Gao N!a. The boys lived in the long ago time when ≠Gao N!a lived on earth. A long, involved tale tells of their doings. In one episode the boys set forth with two lions to hunt and were treacherously killed and buried by the lions. ≠Gao N!a, passing by, met the lions, noticed that his sons were not with them and suspected the lions. He asked the lions to fetch some water, and in their absence he hid a pair of magic horns in a tree. Then by flattery he induced the lions to show what good dancers they were and tricked them into dancing under the tree. At his signal the horns sprang down and pierced the lions to the heart. ≠Gao N!a then resurrected his sons.

The tale does not say he turned the boys into stars. The !Kung say the stars have always been stars, never people. The stars are only named for the sons of ≠Gao N!a, Old Gaú explained.

No lore about the stars of the Southern Cross and the Pointers was brought forth by the Tshimbaranda !Kung, the !Ko, or the Nharo. The //Gana and the /Gwi call these stars Giraffe Eyes. The Pointers are said to be male giraffes; the four stars of the Cross are female. /Gishay, our interpreter, agreed with this concept and added that *a* and *b* Crucis were mother giraffes, *d* and *y* Crucis were daughters. Ukwane said that the /Gwi call the Pointers male giraffes, the stars in the Cross female giraffes, but he had not been told the latter were mothers and daughters.

When the Pointers were near the horizon and parallel to it, I enjoyed imagining that they were wide-apart eyes of one gigantic celestial giraffe sedately peering over the edge of the world.

Old Demi's Hoax

Talking about the stars with a group of Nyae Nyae !Kung one night, I finally asked if they had names for other stars we had not yet mentioned. It was a night of brilliant moonlight; only the big stars were showing. Old Demi, looking up to the zenith, pointed to three stars and said their names were Bau, /Goishay, and /Gam. Old Demi said he knew no stories about these stars; he only knew their names. The names are commonly used women's names. It was surprising to find them used for stars and surprising that no one else among the Nyae Nyae !Kung had mentioned these stars. Bau was Arcturus, /Goishay was Spica, and /Gam was Saturn.

I pondered over this grouping of a planet with two stars, and next day I asked other people. Everyone laughed and claimed that never in their lives had they heard of those stars being so named. Old Demi, they said, had hoaxed me. ("To lie" is *jing;* "to hoax" is *tshwa.*)

Old Demi, challenged, insisted with quiet dignity that those were the names of the stars. His father had said that the great god, ≠Gao N!a, told those names to the Old Old People. No one confirmed Old Demi's assertion, and I was left wondering if there had been three women in Old Demi's life or his father's life who had been greatly honored, for it seemed to me a very great honor to have one's name bestowed upon a glorious star or a planet.

Orion and the Great Magellan Cloud

The most dramatic celestial event that the Nyae Nyae !Kung describe involves the belt and sword of Orion and the Great Magellan Cloud. The Orion stars are called //Kanosi by the !Kung, and the Great Magellan Cloud is //Galli Ding. //Kanosi we could not translate. //Galli is the soft, thornless, grayish-colored grass that the !Kung gather to use for beds; *"ding"* means "base." The !Kung say that the three stars of Orion's belt are three zebras. The stars we call the sword are an arrow. The !Kung word for both "horse" and "zebra" is *"/kwe."* I was making sure that the !Kung meant zebras, the striped ones, not horses, when Old Demi began insisting that they did not have stripes. It turned out he only meant that the stars are not striped. At least one of Old Demi's contradictions was resolved, but not the next. Some !Kung said the middle zebra is male, the outside two are female. Old Demi said no, that the middle zebra was a mare between two stallions.

Be that as it may, the tale tells us that ≠Gao N!a was hunting one evening. When he stood up on the Great Magellan Cloud to look around, he saw the zebras and shot an arrow at the middle one. Just as human hunters often do, he missed. His arrow fell short. One sees it lying there pointing at the zebras. After his unsuccessful attempt he decided to send the zebras down to earth so that Bushmen could hunt them. Slowly, one following the other, as on a game path, the zebras descended and one by one stepped onto the earth.

The tale is not highly dramatic to relate, but enacted in the sky on a clear Kalahari evening, it is memorable to see. We caught it at exactly the right time on May 11, 1955. We were traveling that evening and not distracted by the light of our campfire or evening chores. When thorn trees still showed black against the glowing horizon, the first magnitude stars appeared. Sirius and Canopus, alike in brilliance, were the first. They seemed to be alone for a few seconds in the pale sky above the sunset. Then the other stars appeared: the Southern Cross was well above the horizon, Orion low in the west. As the sky darkened the Great Magellan Cloud began to glow as though a portentous light were being slowly brightened on a silent stage. The zebras and the arrow shone. Finally, at about nine o'clock, the zebras stepped slowly onto the earth, one by one.

The Hottentots have a similar tale reported by Hahn, as Schapera tells us, in which the main elements are the same as those in the !Kung tale. According to the Hottentot tale, the three stars of the belt "are three fugitive zebras against the middle one of which the hunter shoots his arrows." The hunter is Aldebaran, *a* Tauri, the husband of the Pleiades.

> The /Khunuseti (Pleiades) said to their husband, "Go thou and shoot those three Zebras for us; but if thou dost not shoot, thou darest not come home." And the husband went out with only one arrow, and he shot with his bow. But he did not hit, and he sat there because his arrow had missed the Zebras. On the other side stood the Lion and watched the Zebras, and the man could not go and pick up his arrow to shoot again. And because his wives had cursed him he could not return; and there he sat in the cold night shivering and suffering from thirst and hunger. And the /Khunuseti said to the other men: "Ye men, do you think that you can compare yourselves to us, and be our equals? There now, we defy our own husband to come home because he has not killed game" (Schapera 1930:415ff).

Of the other Bushmen groups we visited, only the Nharo of !Go Tsao shared the tale of a hunter standing on the Great Magellan Cloud shooting at three animals. In the Nharo version, the three stars of Orion's belt were said to be giraffes. However, two old men in the group told us that when the tale had been told to them in their youth, the three stars were said to be zebras. The old men went on to explain that nowadays the young people heard from the Tsaukwe, their neighbors to the northeast, that in their tales the stars are giraffes, so that was what they told us.

All the Bushmen we worked with tended to be diffident with us. This particular group of Nharo were exceedingly hesitant. They had begun our discussion by saying they were only ignorant Bushmen and I must not expect them to know the answers to my questions. Possibly in this instance they had given me the Tsaukwe version thinking the Tsaukwe knew better than they.

The Pleiades, Canopus, and Capella

In !Kung tradition the Pleiades, Canopus, and Capella are seen as a constellation. The stars are relatively near together in right ascension. The Pleiades rise only about an hour and a half before Capella. Capella precedes Canopus by about an hour. In celestial latitude, however, the stars are far apart; Capella and Canopus are separated by ninety-eight degrees. To understand how such widely separated stars are seen as a constellation by the !Kung, one must see them at a certain time of year in the eastern sky at dawn.

The !Kung name for the Pleiades is Tshxum. This is a name, they claimed, not a word with translatable meaning. Capella and Canopus together are called the horns of the Tshxum (Tshxum !Khusi). Capella is singled out by the unlikely name of Green Leaf Horn. The Green Leaf Horn is a bara thing, the !Kung said; it comes when the first flowers bloom. (Bara is the season of the rains.)

When I began inquiring about the stars, the Pleiades were among the first stars to be pointed out, and they were identified as the Tshxum. No confusion arose. R. H. Allen, in *Star Names: Their Lore and Meaning,* quotes Pliny as saying of the Pleiades, "So evident in the heaven, and easiest to be known of all others . . ." (Allen 1963:402). Canopus was also easily recognized and was clearly identified as one of the horns of the Tshxum. However, the Green Leaf Horn eluded me. People would point to a place in the northeast sky about forty-five degrees above the horizon and say the star would appear there. But it never seemed to do so. It became a quest confounded by confusion caused largely, I believe, by the fact that the star was visible in the sky much of the time when I was asking about it, but not in the exact position in which it is recognized by the !Kung as the Green Leaf Horn.

In 1961, our expedition arrived in Nyae Nyae on September 17. Old Gaú had remembered that I wanted to see the Green Leaf Horn, and the first morning after our arrival he came before dawn to waken me, saying he could show me the star. I quickly pulled on some clothes, climbed out of my sleeping tent, and saw a moonless sky blazing with a myriad of stars. The Pleiades were nearing the zenith. Aldebaran, their husband according to Hottentot myth, was near. Sirius and Canopus in their brilliance dominated the lower east and southeast sky. Away in the northeast was the star Old Gaú pointed to. It had not occurred to me that the star would be so distant from the others or so far to the north. I had not learned to identify the northern stars and had to get out the star atlas and a flashlight to learn that the star was Capella, *a* Aurigae. While I was studying the atlas, dawn came. The lesser stars faded away. The horizon began to glow in sunrise crimson. Venus had risen and gleamed near Sirius in the crimson light. For a moment of breathtaking beauty, in a seeming arc soaring over the sunrise glow, Capella and Canopus were paired, matched in brilliance and color, marking the north and the south. An arc drawn between them would bracket the earth. With the Pleiades they formed a great embracing triangle.

At last I had seen the stars as the constellation. Furthermore, to my pleasure, I had seen them at exactly the right time of the year. In that arid land, some of the drought-resistant vegetation does not wait to be quickened by the rains. Not a drop of rain had fallen as yet that season, but we had noticed green blades in the sere golden grass clumps. Lilies had thrust shoots up through the dry sand from their succulent bulbs and had burst into patches of great pink blossoms. The first rain fell on September 24, the first great single drops from a passing cloud of the so-called little rains. They spattered separate circles in the sand and filled the air with the fragrance of wet earth. Flowers and stars had signalled the rains, as the !Kung had said.

While Old Gaú and I were looking at the stars, I had set a pot of cocoa to heat on the coals of our campfire. In excitement and delight at seeing the Tshxum and both its horns in such glory, I got out some bread and a can of bully beef. Old Gaú and I sat down to a little feast of celebration. Over the ages the Pleiades, Canopus, and Capella, as separate entities, have had special importance in many cultures. Allen tells us that each has been chosen to mark the beginning of the year in one ancient culture or another. All have been associated with rain and have been worshiped and prayed to. Capella (the Goat) was called the Rainy Goat-Star by the Romans (Allen 1963:86). The Pleiades appear in the myths about the flood and are especially prominent in the deluge myth of the Chaldaea (Allen 1963:398). Canopus was called god of the waters in Egypt (Allen 1963:71). Four great Egyptian temples built in 6400 B.C. were oriented to Canopus's rising before sunrise at the autumnal equinox (Allen 1963:70). Many people may have feasted in honor of these stars. Old Gaú and I were just another pair of feasters.

I wondered, however, if ever before these stars together as a triadic constellation had been honored by a feast. The early Arabs drew the Pleiades and Capella together into a constellation, calling the Pleiades a "troop of camels" and Capella their driver (Allen 1963:87), but the three together are not recorded as a constellation in any of the cultures mentioned by Allen. Nor are they seen as a constellation by the other Bushman groups we visited—including the !Kung of Tshimbaranda. Those !Kung call the Pleiades Tshxum, as do the Nyae Nyae !Kung, but they do not join Capella and Canopus with the Tshxum in any way, certainly not as "horns." They must have thought me more than a little daft when I asked if the Tshxum had horns, for they gravely stated that stars do not have horns. The concept of this triadic constellation may be unique to the Nyae Nyae !Kung. I do not know. I felt quite certain, however, that our little feast of celebration was a unique event—an old Bushman and a middle-aged American woman feasting at sunrise on bully beef, bread, and cocoa to celebrate a certain triad of stars and the coming rains.

Calling both Canopus and Capella horns of the Tshxum may be unique to the Nyae Nyae !Kung, but the association of horn with Canopus is not unique. Dr. N. J. van Warmelo told me by personal communication that the interior Bantu tribes of South Africa call Canopus by a name that has the same root as the word for horn. For example, he says that the North Sotho name for Canopus is Naka, which is related to *lenaka*, "horn of beast." He added the information that the star Achernar, not far from Canopus and rising four hours earlier at fifty-seven degrees south, is called Little Horn. In the tradition of the Sotho and Venda tribes, the year commences when Canopus is first seen just before sunrise in the southeast sky. People get up to watch for the rising. In the tradition of some Sotho peoples, the first to see the star will reap much maize. Among the North Sotho, young men spend the night on a mountaintop to watch for the star's first gleam and take the news of its rising to their chief. They celebrate the beginning of the new year with feasting.

I was disappointed that the !Kung had no fascinating myth to explain more about their concept of the Tshxum and its horns. If they had had such a myth in the past it was now lost to memory. I believe that the theme of such a myth would have been rain. The stars herald the rains, and horn is strongly associated with rain and rain symbolism.

Patricia Vinnicombe gives an instance of the beliefs of the extinct /Xam Bushmen:

> Rain specialists among the Xam were attributed with the power to disperse as well as to create rain. . . . [A] report claimed that Bushmen who had raided stock from the Bushman's river repelled their attackers by summoning a torrent of rain through the medium of an eland horn. Supporting evidence for the use of horns in rites connected with rain can be found among other Bushman groups. The mythological hero of the Kung in the Kalahari was said to have made 'rain, sky rain, until it poured much upon the women. Then he

forbade it: "Rain, vanish, hi, hi, hi," and was silent, then blew upon a buck's horn and sang. And the rain disappeared.' The Xam Bushmen in the northern Cape burnt horn in order to disperse rain. It was believed that the unpleasant smell rose into the sky and counteracted the ominous-looking green storm clouds whose potential violence was dreaded. Heavy or damaging storms were regarded as masculine and were represented by the rain-bull, and mist was thought of as breath from its nostrils. When Bushmen heard a rain-bull come thundering, they would light fires in the hope that the bull would take fright and retreat. A rain-cow, on the other hand, represented gentle rain:

> I will cut a she-rain which has milk, I will milk her, then she will rain softly on the ground, so that it is wet deep down in the middle. . . . by cutting her I will let the rain's blood flow out, so that it runs along the ground.
>
> (Vinnicombe 1976:340)

In one of the myths collected by W. H. I. Bleek and L. C. Lloyd in the late nineteenth century and recorded in *Specimens of Bushman Folklore* (Bleek and Lloyd 1911:193ff), Rain is a mythical horned beast. He has the form of a bull. He comes to court a young woman. She is lying down in her hut holding her child. Rain senses her and comes to her. His breath is like mist; his scent is fragrant; there is no scent as sweet as Rain's. The young woman lays her child away nicely in a kaross for her husband to care for because she fears that she will die when Rain takes her and that she will become a frog. She presses fragrant *buchu* upon Rain's forehead. Rain takes her on his back and carries her, trotting toward the water pit. As they go along, the young woman watches the trees. When she sees a big one she induces Rain to stop and rest under it, saying that she aches from riding on his back. She asks him to go close to the trunk of the tree. He does so and lies down. She rubs his forehead again with buchu and he falls asleep. Quickly she climbs into the tree and along a widespreading branch until she is at a distance from the sleeping Rain. She then climbs down and steals away home. Rain wakens, and believing that the young woman is still on his back, he walks on and enters the water pit.

This myth ends by saying that, "The old women who had been out seeking food were those who came to burn horns, while they desired that the smell of the horns should go up, so that the Rain should not be angry with them" (Bleek and Lloyd 1911:199). The person telling this myth added the comment that if the young woman had not acted so intelligently and wisely toward Rain, her people might all have been turned into frogs.

In the rock paintings of the southern Bushmen, the numerous rain animals have various forms. Some resemble hippopotami, some are snakes, some are imagined beasts not quite like any living species, some are elands.

In two splendid volumes on the rock paintings by J. David Lewis-Williams (1981b) and by Vinnicombe (1976), the symbolism is traced through the mythology of the /Xam, through the paintings, and through the rituals and beliefs of living Bushmen, with scholarly acumen and with insight. Through its association with life-giving things—rain, water, fat, meat, nonaggression—the eland becomes a symbol of plenty and well-being.

In Nyae Nyae !Kung culture, the symbolic association of the eland with rain, plenty, and well-being is strong. This concept is not expressed in pictorial images. The !Kung are not painters, possibly because they have no rock surfaces or other suitable surfaces on which to paint. They make their symbolic associations by naming one thing for another, in metaphors, and in music. They make the association of the eland with rain specifically in the music in the Rain-Eland Scale.

Going back to the stars, the !Kung I spoke with had only one thing to say that suggested that the horns of the Tshxum represented horns of a mythical beast. I was told that Canopus is the male horn, Capella is the female horn. In !Kung culture the right side is associated with maleness, the left side with femaleness. The remark evokes an image of a great celestial beast facing eastward. With all the association these stars have with rain, the celestial beast might with reason be thought of as a rain animal.

I would like that rain animal to be a magnificent eland. I would imagine it projected upon the stars as images of the constellations of the Zodiac, the Bear, and others have been projected in European tradition. I would have the eland crowned by the gleaming Pleiades to honor him for being life-giving Rain. But such a pictorial fancy must be abandoned. In no way could an eland's horns be made to fit Capella and Canopus. Only the widespread horns of a pictorial buffalo could be made to do so, and there is no trace of symbolism that I know of in Bushman lore to associate those dangerous glaring, snorting, stampeding animals with the goodness of rain and its gifts.

Putting pictorial images aside, we may still conjecture that the Tshxum and its horns are a *sign* of a rain animal, standing for rain, plenty, and well-being.

EPILOGUE

Since the time of our first expeditions to the Kalahari Desert, much change has come to the !Kung Bushmen of Nyae Nyae. Hence, this book represents an ethnographic past. Since the time of our visits, conditions have changed very greatly and with them the hunter-gatherer way of life once lived by the !Kung, a life of great antiquity and great stability.

As early as the 1950s, however, the seeds of change were being sown. White farmers, with their ever-present need for servants and cheap farm labor, had begun to venture into the Kalahari to lure or even capture Bushmen, whom they brought to their farms. Some captives were able to escape and to find their way home, but others, especially children, were not able. If the parents of these children could not find them by tracking the vehicles, the children were lost to their families forever. Partly to discourage the kidnapping and partly to attempt an educational program whereby the Bushmen could, if they chose, learn agricultural practices and abandon what was perceived as an unpleasant nomadic life—a change seen as desirable by the administration of South West Africa (now Namibia) and indeed by most westerners—the Commissioner of Native Affairs established a government post at Tsumkwe. In time, rows of small cinder-block dwellings were erected for the Bushmen, water taps and latrines were installed, and a clinic and a church were established. Later, a store was opened, and later still, a school. Within a few years, Tsumkwe had become a fair-sized post with many branches of government represented, among them the Police, the Department of Nature Conservation, and the Department of Agriculture. Eventually, the South African Army established a military post near Tsumkwe from which to combat the SWAPO forces in Angola.

Under the first administrator, Claude McIntyre, a training program was started to teach the Bushmen various skills. Certain men were taught to drive tractors and other vehicles. Women were taught some of the skills of Western housekeeping, skills such as dishwashing, laundering, and sewing. Both sexes received instruction in gardening and in animal husbandry. As jobs became available, Bushmen were hired to fill them and were paid for their services, either with the going wage in cash or with the equivalent in livestock—in those days sheep and goats. Participation in the program was voluntary, and at first the program itself was motivated by the desire on the part of the government to assume responsibility for the well-being of the Bushmen. McIntyre, who was generally regarded as a friend to the Bushmen, attempted to offer the !Kung a secure and more stable life in an environment that he perceived, correctly, to be changing for the worst as large segments of Nyae Nyae were taken over for ranches and farms.

Unfortunately, after McIntyre's failing health forced his retirement, the situation at Tsumkwe deteriorated. The administrative officials who replaced McIntyre apparently lacked his commitment to bettering the Bushmen's way of life. Educational efforts declined along with agricultural development so that the only employment available to Bushmen was at a menial level, such as carrying baskets full of dirt to build the road.

By then, however, a return to the hunter-gatherer life had become virtually impossible. For miles around Tsumkwe most of the game had been hunted out, and the patches of wild vegetable foods had been picked clean. In fact, what once had been a productive area of open savanna had deteriorated to an expanse of thornbush and sand, perhaps in part because the ancient Ju/wa (Bushman) practice of burning dead grass to encourage new green grass had been deemed destructive by the administration and was discouraged. To obtain food, people had to buy it, and to earn the money people had to seek jobs.

Perhaps more than any other factor contributing to the destruction of the old way of life, wage work dealt the heaviest blow. The administration, of course, was virtually the only employer, with the employment policy—so characteristic of Western culture—of hiring only adult men to fill the limited array of jobs. Thus the Ju/wa women, who once had been productive members of society, became dependents. To a lesser extent the same was true of children and the elderly, who in the new economy were left with no way to contribute either to their own well-being or to the general good. Then too, the pay earned by the men was very low. By Western standards, the Ju/wa men were at the bottom of the ladder, being not only unskilled but also quite unfamiliar with Western ways. They knew nothing of machinery, for instance, or even of ordinary western tools, nor were they equipped to use them. For instance, in order to use a shovel one needs to wear shoes. But in the eyes of the administration, Tsumkwe was a distant and unimportant outpost, where even road building lacked urgency. No effort was made to teach or equip the Ju/wa labor force. Thus the low value placed upon the laborers combined with the low priority of the jobs set the Ju/wasi at the very bottom of the wage scale.

Yet for many people, the low wages were the only means of getting food. And for many of the same reasons that the pay was low, the price of food was high—Tsumkwe was far away. People could afford only the cheapest food, which was the white cornmeal known as mealie meal, the staple food of the southern African poor. With little or no wild foods to supplement the diet of boiled cornmeal, the people began to experience varying degrees of malnutrition.

Completing the people's physical decline was the failure of sanitation. By the old way, in which people had moved their residences fairly often, good sanitation was fostered by the dry climate and the open air and had been easily and efficiently maintained. In the new way, the inadequate latrines were soon overflowing, attracting large swarms of flies and other insects, which found their way to the faces of infants and to people's little caches of unrefrigerated food. Foremost among the diseases to overtake the sedentary population were TB, meningitis, dysentery, measles, and venereal disease, all new to the Ju/wasi of Nyae Nyae. The death rate rose, particularly among the very young and very old.

Perhaps the hardest part of deculturation for the Ju/wasi, however, was the loss of the numerous cultural mechanisms with which they had maintained their social stability and the equitable, peaceful intercourse of their lives. Cooperation and sharing had been the most prominent peacekeeping mechanisms of Ju/wa culture, and these became seriously damaged in the new economy if by nothing else than the small physical size of cash money itself—bills and coins that could be easily hidden and therefore not shared. In addition, this scarce commodity soon came to be treated by the Ju/wasi as it was treated by the Westerners who brought it: with considerable secrecy. Failure to share had traditionally been an unspeakable malfeasance to the Ju/wasi, and the widespread failure caused tensions that were hard to endure. In the past, such tensions had been relieved in a number of ways, foremost among which was the people's mobility, by which groups experiencing dissent could separate to live apart until the tensions subsided. But after ranching interests took over the permanent sources of dry-season water in the north and south of Bushmanland, most of the Ju/wasi living at Tsumkwe had nowhere else to go and had to suffer the tensions in their groups as best they could.

This became virtually impossible after alcohol was introduced into Bushmanland. After the South African Army established its base near Tsumkwe, the Tsumkwe storekeeper, with the aid of a government loan, began to sell liquor to the troops. The Ju/wasi also bought liquor, spending their food money for it, but unlike the soldiers they were not accustomed to it. As hunter-gatherers, they had used no intoxicant except very occasional marijuana, which they had obtained in trade. Hence the effects of alcohol were completely unfamiliar to them, especially the loss of self-control, so that flashes of anger, which under ordinary circumstances would have been suppressed, became translated into action. Tsumkwe became known as Face of Fighting and Where the Fight Follows You. Knife fights and fist fights became frequent occurrences. Violence bred violence, leading to wife-beating and child abuse. Most serious of all was that the intoxicated people readily went for their weapons, which traditionally being hunting tools were always kept at hand. Yet the arrows were poisoned arrows, and a drunken brawl of the Ju/wasi was hard to survive. The death rate soared. Among the people we knew best in Nyae Nyae, at least twenty met their deaths through alcohol-induced violence.

Even so, in spite of the terrible conditions that the people of Nyae Nyae endured as a result of the degradation of their environment and culture, Bushmanland is not entirely without hope for the future. Interestingly, certain people who in the past were known for leadership qualities, people such as the late ≠Toma, saw to the roots of the terrible troubles that beset their people. To do this cannot have been easy or simple. Rather, to their infinite credit, the Ju/wa leaders of Nyae Nyae had to grope their way in areas that were completely outside their former experience. As a result, when possible solutions appeared, these leaders were ready to adopt them.

Perhaps the most significant form of assistance to appear in Nyae Nyae has been the Ju/wa Bushman Development Foundation (JBDF). Funded initially with a small grant from the estate of Laurence Marshall, this foundation was started by John Marshall, who with ≠Toma and certain other people, began an effort to move Ju/wa families away from the violence and diseases of Tsumkwe. To any group willing to return to its former area, where the group owned the hunting and water rights, the foundation would provide the basic necessities of farming—fencing, tools, seeds, and a starter herd of cattle complete with inoculations. In areas that lacked water, the foundation would dig wells. Slowly at first, the people at Tsumkwe began to take advantage of the foundation's offer, and at the time of this writing, there are a number of little farming communities scattered throughout Nyae Nyae, some at traditional water holes such as Gautscha, others at newly dug sources of water. At these communities people have a mixed economy, which allows for some hunting and gathering as well as some gardening and husbandry. Many people earn cash by making craft items for sale to the tourist trade.

Gardening has perhaps been less successful than ranching in Bushmanland. Even though ≠Toma and his wife !U, by then an elderly couple, once dug an entire garden, planted it with pumpkin seeds, raised the pumpkins, and shared them generously to demonstrate how beneficial a garden could be, making and tending a garden has so far not proved to be work that the Ju/wasi enjoy. Cattle on the other hand are greatly enjoyed and are tended quite carefully by most of the groups that own them. And cattle ranching, if practiced rightly, has considerable tenacity. Unlike sheep and goats, cattle do not denude a pasture and are too big and too important to kill for casual meat meals. Alive, the cattle provide nourishing food in the form of milk, which to render digestible the Ju/wasi make into clabber. The cattle can also be sold for cash or slaughtered for meat. The hides can also be sold or used for leather.

In a number of ways the experiment of the Ju/wasi in subsistence farming has proved to be quite successful, not the least of its benefits being that the health and social stability of the people have greatly improved. Also important is that the ranching practices of the Ju/wasi are somewhat modern. Unlike some of the surrounding ranching peoples, the Ju/wasi do not keep cattle in numbers too great for the pasture to support. Thus the foundation has put what was regarded as underutilized land to a supposedly more acceptable use. As long as Ju/wa ranching does not degrade the environment, the development of Nyae Nyae will have helped independent Namibia, as well as the people it was originally designed to serve.

John Marshall and ≠Toma's son, Tsamko, were instrumental in beginning the work of the foundation and in carrying it forward to the time of Namibian independence. Throughout the 1980s they were joined by Claire Ritchie, and in 1988 by Megan Biesele. It is hoped that the new government of Namibia will respect the rights of the Ju/wasi—surely the oldest of Namibia's inhabitants—and allow them the freedom to develop the small amount of Nyae Nyae that remains in their hands.

AFTERWORD

Change Put in Perspective

Since the 1960s, when the Marshalls completed research among the !Kung of Nyae Nyae, profound changes have come to Ju/'hoan (!Kung) society. They have made a transition of immense proportions in a single generation, one greater, perhaps, than by any other societies in such a short time. Some of the elements of this transition were chosen by the !Kung people as they became aware of new possibilities; most, however, were imposed on them by their geographical and historical circumstances. In general, they have made a lively and creative attempt to integrate the changes that have been necessary. Attention should be drawn to the courage of the !Kung people in facing the great challenges of the last few decades and to the importance of help they have received from hardworking friends in the international community, who have involved themselves in detail in their lives.

At the time of the research, the people whose beliefs are described in this book had been the only permanent residents of Nyae Nyae for many thousands of years. In the 1950s, about 1,200 !Kung living there were the last independent, self-sufficient hunters and gatherers in southern Africa. Living by hunting and gathering in this area required approximately 37 square kilometers per person to support a stable population. It also required that people live in small, widely scattered groups in order not to put too much pressure on local resources. Hunting supplied about twenty percent and gathering about eighty percent of the diet.

From the 1950s to the 1970s the Ju/'hoan (!Kung) way of life in Nyae Nyae changed rapidly. The first commissioner placed at Tjum!kui (Tsumkwe) by the South West African administration, Claude McIntyre, was a compassionate man who saw that the size of the land area of Nyae Nyae was threatened by plans to create apartheid "homelands" like those in South Africa. He encouraged the !Kung to learn alternative ways of supporting themselves, given that the large hunting and gathering areas that had sustained their culture would in all likelihood be reduced. Over 900 !Kung people migrated from their traditional *n!ore* areas (the areas of wild food and water resources to which extended family groups had long-term ties) to the administrative center at Tjum!kui. Though the intention to provide agricultural training and jobs to the people was well meant, the project was overwhelmed by numbers and practical difficulties.

At Tjum!kui a school, a clinic, a church, a jail, and a store were built, and jobs making roads and clearing grounds for structures were made available to a few able-bodied men. Women had no productive work, and what they were able to contribute to their families' diets by gathering wild foods decreased rapidly as resources near Tjum!kui were eaten out completely. A large part of the !Kung population became dependent on government handouts. Crowding and hunger led to public health problems, and enforced idleness led to discontent. Feelings boiled over into fighting when a bottle store was established by a local trader and alcohol became available for the first time. Worse, as the !Kung were no longer occupying their land, it became the target of attempts by the Directorate of Nature Conservation to set it aside as a game reserve, from which ordinary human habitation would be excluded.

A few !Kung would be allowed to remain in Nyae Nyae, dressed in traditional skin clothing, as picturesque guides for tourists. John Marshall has called this approach to developing the tourist potential of the area "a plastic Stone Age." Clearly such a plan would have had devastating effects on both the community life and the livelihood of the !Kung.

In 1970, following the work of the Odendaal Commission, the !Kung lost, as Claude McIntyre had predicted, some seventy percent of their previous foraging territory in South West Africa and all but one of their permanent waters. Over 30,000 square kilometers of northern Nyae Nyae, where only !Kung and three Kavango families lived, were incorporated into the Kavango homeland. About 4,000 square kilometers were later proclaimed the Kaudum Game Reserve. The !Kung people were left with about 6,000 square kilometers of land, enough to support only about 170 residents by hunting and gathering.

By the late 1970s, the Nyae Nyae people were realizing that they would have to go back to their n!ores if they hoped to hold on to them. They also saw that they would have to develop some alternative economic means to supplement their hunting and gathering if they were to survive on a reduced land area. As they discussed their problems in Tjum!kui, stronger leadership for the n!ore groups evolved from necessity. People put their hearts behind individuals they thought could lead them out of the "place of death," as Tjum!kui had come to be called. One such leader was ≠Toma of /Aotcha, who led his people back to their n!ore in the early 1980s, where they have remained to this day. His group said of him, "he stopped our feet" (from wandering).

≠Toma and several other leaders in fact led a movement back to the land that has been the decisive factor in the !Kung's establishment of their land rights. In 1981 the first three groups departed from Tjum!kui to re-form their ties to their ancestral n!ores. By 1991 there were actually thirty returned n!ore groups living again on the land in Nyae Nyae. This widespread social movement paralleled the so-called Outstation Movement in Australia, where Aboriginal peoples have reestablished their communities in the outback and sought means to sustain themselves communally by various subsistence combinations. The !Kung communities aimed at a mixed subsistence as well, and they had help in doing so from an old friend, John Marshall, who with Claire Ritchie arrived in Tjum!kui in 1978 and began to explore new economic possibilities with the people of Nyae Nyae.

John and Claire saw that with the people's will to hold on to their land what was required was some strategic support to help them withstand the threat of the game reserve. With private donations they began what was originally called The Cattle Fund, which made small sums of money available to communities to develop water resources and to begin cattle herds and dryland gardens to supplement their hunting and gathering. The fund eventually became the Ju/wa Bushman Development Foundation (JBDF), and it raised substantial money from international agencies to help strengthen the !Kung's claim to be making productive use of their land. The intent throughout this time was to find a way to counter the forces of disintegration, including hunger, poverty, unemployment, illness, and anomie, which had so changed !Kung life from the self-sufficient one it had been before the people went to Tjum!kui. Most importantly, both the !Kung and their foundation tried to make the point that they were intelligent users of their land and resources, in order to reinforce their right to secure tenure of the land no matter what politics might bring.

Outside politics became an inescapable factor in the !Kung's life in the late 1970s, when attempts were made by the South African military to recruit Bushman trackers for their war against the South West African Peoples Organization (SWAPO). Military camps were set up at Tjum!kui and at several places in Western Bushmanland, and several hundred !Kung took jobs in the army, little realizing what kind of work they were getting into. The relatively enormous army salaries created income differentials that led to conflict within the !Kung communities. They also made it possible for dangerously large amounts of money to be spent on liquor by inexperienced young soldiers, with chaotic and sometimes violent results.

!Kung people, realizing the many forces arrayed against their community harmony and progress, reacted by starting a grassroots organization to tackle problems. In 1986, with the help of the JBDF, the Ju/wa (Ju/'hoan, !Kung) Farmers Union (JFU) was formed; its name in both English and !Kung was designed to underscore the hope of the people to establish a self-determined mixed subsistence based on more than hunting and gathering. Together, the members of the JFU struggled to combat problems such as the cattle predations of a large lion population (artificially increased by Nature Conservation officials for tourism purposes), the destruction of water installations by elephants, and the hostility of the administration officials who did not believe the !Kung capable of managing their own communities. The JFU represented the n!ore groups from Tjum!kui who had gone back to their own land, and it also worked to enable dispossessed groups from other areas, such as the Gobabis farming district to the south, to settle on available land along the old n!ore lines of settlement.

The most important work of the Farmers Union, which later became the Nyae Nyae Farmers' Cooperative (NNFC), was communicating new understanding and skills needed to reestablish the !Kung communities at a time of great political change in southern Africa. Traditionally, the !Kung did not have an overarching political organization larger than their localized kin-based living groups. To meet the challenges of becoming self-sufficient and of developing a voice to speak in external forums about land rights and development, they began to explore the extension of their familiar tolerant, egalitarian way of governing themselves into a version of representative democracy to support the interests of the region as a whole.

The structure of the NNFC was formalized in 1988 with the writing of a document of statutes in the !Kung language and in English. Each of the communities in Nyae Nyae was to elect two representatives to the council of the NNFC to act as voices for their communities on matters of n!ore allocation, n!ore group viability, cattle allocation, and the organization of farming labor. A leadership structure was formalized as well: ongoing debate and refinement of this structure have provided continuous opportunity for engagement of community members in the creation of their own community and regional rules. One of the most demanding aspects of change for the !Kung has been the struggle within their communities to adapt the cultural rules and values that underwrote the old foraging way of life to the very different one of agriculture and mixed subsistence.

The NNFC deliberates upon regional matters such as the applications of new groups for n!ore waterpoints and materials to build infrastructure, the best way to interact with local government entities, and the necessity for cooperative members to support each other in questions of new settlement by outsiders who do not agree to abide by coop rules. It emphasizes that the health of the land will only be preserved by careful limitation of the numbers of introduced stock such as cattle. It disseminates information about the availability of community services such as health care, schooling, and vocational training, and it keeps members abreast of national and international news likely to impinge on the communities.

The single most important area of awareness promoted by the Farmers' Cooperative has been the relation of their land rights struggle to the independence process, as South West Africa at last became Namibia. NNFC leaders accomplished prior to independence an extraordinary public-awareness program, carrying to the far-flung villages of Nyae Nyae the knowledge of UN Resolution 435, the meaning of SWAPO's war for liberation, and the challenges and opportunities they would face as new citizens of a nonracial state. By the time of the first free election, a large proportion of the !Kung population turned out as informed voters. Thanks to the JBDF, the NNFC was able to establish close contact with United Nations officials stationed in Tjum!kui and learned to rebut the anti-liberation propaganda of the departing South African Defense Forces. Farmers' Cooperative communities were enabled to vote at polling booths helicoptered into their remote area. Being part of the process that brought about the absolute end of the repressive Afrikaner-dominated South West African regime and ended petty apartheid in their area for good made a change in the consciousness of the !Kung people, which can never be changed back again. They discovered that their own efforts could make a difference.

One year after independence, which !Kung people celebrated by dancing in the streets with other Namibians, they raised their new-found political voice to good advantage at the Namibian National Conference on Land Reform and the Land Question. Representatives from the Nyae Nyae Farmers' Cooperative were formally invited to make a presentation at the conference, and they presented their case for security of communal land tenure most effectively. The leaders of the coop were accompanied by their own translators, written materials and graphics describing their traditional n!ore system of land stewardship, and the knowledge that the people they represented fully trusted them to present the regional case for communal rights. The conference acknowledged their presentation by resolving special protection for the land rights of their communities, and it recognized the n!ore system as the basis for future land allocation in Nyae Nyae.

While political awareness was growing for the !Kung, they were also consolidating their communities economically. With the combined help of the Farmers' Cooperative and the JBDF, which after independence changed its name to the Nyae Nyae Development Foundation of Namibia (NNDFN), the people of Nyae Nyae drilled boreholes for water, built stout kraals for small cattle herds, started dryland and in some cases small irrigated gardens, began selling their handicrafts on an expanded basis in Windhoek, and made plans for community stewardship of natural resources. Some of these activities became possible only as the apartheid government's lid on local initiative was removed, and the new Namibian government sought at last to support self-help efforts.

These improvements did not come without some turmoil within the communities. The once egalitarian !Kung, whose economic activities centered on individualistic pursuits such as hunting, had to face new challenges both in leadership and in the organization of work and its rewards. They had to find ways of adapting the strengths of their reliable sharing system to new demands. They also had to adapt their face-to-face method of relating in small groups, where each person had a say in decisions, to the exigencies of decision-making by representatives charged with community trust. The creative ideas that have come forward in solving these cultural problems seem among the most hopeful indicators that the !Kung are surviving great change in psychological health.

What the next years will bring, given the enormous strength of economic forces working against self-determination for a group as small and unaggressive as the !Kung, is anybody's guess. One thing on the people's side now is the turning tide of world sentiment in favor of multiculturalism. Human rights activism, environmental concern allying itself with self-determination efforts by indigenous peoples, and the global nature of communication are all on the side of small-scale peoples like the !Kung. We can only hope that the contexts in which they have to do their great changing in order to survive will value the philosophies, beliefs, spiritual practices, and knowledge that have sustained them, as well as their ability to change those things. Maybe in that way their new society can be a true outgrowth of those beliefs. Maybe it can be one chosen and molded by them for themselves.

MEGAN BIESELE
1992

APPENDIX:
BAND CHARTS

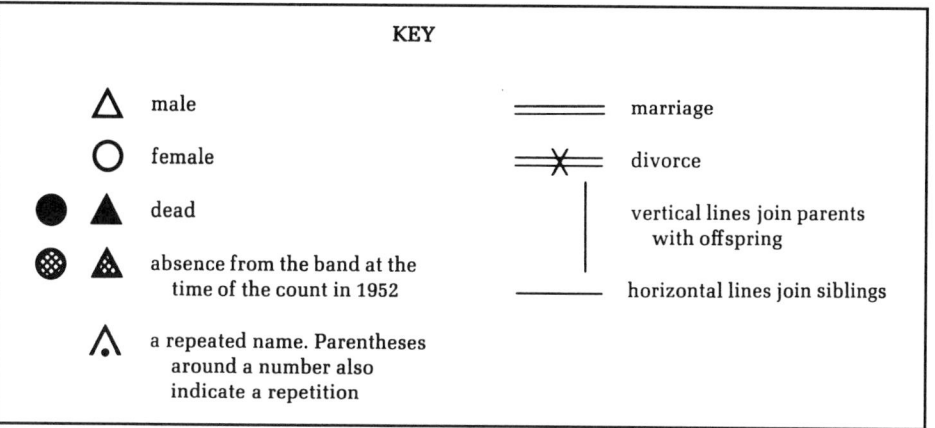

KEY			
△	male	══════	marriage
○	female	══✗══	divorce
● ▲	dead	│	vertical lines join parents with offspring
⊗ ▲	absence from the band at the time of the count in 1952	─────	horizontal lines join siblings
⟁	a repeated name. Parentheses around a number also indicate a repetition		

Numbers have been assigned to the individuals in the band charts for the purpose of identification. The numbers are composed of the band number and a number for the individual within the band—1.1, 1.2, 2.1, 2.2, etc. An X in the number—e.g., 1.X3—means that the person is dead. A Q in the number—e.g., 1.Q2—means that the person is counted as a member of the band but was temporarily living elsewhere at the time of the count in 1952. The numbers do not express any hierarchical order of persons.

Segments, groupings of families within the large bands (Bands 1, 2, 10, and 12), are separated by heavy vertical lines. The numbering of the segments is not sequential on the page. The segments and the order in which they are numbered are explained below.

Age is indicated approximately as follows:

YC	0–7 years old
C	8–15 years old
YA	16–24 years old
A	25–50 years old
O	50 years or older

In the three charts that follow the band charts (see pp. 305–9), forebears who do not appear on the band charts have not been assigned numbers, e.g., //Ao and !U in the chart about the relationships of members of Bands 1 and 2 on page 305. For spouses and offspring (omitted in these "relationship" charts) of persons listed in boxes, see the band charts. Siblings of the generations listed in boxes are given in order of age. Relative age of siblings in ascending generations is not indicated. Dead siblings are not recorded.

Charts are provided of ten bands in the Nyae Nyae area to show examples of large and small bands and to show the relationships through which people come together to form bands. The charts record the living people who were the members of the bands at the time the first count was made in 1952. If charts were to be made of these same bands at another time, they would show some of the same people in the band together, but there would be movement and change to record also. Only a few dead forebears are included to show key relationships. Space does not permit the inclusion of abundant genealogical material, but in the "relationship" charts, a sampling of genealogies shows how relationships extend throughout the area. Bands that neighbor each other are especially rich in linking relationships. The two Gautscha bands provide an example. The Deboragu and Nam Tshoha bands and the Tsumkwe and Khumsa bands do also. Genealogies of the members of Band 12 are not given, but this band has similar interwoven relationships with the other southern bands, Bands 13–16.

Bands 3, 4, 5, 6, and 9 are not complex. The charts show quite simply all the relationships involved—who are the "owners" of the territory, who are the incoming members of the bands.

The larger bands, Bands 1, 2, 10, and 12, and Band 7, though it is not large, are complex. They are composed of groups that I call segments. Each segment has its own internal bonds of relationships that make it a unit. The segments are joined in the band by consanguineous or affinal bonds; in the instances before us, each is held by a single bond to one other segment.

In Band 1, Segments 1 and 2 are both composed of the "owners" of the territory, the kxai k"xausi, and their incoming spouses. See page 305 for the relationship between Old N/aoka [1.13] and Old Gaú [1.20] as "owners," as well as the relationship with Debe [1.X1] and /Khoa [1.X2], who were incoming members in their generation. Old N/aoka and Old Gaú pass the "ownership" to their descendents. Although the members of Segments 1 and 2 are related, and although they live together closely most of the time, I count them as two segments because they do cleave at the segment line when they separate to go to different places to visit or gather. They do not live as one "household," but as two separate but adjacent family groups. Segment 3 in Band 1 is composed of people who belong to Band 4. Gao [1.8] is the son of old /Gaishay [4.1]. He comes into Band 1 and brings his first wife, N/aoka [1.7] and his whole extended family, through his marriage with his second wife, Di!ai [1.9], daughter of Old N/aoka, sister of !U [1.15] and Lame ≠Gao [1.14].

Note that in Band 1, in Segments 1 and 2, the living incoming spouses happen to be men married to women Gautscha "owners." They are ≠Toma [1.16] from /Gam (the band he belonged to is disbanded, its affiliations were with Band 14) and /Qui [1.24]. Gao [1.8] in Segment 3 is another male incoming spouse to Band 1. (See the charts on pp. 306–9 for the genealogical background of Gao and pp. 306–7 for that of /Qui.)

In Band 2, Segments 1 and 2, like those of Band 1, are composed of "owners" of Gautscha and their incoming spouses. The chart on page 305 shows the relationship between the two segments. They live as two separate but adjacent family groups, as do Segments 1 and 2 in Band 1. Note that whereas in Band 1 the incoming spouses happen to be men, in Band 2 it happens that of seven incoming spouses married to Gautscha "owners" five are women. Old Xama [2.7] came from Band 7. /Gasa [2.5] came from Band 5. Old /Gam [2.17] and N≠isa [2.21] came from /Gam. //Kushay II [2.8] came from Band 4. //Kushay I [2.10] is an "owner" of Gautscha, as is her husband, Gao Beard [2.9]. Of the two men, Gao [2.1], a son of Debe of Band 24, came from Tsho/ana, /Tuka [2.15] came from the vicinity of Epata.

Segment 3 in Band 2, like Segment 3 in Band 1, is not an integral part of the band. Segment 3 comes into Band 2 through the marriage of Gau [2.25] to Khuan//a [2.24], sister of Old /Gam [2.17]. Gau was in bride service. Gau, Old /Gasa [2.35], his mother, and his two sisters, ≠Gisa [2.31] and N/aoka [2.36], belong to Band 3 where ≠Gao [3.4], also a son of Old /Gasa, is the present k"xau n!a. Short /Qui [2.37], husband of N/aoka, and Dam [2.32], husband of ≠Gisa, belong to Band 12. Short /Qui and Dam and their families were living in Band 12 when we first saw them. They came to live with Gau in Band 2 shortly after. The people of Segment 3 have three choices of residence, Band 3, Band 12, or Band 2, that is, as long as Gau chooses to stay in Band 2.

In Band 7, Segment 1 was composed of the old k"xau n!a, Old /Qui [7.2], his wives, offspring, and his son's wife's mother, //Kushay [7.6]. Segment 2 was only briefly present in Band 7. It was composed of Gao [7.12], another son of Old /Gasa, and his wife, Di!ai [7.13], daughter of Old Xama [2.7], sister of Gao Beard [2.9]. Gao [7.12] belongs to Band 3 where his brother ≠Gao [3.4] is k"xau n!a. He had recently married /Doĩn [7.11], granddaughter of Old /Qui, as his second wife and was in bride service for her. In 1953, that marriage dissolved in divorce, and Gao and Di!ai went back to live in Band 3.

In Band 10, Segment 1 is composed of the "owners" of Tsumkwe and their spouses (see pp. 308–9). Segment 2 is composed of the family of //Ao [10.21] from Tsho/ana. They are in Band 10 temporarily through the marriage of /Qui [10.7], the son of //Ao and N≠isa, to two daughters of Baú [10.12] and ≠Gao [10.13].

Band 12 at /Gam was more complex than any of the others. When we were with the band it had six segments. Unfortunately, the genealogical superstructure that would show the relationship between some of the segments was lost to memory. Band 12 people appeared to be singularly uninformed about their forebears. One of our interpreters, with whom we had only recently begun to work and whom we had not yet trained to avoid interjecting his own questions or remarks into an interrogation, became exasperated with the replies of "I do not know" and said to Khwova [12.7], "You seem to be an old woman. How is it you are so ignorant about your relatives?" She replied, apparently without taking offense, "I am not old. It is hunger makes me seem so." She left his accusations of ignorance without comment.

Gao [12.29] in Segment 1 was the k"xau n!a of the band. He was a young man; his first child was only about two years old. Gao's father, !Kham [12.X11], had been k"xau n!a before him. Gao could tell us little about his father except that he had been, as Gao said, the "biggest" k"xau n!a at /Gam. That would mean probably that his family had been established at the /Gam water longer than the family of the k"xau n!a of Band 13, a position claimed by /Ti!kay [13.14]. /Ti!kay's position was not substantiated by the rather confused genealogical data we managed to gather from that band, but that !Kham had been the "big" k"xau n!a and the person who gave people from other places permission to take the /Gam water was substantiated by the explicit statements of several persons in addition to those of his son, Short Gao [12.6], Short /Qui [2.37], Dam [2.32], Old Debe, leader of Band 13, and Old /Ti!kay, k"xau n!a of Band 14, all of whom concurred.

Segment 2 of Band 12 was composed of Kuara [12.22] and his family. Kuara is a brother of Gao's deceased mother, Baú [12.X9], and of her old sister, Old Khwova [12.28], who lives with Gao, and of another of Baú's sisters, /Khoa [12.17], who lives with her family in Segment 3. Kuara and his family were present in Band 12 because of the drought. Ordinarily, they live with Band 15 of Domn!a. That is the band from which Kuara, Gao's mother, and the two other sisters stem. When the water hole at Domn!a dried, Kuara took advantage of his Band 12 connections and settled down between his two old sisters. He expected to return to Band 15 when the water permitted. Old Khwova and /Khoa live permanently with Gao, insofar as any residential pattern is permanent. I count /Khoa and her family as living in a separate segment from Gao's, however, because they lived separately in the encampment, next to their daughter's husband's people, i.e., the people of Segment 4. The daughter is N≠isa [12.15]; her husband is /Qui [12.14]. They provide an example, incidentally, of a marriage between two people in the same band. Although not prohibited by the marriage regulations, provided the couple's consanguineous or affinal bonds permit it, a marriage within a band is nevertheless unusual.

Segment 4 was composed of Short Gao [12.6] and his family. Short Gao felt that he was as firmly and clearly an integral part of Band 12, as much a kxai k"xau, as Gao.

/Ti!kay [12.X6], Short Gao's father, and !Kham [12.X11], Gao's father, had been related and had belonged together in Band 12. When !Kham died and Gao, his son, was still a young boy, /Ti!kay had become the leader of the band. The two young men, Short Gao and Gao, were equally ignorant of the relationship that united their fathers. They could tell me the names of their grandparents (apparently none of the grandparents were siblings), but nothing at all about their great grandparents. In all probability, a sibling relationship in the great grandparents' generation existed, and the two young men are second cousins.

The one person who came into a band on the basis of a name relationship, rather than through a consanguineous or affinal bond, is Old //Kushay [12.12]. Her deceased daughter was named Baú and that gave her a name bond with Old Baú [12.13] with whom she lives. Old Baú lives with her daughter, Khwova [12.7], and her son, /Qui [12.14]. Old //Kushay left Band 13 because she hated //Aha [13.13], the first wife of her deceased daughter's husband, /Ti!kay [13.14]. /Khoa [12.10] was /Ti!kay's third wife before //Aha drove her away with her shrill, vociferous jealousy.

Tshi!ko [12.1] and her family, Segment 5 of Band 12, came from the band to which Dam [2.32] had belonged, a band that broke up because their water hole dried completely, not in the present drought but some years before. Dam and Tshi!ko had connections with Band 12 through an ascending generation that are now forgotten, like the relationship between !Kham [12.X11] and /Ti!kay [12.X6]. Tshi!ko has additional affinal connections. Her two sons married daughters of Khwova [12.X5], who was a sister of /Ti!kay [12.X6].

Old Gao [12.37] and his family, Segment 6, came into Band 12 from Band 13 through the marriage of Sebe [12.30] to Gao [12.29], the young k"xau n!a. The connection between Old Gao and Sebe is one of the stretched-out connections. Sebe is Old Gao's son's second wife's daughter by a former marriage of the son's second wife. Old Gao's son and his wife came to live with Sebe, and Old Gao and his wives came to live with his son, all simply because they prefer living in Band 12 than in Band 13. They might return to Band 13 any time they wished to do so.

I enjoyed Old Gao immensely. He was cheerful, agreeable, and willing to talk with me about anything under the sun. His second wife, Old //Khuga [12.41], did not find him so agreeable. She apparently was thoroughly annoyed with him and declared herself divorced from him. However, she liked to live with her sister, Old Gao's third wife, //Kushay [12.38], so they made a little ménage á trois in spite of the declared divorce. I may add that Old Gao and //Kushay lived at one fire, and Old //Khuga at another, but the fires were only about eight feet apart, and I think we should take the declaration of the divorce with a grain of salt.

BAND 1—GAUTSCHA

SEGMENT 3

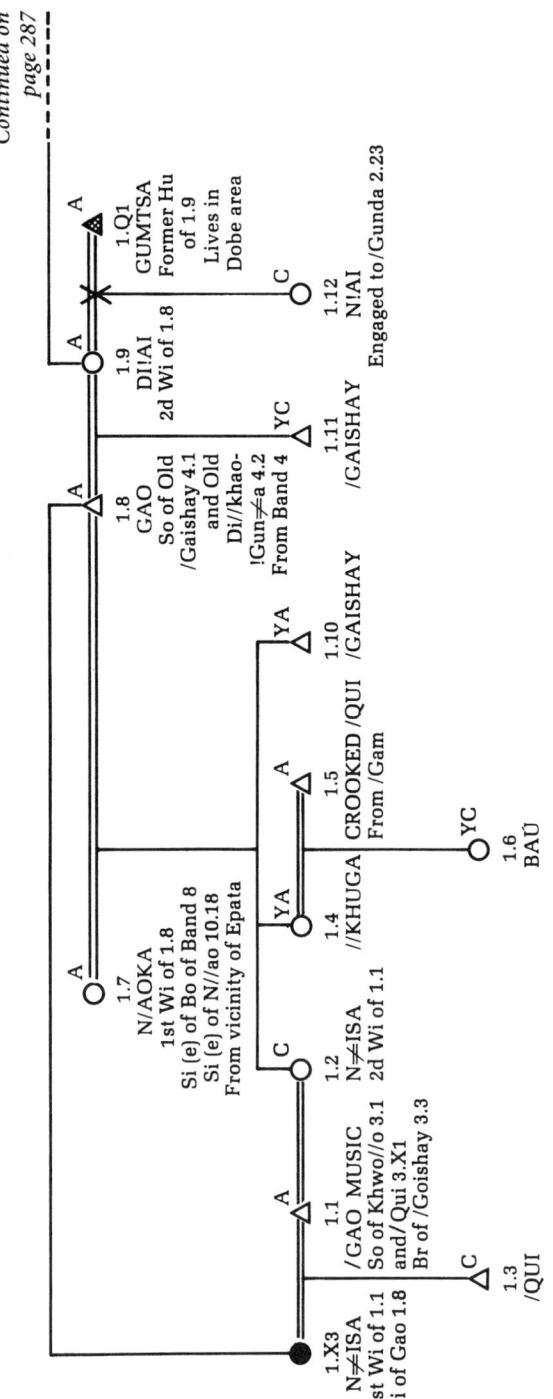

Continued on
page 287

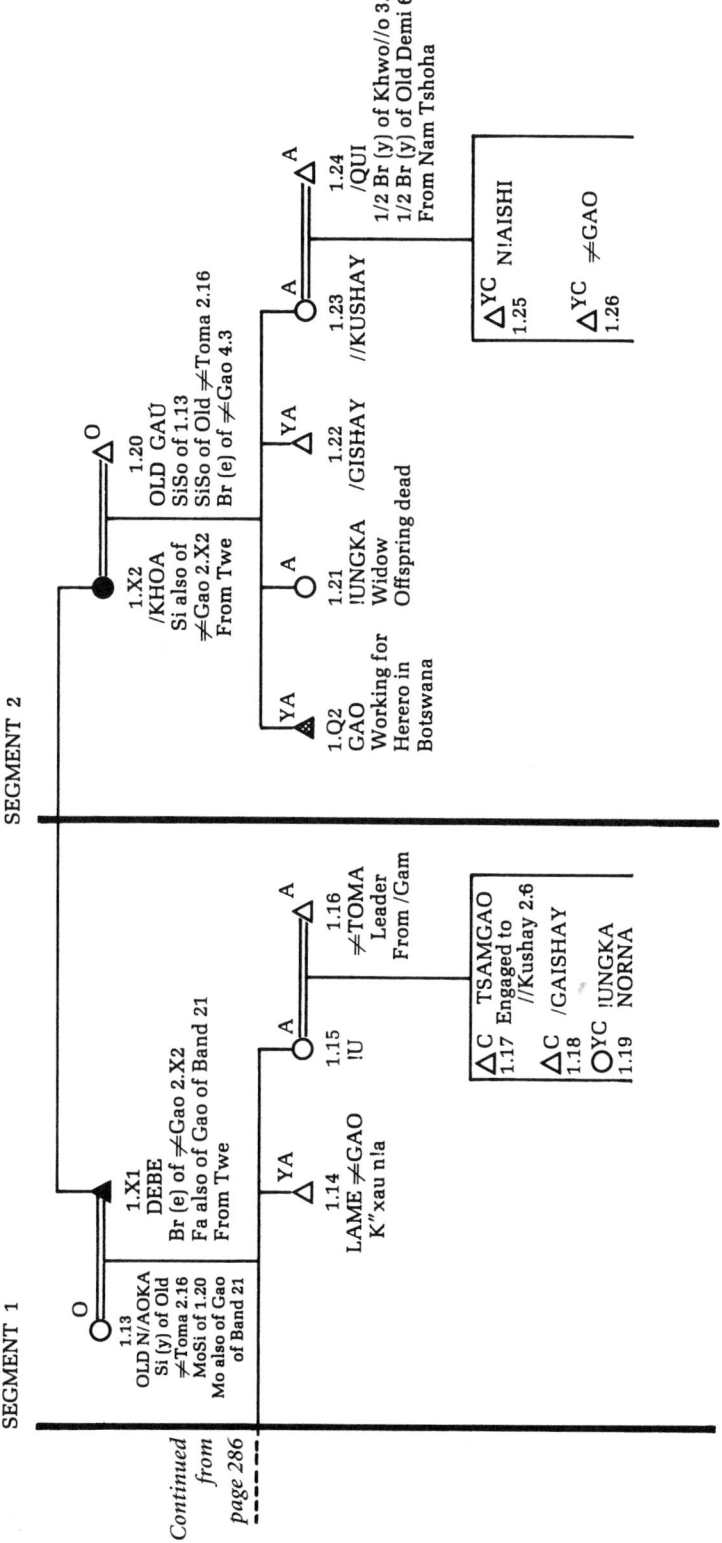

SEGMENT 2

SEGMENT 1

*Continued
from
page 286*

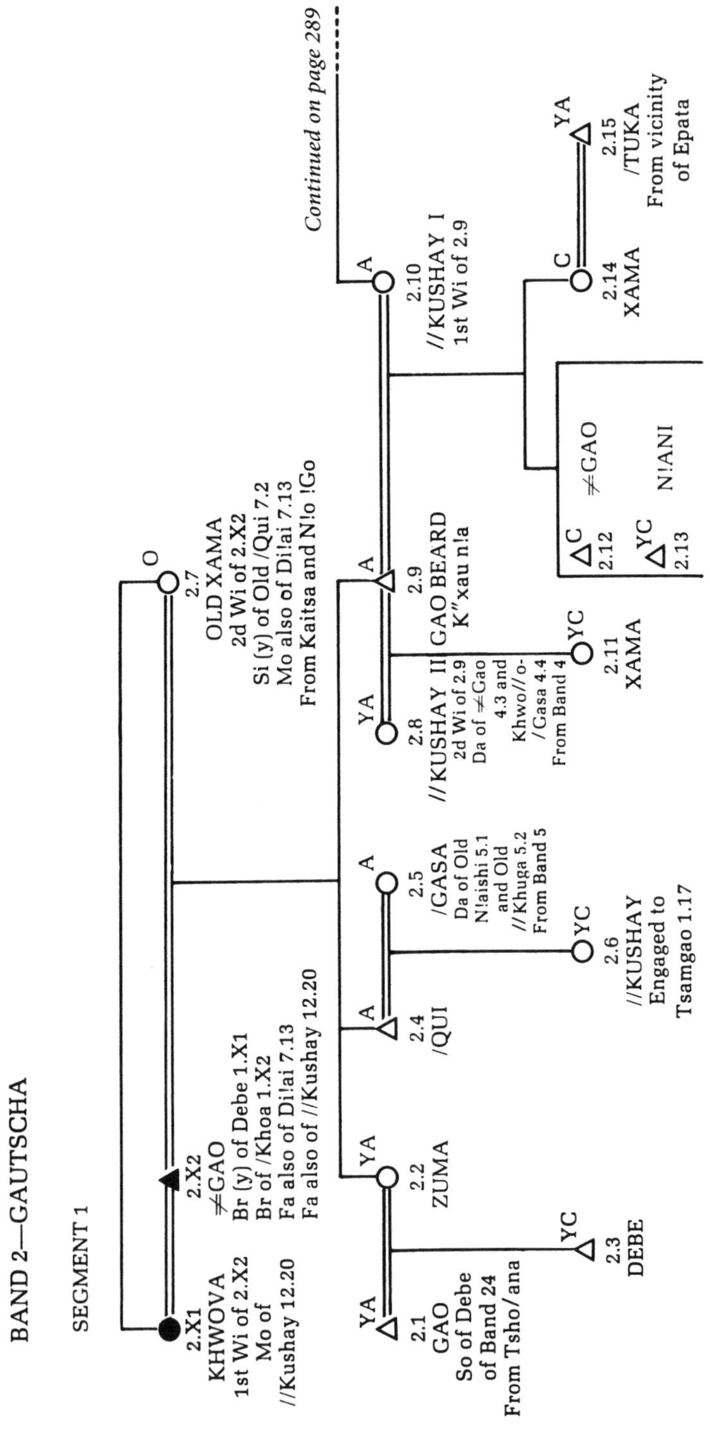

BAND 2—GAUTSCHA
SEGMENT 1
Continued on page 289
2.X1 KHWOVA 1st Wi of 2.X2 Mo of //Kushay 12.20
2.X2 ≠GAO Br (y) of Debe 1.X1 Br of /Khoa 1.X2 Fa also of Di!ai 7.13 Fa also of //Kushay 12.20
O
2.7 OLD XAMA 2d Wi of 2.X2 Si (y) of Old /Qui 7.2 Mo also of Di!ai 7.13 From Kaitsa and N!o !Go
YA
2.1 GAO So of Debe of Band 24 From Tsho/ana
YA
2.2 ZUMA
YC
2.3 DEBE
A
2.4 /QUI
A
2.5 /GASA Da of Old N!aishi 5.1 and Old //Khuga 5.2 From Band 5
YC
2.6 //KUSHAY Engaged to Tsamgao 1.17
YA
2.8 //KUSHAY II 2d Wi of 2.9 Da of ≠Gao 4.3 and Khwo//o-/Gasa 4.4 From Band 4
A
2.9 GAO BEARD K"xau n!a
YC
2.11 XAMA
A
2.10 //KUSHAY I 1st Wi of 2.9
C
2.12 ≠GAO
YC
2.13 N!ANI
C
2.14 XAMA
YA
2.15 /TUKA From vicinity of Epata

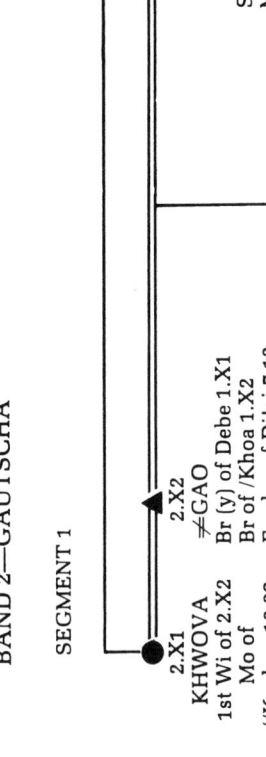

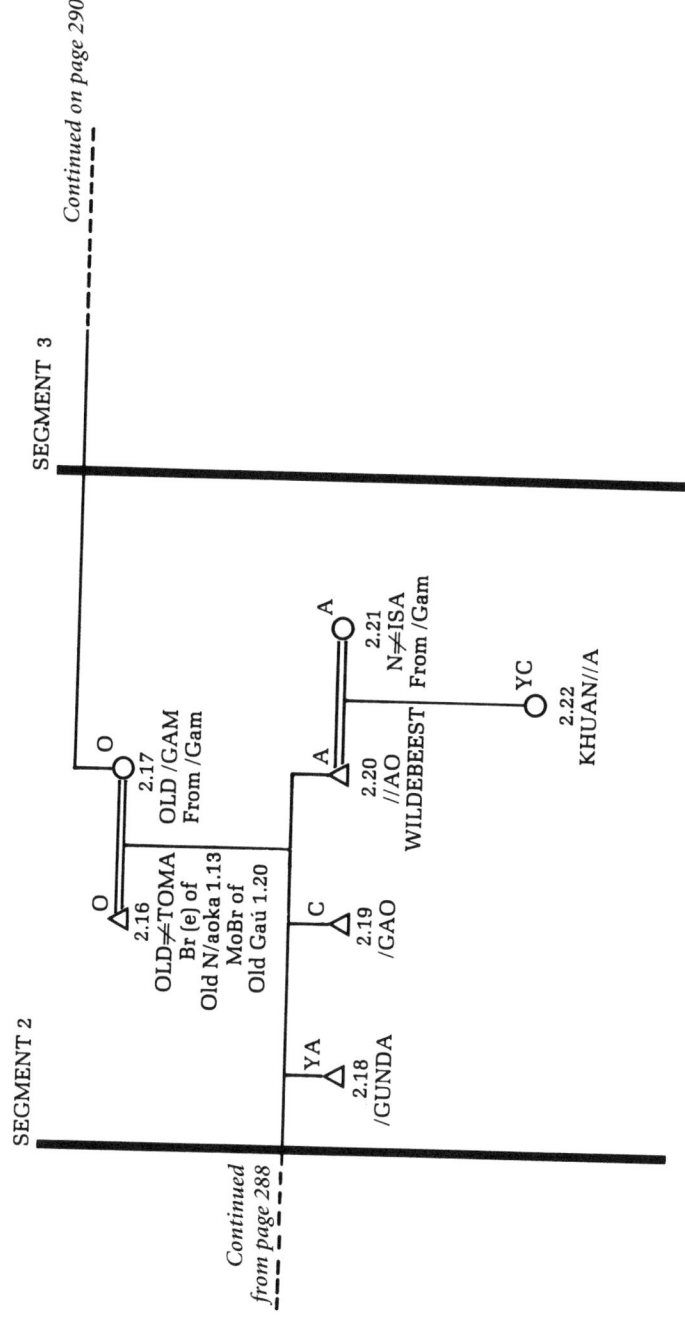

Continued on page 290

SEGMENT 3

SEGMENT 2

Continued from page 288

SEGMENT 3

Continued from page 289

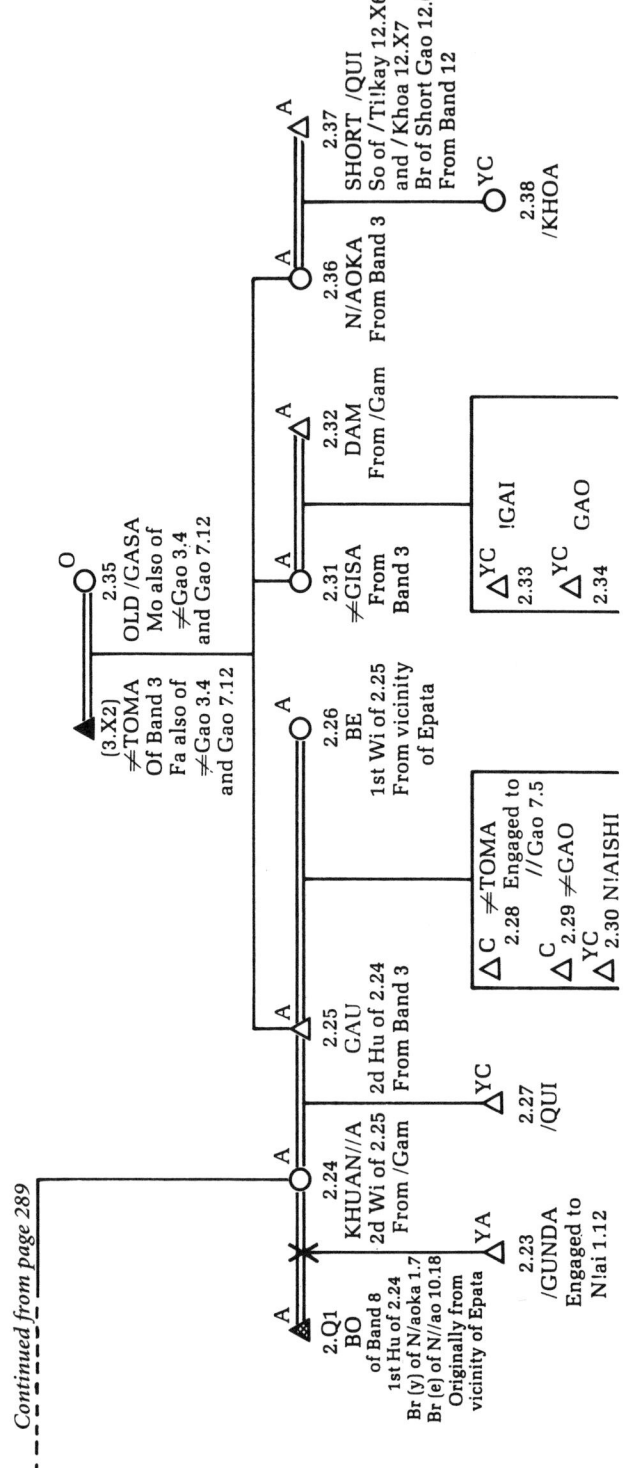

BAND 3—KAUTSA

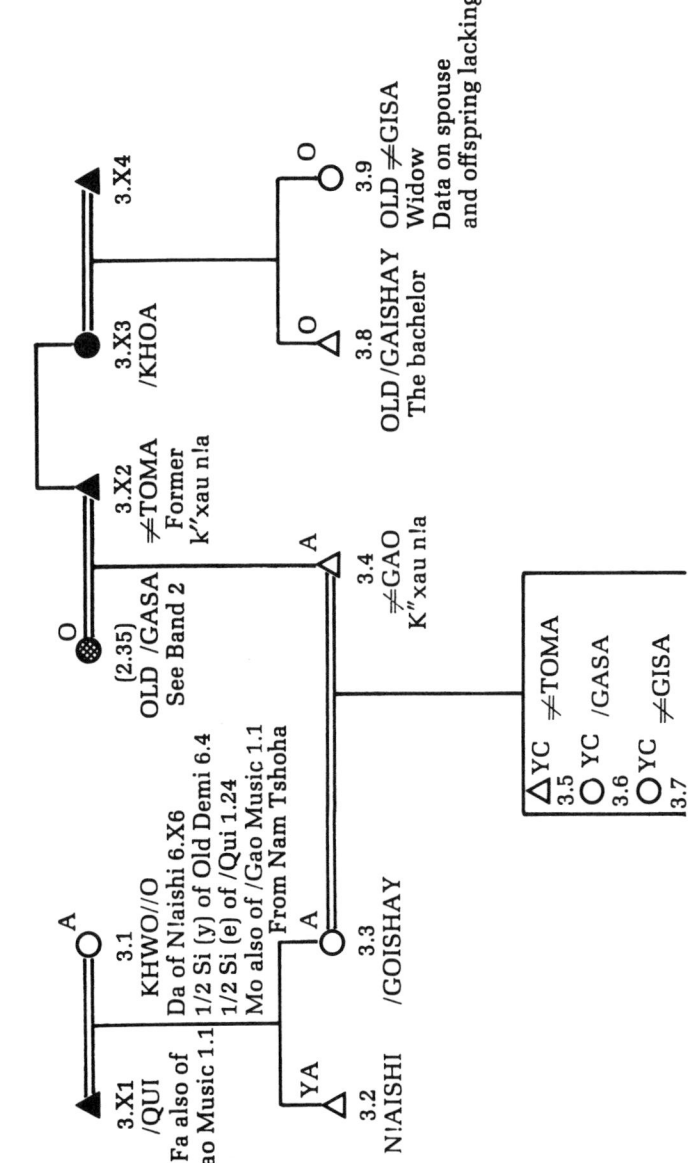

BAND 4—DEBORAGU

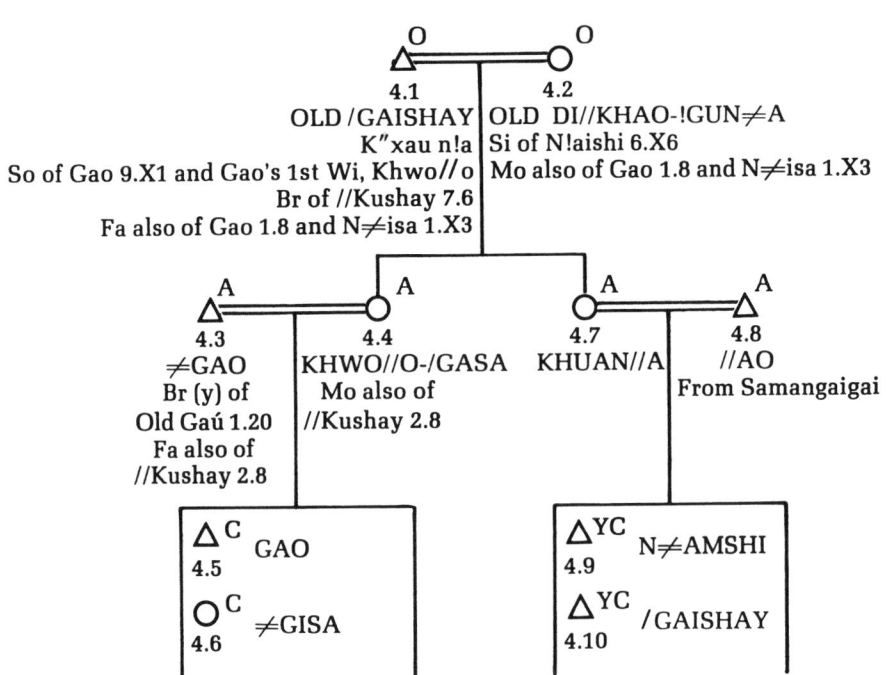

BAND 5—DEBORAGU

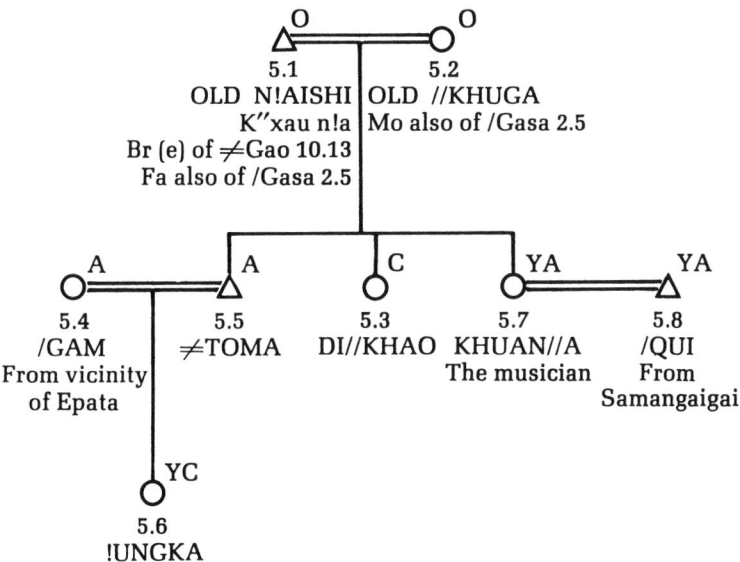

5.1
OLD N!AISHI
K"xau n!a
Br (e) of ≠Gao 10.13
Fa also of /Gasa 2.5

5.2
OLD //KHUGA
Mo also of /Gasa 2.5

5.4
/GAM
From vicinity
of Epata

5.5
≠TOMA

5.3
DI//KHAO

5.7
KHUAN//A
The musician

5.8
/QUI
From
Samangaigai

5.6
!UNGKA

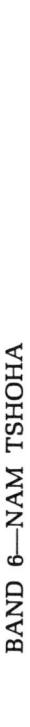

BAND 6—NAM TSHOHA

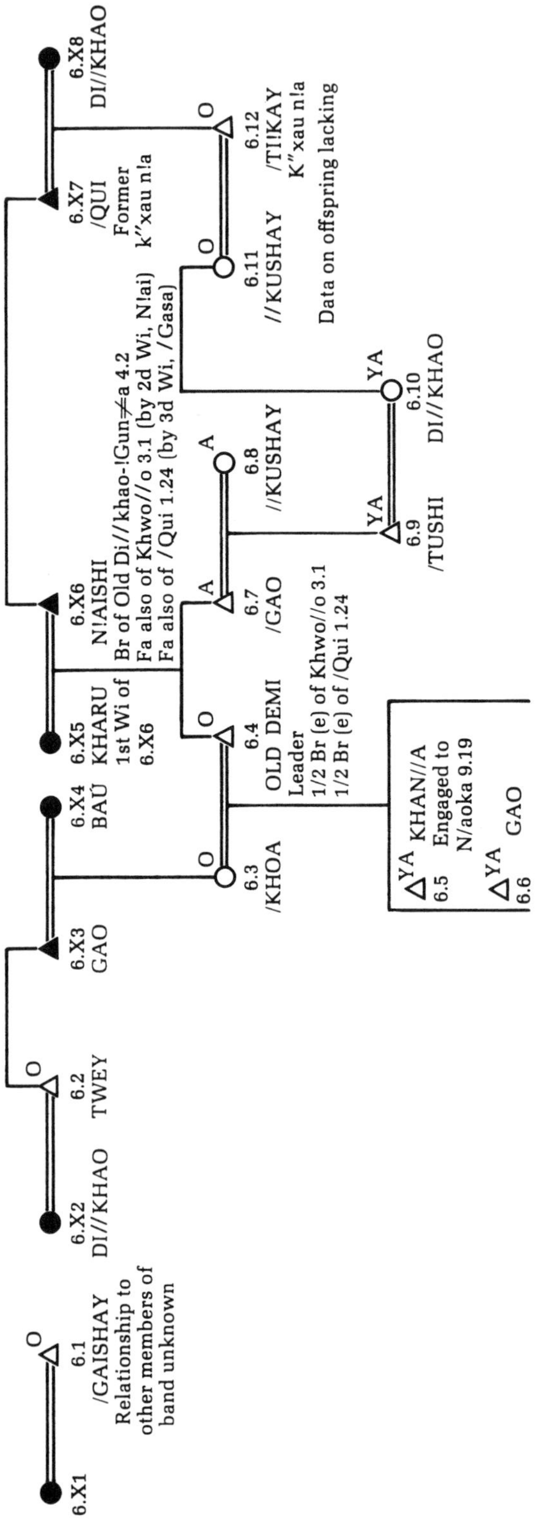
6.X1
O
6.1
/GAISHAY
Relationship to other members of band unknown
6.X2
DI//KHAO
O
6.2
TWEY
6.X3
GAO
6.X4
BAU
O
6.3
/KHOA
O
6.4
OLD DEMI
Leader
1/2 Br (e) of Khwo//o 3.1
1/2 Br (e) of /Qui 1.24
YA
6.5
KHAN//A
Engaged to N/aoka 9.19
YA
6.6
GAO
6.X5
KHARU
1st Wi of 6.X6
6.X6
N!AISHI
Br of Old Di//khao-!Gun≠a 4.2
Fa also of Khwo//o 3.1 (by 2d Wi, N!ai)
Fa also of /Qui 1.24 (by 3d Wi, /Gasa)
A
6.7
/GAO
A
6.8
//KUSHAY
YA
6.9
/TUSHI
YA
6.10
DI//KHAO
6.X7
/QUI
Former k"xau n!a
O
6.11
//KUSHAY
O
6.12
/TI!KAY
K"xau n!a
Data on offspring lacking
6.X8
DI//KHAO

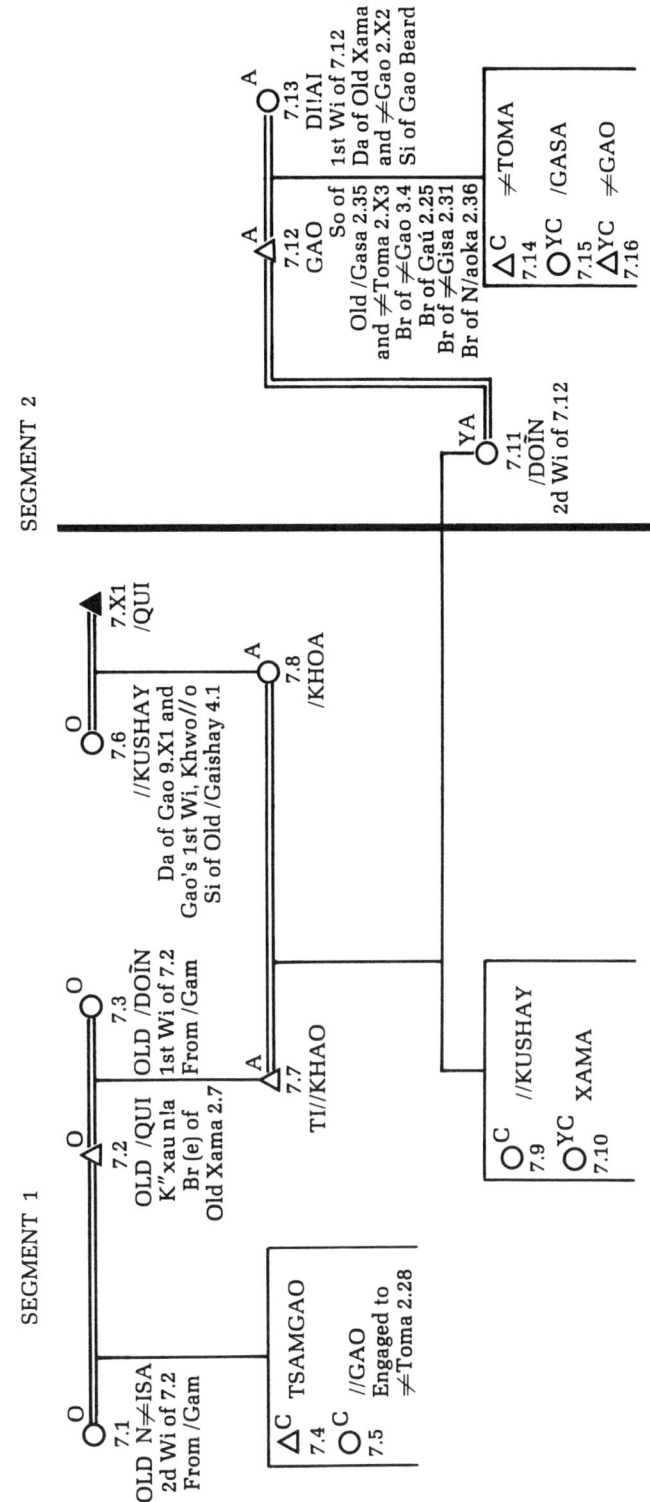

BAND 7—N!O !GO (Winter), KEITSA (Summer)

BAND 9—KHUMSA

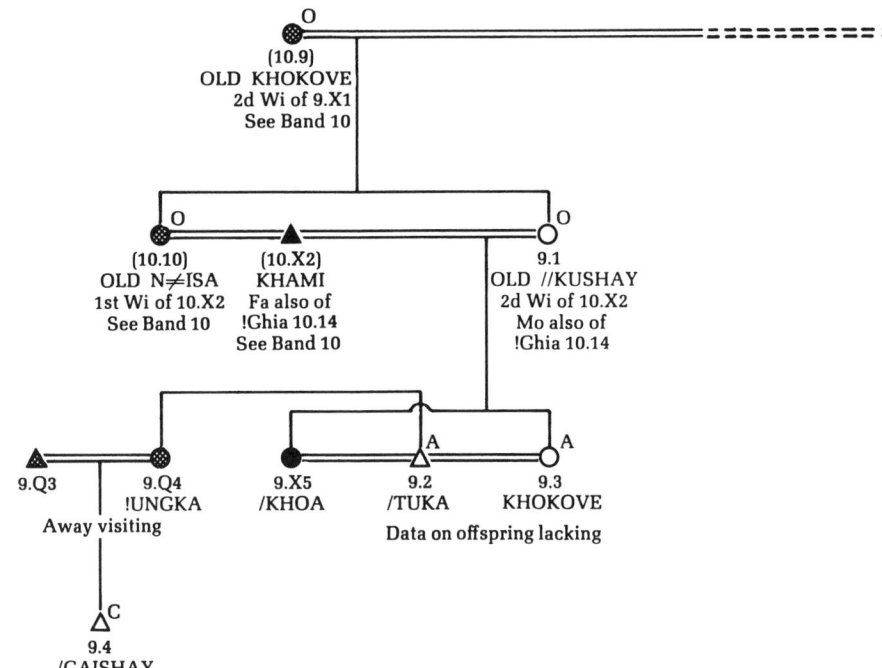

9.4
/GAISHAY
This boy was living with 9.2 and 9.3

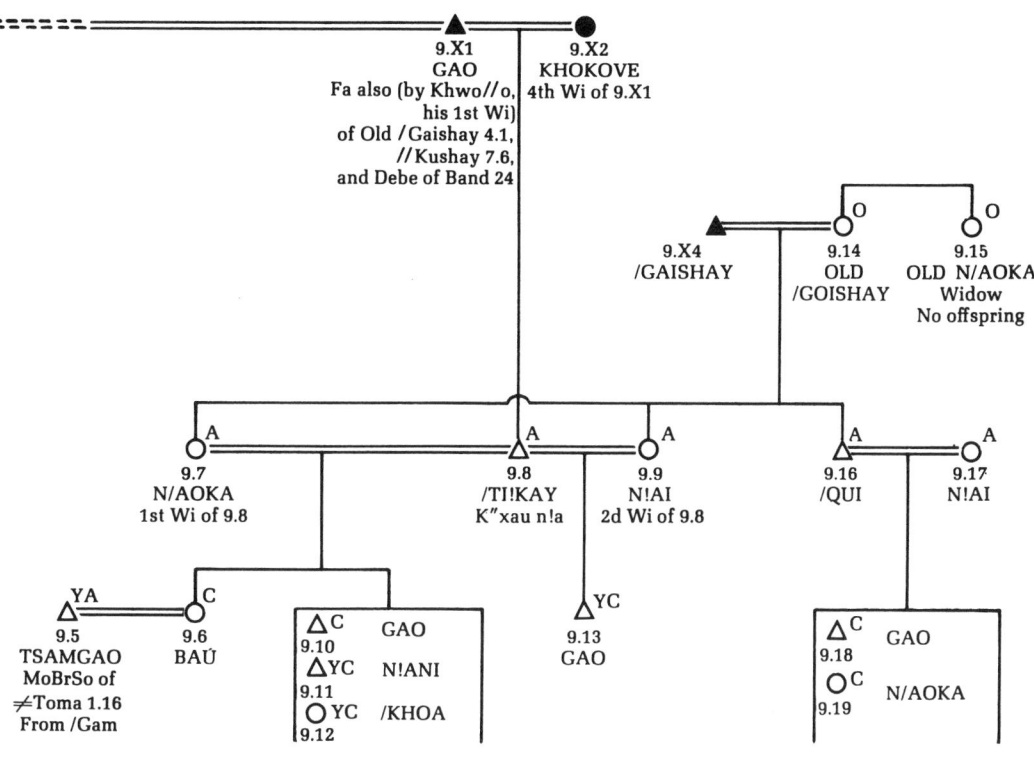

BAND 10—TSUMKWE

SEGMENT 1

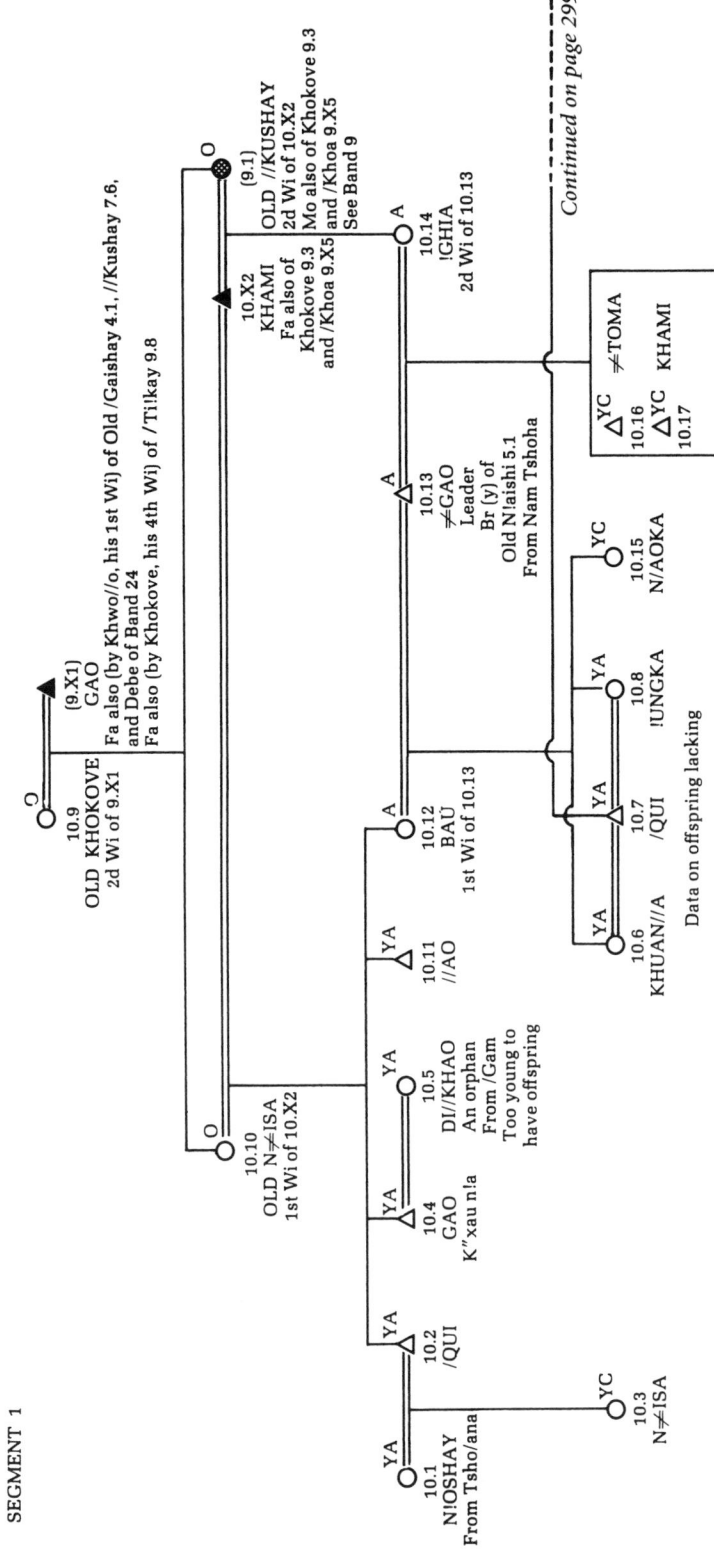

Continued on page 299

SEGMENT 2

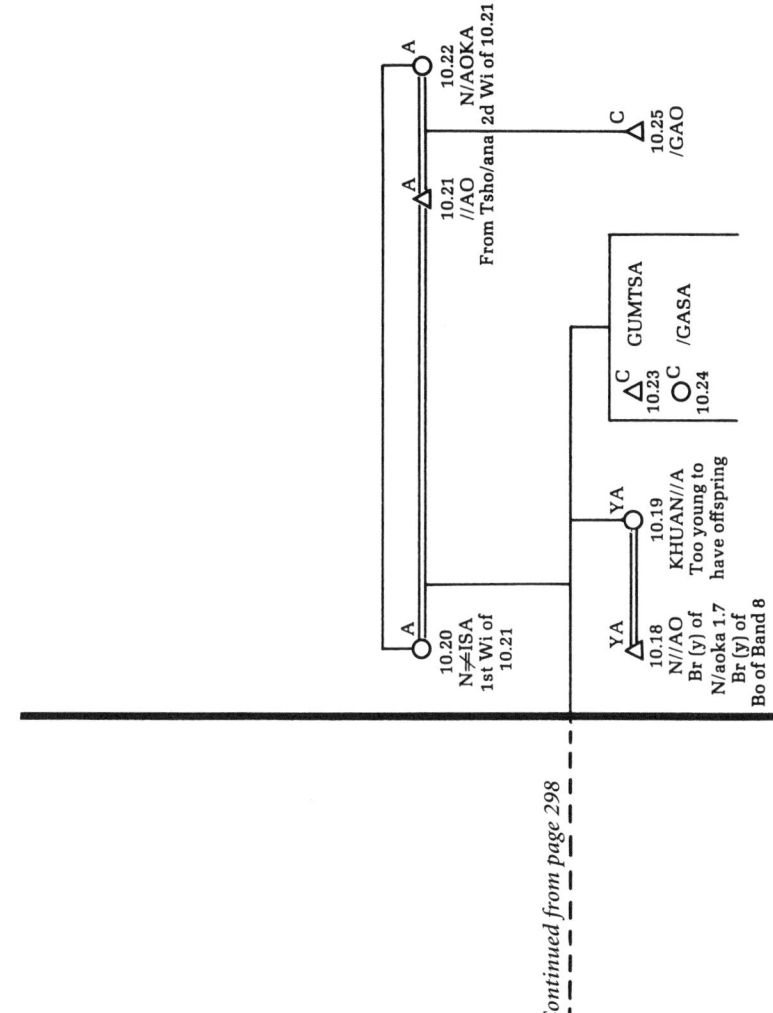

Continued from page 298

BAND 12—/GAM

SEGMENT 5

SEGMENT 4

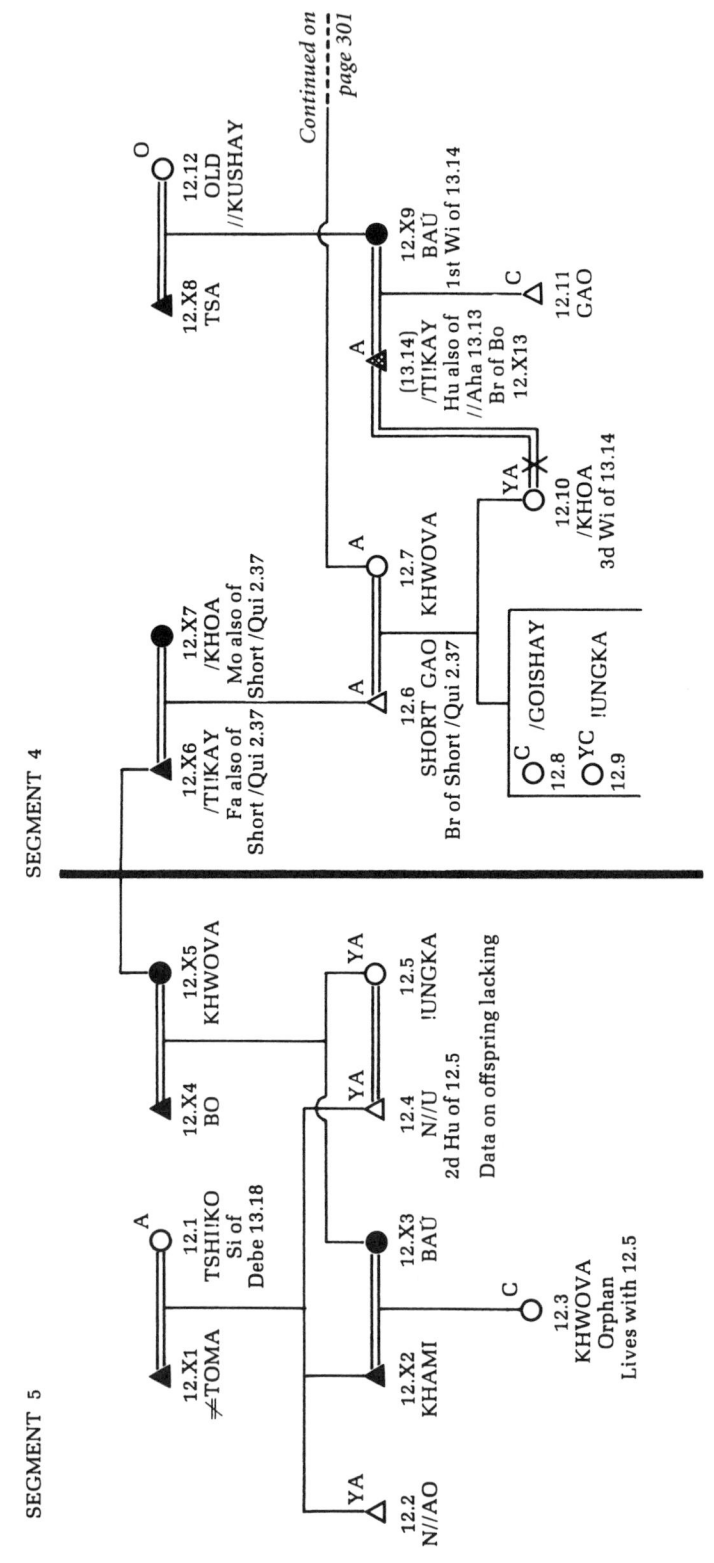

Continued on
page 301

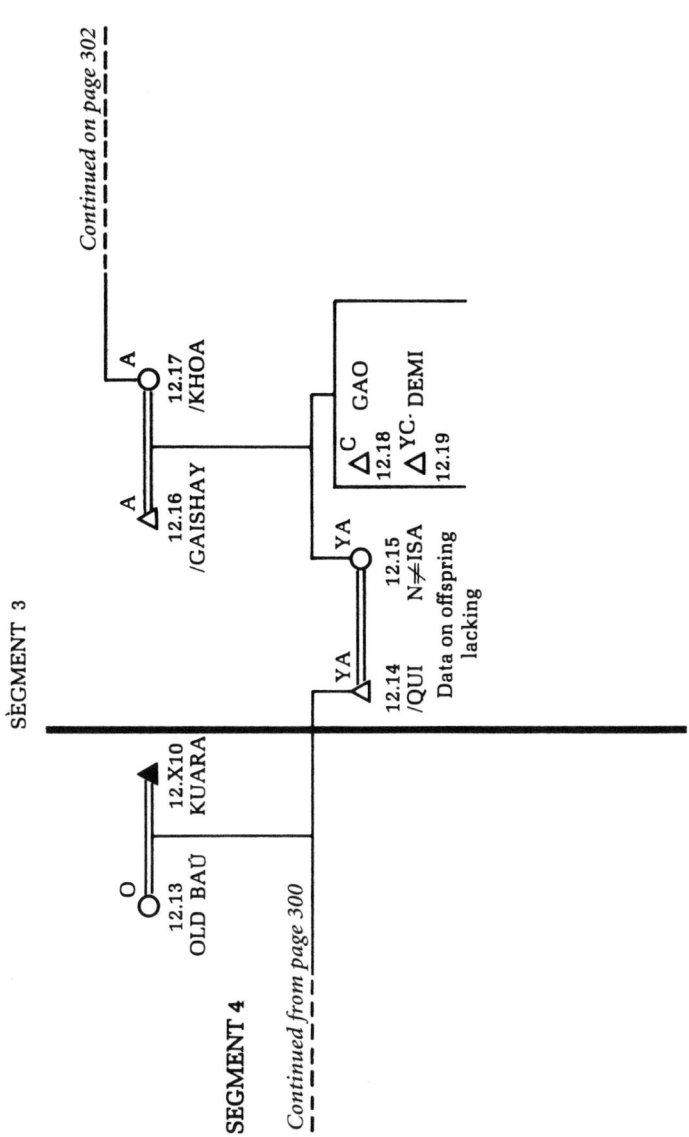

SEGMENT 3

Continued on page 302

A
12.17
/KHOA

A
12.16
/GAISHAY

C
12.18
GAO

YC· DEMI
12.19

YA
12.15
N≠ISA

Data on offspring
lacking

YA
12.14
/QUI

O
12.13
OLD BAÙ

12.X10
KUARA

SEGMENT 4

Continued from page 300

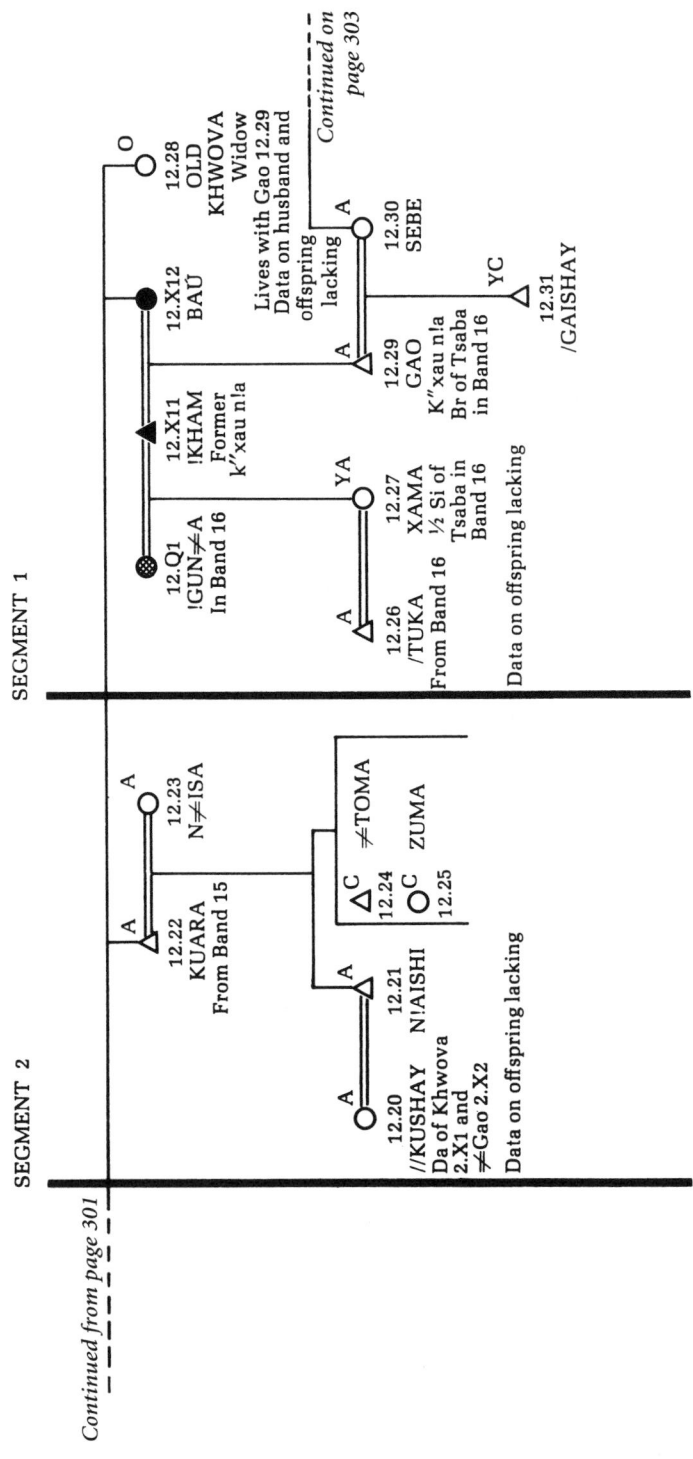

SEGMENT 1

SEGMENT 2

Continued on
page 303

Continued from page 301

SEGMENT 6

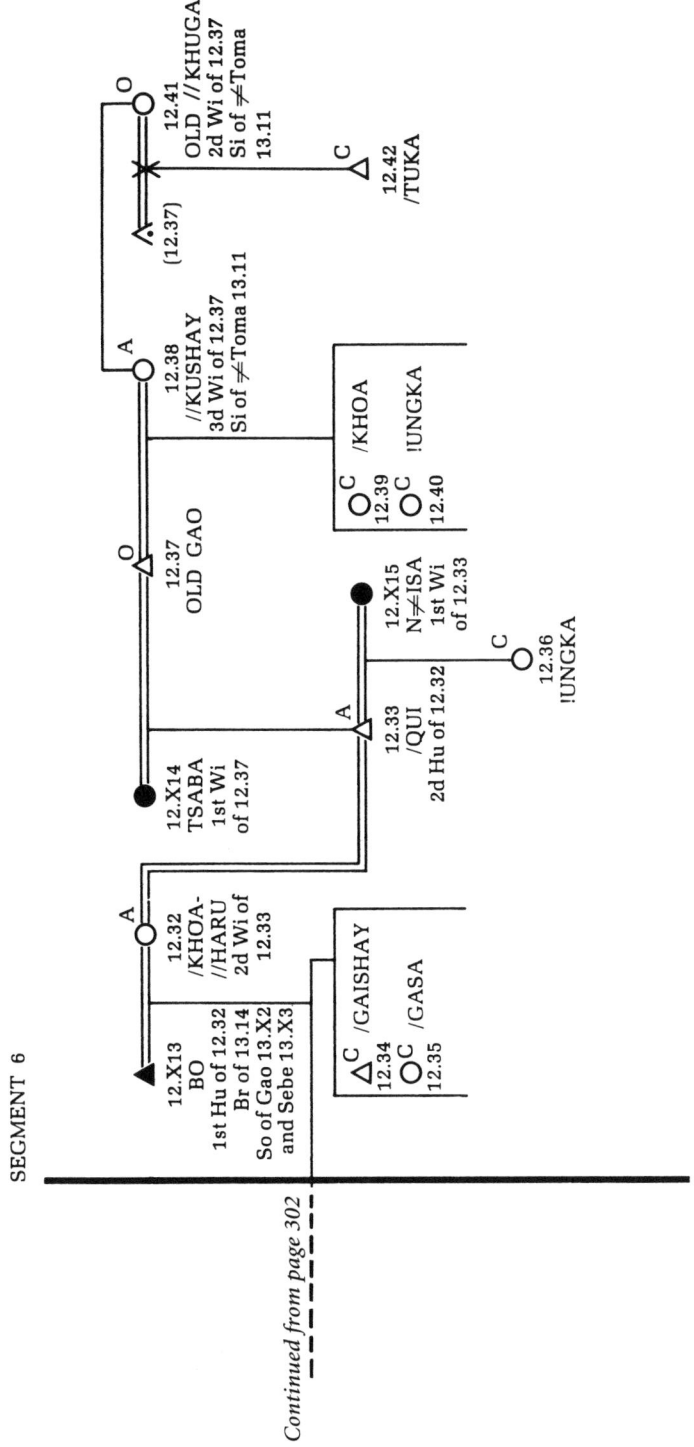

Continued from page 302

Relationships of members of Bands 1 and 2 in Segments 1 and 2 of each band

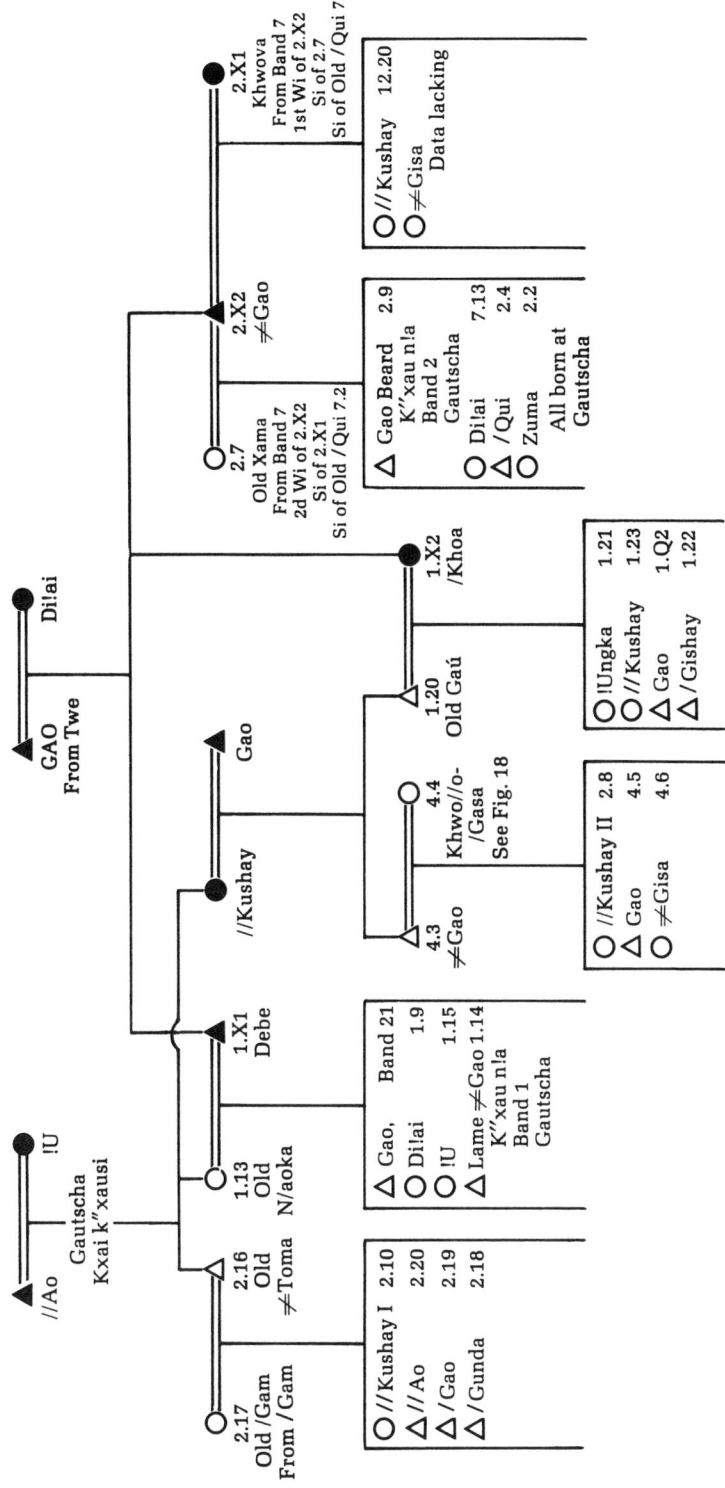

Relationships of members of Bands 4, 5, 6, 10, and Segment 3 of Band 1

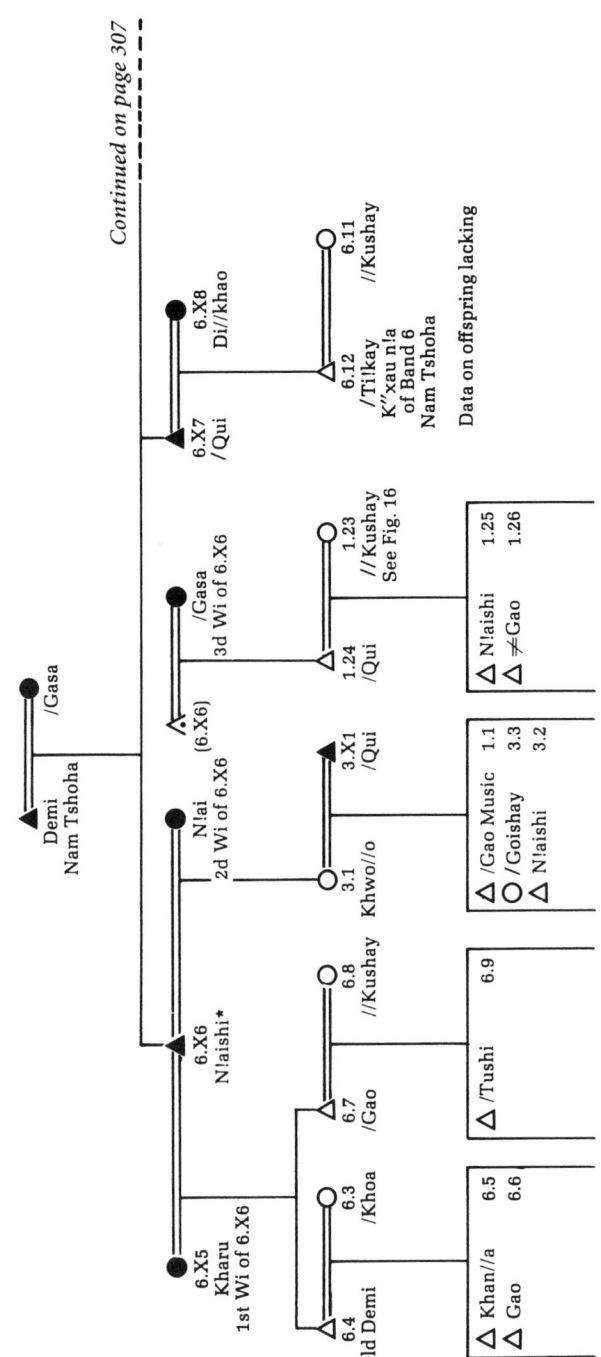

Continued on page 307

*N!aishi 6.X6 provides an example of a broken social rule. He married a woman who had the same name as his mother.

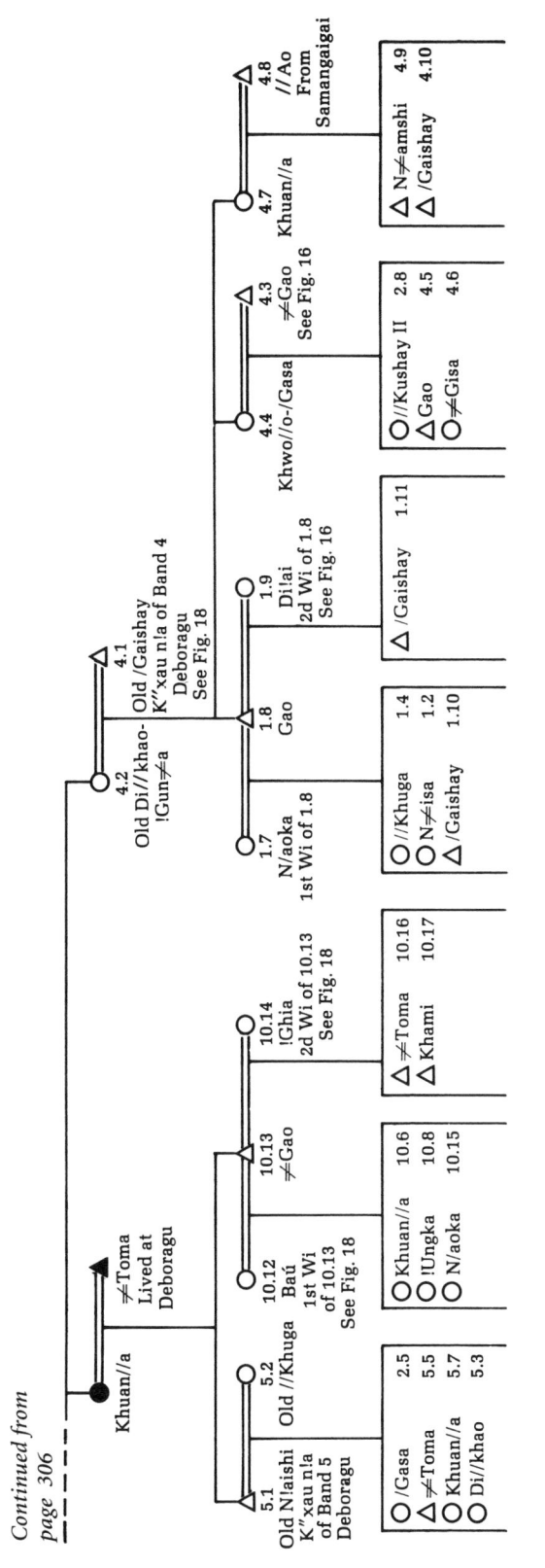

Continued from
page 306

Relationships in Bands 9 and 10: Descendants of Gao 9.X1 and three of his four wives

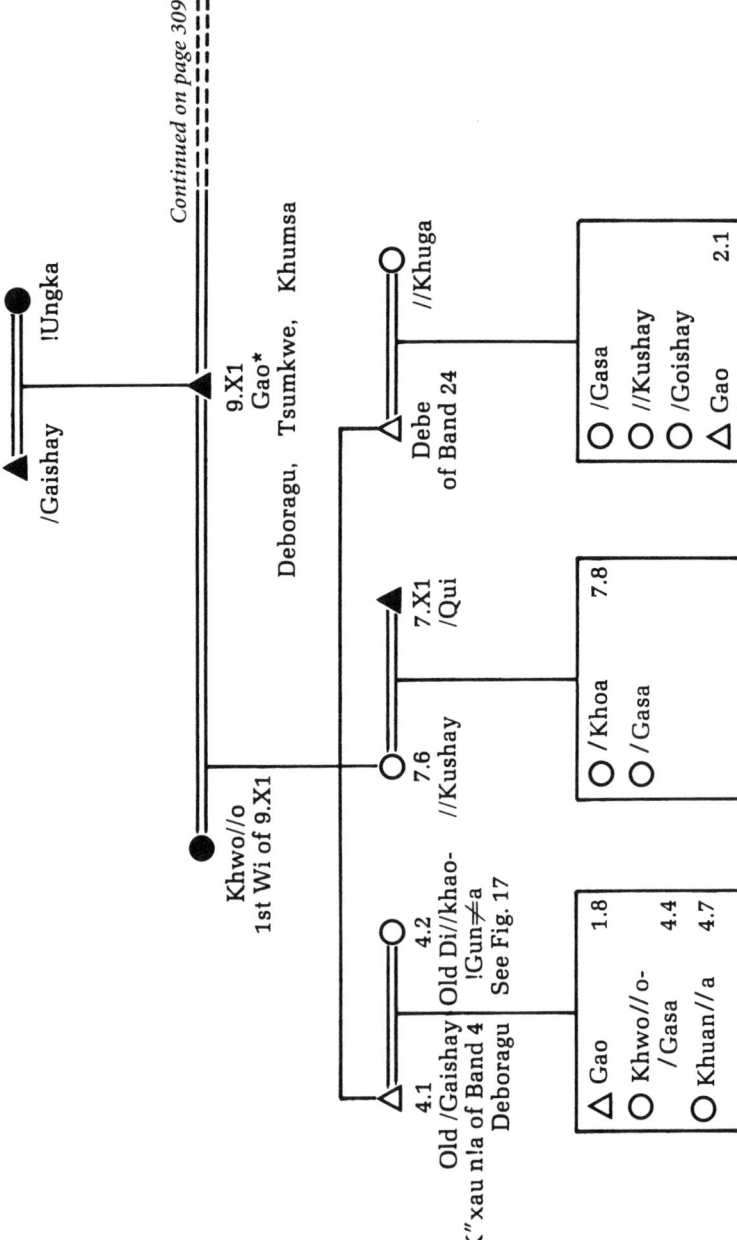

Continued on page 309

* //Gao was the third wife of Gao 9.X1. At Gao's death she went to Botswana, and the people of Nyae Nyae lost track of her.

Continued from page 308

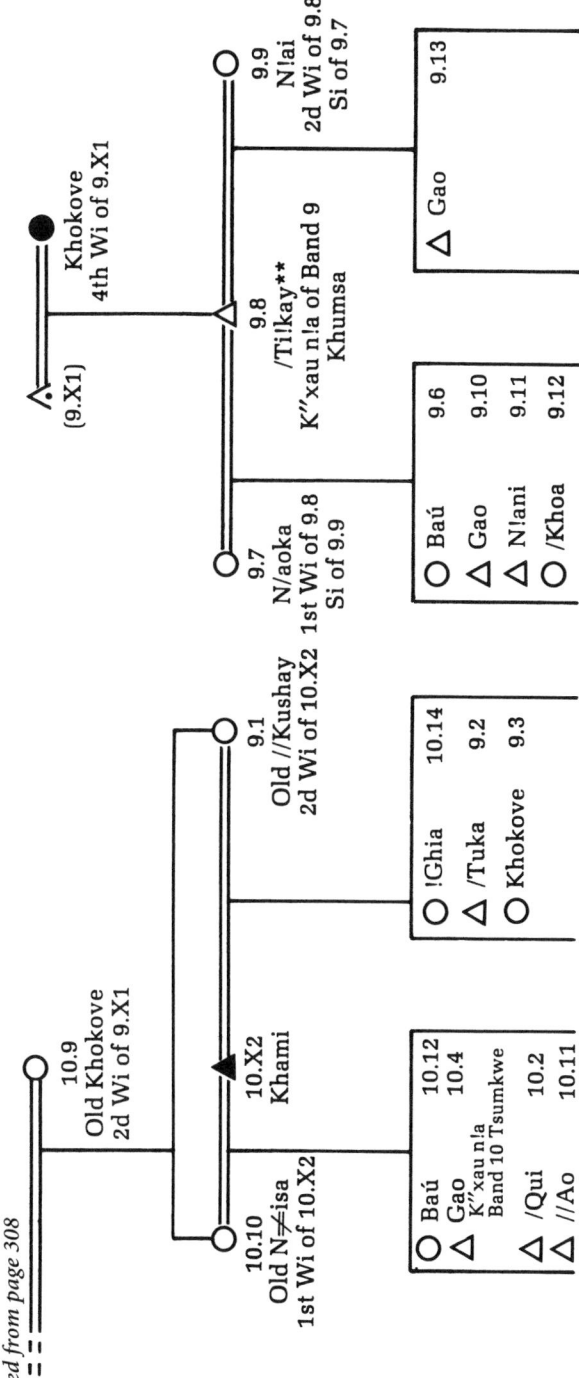

**/Ti!kay 9.8 belongs to the generation of his older half-brother, Old /Gaishay 4.1, but being the youngest of Gao's offspring, he corresponds in age to a younger generation, that of Gao 1.8, ≠Toma 1.16, and !U 1.15, and /Ti!kay's children correspond to theirs in age.

Notes

Introduction

1. Megan Biesele, Richard Katz, and Richard Lee in their studies of !Kung trance have used the word "energy" in this context. I am using the word "force." I prefer it because I think it better suggests the plurality and differentiation that I believe the !Kung supernatural "forces" are thought to have. In fanciful comparison, I think of the differentiated forces of the universe, such as the electromagnetic force and gravity.

2. Sha sha, *Pelargonium* near *senecioides* in the Geraneaceae family. Sha sha is a plant that grows to be about fourteen to eighteen inches in height. The !Kung, who observe plants very carefully, recognize a male and female plant of sha sha and say the female is the larger. Sha sha was not identified by a botanist when we were in the field, but recently a sample was kindly sent to me by Megan Biesele. Dr. Peter F. Stevens of Harvard University made the identification and I thank him very much. I am grateful also to Franklin Ross for gathering information on *Pelargonium,* which he has given me by personal communication. Several species in the Geraneaceae family are to be found in South Africa. Ross tells me that the one found in the Nyae Nyae area in northeastern Namibia is farther north than any others that have been reported. Further work on prepared botanical material will be needed to determine the species of sha sha precisely.

Sha sha is one of the plants I have called medicine plants as distinguished from food plants. Each of the medicine plants is believed to have strong n/um. Twenty-six such plants came to our attention in the field. To my regret we failed to have more than a few identified botanically for various reasons, mostly because the plants grew too far away from where we were. Some of the plants were used in treating mild physical ailments (see chapter 2). Whether any of the plants have actual medicinal properties that are curative according to Western concepts of medicine, we do not know. In any case, it was their n/um the !Kung sought to use. Other plants were used for believed protective properties—to keep lions away, for example, or to keep mamba from biting. Other medicine plants, strong in n/um, were used in various rites and ritual practices. The plants will be mentioned in context.

Of all the medicine plants, sha sha has the widest use in the ritual practices, functioning as a protective force. The root of either the male or female plant is used. Women habitually have a root or two hanging from a thong that they wear around their necks among their bead necklaces, to have a sha sha root always at hand.

The !Kung are not alone in making use of *Pelargonium.* Two characteristics that draw attention to the plants are their agreeable scents and their oiliness. The genus *Sarcocaulou,* a relative of sha sha, has so much oil that it will burn like a torch, and in South Africa it is called Bushman's candle (Ross, personal communication). Other species of *Pelargonium* are used by other southern African peoples for medicinal and for magical purposes (Ross, personal communication).

3. A few of the tales of ≠Gao N!a that my daughter, Elizabeth Marshall Thomas, and I collect-ed appear in chapter 1. Many of the tales in the fine collection made by Megan Biesele in Botswana appear in her book, *"Women Like Meat": The Folklore and Foraging Ideology of the Kalahari Ju/'hoan* (1993).

Chapter 1

Note: This chapter is a somewhat revised version of a paper entitled "!Kung Bushman Religious Beliefs" published in *Africa* 32 (July 1962):221–52. It is reprinted here with the kind permission of the International African Institute and Edinburgh University Press. The revisions consist mainly in omission of some of the introductory paragraphs, the addition of a brief section on the !Kung con-ception of the cosmos, and the omission of the section on the Ritual Healing Dance, which has been expanded into chapter 3 of this book.

1. The !Kung we worked with knew almost nothing about the earth beyond the land they walked on and the Okavango River and the Tsodilo Hills, which they had heard about from visitors. They did not know of the existence of oceans. They were aware of their ignorance and apologetic for it. With a mingling of humility and dignity that I found very appealing, they would explain that they had only been as far as Tsho/ana or Kai Kai and had not seen the land beyond.

2. *Tshi:* "thing"; *dole:* "harmful," "potentially harmful," "strange," "different," "bad," or "worth-less." The metaphor is that the great god is a stranger to man, aloof and distant.

3. I wish to acknowledge with gratitude and pleasure the assistance of my daughter, Elizabeth Marshall Thomas, in making our collection of some twenty tales from the Nyae Nyae !Kung, some in several versions. Megan Biesele's important collection of tales from the !Kung in Botswana, some of which appear in her book, *"Women Like Meat": The Folklore and Foraging Ideology of the Kalahari Ju/'hoan* (1993), contains a few more than we found among the Nyae Nyae !Kung, but most of the tales appear in both collections. We found several of the same tales among the other language groups we visited. Of the ones presented here, three occur among the /Gwi and the Nharo, as well as among the !Kung: "≠Gao N!a, His Tun!ga (the Fat Paouw), and the Pit," "Eyes-on-His-Feet," and "≠Gao N!a and the Fire Sticks."

4. In my Festschrift, *The Past and Future of !Kung Ethnography* (Biesele, ed., 1986), Sigrid Schmidt contributed, to my delight, a chapter on Eyes-on-His-Feet entitled "Tales and Beliefs about Eyes-on-His-Feet." I had wanted to know more about this character but had put off any attempts to learn more. The chapter came as a gift in answer to my wish. Schmidt traces and analyzes the tales about the character, with their variations, through the folktales of several Khoisan peoples. She has found the character Eyes-on-His-Feet only among Khoisan peoples, not in other cultures, and has studied the tales of the Nama and Dama as well as those of the Heikum, Nharo, !Kung in Namibia, and !Kung in Botswana.

In the various versions the eyes of Eyes-on-His-Feet are in different places: on his ankles, on his toes where toenails are, between his toes, and on top of his feet. In some versions Eyes-on-His-Feet is an evil character, an ogre, a cannibal. He can run very fast, and sometimes he catches people; but if they can run in sand or throw sand in his eyes, they may be able to escape. In a Nama version he lures people who are lost into the veld by building a big fire at night to attract them. When they come to him, he cooks and eats them. In other versions, like that of the Nyae Nyae !Kung, Eyes-on-His-Feet is a victim. Someone burns his eyes, which causes his death. In these tales his character is not defined as either good or bad. In the !Kung tale it is ≠Gao N!a who burns the eyes of Eyes-on-His-Feet. The tale does not say why ≠Gao N!a was impelled to do this. Was it simply because the eyes on his feet were so strange an abnormality as to be frightening? According to a Nama-Dama version, the strangeness of finding eyes on a man's feet frightens even an ogre so much that he runs away.

5. "Doro," said to be the name of /Ka /Kani's fire, is given as a noun and a verb in *A Bushman Dictionary* (Bleek 1956). As a verb, "doro" means "to twirl, pierce, bore, or rub fire," and as a noun it is translated as "fire stick" or "tinder box" (p. 28). The words occur in central and northern Bushman languages. In !Kung specifically, according to *A Bushman Dictionary*, /ka/ka:ne is the word for "upper fire stick" (p. 305). For the possessor of fire to be named "upper fire stick" is appropriate. (The !Kung word for "fire" is *da.)*

6. The following description of a djani is an excerpt from *The !Kung of Nyae Nyae*:

> A *djani* is an exquisite winged toy. Tossed high in the air, it floats down verti-cally, spinning. Boys and young men play with the djani; girls never do. The game is a favorite one played almost every day for long periods at a time.
>
> To make a djani, a boy uses a length of hollow segmented reed. The reed, though light, is strong. The length of the piece used varies: those I measured were between 10 and 13 inches long. A tuft of guinea fowl down is thrust into the top of the reed where it stays without glue or binding. About an inch above the middle of the reed, a guinea fowl feather about 5 inches long is bound to the reed in such a way that it slants out from the reed a little. The binding is sinew.
>
> A thong is bound with sinew to the bottom of the reed, and a weight is attached to the djani by this thong. If a mangetti nut is used as the weight, a hole is bored through it with an awl, and the nut is strung on the thong, which is then knotted at the end. A lump of gum from a tree may be used instead: while still moist, it is pressed around the thong and allowed to dry.
>
> When I observed /Gaishay . . . making the djani, . . . I noticed that he took care to trim the thong with a knife until it was the right width and perfectly straight. To trim the feather, he took from the fire a stick that was glowing at the end and burned the ragged edges off making the feather symmetrical (Marshall 1976:345).

7. The god who had a horse and a gun would also have metal implements. According to Richard Lee in *Subsistence Ecology of !Kung Bushmen* (1965), metal was introduced to the !Kung in the 1880s or 1890s by the Tawana tribes who came into western Botswana to graze their cattle in areas where the !Kung lived. The !Kung traded with the Tawana and the Herero who live along the western border of Botswana and thereby obtain knives, adze and assagai blades, and malleable metal for arrowpoints.

8. The only mention of a woman possessing fire that we heard in all our study was this old man's unadorned statement, "The woman had fire," given in his account of the creation. Megan Biesele came upon the theme again when she was collecting !Kung folktales in Botswana in 1971, showing that the theme does exist in the folklore; it was not the old man's aberration. A woman named /Asa gave an account that can hardly be called a tale. Biesele included it in *Folklore and Ritual of !Kung Hunter-Gatherers* (1975a), and she has kindly given me permission to present it here. It is interesting to note that it has one detail in common with the tale of /Ka /Kani and his fire called "Doro": what is important about fire is that it enables people to cook food.

> The person who first found fire was a woman. A woman discovered fire, a woman was first to see it; that's what I, your grandmother, am always telling you. Well, this woman had children and they all ate together around the fire. But her husband slept in the dark. He had no fire (giggle!), no fire at all and just slept in the dark. The rest of them cooked their food and ate it. And he ate raw things.

But once the man caught his wife making a fire, and he was very surprised. When she had the fire started, he came and stole it. He stole it and went off and started a fire of his own. He started his own fire.

Women had fire first, because a woman is just naturally a great thing! Yes, my daughter, that's how it was, that's how people who have fire have become many and have used fire to cook with. Yes, that's how it was (Biesele 1975a:222).

9. In the original publication of the material presented in this chapter (Marshall 1962), I stated that I had been told that this tree had no name. Seven !Kung had concurred in telling me this. Because the trees at the dwelling place of the lesser god did have names, I mentioned in the earlier paper that I thought it possible that the tree of ≠Gao N!a's dwelling place had a name but that this name was secret and not to be told to me. Also, I thought it quite possible that individuals might not know the name, not having been told it by their elders. Later, in working over the material again, I found a note in which I recorded that one person had told me that the name of the tree was "≠Gao." Since I had failed to pursue this question further in the field, I am uncertain of the datum and the spelling.

10. Kernel Ledimo and I worked carefully over this translation. We think we have the correct idea.

Chapter 2

1. I use the words "healers," "healing," and "curing," making a distinction between "healing" and "curing." I am using "curing" in a limited sense to refer to the curing of actual sickness. In "healing" I want to include large concepts, such as the healing of conflict in the group or the healing of anxiety as well as the healing of ailments. The Ritual Healing Dances have such purposes. What I call "special curings" are the healers' using their curing processes over an individual who is actually ill.

2. The Nyae Nyae !Kung knew of and named four diseases that have specific symptoms. They considered them diseases of the black people. From the descriptions given, I think it very likely that these diseases were smallpox *(n/qui)*, measles *(cho che)*, influenza or other respiratory diseases *(/toa)*, and malaria *(g≠ai)*. The !Kung knew that smallpox and measles could be contracted by contact. John Marshall, in later years of fieldwork, found vague knowledge of a few other diseases. From talking with their Tswana and Herero neighbors in Botswana, the Nyae Nyae !Kung also knew something about venereal diseases but had no names for them. They believed that these also are diseases of the black people. ≠Toma said he would not touch a Herero or a Tswana woman. The !Kung with whom we worked thought that smallpox, measles, and venereal diseases had not been contracted by any of the Nyae Nyae people they knew. Of course we do not know, but we do not have any evidence that this belief was wrong. There was no history of past epidemics of these diseases. The Nyae Nyae !Kung were more fortunate than the /Gwi we worked with in Botswana, who had suffered a devastating epidemic of smallpox. In addition to the ailments I describe in this chapter, we think that the Nyae Nyae !Kung had touches of malaria, and we experienced an epidemic of influenza.

None of my family or other members of the expeditions had had medical training. Our only medical resources were *The Merck Manual of Diagnosis and Therapy* and a medicine chest thoughtfully assembled by our friend, the late Dr. Jacob Fine, in Boston. We had not known what attitudes to expect among the !Kung about health matters or about anything, and had not set out to provide medical care. Our medicine chest was planned for the expedition members. Very early in our fieldwork, however, we found ourselves involved. A boy's toe was broken by accident in one of our trucks. Until our advent these people had not experienced wheels and their dangers. We could see the broken bone sticking up. Elizabeth and I ran for the medicine chest and began to pull out antibiotic ointments, bandages, a splint, feeling abysmally inadequate to setting a bone and guilty about our activities' having been the cause of the accident. I was hoping I could keep from vomiting. The boy was stoically quiet. At this point a pair of brown hands appeared among our own. They took hold of the boy's foot and deftly set the bone so that the toe was straight and normal-looking except for the bloody gash across the top. We looked up into the face of Gaú, one of the healers in Band 2. He was smiling and nodding, indicating that we should proceed with our bandaging. We continued to care for the toe, and in due time it healed well without infection or any other complications. After the episode of the toe we felt at ease in our relationship with the healers as healers, and we treated as best we could anyone who came to us asking for our care, including the healers.

We tried to keep on a very low key, not to seem to supplant the healers. We said that our medicines were not powerful like the healers' n/um. They were more like the medicine plants that might be used in conjunction with the healers' n/um. Nevertheless, the people believed that our medicines were strong and well worth trying. Combining our resources with theirs was considered to be all to the good, and to increase the healing potential.

Except for the epidemic of influenza that occurred late in November 1952, the !Kung we worked with most closely that year—those of the interior Nyae Nyae bands, Bands 1 through 7 and 9, a population of about 138—were in good health. Their ailments were mild; their injuries, except for the broken toe, were minor. There were many instances of inflamed eyelids, but this inflammation did not lead to infection of the eye and blindness. We were impressed with the fact that we saw only one blind person in the whole of the Nyae Nyae area, an old woman who was led about by her sister with whom she lived. This was in contrast to the many instances of blindness we saw among the Herero and the Tswana in Botswana.

Burns and gashes in the feet were the next most common conditions that we treated. Children were frequently burned as they played around the family fires, and healers were burned in handling the fire at the Healing Dances. Hunters often gashed their feet running over stones or sharp sticks. Several nursing mothers had infected, swollen breasts; that condition responded very well to our antibiotics. Several babies were sick. None died where we were, but we heard of the death of three babies elsewhere. Four people had boils; several had colds; several had diarrhea. Several had moderate fevers from causes we could not determine. We thought that possibly we were seeing touches of malaria. None of these people were very sick. Two men had suffered more serious illness in the past. !Kham and Lame ≠Gao had suffered a bone disease that left them lame. !Kham walked with crutches of his own contriving; ≠Gao limped with a cane. Both managed their nomadic lives very well.

In 1955 we saw two cases of diseases brought from outside into the area. A woman returned from Samangaigai with scabies; another woman returned from Botswana with mumps. We left not long after their arrival and do not know if their diseases spread to others.

The influenza epidemic in November 1952 was wholly another experience from our treating minor ailments in our little makeshift clinic. A visitor, Gumtsa, the father of N!ai, arrived at Gautscha from Botswana. He had come to protest his daughter's engagement (see Marshall 1976). Unfortunately Gumtsa was sick with influenza, though no one noticed at first. There was much tension in the camp; people grouped together talking and for four days were exposed to Gumtsa's germs. He returned to Botswana, and our people began to go down in waves like grass before the scythe, ten to twenty at a time. Seventy-four people in all took sick, not including ourselves. My family and I eventually took sick also, but our immunities, probably well developed during many years of Massachusetts winters, proved to be strong, and we were not very sick. The !Kung, however, were very sick. We divided ourselves into shifts for the nursing day and night. People were too sick to hunt and gather, so we provided food and water as well as our antibiotics and vitamins. We sent a party out to Grootfontein for supplies and, if possible, a doctor. To our astonishment and excitement, the doctor, days earlier than we could have expected, arrived in a little chartered airplane instead of our truck. People were wildly excited. They had never seen an airplane before, and after that the boys played "airplane" every day as well as "truck." The doctor examined everyone, let us know who had developed pneumonia and what antibiotics to give to them, approved our treatment in general, replenished our medicines, and flew away.

No one died at Gautscha. In about two weeks people began to recover, and as they did, they moved away. Visitors returned to their own water holes. Half of Band 1 dispersed. Two old people who had not come down with the influenza at Gautscha fell ill after they moved away. They both died. We think that our being able to supply food and water was of critical importance in the people's recovery, probably of greater importance than the antibiotics, except for those with pneumonia.

3. My impression is that, at the time we were in the field, the Nyae Nyae !Kung had sufficient food of one kind or another—meat, tsi, other plant foods—to sustain them in health and vigor but not enough to fatten them. All are slender or thin. Drs. A. S. Truswell and J. D. L. Hansen of the University of Cape Town examined the !Kung in the Dobe area in 1967 and 1968, and their observations substantiate my impressions. They said they found little or no evidence of mineral or vitamin deficiency, they observed no kwashiorkor, edema, or pellagra, but that toward the end of the dry season protein intake became critical. They went on to say:

> Although they were not usually malnourished, the Bushmen's adult weights averaged only 80% of standard for their heights. Weight/height ratio declined with age in both sexes, and mean mid-triceps skinfolds were only 5.0 mm. in men and 9.4 mm. in women. Skinfolds increased significantly between the dry season and the examination after the rains. By these and other criteria the Bushmen were moderately undernourished.

> It appears that the hunter-gatherer diet of nuts, fruit, roots and meat is fairly well balanced in specific nutrients, but the Bushmen's problem is how to obtain sufficient total calories for the large amount of energy they have to spend walking from their water holes to collect their food (Truswell and Hansen 1968:1338).

4. Sa is a pleasantly scented powder made of the dried bulb of a plant. It has other uses besides being tossed into a wind blowing over a grave. It is regularly used in greeting visitors. We watched Old N≠isa greeting a man named ≠Gao who came to visit at Gautscha. When he sat down at her fire, she took a pinch of sa powder and sprinkled it from the back of his head, down his forehead, down his nose, around his eyes, then under his chin and around his neck. "This will keep sickness of the sky from coming to him," N≠isa explained. There was nothing special in N≠isa's greeting except that it was more meticulously carried out than most.

Sa is used by all !Kung women as a cosmetic. The women keep a supply of it in a little tortoise shell hung from their necks by a string of beads or a thong. In the shell the women also keep a bit of fur or the nest of a penduline titmouse, which they use as a powder puff to dust the sweet-smelling sa powder under their arms and chins. Sa is said to be cooling. The powder is tossed on healers whose n/um is too hot.

5. John Marshall and Claire Ritchie, in their extended collection of !Kung genealogies in Nyae Nyae, found several accounts of hunters killed by leopards but no accounts of people killed by lions.

6. Roughly a decade later in the Dobe area in Botswana, Megan Biesele and Richard Katz with the Harvard Kalahari Research Group found a number of women healers. Katz in 1968 estimated that about ten percent of the women in that area became healers (see Katz 1982). He says that one of the women, Wa Na, was considered to be the most powerful healer in the entire Dobe area.

Katz and Biesele (1986) tell of a dance called "Drum Dance," which was introduced into the Dobe area in the 1960s, probably from a Bantu-speaking source. In the Drum Dance, as Katz and Biesele describe it, the women sing, clap, dance, and go into trance. One man drums, others watch and from time to time take turns at the drumming; the men do not dance. The dancing women soon begin to fall into trance in groups. The trembling, staggering ones in trance are helped by other dancers, but the women do not heal anyone, themselves or others. The trancing seems to be an end in itself. The authors say:

> Though healing in Drum is not actively sought, some women do go on to become healers in other contexts. They may heal in special curings held for the seriously ill, and many become healers in Giraffe, as well. (Giraffe is one of the Healing Dances.) In general, a healing role is confined to older women past child-bearing age, because of a strong belief that working with n/um is harmful to unborn babies. At present, the n/um of the Drum Dance is "put into" young girls by older women experts, then removed by these women when the girls marry and start their families. Later, after menopause, a woman may choose to have her n/um reactivated. Then she may go on to *!kia* in Drum and sometimes to !kia and heal in Giraffe.
>
> The putting of n/um into the young girls is described in terms of invisible arrows shot into their midriffs by the initiated women. It is also believed that developing n/um is aided by drinking a tea made from *!gwa,* a local shrub, but this tea is used ritually only for the first experience and not taken each time thereafter (Katz and Biesele 1986:203).

7. In *The !Kung of Nyae Nyae* (Marshall 1976), I say of Old /Gaishay: "For reasons no one understood he could not hunt; he gathered plant foods like a woman. Gossip had it that twice he had tried to drag a woman against her will into his shelter, but had not succeeded. The !Kung remarked, 'Women like meat'" (Marshall 1976:270). Carlton Coon (personal communication) suggested that Old /Gaishay may have been unable to hunt because he was color-blind. I have regretted ever since that this possibility did not occur to any of us in the field. We might have tested the old man.

8. I am grateful to Dr. Ernest W. Williams of the Museum of Comparative Zoology, Harvard University, for the identification of the tortoises.

9. The !Kung know about *Cannabis sativa;* they call it dagga. I am grateful to Robert Story (personal communication) for the information he has given me about it. "Dagga" is the Hottentot word for *Cannabis sativa,* from which hashish and marijuana are made. The !Kung say that dagga grows far away, somewhere in Botswana, not in their area. Story confirms their statement that it does not grow in the Gautscha area. Gao Feet said he would like to get some from his Tswana or Herero neighbors, but he was vague about who would have any and said it would probably cost too much in trade. We saw no indication of the !Kung using dagga at dances to induce trance or on any occasions, and I can state with assurance that it was not a significant element in their culture.

Chapter Three

Note: This chapter is a revised version of a paper entitled "The Medicine Dance of the !Kung Bushmen," *Africa* 39(4)(October 1969):347–81. The paper is reprinted here with the kind permission of the International Africa Institute and Edinburgh University Press. The revisions consist mainly of the omission of some material that is placed elsewhere in this book and the revision of the list of songs, with the addition of one, "The Great Eland Song." A section on the music of the songs has been added.

1. /Qui's misfortune has been described by Elizabeth Marshall Thomas in *The Harmless People,* (1959:230–39).

2. The tapes of the Nyae Nyae !Kung Healing Dance music are in Nicholas England's collection. Two records of !Kung music were produced by Folkways Records: Album No. FE 4315, *Instrumental Music of the Kalahari San,* recorded by Marjorie Shostak, Megan Biesele, and Nicholas England; Album No. FE 4316, *Healing Dance Music of the Kalahari San,* recorded by Richard Katz, Megan Biesele, and Marjorie Shostak in 1983. The recordings of Nicholas England were made in the Nyae Nyae area in the decade of the 1950s. The other recordings were made in Botswana in the 1970s. Album 1415 includes recordings of the thumb piano, which had become popular.

3. I describe them and my delight in them in *The !Kung of Nyae Nyae* (Marshall 1976: chap. 11).

4. Megan Biesele and Richard Katz have more detailed accounts from healers in Botswana who told of out-of-body visions. One of the men Katz talked with said he had been to the sky while in trance, and added matter-of-factly that he had not seen any of his own people there. This man when in trance had visions of traveling to places on the earth. He traveled to his daughter's place miles away and saw that she was doing well (Katz 1982:187).

Biesele transcribed a long, detailed account of a healer named K"xau Giraffe. With Biesele's permission I give a brief synopsis:

> God himself came to K"xau. (The name given to god was Kauha.) Together they went into a river and traveled a long way, carried by the water. They came to a place where spirits were dancing. Kauha and K"xau joined them. K"xau danced badly and Kauha said he must learn and showed him how. They danced and danced. Then Kauha took K"xau to one of the spirits who would be what was translated as his "protector." The protector put n/um into K"xau. They were still under water and K"xau was struggling. They struggled and sang and danced until daybreak. K"xau had danced well and the protector said that now he would be able to trance and to cure. After that Kauha and K"xau entered the earth and traveled a long way within it. When they emerged, they climbed the thread of the sky and met the spirits of the dead up there. The spirits sang for K"xau to dance. (Biesele 1979)

Chapter Four

1. The emphasis on madness as a result of an infraction in food avoidance was out of proportion with reality. Madness was rare in this !Kung population. The !Kung we questioned knew of only four instances of madness within anyone's memory in the whole Nyae Nyae area. /Gunda Legs was one. We were told also of a woman whose madness took the form of open sexual expression, shocking to the !Kung whose sexual activity is modestly hidden. Another was a man who killed someone. A boy who ate korhaan was the fourth. I think that because mad behavior is so egregious and frightening to the !Kung, it looms high in their imagination, although it is so infrequent.

2. As to physical cleanliness, the !Kung are neither markedly concerned or unconcerned with dirt. According to my notions, they are reasonably clean without being fastidious. It is easy to be reasonably clean in a semi-desert. The !Kung live on dry, sandy ground, which brushes off easily. Their bare bodies, leather garments, grass shelters, and the earth on which they live are exposed most of the time to dry air and sun. They wash when there is water enough. Food is handled carefully. No putrid refuse lies about. Much of their food is cooked on coals and in the ashes. The ash is tapped off and the little that clings to the foods is eaten without repugnance. Like earth, ash is not dirt to

the !Kung. Feces and urine are dirt to the !Kung; they keep their encampments entirely clean of them, going to a distance to defecate and urinate, modestly disappearing from view in the bushes.

3. It was hard for me to judge the age of the children by size. These are a small people. A group of thirty women we measured averaged 4' 11" in height. The shortest adult woman was 4' 8". A group of sixteen men averaged 5' 2". At the time I took N!ai as my measure of age for the beginning of girls' food avoidances, she was 3' 11" in height. When she was fully grown, when, as the !Kung say, she "reached her head's place," she was 4' 9". Her breasts had not begun to grow when she was 3' 11". Six years later she menstruated for the first time, and she did not have her first child for two years more.

4. One of the folktales told by the !Kung makes a clear distinction between scavenging animals (hyenas and jackals) and the animals whose meat is good to eat (antelopes or zebras, for instance). The story compares the meat animals to hunters who receive scarifications at their first kill. The scavengers are set apart as inferior and do not receive the beautiful scarifications. The jackal instead has his back burned and the hyena has flung after him a bag of bones, which he is condemned to eat from then on instead of fresh meat. The story and an analysis appear in Megan Biesele's "The Black-Backed Jackal and the Brown Hyena: A !Kung Bushman Folktale," in *Botswana Notes and Records* (1972).

5. I shall use the word "root" when referring in general to plant foods that are the underground part of the plant, i.e., tuber, bulb, storage organ, corm, or root. I call them roots in the way we use the word in referring to "root vegetables."

Chapter Seven

Note: "N!ow" was originally published as a paper in *Africa* 27(3)(July 1957):232–40. It is reprinted here with the kind permission of the International African Institute and Edinburgh University Press. The paper has been partially rewritten and has been shortened by taking out material that appears elsewhere in this book.

1. "N!ow" as a noun is the name of a force like n/um, and I am told by Megan Biesele that the word is also a transitive verb. One can *n!ow !ga* (rain), or *n!ow /em* (sun), or *n!ow ≠gau* (cold).

2. It was a custom of the southern Bushmen to burn horns to stop rain. "They burn the outer covering of horns, when they want the rain to disperse, when they see that the rain seems to be bringing danger, because its darkness is like night" (Bleek and Lloyd 1911).

Chapter Eight

1. From a documentary film *N!ai, the Story of a !Kung Woman*, produced in 1980 by Michael J. Ambrosino, John Marshall, and Sue Cabezas through Documentary Educational Resources, Inc., and Public Broadcasting Associates, Inc. Filmed by John Marshall. N!ai's words translated by Megan Biesele.

2. From Polly Wiessner's paper, "Social and Ceremonial Aspects of Death Among the !Kung San," published in *Botswana Notes and Records* 15(1983):1–5. The Botswana Society has kindly granted permission to reprint the passage. The burial Wiessner describes took place near Dobe in Botswana during a period of her fieldwork between 1973 and 1975.

> The grave . . . was about two metres deep. The men passed Cwa's body down into the grave and took ten to fifteen minutes to arrange it in place, all the while discussing how important it was that the body was correctly positioned. The grave ran north/south and she was put on her right side facing east with her legs slightly flexed. In the two /xai/xai burials, an additional chamber of ca. twenty cm width had been dug into the wall at the bottom of the grave and the back of the corpse

tucked into this. The Dobe San had not done this because they did not feel that the extra work was necessary in the hard ground. While the men were arranging the body, those who had walked arrived and stood about five metres from the grave, talking, smoking, and laughing with intermittent outbursts of tears. Topics of conversation ranged from discussion of what people were doing and how they felt when they heard of Cwa's death, to speculations about the destination and mission of a passing overhead jet. During this time, I asked several San what they believed would happen to Cwa after her burial, but only got the answer, "We will not tell you about things we do not know about."

When Cwa's body was in place, Tsao, who had by this time worked himself into trance without the aid of any singing or dancing, sprinkled scented powder into the grave while making an elaborate speech, once more asking that Cwa find the right path to join her ancestors in the eastern sky. Finally he said good-bye to her. Then the children were summoned and Cwa's eldest daughter handed them sand. One by one they threw the sand in the grave, followed by the women, who did the same. Then the men came and pushed the sand in with their elbows until the body was covered. Old Tsao then took the shovel, reached across the grave to the pile of dirt on the other side and threw a shovelful in. After that the men filled the grave quickly and no more tears were shed. While doing this, they chatted constantly about the details of the job. When they had finished, they made a mound of earth about sixty cm high on top of the grave, flattened the top and placed a large stone at the head to mark the grave, so that others walking in the bush would see the stone and not walk on the grave. When this was done, the women brought some water in a large bowl, placed it carefully at the side of the grave and lined up the shovels on each side of the bowl. The men who had worked on the grave then washed, not symbolically but vigorously, scrubbing themselves clean, while laughing about so many people taking a real bath in a bowl of water. The tension of death had clearly broken as soon as Cwa's body was out of sight. The other participants followed suit and washed their hands as a symbolic gesture. Cwa's nephew took the rest of the water and poured it over the grave saying, "Here is the water for your journey."

After washing, Tsao n!a and Cwa's husband, Bo, took powder from a tortoise shell compact and summoned the participants one by one, rubbing the powder up over their nose, between their eyes and then blowing the rest into the air over their heads. They repeated the same gestures over both cheeks, blowing the powder towards each ear with great ceremony, saying, "Here is your beloved _____, your relative who has come to say goodbye and wish you well." They did this to each person while the San laughed and chatted. When they had finished with everybody, the participants slowly made their ways back to their camps.

3. Suicide is extremely rare among the !Kung, but we did hear of one young woman killing herself. This happened long ago. /Qui explained that she did not like the people she lived with. She was sad in her heart. She got her father's arrow and stuck it into her thigh. The people cut the wound and tried to suck the poison out, but they failed. The girl cried and cried, saying "I have killed myself." The girl's father and husband dug a very deep grave, and all the people present attended her burial. /Qui said this was a very sad thing, and people still feel sad when they think about it.

Chapter Nine

1. Comparisons may be made between the Nyae Nyae !Kung Menarcheal Rite and that of two other Bushman cultures, the /Gwi and the !Ko, by reading two fine informative papers by G. B. Silberbauer (1963) and H.-J. Heinz (1975) respectively. Heinz has produced a film on a !Ko Menarcheal Rite entitled: *!ko-Buschmänner (Südafrika, Kalahari) Mädchen-Initiation,* Film E 1849, Institut für den Wissenschaftlichen Film-Göttingen, 1975.

2. In the foreword to J. David Lewis-Williams' *Believing and Seeing* (1981b), when listing the Bushman groups we found to have the Eland Dance, I included the /Gwi inadvertently. This is an embarrassing error, which I regret very much. We visited the /Gwi, but we did not find the Eland Dance among them. Silberbauer made the same observation—that the /Gwi do not have the Eland Dance (Silberbauer 1963:21).

3. It is with the fertility of vegetation, especially the fertility of the plant foods, that a strong ritual association is made through the association with rain. The fertility of the menstruating girl is not ritually emphasized. !Kung want children, and they want the girl to be fertile—but not too fertile. The !Kung have no soft foods to supplement mother's milk, and !Kung mothers want to nurse a baby for three or four years. They cannot satisfactorily nurse two at once so they hope to space their children.

Chapter Ten

1. Nicholas England's study of !Kung music includes a study of the recordings that we made in 1951 and from 1952 to 1953, and recordings that he himself made when he was in the field with Laurence Marshall and John in 1957 and with Laurence and me in 1959 and 1961.

Chapter Eleven

1. Any man among the !Kung can divine. The men use sets of disks *(/xusi),* which I call oracle disks. In *A Bushman Dictionary,* they are called divining pieces (Bleek 1956:366). The !Kung disks are a set of five or six circular pieces of leather or, rarely, of wood. A man throwing the disks attributes identity to each, asks a question, and tosses the disks. He reads his answer in their distribution. The disks are in almost daily use. The men gather together in a group to read them, often arguing among themselves about the interpretation. In most of the sessions the concern is hunting. The men ask which direction to take to find animals and what luck they will have. They also consult the disks frequently about the activities and whereabouts of relatives and friends—all mundane matters, not occult. Women may watch a disk-throwing session, but they never throw the disks. I have described the disks and the sessions in *The !Kung of Nyae Nyae* (Marshall 1976:152–55).

Chapter Twelve

1. I am grateful to Franklin Ross at the Museum of Comparative Zoology at Harvard University for the information on mantises. He says: "Among insects in general, although cockroaches, wasps, flies, and dragonflies can move their heads to a lesser degree, mantids are unique among insects in their highly developed head-turning ability. Only mantids can turn their heads distinctly sideways, perpendicular to the body axis, to stare at you, two eyes at a time, as a person might. Mantids appear

unique among insects also by having the habit of hunting at points of light in the darkness. Why insects are drawn to bright light points helplessly is not understood clearly, but mantids are drawn to these places as predators of other insects, or of other predators drawn to the light for the same reasons. I've heard of scorpions, spiders, frogs, geckos, mantids, and snakes using this behavior. Mantis is the only insect" (personal communication).

2. Dr. Robert Story reminded us that the concept of having no knee joints is found in Caesar's *Gallic Wars*. I am indebted to Dr. Mary Lou Lord for giving me the reference for Caesar and another for Pliny, who takes up Caesar's account and gives additional descriptive details as follow:

> There are also elks so-called. Their shape and dappled skin are like unto goats, but they are somewhat larger in size and have blunted horns. They have legs without nodes or joints, and they do not lie down to sleep, nor, if any shock has caused them to fall, can they raise or uplift themselves. Trees serve them as couches; they bear against them, and thus, leaning but a little, take their rest (Caesar, *The Gallic Wars*, with an English translation by H. J. Edwards, Cambridge, Mass., Harvard University Press, 1958, Book VI, Chapter 27).

> . . . also the achlis, born in the island of Scandinavia and never seen in Rome, although many have told stories of it—an animal that is not unlike the elk but has no joint at the hock and consequently is unable to lie down but sleeps leaning against a tree, and is captured by the tree being cut through (by hunters) to serve as a trap, but which nevertheless has a remarkable turn of speed. Its upper lip is exceptionally big: on account of this it walks backward when grazing, so as to avoid getting tripped up by it in moving forward (Pliny, *Natural History*, Book VIII, Chapter XVI, Paragraph 39. Translation by H. Rackham, The Loeb Classical Library).

3. Richard Lee tells me that the Dobe !Kung believe that the Knee Knee None have abnormal sexual appetite as well as other characteristics mentioned here in this account.

4. Ledimo, our Tswana interpreter, told us that in Tswana mythology there is also a people who eat the sun when it sets. These people are small in stature like Bushmen. They have normal knees. Their outstanding characteristic is that they have two mouths, one in the front of their heads for talking, the other, with huge teeth, at the back of their heads for eating.

Chapter Thirteen

Note: This chapter is a shortened version of a paper entitled "Some Bushman Star Lore" that appeared in *Contemporary Studies on Khoisan 2*, Band 5.2, Quellen zur Khoisan-Forschung, Rainer Vossen and Klaus Keuthmann, editors. Hamburg: Helmut Buske Verlag, 1986, pp. 169–204. Portions of the paper are reprinted here.

Appendix

Note: This appendix has been reprinted from *The !Kung of Nyae Nyae* (Marshall 1976). The text and charts have not been substantively updated or edited.

BIBLIOGRAPHY

Allen, R.
1963   *Star Names: Their Lore and Meaning.* Dover, New York.

Anderson, C., and T. Benson
1991   "Setz die Kamera ab und greif zur Schaufel: Ein Interview mit John Marshall," in *Jäger und Gejagte, John Marshall und seine Film,* R. Kapfer, W. Petermann, and R. Thoms, eds. Trickster Verlag, Munich.

Asch, T.
1991   "Das Filmen in Sequenzen und die Darstellung von Kultur," in *Jäger und Gejagte, John Marshall und seine Film,* R. Kapfer, W. Petermann, and R. Thoms, eds. Trickster Verlag, Munich.

Asch, T., and P. Asch
1986   "Images That Represent Ideas: The Use of Films on the !Kung to Teach Anthropology," in *The Past and Future of !Kung Ethnography: Critical Reflections and Symbolic Perspectives. Essays in Honour of Lorna Marshall,* M. Biesele, ed., with R. Gordon and R. Lee, pp. 327–58. Helmut Buske Verlag, Hamburg.

Balikci, A.
1991   "Hommage an John Marshall," in *Jäger und Gejagte, John Marshall und seine Film,* R. Kapfer, W. Petermann, and R. Thoms, eds. Trickster Verlag, Munich.

Barnard, A.
1980   "Kinship and Social Organization in Nharo Cosmology." Paper presented at Second International Conference on Hunting and Gathering Societies. Department of Anthropology, Laval University, Quebec, 19–24 Sept.
1988   "Structure and Fluidity in Khoisan Religious Ideas." *Journal of Religion in Africa* 18(3):216–36.

Beake, L.
1991   *The Song of Be.* Young Africa Series. Maskew Miller Longmans, Cape Town.

Bicchieri, M., ed.
1972   *Hunters and Gatherers Today.* Holt, Rinehart and Winston, New York.

Biesele, M.
1972   "The Black-Backed Jackal and the Brown Hyena: A !Kung Bushman Folktale." *Botswana Notes and Records* 4.
1975a   "Folklore and Ritual of !Kung Hunter-Gatherers," 2 vols. Ph.D. dissertation, Harvard University, Department of Anthropology, Cambridge.
1975b   "Song Texts by the Master of Tricks: Kalahari San Thumb Piano Music." *Botswana Notes and Records* 7.
1976a   "Aspects of !Kung Folklore," in *Kalahari Hunter-Gatherers: Studies of the !Kung San and Their Neighbors,*

R. Lee and I. DeVore, eds., p. 322. Harvard University Press, Cambridge.

1976b "Basarwa Development, Northwest District: A Research Note." *Botswana Notes and Records* 8:297–98.

1976c "Environmental Planning and Botswana's Basarwa (Bushman) Citizens: A Progress Report." Paper prepared for IDEP/UNEP Conference on Environmental Planning and "Poorly Integrated" Minorities in Africa. Mauritius, June.

1978 "Religion and Folklore," in *The Bushmen: San Hunters and Herders of Southern Africa.* P. V. Tobias, ed., pp. 162–72. Human and Rousseau, Cape Town.

1979 "Old K"xau," in *Shamanic Voices: A Survey of Visionary Narratives,* J. Halifax, ed., pp. 54–62. Dutton, New York.

1983 "Interpretation in Rock Art and Folklore: Communication Systems in Evolutionary Perspective," in *New Approaches to Southern African Rock Art,* J. Lewis-Williams, ed. pp. 54–60. Goodwin Series 4. South African Archaeological Society, Cape Town.

1986 "Anyone with Sense Would Know": Tradition and Creativity in !Kung Narrative and Song," in *Contemporary Studies on Khoisan Part 1,* R. Vossen and K. Keuthmann, eds., pp. 83–106. Quellen zur Khoisan-Forschung vol. 5.1. Helmut Buske Verlag, Hamburg.

1989 *Learning a "New" Language of Democracy? Bushmen in an Independent Namibia.* Nyae Nyae Development Foundation of Namibia, Windhoek.

1990 *Shaken Roots: Photographs by Paul Weinberg.* EDA Publications, Marshalltown, South Africa.

1993 *"Women Like Meat": The Folklore and Foraging Ideology of the Kalahari Ju/'hoan.* Witwatersrand University Press, Johannesburg, and Indiana University Press, Bloomington.

1996 "'He Stealthily Lightened at His Brother-in-law' (and Thunder Echoes in Bushman Oral Tradition a Century Later)," in *Voices from the Past: /Xam Bushmen and the Bleek and Lloyd Collection,* J. Deacon and T. Dowson, eds., pp. 142–60. Witwatersrand University Press, Johannesburg.

Biesele, M., ed.
1986 *The Past and Future of !Kung Ethnography: Critical Reflections and Symbolic Perspectives. Essays in Honour of Lorna Marshall,* with R. Gordon and R. Lee. Helmut Buske Verlag, Hamburg.

Biesele, M., M. Guenther, R. Hitchcock, R. Lee, and J. MacGregor
1989 "Hunters, Clients and Squatters: The Contemporary Socioeconomic Status of Botswana Basarwa." *African Study Monographs* 9(3):109–51.

Biesele, M., D. Hubbard, and J. Ford
1991 "Land Issues in Nyae Nyae: A Communal Areas Example," in *National Conference on Land Reform and the Land Question, Windhoek, 25 June–1 July, 1991.* Vol. 1, *Research Papers, Addresses, and Consensus Document,* Office of the Prime Minister, ed., pp. 517–44. Government of the Republic of Namibia, Windhoek.

Biesele, M., and B. Jones
1991 *Integrating Conservation and Development in Eastern Bushmanland (Nyae Nyae).* Ministry of Wildlife and Tourism/Nyae Nyae Development Foundation of Namibia, Windhoek.

Biesele, M., J. Lambert, and P. Dickens
1990 "Educational Policy Affecting Ju/'hoansi in Independent Namibia: Minority Needs in Nation Building Context." Paper presented at Sixth

International Conference on Hunting
and Gathering Societies, Symposium
on Education and Language Policies
Toward Hunter and Gatherer
Societies in the Context of Modern
Nation States. University of Alaska at
Fairbanks, May 28–June 1.

Bleek, D.
1928 *The Naron: A Bushman Tribe of the
      Central Kalahari.* Cambridge Univer-
      sity Press for University of Cape
      Town, Publications of the School of
      African Life and Languages, Cape
      Town.
1929a "Bushman Folklore." *Africa* 2:302–13.
1929b *Comparative Vocabularies of Bushman
      Languages.* Cambridge University
      Press, Cambridge.
1935 "Beliefs and Customs of the /Xam
      Bushmen, Part VII: Sorcerors." *Bantu
      Studies* 9:1–47.
1936 "Beliefs and Customs of the /Xam
      Bushmen, Part VIII: More about
      Sorcerors and Charms." *Bantu Studies*
      10:131–62.
1956 *A Bushman Dictionary,* H. Hoenigs-
      wald, ed. American Oriental Society,
      New Haven, Conn.

Bleek, D., ed.
1923 *The Mantis and His Friends: Bushman
      Folklore.* Collected by the late Dr. W.
      H. I. Bleek and the late Dr. Lucy C.
      Lloyd. Blackwell, London and Oxford,
      and T. Maskew Miller, Capetown.

Bleek, W., and L. Lloyd
1911 *Specimens of Bushman Folklore.*
      George Allen, London. Reprinted
      1968 by C. Struik, Cape Town.

Blurton Jones, N., and M. Konner
1976 "!Kung Knowledge of Animal
      Behavior (or: The Proper Study of
      Mankind Is Animals)," in *Kalahari
      Hunter-Gatherers: Studies of the !Kung
      San and Their Neighbors,* R. Lee and

I. DeVore, eds., pp. 325–48. Harvard
University Press, Cambridge.

Brew, J.
1972 "Review of the Film *!Kung Bushman
      Hunting Equipment.*" *American
      Anthropologist* 74(1, 2):188–89.

Breyer-Brandwijk, M.
1937 "A Note on the Bushman Arrow
      Poison, *Diamphidia Simplex*
      peringuey," in *Bushmen of the
      Southern Kalahari,* J. Rheinallt-Jones
      and C. Doke, eds., pp. 221–26.
      Witwatersrand University Press,
      Johannesburg.

British Association for the Advancement of
Science
1929 *Notes and Queries in Anthropology.*
      5th ed. The Royal Anthropological
      Institute, London.

Brooks, A., D. Gelburd, and J. Yellen
1984 "Food Production and Culture
      Change among the !Kung San:
      Implications for Prehistoric
      Research," in *From Hunters to
      Farmers: The Causes and Conse-
      quences of Food Production in Africa,*
      J. Clark and S. Brandt, eds., pp.
      293–310. University of California
      Press, Berkeley.

Brown, S.
1969 "Exploding the Myth of the
      Bushmen's God." *Cape Times
      Weekend Magazine.* September 13.

Brues, A.
1959 "The Spearman and the Archer."
      American Anthropologist 61:457–69.

Caesar, Julius
1958 *The Gallic Wars,* with an English
      translation by H. Edwards. Harvard
      University Press, Cambridge.

Carstens, P.
1975   "Some Implications of Change in
        Khoikhoi Supernatural Beliefs," in
        *Religion and Social Change in
        Southern Africa: Anthropological
        Essays in Honour of Monica Wilson,*
        M. Whisson and M. West, eds., pp.
        78–95. David Philip, Cape Town.

Carstens, P., G. Klinghardt, and M. West, eds.
1987   *Trails in the Thirstland: The Anthro-
        pological Field Diaries of Winifred
        Hoernlé.* Centre for African Studies,
        University of Cape Town, Communi-
        cations, no. 14. Cape Town.

Cashdan, E.
1980   "Egalitarianism among Hunters and
        Gatherers." *American Anthropologist*
        82:116–20.
1983   "Territorialism among Human For-
        agers: Ecological Models and an
        Application to Four Bushman
        Groups." *Current Anthropology*
        24(1):47–66.

Chagnon, N.
1968   *Yanomamo: The Fierce People.* Holt,
        Rinehart and Winston, New York.
1988   "Life Histories, Blood Revenge, and
        Warfare in a Tribal Population."
        Science 239:985–92.

Clark, J.
1970   *The Prehistory of Africa.* Praeger, New
        York.

Clark, J., and S. Brandt, eds.
1984   *From Hunters to Farmers: The Causes
        and Consequences of Food Production
        in Africa.* University of California
        Press, Berkeley.

Conkey, M.
1984   "To Find Ourselves: Art and Social
        Geography of Prehistoric Hunter
        Gatherers," in *Past and Present in
        Hunter Gatherer Studies,* C. Schrire,
        ed., pp. 253–76. Academic Press,
        Orlando, Fla.

Connor, L., P. Asch, and T. Asch
1986   *Jero Tapakan, Balinese Healer: An
        Ethnographic Film Monograph.*
        Cambridge University Press,
        Cambridge.

Coon, C.
1965   *The Living Races of Man.* Alfred A.
        Knopf, New York.
1971   *The Hunting Peoples.* Little, Brown
        and Company, Boston.

Dart, R.
1937a   "The Hut Distribution, Genealogy
        and Homogeneity of the /'Auni-
        ≠Khomani Bushmen." *Bantu Studies*
        11:159–74.
1937b   "Racial Origins," in *The Bantu-
        Speaking Tribes of Southern Africa,*
        I. Schapera, ed., pp. 1–31. George
        Routledge and Sons Ltd., London.
1957   *The Osteodontokeratic Culture of
        Australopithecus Prometheus.*
        Transvaal Museum, Memoir no. 10,
        Transvaal Museum, Pretoria.

Davis, D., ed.
1964   *Ecological Studies in Southern Africa.*
        D. W. Junk, The Hague.

Deacon, J.
1986   "My Place is the Bitterputs: The
        Country of Bleek and Lloyd's /Xam
        San Informants." *African Studies*
        45:135–55.

de Brigard, E.
1991   "Kulturheros," in *Jäger und Gejagte,
        John Marshall und seine Film,* R.
        Kapfer, W. Petermann, and R. Thoms,
        eds. Trickster Verlag, Munich.

Denbow, J.
1984   "Prehistoric Herders and Foragers of
        the Kalahari: The Evidence for 1500
        Years of Interaction," in *Past and
        Present in Hunter Gatherer Studies,* C.
        Schrire, ed., pp. 175–93. Academic
        Press, Orlando, Fla.

Denbow, J., and E. Wilmsen
  1983 "Iron Age Pastoral Settlements in Botswana." *South African Journal of Science* 79:405–8.
  1986 "The Advent and Course of Pastoralism in the Kalahari." *Science* 234:1509–15.

DeVore, I.
  1971 "The Evolution of Human Society," in *Man and Beast: Comparative Social Behavior,* J. F. Eisenberg and W. S. Dillon, eds. Smithsonian Institution Press, Washington, D.C.

DeVore, I., and M. Konner
  1974 "Infancy in Hunter-Gatherer Life: An Ethological Perspective," in *Ethology and Psychiatry,* N. White, ed., pp. 113–41. University of Toronto Press, Toronto.

Dickens, P.
  1991 "Ju/'hoan Orthography in Practice." *South African Journal of African Languages* 11(1):99–104.

Doke, C.
  1925 "An Outline of the Phonetics of the Language of the ͻhũ Bushmen of North-West Kalahari," *Bantu Studies* 2:129–65.

Dornan, S.
  1928 "Rainmaking in South Africa." *Bantu Studies* 3(2):185–96.

Douglas, M.
  1966 *Purity and Danger: An Analysis of Concepts of Pollution and Taboo.* Routledge and Kegan Paul, London.
  1970 *Natural Symbols: Explorations in Cosmology.* Pantheon Books, New York.
  1975 *Implicit Meanings: Essays in Anthropology.* Routledge and Kegan Paul, London.

Douglas, M., ed.
  1973 *Rules and Meanings: The Anthropology of Everyday Knowledge: Selected Readings.* Penguin Books, Harmondsworth.

Dowson, T.
  1988 "Revelations of Religious Reality: The Individual in San Rock Art." *World Archaeology* 20:116–28.
  1991 *Rock Engravings of Southern Africa.* Witwatersrand University Press, Johannesburg.

Draper, P.
  1972 "!Kung Bushman Childhood." Ph.D. dissertation, Harvard University, Department of Anthropology, Cambridge.
  1975 "!Kung Women: Contrasts in Sex Role Egalitarianism in the Foraging and Sedentary Contexts," in *Toward an Anthropology of Women,* R. Reiter, ed., pp. 77–109. Monthly Review Press, New York.
  1976 "Social and Economic Constraints on !Kung Childhood," in *Kalahari Hunter Gatherers: Studies of the !Kung San and Their Neighbors,* R. Lee and I. DeVore, eds., pp. 200–217. Harvard University Press, Cambridge.
  1978 "The Learning Environment for Aggression and Antisocial Behavior among the !Kung," in *Teaching Non-Aggression,* A. Montagu, ed., pp. 31–53. Oxford University Press, New York.

Draper, P., and E. Cashdan
  1974 "The Impact of Sedentism on !Kung Socialization." Paper prepared for Annual Meeting of American Anthropological Association, Mexico City.
  1988 "Technological Change and Child Behavior among the !Kung." *Ethnology* 27(4):339–65.

Durkheim, E.
  1965 *The Elementary Forms of the Religious Life.* The Free Press, New York.

Ebert, J.
1976   *Hunting in Botswana's Past and Its
        Role in a Developing Botswana.*
        University of New Mexico Develop-
        ment Report to the Botswana
        Government, No. 13.

Eibl-Eibesfeldt, I.
1971   *Love and Hate: The Natural History
        of Behavior Patterns.* Translated by
        G. Strachan. Holt, Rinehart and
        Winston, New York.
1972   *Die !Ko-Buschmann Gesellschaft:
        Gruppenbindung und Aggressions-
        Kontrolle.* Piper, Munich.

Eliade, M.
1958   *Rites and Symbols of Initiation: The
        Mysteries of Birth and Rebirth.* Harper
        Torchbooks, New York.
1964   *Shamanism: Archaic Techniques of
        Ecstasy.* Bollingen Foundation.
        Pantheon Books, New York.

Endicott, K.
1979   *Batek Negrito Religion: The World-
        View and Rituals of a Hunting and
        Gathering People of Peninsular
        Malaysia.* Clarendon Press, Oxford.

Endicott, K., and K. L. Endicott
1986   "The Question of Hunter-Gatherer
        Territoriality: The Case of the Batek
        of Malaysia," in *The Past and Future
        of !Kung Ethnography: Critical
        Reflections and Symbolic Perspectives.
        Essays in Honour of Lorna Marshall,*
        M. Biesele, ed., with R. Gordon and
        R. Lee, pp. 136–62. Helmut Buske
        Verlag, Hamburg.

England, N.
1967   "Bushman Counterpoint." *Journal of
        the International Folk Music Council*
        9:1–66.
1995   *Music among the Zũ'/'wã-si and
        Related Peoples of Namibia, Botswana,
        and Angola.* Garland Publishing Inc.,
        New York.

Esterhuyse, J.
1968   *Southwest Africa, 1880–1894.* The
        Rustica Press, Cape Town.

Esterman, R.
1946–49 "Quelques observations sur les
        Bochimans !Kung de l'Angola merid-
        ionale." *Anthropos* 41(4):711–22.

Fernandes-Costa, F., J. Marshall, C. Ritchie,
S. van Tonder, D. Dunn, T. Jenkins, and J. Metz
1984   "Transition from a Hunter-Gatherer
        to a Settled Lifestyle in the !Kung
        San: Effect on Iron, Folate, and
        Vitamin B_{12} Nutrition." *The American
        Journal of Clinical Nutrition*
        40:1295–1303.

FitzSimons, V.
1962   *Snakes of Southern Africa.* Purnell and
        Sons (S. A.)(Pty.) Ltd., Cape Town
        and Johannesburg.

Forde, D., ed.
1954   *African Worlds: Studies in the Cosmo-
        logical Ideas and Social Values of
        African Peoples.* Oxford University
        Press for International African
        Institute, London.

Forde, D., M. Fortes, M. Gluckman, and
V. Turner
1962   *Essays on the Ritual of Social
        Relations.* Manchester University
        Press, Manchester, England.

Fortes, M.
1949   *The Web of Kinship among the
        Tallensi.* Oxford University Press for
        International African Institute,
        London.

Fortes, M., and S. Patterson, eds.
1975   *Studies in African Social Anthropology.*
        Academic Press, London.

Fourie, L.
1926   "Preliminary Notes on Certain
        Customs of the Hei-//om Bushmen."
        *Journal of the South West African
        Scientific Society* 1:49–63.

1928 "The Bushmen of South West Africa,"
in *The Native Tribes of South West
Africa,* C. Hahn, H. Vedder, and
L. Fourie, eds., pp. 79–105. Cape
Times, Ltd., Cape Town.

Frazer, J.
1926 *The Golden Bough: A Study in Magic
and Religion.* MacMillan Company,
New York.

Frisch, R.
1975 "Critical Weights, A Critical Body
Composition, Menarche, and the
Maintenance of Menstrual Cycles," in
*Biosocial Interrelations in Population
Adaptation,* E. Watts, F. Johnston, and
S. Laskar, eds., pp. 319–52. Mouton,
The Hague.

Frisch, R., R. Revelle, and S. Cook
1973 "Components of Weight at Menarche
and the Initiation of the Adolescent
Growth Spurt in Girls: Estimated
Total Water, Lean Body Weight and
Fat." *Human Biology* 45(3):469–83.

Gardner, R.
1957 "Anthropology and Film." *Daedalus*
86(4):344–51.
1964 *A Human Document.* The Gehenna
Press, Northampton, Mass.

Gibbs, J., Jr., ed.
1965 *Peoples of Africa.* Holt, Rinehart and
Winston, New York.

Giess, W., and J. Snyman
1986 "The Naming and Utilization of
Plant Life by the Žu/'hōasi Bushmen
of the Kaukauveld," in *Contemporary
Studies on Khoisan Part 1,* R. Vossen
and K. Keuthmann, eds., pp. 237–346.
Queller zur Khoisan-Forschung vol.
5.1. Helmut Buske Verlag, Hamburg.

Goodwin, A.
1953 *Method in Prehistory: An Introduction
to the Discipline of Prehistoric Archae-*
*ology with Special Reference to South
African Conditions.* The South
African Archaelogical Society
Handbook Series No. 1. The South
African Archaeological Society,
Capetown.

Gordon, R.
1983 "The !Kung San: A Labour History."
Cultural Survival Quarterly
7(4):14–16.
1984a *The San in Transition,* Vol. 2, *What
Future for the Ju/wasi of Nyae-Nyae?"*
Occasional Papers No. 13 (July).
Cultural Survival, Inc., Cambridge,
Mass.
1984b "The !Kung in the Kalahari Exchange:
An Ethnohistorical Perspective," in
*Past and Present in Hunter Gatherer
Studies,* C. Schrire, ed., pp. 195–224.
Academic Press, Orlando, Fla.
1986a "A Namibian Perspective on Lorna
Marshall's Ethnography," in *The Past
and Future of !Kung Ethnography:
Critical Reflections and Symbolic
Perspectives. Essays in Honour of
Lorna Marshall,* M. Biesele, ed., with
R. Gordon and R. Lee, pp. 359–74.
Helmut Buske Verlag, Hamburg.
1986b "Once Again: How Many Bushmen
are There?" in *The Past and Future of
!Kung Ethnography: Critical
Reflections and Symbolic Perspectives.
Essays in Honour of Lorna Marshall,*
M. Biesele, ed., with R. Gordon and
R. Lee, pp. 53–68. Helmut Buske
Verlag, Hamburg.
1987a "Namibia—Africa's Longest (and
Forgotten) War." *Cultural Survival
Quarterly* 11(4):56–57.
1987b "Anthropology and Apartheid—The
Rise of Military Ethnology in South
Africa." *Cultural Survival Quarterly*
11(4):58–60.
1992 *The Bushman Myth.* Westview Press,
Boulder, Colo.

Greenberg, J.
1950 "The Click Languages." *Southwestern Journal of Anthropology* 6(3):223–37.
1955 *Studies in African Linguistic Classification.* Compass Publishing Co., Branford, Conn.
1966 *Languages of Africa,* 2d ed. Indiana University Research Center in Anthropology, Folklore and Linguistics Publication 25. Indiana University, Bloomington.

Guenther, M.
1975a "San Acculturation and Incorporation in the Ranching Areas of the Ghanzi District: Some Urgent Anthropological Issues." *Botswana Notes and Records* 7:167–70.
1975b "The Trance Dancer as an Agent of Social Change among the Farm Bushmen of the Ghanzi District," *Botswana Notes and Records* 7:161–66.
1976 "From Hunters to Squatters: Social and Cultural Change among the Farm San of Ghanzi," in *Kalahari Hunter-Gatherers: Studies of the !Kung San and Their Neighbors,* R. Lee and I. DeVore, eds., pp. 120–33. Harvard University Press, Cambridge.
1979 "Bushman Religion and the (Non)sense of Anthropological Theory of Religion." *Sociologus* 29:102–32.
1986a *The Nharo Bushmen of Botswana.* Helmut Buske Verlag, Hamburg.
1986b "Acculturation and Assimilation of the Bushmen of Botswana and Namibia," in *Contemporary Studies on Khoisan Part 1,* R. Vossen and K. Keuthmann, eds., pp. 347–73. Quellen zur Khoisan-Forschung vol. 5.1. Helmut Buske Verlag, Hamburg.
1986c "'San' or 'Bushmen'?" in *The Past and Future of !Kung Ethnography: Critical Reflections and Symbolic Perspectives. Essays in Honour of Lorna Marshall,*

M. Biesele, ed., with R. Gordon and R. Lee, pp. 27–51. Helmut Buske Verlag, Hamburg.
1988 "Animals in Bushman Thought, Myth and Art," in *Hunters and Gatherers 2: Property, Power and Ideology,* T. Ingold. D. Riches and J. Woodburn, eds., pp. 192–202. Berg, London.
1989 *Bushman Folktales: Oral Traditions of the Nharo of Botswana and the /Xam of the Cape.* Franz Steiner Verlag Wiesbaden, Stuttgart.

Guerreiro, M.
1968 *Bochimanes !Khu de Angola.* Instituto de Investigaçao Cientifica de Angola, Lisbon.

Gusinde, M.
1965 "Die Religionsform der !Kung-Buschleute in Süd-Afrika." *Mitteilungen der Anthropologischen Gesellschaft* 92:36–42.
1966 *Von gelben und schwarzen Buschmännern: Eine untergehende Altkultur im Süden Afrikas.* Akademische Druck u. Verlagsanstalt, Graz, Austria.

Hahn, T.
1881 *Tsuni-//Goam, the Supreme Being of the Khoi-Khoi.* Trubner and Co., London.
1882 *On the Science of Language and Its Study, with Special Regard to South Africa.* Herrmann Michaelis, Cape Town.
1901 "Collectanea Hottentotica." Ms. in 2 vols. City Library, Johannesburg.

Halifax, J.
1979 *Shamanic Voices: A Survey of Visionary Narratives.* E. P. Dutton, New York.

Harpending, H.
1976 "Regional Variation in !Kung Populations," in *Kalahari Hunter-*

Gatherers: Studies of the !Kung San and Their Neighbors, R. Lee and I. DeVore, eds., pp. 152–65. Harvard University Press, Cambridge.

Harpending, H., and T. Jenkins
1973   "Genetic Distance among Southern African Populations," in *Methods and Theories of Anthropological Genetics*. M. Crawford and P. Workman, eds. pp. 177–99. University of New Mexico Press, Albuquerque.
1974   "!Kung Population Structure," in *Genetic Distance*, J. Crow and C. Denniston, eds. Plenum Press, New York.

Heffner, R-M.
1960   *General Phonetics*. University of Wisconsin Press, Madison.

Heinz, H.-J.
1967   *Conflict, Tensions, and Release of Tensions in a Bushman Society*. Institute for the Study of Man in Africa Paper No. 23. Johannesburg.
1975   "Elements of !Ko Bushman Religious Beliefs," in *Anthropos* 70:17–41.
1978–79   "The Ethnobiology of the !Xō Bushmen: Knowledge Concerning Medium and Smaller Mammals." *Ethnomedizin* 5:319–40.
1979   "The Nexus Complex among the !Xō Bushmen of Botswana." *Anthropos* 74:465–80.
1986   "A !Xō Bushman Burial," in *Contemporary Studies in Khoisan Part 2*, R. Vossen and K. Keuthmann, eds., pp. 23–36. Quellen zur Khoisan-Forschung, vol. 5.2. Helmut Buske Verlag, Hamburg.

Heinz, H.-J., and M. Lee
1979   *Namkwa: Life among the Bushmen*. Houghton Mifflin Co., Boston.

Heinz, H.-J., and B. Maguire
1974   *The Ethno-Biology of the !Xō Bushmen: Their Ethnobotanical Knowledge and Plant Lore*. Occasional Paper No. 1. Botswana Society, Gaborone.

Heinz, H.-J., and O. Martini
1980   "The Ethno-Biology of the !Xō Bushmen: The Ornithological Knowledge." *Ethnomedizin* 6(1–4):31–59.

Helgren, D., and A. Brooks
1983   "Geoarchaeology at Gi, a Middle Stone Age and Later Stone Age Site in the Northwest Kalahari." *Journal of Archaeological Science* 10:181–97.

Hermans, J.
1980   "The Basarwa of Botswana: A Case Study in Development." Master's thesis, Applied Anthropology, American University. Washington, D.C.

Hewitt, R.
1986   *Structure, Meaning and Ritual in the Narratives of the Southern San*. Quellen zur Khoisan Forschung, vol. 2. Helmut Buske Verlag, Hamburg.

Hitchcock, R.
1978a   *A History of Research among the Basarwa in Botswana*. National Institute for Research in Development and African Studies, Documentation Unit, Working Paper No. 19. National Institute of Research, Gaborone.
1978b   "Patterns of Sedentism among Hunters and Gatherers in Eastern Botswana." Paper prepared for First International Conference on Hunter-Gatherers. Paris.
1982   "Patterns of Sedentism among the Basarwa of Eastern Botswana," in *Politics and History in Band Societies*, E. Leacock and R. Lee, eds., pp. 223–67.

Cambridge University Press, Cambridge, and Maison des Sciences de l'Homme, Paris.

1986a "Impacts of Drought upon Kalahari San Populations." *International Work Group for Indigenous Affairs (IWGIA) Newsletter* 45:9–14.

1986b "Ethnographic Research and Socioeconomic Development among Kalahari San," in *The Past and Future of !Kung Ethnography: Critical Reflections and Symbolic Perspectives. Essays in Honour of Lorna Marshall,* M. Biesele, ed., with R. Gordon and R. Lee, pp. 375–423. Helmut Buske Verlag, Hamburg.

1987a "Hunters and Herding: Local Level Livestock Development among Kalahari San." *Cultural Survival Quarterly* 11(1):27–30.

1987b "Anthropological Research and Remote Area Development among Botswana Basarwa," in *Research for Development in Botswana,* R. Hitchcock, N. Parsons, and J. Taylor, eds., pp. 285–341. Botswana Society, Gaborone, Botswana.

1988 "Decentralization and Development among the Ju/wasi, Namibia." *Cultural Survival Quarterly* 12(3):31–33.

Hitchcock, R., and J. Ebert
1984 "Foraging and Food Production among Kalahari Hunter-Gatherers," in *From Hunters to Farmers: The Causes and Consequences of Food Production in Africa,* J. Clark and S. Brandt, eds., pp. 328–48. University of California Press, Berkeley.

Hitchcock, R., and J. Holm
1985 "Political Development among the Basarwa of Botswana." *Cultural Survival Quarterly* 9(3):7–11.

1993 "Bureaucratic Domination of Hunter-Gatherer Societies: A Study of the San in Botswana." *Development and Change* 24(2):305–38.

Hockings, P., ed.
1975 *Principles of Visual Anthropology.* Mouton and Co., The Hague.

Hoernlé, A. W.
1918 "Certain Rites of Transition and the Conception of !Nau among the Hottentots." in *Harvard African Studies 2,* O. Bates, ed., pp. 75-77. African Department of the Peabody Museum of Harvard University, Cambridge.

1922 "A Hottentot Rain Ceremony." *Bantu Studies* 1(2):3–4.

Howell, N.
1973 "Feasibility of Demographic Studies in 'Anthropological' Populations," in *Methods and Theories in Anthropological Genetics,* M. Crawford and P. Workman, eds., pp. 249–62. University of New Mexico Press, Albuquerque.

1979 *The Demography of the Dobe !Kung.* Academic Press, New York.

1988 "Understanding Simple Social Structure: Kinship Units and Ties," in *Social Structures: A Network Approach,* B. Wellman and S. Berkowitz, eds., pp. 62–73. Cambridge University Press, Cambridge.

Inskeep, R.
1978 "The Bushmen in Prehistory," in *The Bushmen: San Hunters and Herders of Southern Africa,* P. Tobias, ed., pp. 33–56. Human and Rousseau, Cape Town.

Jenkins, T.
1985 "On Health and Acculturation." *Current Anthropology* 26:520.

1986 "The Prehistory of the San and the Khoikhoi as Recorded in Their Blood," in *Contemporary Studies on Khoisan Part 2,* R. Vossen and K. Keuthmann, eds., pp. 51–77. Quellen zur Khoisan-Forschung vol. 5.2. Helmut Buske Verlag, Hamburg.

Jenkins, T., and G. Nurse
1976 "Biomedical Studies on the Desert-Dwelling Hunter-Gatherers of Southern Africa" *Progress in Medical Genetics,* n.s., 1:211–81.
1977 *Health and the Hunter-Gatherer.* Witwatersrand University Press, Johannesburg.

Kapfer, R., W. Petermann, and R. Thoms, eds.
1991 *Jäger und Gejagte, John Marshall und seine Film.* Trickster Verlag, Munich.

Katz, R.
1976 "Education for Transcendence: !Kia-Healing with the Kalahari !Kung," in *Kalahari Hunter-Gatherers: Studies of the !Kung San and Their Neighbors,* R. Lee and I. DeVore, eds., pp. 281–301. Harvard University Press, Cambridge.
1981 "Education as Transformation: Becoming a Healer among the !Kung and Fijians." *Harvard Educational Review* 51(1).
1982 *Boiling Energy: Community Healing among the Kalahari Kung.* Harvard University Press, Cambridge.

Katz, R., and M. Biesele
1980 "Male and Female Approaches to Healing among the Kalahari !Kung." Paper presented at Second International Conference on Hunting and Gathering Societies. Department of Anthropology, Laval University, Quebec, 19–24 Sept.
1986 "!Kung Healing: The Symbolism of Sex Roles and Culture Change," in *The Past and Future of !Kung Ethnography: Critical Reflections and Symbolic Perspectives. Essays in Honour of Lorna Marshall,* M. Biesele, ed., with R. Gordon and R. Lee, pp. 195–230. Helmut Buske Verlag, Hamburg.

Katz, R., M. Biesele, and M. Shostak
1982 *Community Healing Dance Music of the Kalahari !Kung.* Folkways Records, New York. (Now available

from Kalahari Peoples Fund, P. O. Box 7855, University Station, Austin, TX 78713-7855.)

Katz, R., M. Biesele, and V. St. Denis
1997 *Healing Makes Our Hearts Happy: Spirituality and Cultural Transformation among the Kalahari Ju/'hoansi.* Inner Traditions International, Rochester, Vt.

Köhler, O.
1961 "Die Sprachforschung in Südwestafrika," in *Ein Leben für Sudwestafrika* (Festschrift Dr. h. c. Heinrich Vedder), W. Drascher and H. Rust, eds., pp. 61–77. S.W.A. Wissenschaftliche Gesellschaft, Windhoek.
1971 "Noun Classes and Grammatical Agreement in !Xũ (Zû-/hoà Dialect)," in *Actes du Huitieme Congres International de Linguistique Africaine, Abidjan 24–28 Mars 1969,* vol. 2, pp. 489–522. Université d'Abidjan.
1977 "New Khoisan Linguistic Studies: Summary and Comments." *African Studies* 36(2):255–78.
1978–79 "Mythus, Glaube und Magie bei den Kxoe—Buschmännern." *Journal der SWA Wissenschaftlichen Gesellschaft* 33:9–49.

Köhler, W.
1971 "Die 'Krankheit' im Denken der Kxoe-Buschmänner: Afrikanische Sprachen und Kulturen—Ein Querschnitt." *Hamburger Beitrage zur Afrika-Kunde.* Deutsches Institut für Afrika-Forschung, Hamburg.

Kolata, G.
1974 "!Kung Hunter-Gatherers: Feminism, Diet and Birth Control." *Science* 185:932–34.

Konner, M.
1972 "Aspects of the Developmental Ethology of a Foraging People," in

Ethological Studies of Child Behavior,
N. Blurton-Jones, ed., pp. 285–304.
Cambridge University Press,
Cambridge.

1976 "Maternal Care, Infant Behavior and
Development among the !Kung," in
*Kalahari Hunter-Gatherers: Studies of
the !Kung San and Their Neighbors,* R.
Lee and I. De Vore, eds., pp. 218–45.
Harvard University Press, Cambridge.

1983 *The Tangled Wing: Biological
Constraints on the Human Spirit.*
Harper and Row, Cambridge, Mass.

Konner, M., and M. Shostak

1986 "Ethnographic Romanticism and the
Idea of Human Nature: Parallels
between Samoa and the !Kung San," in
*The Past and Future of !Kung Ethnog-
raphy: Critical Reflections and Symbolic
Perspectives. Essays in Honour of Lorna
Marshall,* M. Biesele, ed., with R.
Gordon and R. Lee, pp. 69–76.
Helmut Buske Verlag, Hamburg.

1987 "Timing and Management of Birth
among the !Kung: Biocultural Interaction in Reproductive Adaptation."
Cultural Anthropology 2(1):11–28.

Konner, M., and C. Worthman

1980 "Nursing Frequency, Gonadal
Function and Birth Spacing among
!Kung Hunter-Gatherers." *Science*
207:788–91.

Kuper, A.

1970 *Kalahari Village Politics: An African
Democracy.* Cambridge University
Press, London.

Leacock, E., and R. Lee, eds.

1982 *Politics and History in Band Societies.*
Cambridge University Press, Cambridge, and Maison des Sciences de
l'Homme, Paris.

Lebzelter, V.

1934 *Eingeborenen Kulturen in Südwest-
und Südafrika.* Hiersemann, Leipzig.

Lee, R.

1965 *Subsistence Ecology of !Kung Bushmen.*
University Microfilms, Ann Arbor,
Mich.

1968a "What Hunters Do for a Living, or,
How to Make Out on Scarce
Resources," in *Man the Hunter,* R. Lee
and I. DeVore, eds., pp. 30–48.
Aldine, Chicago.

1968b "Sociology of !Kung Bushman Trance
Performances," in *Trance and Posses-
sion States,* R. Prince, ed., pp. 35–54.
R. M. Bucke Memorial Society,
Montreal.

1969a "Eating Christmas in the Kalahari."
Natural History (December).

1969b "!Kung Bushman Subsistence: An
Input-Output Analysis," in *Environment and Cultural Behavior,* A. Vayda,
ed., pp. 73–94. Natural History Press,
New York.

1972 "Population Growth and the Begin-
nings of Sedentary Life among the
!Kung Bushmen," in *Population
Growth: Anthropological Implications,*
B. Spooner, ed., pp. 329–42. MIT
Press, Cambridge.

1973 "Mongongo: The Ethnography of a
Major Wild Food Resource." *Ecology
of Food and Nutrition* 2:307–21.

1976 "!Kung Spatial Organization: An
Ecological and Historical Perspec-
tive," in *Kalahari Hunter-Gatherers:
Studies of the !Kung San and Their
Neighbors,* R. Lee. and I. DeVore, eds.,
pp. 73–97. Harvard University Press,
Cambridge.

1978a "The Ecology of a Contemporary San
People," in *The Bushmen: San
Hunters and Herders of Southern
Africa,* P. Tobias, ed., pp. 94–114.
Human and Rousseau, Cape Town.

1978b "Hunter-Gatherers in Process: The
Kalahari Research Project, 1963–76,"
in *Long Term Field Research in Social
Anthropology,* G. Foster et al., eds., pp.
303–21. Academic Press, New York.

1979   *The !Kung San: Men, Women and Work in a Foraging Society.* Cambridge University Press, Cambridge.

1984   *The Dobe !Kung.* Holt, Rinehart and Winston, New York.

1985   "Foragers and the State: Government Policies toward the San in Namibia and Botswana," in *The Future of Former Foragers in Australia and Southern Africa,* C. Schrire and R. Gordon, eds., pp. 37–45. Occasional Papers No. 18. Cultural Survival, Inc., Cambridge, Mass.

1986   "!Kung Kin Terms, the Name Relationship and the Process of Discovery," in *The Past and Future of !Kung Ethnography: Critical Reflections and Symbolic Perspectives. Essays in Honour of Lorna Marshall,* M. Biesele, ed., with R. Gordon and R. Lee, pp. 77–102. Helmut Buske Verlag, Hamburg.

1992   "Art, Science, or Politics? The Crisis in Hunter-Gatherer Studies." *American Anthropologist* 94(1):23–46.

Lee, R., and M. Biesele

1991   "Dependency or Self-Reliance: The Ju/'hoansi—!Kung Forty Years On." Paper presented at annual meeting of American Anthropological Association, Chicago, Ill. November.

Lee, R., and I. DeVore

1976   *Kalahari Hunter-Gatherers: Studies of the !Kung San and Their Neighbors.* Harvard University Press, Cambridge.

Lee, R., and M. Guenther

1991   "Oxen or Onions? The Search for Trade (and Truth) in the Kalahari." *Current Anthropology* 32(5):592–601.

Lee, R., and S. Hurlich

1982   "From Foragers to Fighters: The Militarization of the !Kung San," in *Politics and History in Band Societies,* E. Leacock and R. Lee, eds., pp. 327–45. Cambridge University Press, Cambridge, and Maison des Sciences de l'Homme, Paris.

Lepionka, L.

1979   "Ceramics at Tautswemogala," in *Iron Age Studies in Southern Africa,* N. van der Merwe and T. Huffman, eds., pp. 62–71. Goodwin Series 3. South African Archaeological Society, Claremont.

Lessa, W., and E. Vogt, eds.

1958   *Reader in Comparative Religion: An Anthropological Approach.* Row, Peterson and Company, Evanston, Ill.

Lévi-Strauss, C.

1966   *The Savage Mind.* University of Chicago Press, Chicago.

Lewis-Williams, J.

1981a   "The Thin Red Line: Southern San Notions and Rock Paintings of Supernatural Potency." *South African Archaeological Bulletin* 36:5–13.

1981b   *Believing and Seeing: Symbolic Meanings in San Rock Paintings.* Academic Press, London.

1982   "The Social and Economic Context of Southern San Rock Art." *Current Anthropology* 23:429–49.

1983   *The Rock Art of Southern Africa.* Cambridge University Press, Cambridge.

1984   "Ideological Continuities in Prehistoric Southern Africa: The Evidence of Rock Art," in *Past and Present in Hunter-Gatherer Studies,* C. Schrire, ed., pp. 225–52. Academic Press, New York.

1987   "Paintings of Power: Ethnography and Rock Art in Southern Africa," in *The Past and Future of !Kung Ethnography: Critical Reflections and Symbolic Perspectives. Essays in Honour of Lorna Marshall,* M. Biesele, ed., with R. Gordon and R. Lee, pp. 231–73. Helmut Buske Verlag, Hamburg.

1990   *Discovering Southern African Rock Art.* David Philip, Cape Town.

Lewis-Williams, J., and M. Biesele
1978   "Eland Hunting Rituals among Northern and Southern San Groups: Striking Similarities." *Africa* 48(2):117–34.

Lewis-Williams, J., and T. Dowson
1989   *Images of Power.* Southern Book Publishers, Johannesburg.
1990   "Through the Veil: San Rock Paintings and the Rock Face." *South African Archaeological Bulletin* 45:5–16.

Lloyd, L.
1889   *A Short Account of Further Bushman Material.* David Nut, London.

Lomax, A.
1972   "Review of the Film *Bitter Melons.*" *American Anthropologist* 74:1018–20.

Maguire, B.
1954   "A Report on the Food Plants of the !Kung Bushmen of North-eastern South West Africa." Unpublished ms.; in collaboration with the Harvard-Peabody Anthropological Mag. 54 Expedition to South-West-Africa, 1952–1953.

Marshall, J.
1957   "Ecology of the !Kung Bushmen of the Kalahari." Senior honors thesis, Department of Anthropology, Harvard University, Cambridge.
1958   "Man the Hunter, Part I." *Natural History* 67 (June-July):291–309; "Man the Hunter, Part II." *Natural History* 67 (Aug.–Sept.):376–95.
1984   "Death Blow to the Bushmen. A Proposed Game Park in Namibia Would Force the Last Ju/wasi off Their Traditional Lands." *Cultural Survival Quarterly* 8(3):13–16.
1985   "Plight of the Bushmen." *Leadership.* Johannesburg. Photographs by Paul Weinberg. First Quarter, 1985:36–49.
1988   "Bushmanland: Lives in the Balance" (Letter). *African Wildlife* 42(6):357.

1989   *The Constitution and Communal Lands in Namibia. Land Rights and Local Governments: Helping 33,000 People Classified as "Bushmen." The Ju/wa Case.* Nyae Nyae Development Foundation of Namibia, Windhoek.
1991a   *Local Development or Poverty and Debt? The Future of Communal Lands in Namibia.* Nyae Nyae Development Foundation of Namibia, Windhoek. Serialized in *The Namibian* (Newspaper), June.
1991b   "Tödliche Mythen (Deadly Myths), Die sichtbare und die unsichtbare Realität (Visible and Invisible Reality), The Hunters," in *Jäger und Gejagte, John Marshall und seine Film,* R. Kapfer, W. Petermann, R. Thoms, eds. Trickster Verlag, Munich.

Marshall, J., R. Gordon, and C. Ritchie
1984   "Open Letter on the Ju/wasi of Bushmanland." *Cultural Survival Quarterly* 8(1):84.

Marshall, J., and O. Levinson
1984   "A People in Jeopardy." *Windhoek Observer,* December 14.

Marshall, J., and C. Ritchie
1982   "Husbandry in Eastern Bushmanland." Development plan submitted to the administration of South West Africa, Windhoek, Namibia.
1984   *Where are the Ju/wasi of Nyae Nyae? Changes in a Bushman Society, 1958–1981.* Center for African Studies, University of Cape Town. Rondebosch, South Africa.

Marshall, L.
1957a   "N!ow." *Africa* 27(3):232–40.
1957b   "The Kin Terminology System of the !Kung Bushmen." *Africa* 27(1):1–25.
1959   "Marriage among !Kung Bushmen." *Africa* 29(4):335–65.
1960   "!Kung Bushman Bands." *Africa* 30(4):325–55.

1961 "Sharing, Talking and Giving: Relief of Social Tensions among !Kung Bushmen." *Africa* 31(3):231–49.

1962 "!Kung Bushman Religious Beliefs." *Africa* 32(3):221–52.

1965 "The !Kung Bushmen of the Kalahari Desert," in *Peoples of Africa.* J. Gibbs, Jr., ed., pp. 241–78. Holt, Rinehart and Winston, New York.

1968 "Discussion," in *Man the Hunter,* R. Lee and I. DeVore, eds., pp. 152–53. Aldine Publishing Co., Chicago.

1969 "The Medicine Dance of the !Kung Bushmen." *Africa* 39(4):347–81.

1975 "Two Ju/wa Constellations." *Botswana Notes and Records* 7:153–59.

1976 *The !Kung of Nyae Nyae.* Harvard University Press, Cambridge.

1980 "The Marshall Chronicles," in *Odyssey,* pp. 10–15. Public Broadcasting Associates, Inc., Boston, Mass.

1986 "Some Bushman Star Lore," in *Contemporary Studies on Khoisan Part 2,* R. Vossen and K. Keuthman, eds., pp. 169–204. Quellen zur Khoisan-Forschung vol. 5.2. Helmut Buske Verlag, Hamburg.

Marshall, L., and M. Biesele

1974 *N/um Tchai: The Ceremonial Dance of the !Kung Bushmen. A Study Guide.* Documentary Educational Resources, Somerville, Mass.

Marshall, L., and L. K. Marshall

1956 "!Kung Bushmen of South West Africa." *South West Africa Annual* 1956:11–27.

Mauss, M.

1954 *The Gift: Forms and Functions of Exchange in Archaic Society.* Cohen and West Ltd., London.

1972 *A General Theory of Magic.* Translated from the French by R. Brain. Routledge and Kegan Paul, London.

Mbuende, K.

1989 "The San People and the Transition to Independence in Namibia: Problems and Prospects." South West African Peoples Organization Background Paper, Windhoek, Namibia.

McCall, D.

1970 *Wolf Courts Girl: The Equivalence of Hunting and Mating in Bushman Thought.* Papers in International Studies, Africa Series No. 7. Ohio University Center for International Studies, Athens, Ohio.

Meillassoux, C.

1973 "On the Mode of Production of the Hunting Band," in *French Perspectives in African Studies,* P. Alexandre, ed., pp. 187–203. Oxford University Press, Oxford.

Menzel, D.

1964 *A Field Guide to the Stars and Planets.* The Riverside Press, Cambridge.

Merriam, A.

1964 *The Anthropology of Music.* Northwestern University Press, Evanston, Ill.

Mertens, A.

1966 *South West Africa and Its Indigenous People.* Introduction by S. Cloete. Collins, London.

Metzger, F.

1950 *Narro and His Clan.* John Meinert Ltd., Windhoek, South West Africa.

Metzger, F., and P. Ettighofer

1952 *Und seither lacht die Hyaene.* John Meinert Ltd., Windhoek.

Middleton, J., ed.

1967 *Myth and Cosmos: Readings in Mythology and Symbolism.* University of Texas Press, Austin.

Murdock, G.
1949   *Social Structure*. Macmillan, New York.
1959   *Africa: Its Peoples and Their Culture History*. McGraw-Hill, New York.

Norberg, A.
1987   *A Handbook of Musical and Other Sound-Producing Instruments from Namibia and Botswana*. Musik-mupeets skrifter 13, Stockholm.

Norton, A., and J. Gall Inglis
1954   *A Star Atlas*. Gall and Inglis, London.

Nurse, G., and T. Jenkins
1974   "Lactose Intolerance in San Popula-tions." *British Medical Journal* 2:728.
1977   *Health and the Hunter-Gatherer*. Monographs in Human Genetics, no. 8. S. Karger, Basel.

Nurse, G., J. Weiner, and T. Jenkins
1985   *The Peoples of Southern Africa and Their Affinities*. Clarendon Press, Oxford.

Nyae Nyae Farmers' Cooperative
1989   "≠Hanu a N!an!a'an: N//oaq!'ae Farmakxaosi //Koa//Kae" (Constitu-tion of the Nyae Nyae Farmers' Cooperative). /Aotcha, Namibia.

Orpen, J.
1874   "A Glimpse into the Mythology of the Maluti Bushmen." *Cape Monthly Magazine* 9:1–13.

Pager, H.
1971   *Ndedema*. Akademische Druck u. Verlagsanstalt, Graz, Austria.
1982   "The Ritual Hunt: Parallels between Ethnological and Archaeological Data." *South African Archaeological Bulletin* 38:80–87.

Parkington, J.
1984   "Soaqua and Bushmen: Hunters and Robbers," in *Past and Present in Hunter-Gatherer Studies*, C. Schrire, ed., pp. 151–74. Academic Press, Orlando, Fla.

Parrinder, G.
1967   *African Mythology*. Paul Hamlyn, London.

Passarge, S.
1907   *Die Buschmänner der Kalahari*. Dietrich Reimer (Ernest Vohsen), Berlin.

Peterson, N.
1970   "Territorial Adaptation among Desert Hunter-Gatherers: The !Kung and Australians Compared," in *Social and Ecological Systems*, P. Burnham and R. Ellen, eds., pp. 111–29. A.S.A. Monograph 18. Academic Press, New York.

Pfeiffer, J.
1982   *The Creative Explosion: An Inquiry into the Origins of Art and Religion*. Harper and Row, New York.

Prozesky, O.
1970   *A Field Guide to the Birds of Southern Africa*. Collins, London.

Radin, P.
1956   *The Trickster: A Study in American Indian Mythology*. Philosophical Library, New York.

Reichlin, S.
1974a   *"The Wasp's Nest": A Study Guide*. Documentary Educational Resources, Watertown, Mass.
1974b   *"The Meat Fight": A Study Guide*. Documentary Educational Resources, Watertown, Mass.
1975   *"A Rite of Passage": Film Notes*. Docu-mentary Educational Resources, Watertown, Mass.

Reichlin, S., and J. Marshall
1974   *"An Argument about a Marriage": The Study Guide*. Documentary Educa-tional Resources, Watertown, Mass.

Ritchie, C.
1984   "Update on the Bushmen." *Cultural Survival Quarterly* 8(3):16–17.

1986a   "Stress, Culture Change and Healing
        in a Ju/wa Society." Unpublished ms.,
        Department of Anthropology, Boston
        University.
1986b   "From Foragers to Farmers: The
        Ju/wasi of Nyae Nyae Thirty Years
        On," in *The Past and Future of !Kung
        Ethnography: Critical Reflections and
        Symbolic Perspectives. Essays in Hon-
        our of Lorna Marshall,* Megan Biesele,
        ed., with R. Gordon and R. Lee,
        pp. 311–25. Helmut Buske Verlag,
        Hamburg.
1987   "The Political Economy of Resource
        Tenure in the Kalahari: San Survival
        in Namibia and Botswana." Master's
        thesis, Department of Anthropology,
        Boston University, Boston.
1988a   "≠Toma: A Tribute." *Cultural Survival
        Quarterly.* 12(3):36–38.
1988b   "Update on the Status of Bushman-
        land." *Cultural Survival Quarterly*
        12(3)34–35.

Rosenberg, H.
1990   "Complaint Discourse, Aging, and
        Caregiving among the !Kung San of
        Botswana," in *The Cultural Context of
        Aging,* J. Sokolovsky, ed., pp. 19–41.
        Bergin and Garvey, Boston.

Ruby, J.
1989   "Robert Gardner und der anthropol-
        ogische Film," in *Rituale von Leben
        und Tod,* R. Kapfer, W. Petermann,
        and R. Thoms, eds., pp. 51–67.
        Quoted from the English manuscript,
        "Robert Gardner and Anthropological
        Cinema." Trickster Verlag, Munich.

Rudner, J., and I. Rudner
1970   *The Hunter and His Art.* Struik, Cape
        Town.

Russell, M.
1976   "Slaves or Workers? Relations
        between Bushmen, Tswana and Boers
        in the Kalahari." *Journal of Southern
        African Studies* 2(2):178–97.

Sahlins, M.
1974   *Stone Age Economics.* Tavistock Publi-
        cations, London.
1976   *Culture and Practical Reason.* Univer-
        sity of Chicago Press, Chicago.

Sandelowsky, B.
1971   "Ostrich Eggshell Caches from
        S. W. A." *South African Archaeological
        Bulletin* 26, Parts 3 and 4.
1974   "Pre-historic Metal Working in
        S. W. A." *Journal of the South African
        Institute of Mining and Metallurgy*
        74(10).
1983   "Archaeology in Namibia." *American
        Scientist* 71(Nov.–Dec):606–15.

Sandelowsky, B., J. Van Rooyen, and J. Vogel
1979   "Early Evidence for Herders in the
        Namib." *South African Archaeological
        Bulletin* 34:50–51.

Sbrzesny, H.
1976   *Die Spiele der !Ko-Buschleute.* Piper
        Verlag, Munich.

Schapera, I.
1926   "A Preliminary Consideration of the
        Relationship between the Hottentots
        and the Bushmen." *South African
        Journal of Science* 23:833–66.
1930   *The Khoisan Peoples of South Africa.*
        Routledge & Kegan Paul, London.
        Reprinted 1951 by The Humanities
        Press, New York.
1939   "A Survey of the Bushman Question,"
        Race Relations 6(2):68–83.
1952   *The Ethnic Composition of Tswana
        Tribes.* Monographs on Social
        Anthropology, no. 11. London School
        of Economics and Political Science,
        London.
1971   *Rainmaking Rites of Tswana Tribes.*
        African Social Research Documents,
        vol. 3. Afrika-Studiecentrum, Leiden,
        Netherlands.

Schmidt, S.

1973   "Die Mantis religiosa in den Glaubensvorstellungen der Khoesan-Völker." *Zeitschrift für Ethnologie* 98(1):102–25.

1975   "Folktales of the Non-Bantu Speaking Peoples in Southern Africa." *Folklore 86.*

1979   "The Rain Bull of the South African Bushmen." *African Studies* 38(2): 201–24.

1980   *Märchen aus Namibia.* Eugen Diederichs Verlag, Düsseldorf.

1986   "Tales and Beliefs about Eyes-on-His-Feet: The Interrelatedness of Khoisan Folklore," in *The Past and Future of !Kung Ethnography: Critical Reflections and Symbolic Perspectives. Essays in Honour of Lorna Marshall,* M. Biesele, ed., with R. Gordon and R. Lee, pp. 169–94. Helmut Buske Verlag, Hamburg.

Schrire, C.

1980   "An Inquiry into the Evolutionary Status and Apparent Identity of San Hunter-Gatherers." *Human Ecology* 8(1):9–32.

1984   "Wild Surmises on Savage Thoughts," in *Past and Present in Hunter Gatherer Studies,* C. Schrire, ed., pp. 1–25. Academic Press, Orlando, Fla.

Schrire, C., ed.

1984   *Past and Present in Hunter Gatherer Studies.* Academic Press, Orlando, Fla.

Schrire, C., and R. Gordon, eds.

1985   *The Future of Former Foragers, Australia and Southern Africa.* Occasional Papers No. 18 (October), Cultural Survival, Inc., Cambridge, Mass.

Schwartzman, H.

1978   *Transformations: The Anthropology of Children's Play.* Plenum Press, New York.

Shaw, E., P. Wooley, and F. Rae

1963   "Bushman Arrow Poisons." *Cimbebasia,* no. 7 (December):2–41.

Shortridge, G.

1934   *The Mammals of South West Africa: A Biological Account of the Forms Occurring in That Region,* vols. 1, 2. William Heinemann, Ltd., London.

Shostak, M.

1976   "A !Kung Woman's Memories of Childhood," in *Kalahari Hunter-Gatherers: Studies of the !Kung San and Their Neighbors,* R. Lee and I. DeVore, eds., pp. 246–77. Harvard University Press, Cambridge.

1981   *Nisa: The Life and Words of a !Kung Woman.* Harvard University Press, Cambridge.

1984   "The Creative Individual in the World of the !Kung San." Paper presented at annual meeting, American Anthropological Association. November.

Silberbauer, G.

1963   "Marriage and the Girl's Puberty Ceremony of the G/wi Bushmen." *Africa* 33(3):12-24.

1965   *Bushman Survey Report.* Bechuanaland Government, Gaberones.

1981   *Hunter and Habitat in the Central Kalahari Desert.* Cambridge University Press, Cambridge.

1982   "Political Process in G/wi Bands," in *Politics and History in Band Societies,* E. Leacock and R. Lee, eds., pp. 23–35. Cambridge University Press, Cambridge, and Maison des Sciences de l'Homme, Paris.

1991   "Morbid Reflexivity and Overgeneralization in Mosarwa Studies." *Current Anthropology* 32:96–99.

Silberbauer, G., and A. Kuper

1966   "Kgalagadi Masters and Bushman Serfs." *African Studies* 25(4):171–79.

Singer, R.
1978   "The Biology of the San," in *The Bushmen: San Hunters and Herders of Southern Africa*, P. Tobias, ed., pp. 115–29. Human and Rousseau, Cape Town.

Smith, A.
1990   "On Becoming Herders: Khoikhoi and San Ethnicity in Southern Africa." *African Studies* 49(2):50–73.

Snyman, J.
1969   *!Xũ (A Bushman Language) Orthography no. 1.* Language and Publications Board of S. W. A., Windhoek.
1970   *An Introduction to the !Xũ Language."* Communication no. 34 of the University of Cape Town School of African Studies. A. A. Balkema, Cape Town.
1974   *The Bushman and Hottentot Languages of Southern Africa.* Limi 2.2. University of South Africa, Pretoria.
1975a   "Some Phonetic and Lexical Aspects of Žu/'hõasi," in *Bushman and Hottentot Linguistic Studies*, A. Traill, ed., African Studies Institute Communication No. 2. African Studies Institute, University of the Witwatersrand, Johannesburg.
1975b   *Žu/'hõasi Fonologie en Woordeboek.* A. A. Balkema, Cape Town.
1978   "The Clicks of Žu/'hõasi (Bushman)," *Tweede Afrikatale-kongres van UNISA. Miscellenea Congregalia 5*, pp. 144–68. University of South Africa, Pretoria.
1980   "The Relationship between Angolan !Xu and Žu/'hõasi," in *Bushman and Hottentot Linguistic Studies*, J. Snyman, ed., pp. 1–58. University of South Africa, Pretoria.

Solway, J., and R. Lee
1990   "Foragers, Genuine or Spurious? Situating the Kalahari San in History." *Current Anthropology* 31(2):109–45.

Stopa, R.
1986   *Clicks: Their Character, Development, and Origin.* Eurolingua, Bloomington, Ind.

Story, R.
1958   *Some Plants Used by the Bushmen in Obtaining Food and Water.* Botanical Survey Memoir No. 30. Union of South Africa, Department of Agriculture, Division of Botany. The Government Printer, Pretoria.
1964   "Plant Lore of the Bushmen," in *Ecological Studies in Southern Africa*, D. Davis, ed. D. W. Junk, The Hague.

Stow, G.
1905   *The Native Races of South Africa.* Swan and Sonnenschein, London.

Tanaka, J.
1976   "Subsistence Ecology of Central Kalahari San," in *Kalahari Hunter-Gatherers: Studies of the !Kung San and Their Neighbors*, R. Lee and I. DeVore, eds., pp. 98–119. Harvard University Press, Cambridge.
1980   *The San: Hunter-Gatherers of the Kalahari.* Translated by D. Hughes. University of Tokyo Press, Tokyo.
1987   *The Recent Changes in the Life and Society of the Central Kalahari San.* African Study Monographs, vol. 7. Kyoto University, Kyoto.
1991   "Egalitarianism and the Cash Economy among the Central Kalahari San," in *Cash Commoditisation and Changing Foragers*, N. Peterson and T. Matsuyama, eds., pp. 117–34. Senri Ethnological Studies 30, National Museum of Ethnology, Osaka, Japan.

Tart, C.
1976   *Altered States of Consciousness.* Dutton, New York.

Testart, A.
1978   "Milieu natural, mythologie et organ-
         isation sociale." *Social Science Infor-
         mation* 15.
1986   "La femme et la chasse." *La Recherche*
         181(17):1194–1201.

Thomas, E. M.
1956   "/Gikwe Bushmen." *Radcliffe Quar-
         terly.* November.
1959   *The Harmless People.* Alfred A. Knopf,
         New York.
1960   "The Shy People of the Kalahari," in
         The Great Travellers, M. Rugoff, ed.
         Simon and Schuster, New York.
1963   "Today the African Bushman Sur-
         vives Only in the Harsh Kalahari."
         National Geographic 123(6):866–88.
1968   "The Bushmen: Gentle Nomads of
         Africa's Harsh Kalahari," in *Vanishing
         Peoples of the Earth*, R. Breeden, ed.,
         pp. 58–75. National Geographic
         Society, Washington, D.C.
1980   "American Family's Poignant Sojourn
         with the Bushmen." *Smithsonian*
         11(1):86–95.
1987   *Reindeer Moon.* Houghton Mifflin
         Company, Boston.
1989   "The Bushmen in 1989." Epilogue in
         The Harmless People (second paper-
         back edition). Vintage Books, New
         York.
1990   *The Animal Wife.* Houghton Mifflin
         Company, Boston.
1994a   "Management of Violence among the
         Ju/wasi of Nyae Nyae: The Old Way
         and a New Way," in *Studying War:
         Anthropological Perspectives*,
         S. P. Reyna and R. E. Downs, eds.,
         pp. 69–84. Gordon and Breach
         Science Publishers, Philadelphia.
1994b   *The Tribe of Tiger: Cats and Their Cul-
         ture.* Simon and Schuster, New York.

Thomas, E. W.
1950   *Bushman Stories.* Oxford University
         Press, Cape Town.

Tobias, P.
1956   "On the Survival of the Bushmen:
         With an Estimate of the Problem
         Facing Anthropologists." *Africa*
         26(2):174–86.
1961   "Physique of a Desert Folk: Genes,
         Not Habitat, Shaped the Bushman."
         Natural History 70(2):16–25.
1962   "On the Increasing Stature of the
         Bushmen." *Anthropos* 57:801–10.
1975   "Fifteen Years of Study on the
         Kalahari Bushmen or San: A Brief
         History of the Kalahari Research
         Committee." *South African Journal of
         Science* 71:74–78.
1978   "Introduction to the Bushmen or
         San," in *The Bushmen: San Hunters
         and Herders of Southern Africa*,
         P. Tobias, ed., pp. 1–15. Human and
         Rousseau, Cape Town.

Tobias, P., ed.
1978   *The Bushmen: San Hunters and
         Herders of Southern Africa.* Human
         and Rousseau, Cape Town.

Tomaselli, K.
1986   "The 'Bushmen' on Film: From
         Colonialism to Romanticism," in
         *Myth, Race and Power: South Africans
         Imaged on Film and TV*, K. Tomaselli
         et al., eds., pp. 77–101. Critical
         Studies in African Anthropology, no.
         1. Anthropos Publishers, Bellville,
         South Africa.

Tracy, H.
1948   *Ngoma: An Introduction to Music for
         Southern Africans.* Longmans, Green
         and Co., Cape Town.

Traill, A.
1978   "The Languages of the Bushmen," in
         *The Bushmen: San Hunters and
         Herders of Southern Africa*, P. Tobias,
         ed., pp. 137–47. Human and
         Rousseau, Cape Town.

1980 "Phonetic Diversity in Khoisan Languages,"in *Bushman and Hottentot Linguistic Studies,* J. Snyman, ed., pp. 167–89. University of South Africa, Pretoria.

Traill, A., ed.
1975 *Bushman and Hottentot Linguistic Studies.* African Studies Institute Communication No. 2. University of the Witwatersrand, Johannesburg.

Truswell, A., and J. Hansen
1968 "Medical and Nutritional Studies of the !Kung Bushmen in Northwest Botswana: A Preliminary Report." *South African Medical Journal* 42:1338–39.

1976 "Medical Research among the !Kung," in *Kalahari Hunter-Gatherers: Studies of the !Kung San and Their Neighbors,* R. Lee and I. DeVore, eds., pp. 166–94. Harvard University Press, Cambridge.

Truswell, A., J. Hansen, P. Wannenburg, and E. Sellmeyer
1969 "Nutritional Status of Adult Bushmen in the Northern Kalahari, Botswana." *South African Medical Journal* 43:1157–58.

Turnbull, C.
1962 *The Lonely African.* Simon and Schuster, a Clarion Book, New York.

1968 "The Importance of Flux in Two Hunting Societies," in *Man the Hunter,* R. Lee and I. DeVore, eds., pp. 132–37. Aldine, Chicago.

1972 *The Mountain People.* Simon and Schuster, a Touchstone Book, New York.

Turner, V.
1967 *The Forest of Symbols: Aspects of Ndembu Ritual.* Cornell University Press, Ithaca.

1969 *The Ritual Process: Structure and Anti-structure.* Aldine Publishing Co., Chicago.

Ury, W.
1990 "Dispute Resolution Notes from the Kalahari." *Negotiation Journal* 6(3).

Valiente-Noailles, C.
1981 *Los Bosquimanos: Africa Austral.* Emece Editores, Buenos Aires.

van der Post, L.
1958 *The Lost World of the Kalahari.* William Morrow and Company, New York.

1961 *The Heart of the Hunter.* Hogarth Press, London.

van Riet Lowe, C.
1941 *Prehistoric Art in South Africa.* Bureau of Archaeology, Archaeological Series, no. 5. Government Printer, Pretoria.

van Warmelo, N.
1935 *A Preliminary Survey of the Bantu Tribes of South Africa.* Department of Native Affairs Ethnological Publications, vol. 5. The Government Printer, Pretoria.

1951 *Notes on the Kaokoveld (South West Africa) and Its People.* Department of Native Affairs, Ethnological Publications, no. 26. Government Printer, Pretoria.

van Zinderen Bakker, E.
1963 "Palaeobotanical Studies. Symposium on Early Man and His Environments in Southern Africa." *South African Journal of Science* 59.

Vedder, H.
1928a "The Berg Damara," in *The Native Tribes of South West Africa,* C. Hahn, H. Vedder, and L. Fourie, eds., pp. 37–78. Cape Times Ltd., Cape Town.

1928b "The Herero," in *The Native Tribes of South West Africa,* C. Hahn, H. Vedder, and L. Fourie, eds., pp. 153–210. Cape Times, Ltd., Cape Town.

1928c "The Nama," in *The Native Tribes of South West Africa,* C. Hahn, H. Vedder, and L. Fourie, eds., pp. 107–152. Cape Times Ltd., Cape Town.

1938 *South West Africa in Early Times.* Oxford University Press, London.

Viereck, A., and J. Rudner

1957 "Twyfelfontein—A Center of Prehistoric Art in South West Africa." *The South African Archaeological Bulletin* 12(45) (March):15–26.

Vierich, H.

1977 *Interim Report on Basarwa and Related Poor Bakgalagadi in Kweneng District.* Ministry of Local Government and Lands, Republic of Botswana, Gaborone.

1982 "Adaptive Flexibility in a Multi-ethnic Setting: The Basarwa of the Southern Kalahari," in *Politics and History in Band Societies,* E. Leacock and R. Lee, eds., pp. 213–22. Cambridge University Press, Cambridge, and Maison des sciences de l'Homme, Paris.

Vinnicombe, P.

1972a "Motivation in African Rock Art." *Antiquity* 46:124–33.

1972b "Myth, Motive, and Selection in Southern African Rock Art." *Africa* 42(3)(July):192–204.

1976 *People of the Eland: Rock Paintings of the Drakensberg Bushmen as a Reflection of Their Life and Thought.* University of Natal Press, Pietermaritzburg.

1982 "Common Ground in South Africa and Australia." *South African Archaeological Society Newsletter,* 5(1)(June).

1986 "Rock Art, Territory and Land Rights," in *The Past and Future of !Kung Ethnography: Critical Reflections and Symbolic Perspectives. Essays*

in Honour of Lorna Marshall, M. Biesele, ed., with R. Gordon and R. Lee, pp. 275–301. Helmut Buske Verlag, Hamburg.

Volkman, T.

1986 "The Hunter-Gatherer Myth in Southern Africa: Preserving Nature or Culture?" *Cultural Survival Quarterly* 10(2):25–32.

1988 "Out of South Africa: The Gods Must be Crazy," in *Image Ethics,* L. Gross, J. Katz, and J. Ruby, eds., pp. 236–47. Oxford University Press, New York.

von Hornbostel, E.

1924 "Die Entstehung des Jodelns," in *Musikwissenschaftliches Kongress-Bericht,* Basel.

Vossen, R., and K. Keuthmann, eds.

1986 *Contemporary Studies on Khoisan Parts 1 and 2: In Honour of Oswin Köhler on the Occasion of His 75th Birthday.* Quellen zur Khoisan-Forschung vols. 5.1 and 5.2. Helmut Buske Verlag, Hamburg.

Wadley, L.

1986 "Private Lives and Public Lives: A Social Interpretation for the Stone Age in Southern Africa." Paper prepared for the workshop "New Understanding of Sub-Saharan Africa's Prehistoric Art," at the conference *The Longest Record: The Human Career in Africa,* Berkeley, Calif.

Wannenburgh, A., P. Johnson, and A. Bannister

1979 *The Bushmen.* C. Struik, Cape Town.

Washburn, S., and C. Lancaster

1968 "The Evolution of Hunting," in *Man the Hunter,* R. Lee and I. DeVore, eds., pp. 293–303. Aldine, Chicago.

Wehmeyer, A., R. Lee, and M. Whiting

1969 "Nutrient Composition and Dietary Importance of Some Vegetable Foods Eaten by the !Kung Bushmen." *South*

African Medical Journal. December: 1529–30.

Wellington, J.
1967 *South West Africa and Its Human Issues.* Oxford University Press, London.

Westphal, E.
1956 "The Non-Bantu Languages of Southern Africa," in *The Non-Bantu Languages of North-Eastern Africa,* A. Tucker and M. Bryan, eds., pp. 158–73. Handbook of African Languages, vol. 13. Oxford University Press for the International African Institute, London.
1962a "A Re-classification of Southern African Non-Bantu Languages." *Journal of African Languages* 1:1–8.
1962b "On Classifying Bushman and Hottentot Languages." *African Language Studies* 3:30–48.

Wiessner, P.
1977 "Hxaro: A Regional System of Reciprocity for Reducing Risk among the !Kung San." Ph.D. dissertation, Department of Anthropology, University of Michigan, Ann Arbor.
1982 "Risk, Reciprocity and Social Influence on !Kung San Economics," in *Politics and History in Band Societies,* E. Leacock and R. Lee, eds., pp. 61–84. Cambridge University Press, Cambridge, and Maison des Sciences de l'Homme, Paris.
1983 "Social and Ceremonial Aspects of Death among the !Kung San." *Botswana Notes and Records* 15:1–5.
1986 "!Kung San Networks in a Generational Perspective," in *The Past and Future of !Kung Ethnography: Critical Reflections and Symbolic Perspectives. Essays in Honour of Lorna Marshall,* M. Biesele, ed., with R. Gordon and R. Lee, pp. 103–36. Helmut Buske Verlag, Hamburg.

Wiessner, P., and F. Larsen
1979 "'Mother! Sing Loudly for Me!': The Annotated Dialogue of a Basarwa Healer in Trance." *Botswana Notes and Records* 11:25–31.

Willcox, A.
1956 *Rock Paintings of the Drakensberg.* Max Parrish, London.
1963 *The Rock Art of South Africa.* Thomas Nelson and Sons, Johannesburg.
1971 "Size and the Hunter." *South African Journal of Science* 67:306–7.

Willcox, A., and H. Pager
1967 "The Petroglyphs of Redan, Transvaal." *Suid-Afrikaanse Tydskrif vir Wetenskap.* November.

Wilmsen, E.
1985 "The Impact of Land Tenure Policies on the Future of the San," in *The Future of Former Foragers in Australia and Southern Africa,* C. Schrire and R. Gordon, eds., pp. 93–98. Occasional Papers No. 18 (October). Cultural Survival, Inc., Cambridge, Mass.
1989a *Land Filled with Flies: A Political Economy of the Kalahari.* University of Chicago Press, Chicago.
1989b "Those Who Have Each Other: Land Tenure of San-Speaking Peoples," in *We Are Here: Politics of Aboriginal Tenure,* E. Wilmsen, ed., pp. 43–67. University of California Press, Berkeley.

Wilmsen, E., and J. Denbow.
1990 "Paradigmatic History of San-Speaking Peoples and Current Attempts at Revision." *Current Anthropology* 31(5):489–522.

Wilson, M.
1975 ". . . So Truth Be in the Field . . ." The Alfred and Winifred Hoernlé Memorial Lecture 1975. The Natal Witness (Pty) Ltd., Pietermaritzburg, Natal.

Wilson, M., and L. Thompson
 1969 *The Oxford History of South Africa.*
 Oxford University Press, London.

Wily, E.
 1973 "An Analysis of the Bere Bushman
 Settlement Scheme." Report to the
 Ministry of Local Government and
 Lands, Gaborone, Botswana.
 1979 *Official Policy towards San (Bushman)
 Hunter-Gatherers in Modern Botswana:
 1966–1978.* National Institute of
 Development and Cultural Research
 Working Paper No. 23. National
 Institute of Research, Gaborone.
 1982 "Botswana's Development Strategy
 for Its Indigenous Desert People, the
 Kalahari Bushmen," in *Alternative
 Strategies for Desert Development and
 Management,* United Nations Insti-
 tute for Training and Research, pp.
 1108–21. Pergamon Press, New York.

Woodburn, J.
 1980 "Hunters and Gatherers Today and
 Reconstructions of the Past," in *Soviet
 and Western Anthropology,* E. Gellner,
 ed., pp. 95–117. Duckworth, London.

Woodhouse, H.
 1969 "Rockpaintings of 'Eland-Fighting'
 and 'Eland-Jumping.'" *South African
 Archaeological Bulletin* 94:63–65.
 1979 *The Bushman Art of Southern Africa.*
 Purnell, Cape Town.

Wright, J.
 1971 *Bushman Raiders of the Drakensberg
 1840–1870.* University of Natal Press,
 Pietermaritzburg.

Yellen, J.
 1976 "Settlement Patterns of the !Kung: An
 Archaeological Perspective," in *Kalahari Hunter-Gatherers: Studies of the
 !Kung San and Their Neighbors,* R. Lee
 and I. DeVore, eds., pp. 47–72.
 Harvard University Press, Cambridge.
 1977 *Archaeological Approaches to the
 Present: Models for Reconstructing the
 Past.* Academic Press, New York.
 1984 "The Integration of Herding into Prehistoric Hunting and Gathering Econ-
 omies," in *Frontiers: Southern African
 Archaeology Today,* M. Hall, G. Avery,
 M. Wilson, and A. Humphreys, eds.,
 pp. 53–64. Cambridge Monographs in
 African Archaeology 10. B. A. R. International Series 207, Oxford, England.
 1985 "Bushmen." *Science 85* 6(4):41–48.
 1990 "The Transformation of the Kalahari
 !Kung: Why After Centuries of Stability Has This Society, an Apparent
 Relic of Ancient Hunting and Gathering Groups, Abandoned Many of
 Its Traditional Ways?" *Scientific
 American* 262(4):96–105.

Yellen, J., and A. Brooks
 1990 "The Late Stone Age Archaeology in
 the /Xai /Xai region: A Response to
 Wilmsen." *Botswana Notes and
 Records* 22:17–19.

Yellen, J., A. Brooks, R. Stuckenrath, and
R. Welbourne
 1987 "A Terminal Pleistocene Assemblage
 from Drotsky's Cave, Western Ngami-
 land, Botswana." *Botswana Notes and
 Records* 19.

Yellen, J., and H. Harpending
 1972 "Hunter-Gatherer Populations and
 Archaeological Inference." *World
 Archaeology* 4(4):244–53.

Yellen, J., and R. Lee
 1976 "The Dobe-/Du/da Environment:
 Background to a Hunting and
 Gathering Way of Life," in *Kalahari
 Hunter-Gatherers: Studies of the !Kung
 San and Their Neighbors,* R. Lee and
 I. DeVore, eds., pp. 27–46. Harvard
 University Press, Cambridge.

INDEX

WITHDRAWN